Guibert's *Defense of the System of Modern War*

History of Warfare

Editors

Kelly DeVries (*Loyola University Maryland*)
Aimée Fox (*King's College London*)
John France (*Swansea University*)
Paul Johstono (*The Citadel, South Carolina*)
Frederick Schneid (*High Point University, North Carolina*)

VOLUME 153

The titles published in this series are listed at *brill.com/hw*

Guibert's *Defense of the System of Modern War*

Annotated and Translated by

Jonathan Abel

BRILL

LEIDEN | BOSTON

Cover illustrations: Portrait of Jacques Antoine Hippolyte, Count de Guibert. Steel engraving, and Stipple engraving by Amedee Felix Barthelemy Geille (1803-1843), after Roubault (fl. 19thC), c. 1835.
Background: Diagram V: Vaussieux and its Environs. © Drawing by Jonathan Abel.

Portions of the archival research for this book were funded by the Military History Center at the University of North Texas (2008 to 2014).

The Library of Congress Cataloging-in-Publication Data is available online at https://catalog.loc.gov
LC record available at https://lccn.loc.gov/2025023057

Typeface for the Latin, Greek, and Cyrillic scripts: "Brill". See and download: brill.com/brill-typeface.

ISSN 1385-7827
ISBN 978-90-04-72783-0 (hardback)
ISBN 978-90-04-73020-5 (e-book)
DOI 10.1163/9789004730205

Copyright 2025 by Koninklijke Brill BV, Plantijnstraat 2, 2321 JC Leiden, The Netherlands.
Koninklijke Brill BV incorporates the imprints Brill, Brill Nijhoff, Brill Schöningh, Brill Fink, Brill mentis, Brill Wageningen Academic, Vandenhoeck & Ruprecht, Böhlau and V&R unipress.
All rights reserved. No part of this publication may be reproduced, translated, stored in a retrieval system, or transmitted in any form or by any means, electronic, mechanical, photocopying, recording or otherwise, without prior written permission from the publisher. Requests for re-use and/or translations must be addressed to Koninklijke Brill BV via brill.com or copyright.com.
For more information: info@brill.com.

This book is printed on acid-free paper and produced in a sustainable manner.

Dedicated to the memories of Tom Carver and Marilyn Morris

∴

Contents

Acknowledgments   IX
List of Figures   X
On the Translation and Sourcing   XI
Introduction   XV
　　Jonathan Abel

Avant-Propos   1

BOOK 1

FIRST PART

1   [The] System of Mesnil-Durand, Originally Drawn from That of Folard. Who Folard Was. Exposition of His System   9

2   [The] System of Mesnil Durand Enunciated in His Diverse Works. [The] Form by Which I Propose to Analyze It   16

3   [The] System of Mesnil-Durand as It Is in His First Work, Titled *Projet d'un ordre français*   17

4   [The] System of Mesnil-Durand Accommodated to Our Constitution and Named [the] "French Order"   27

5   New Variations of the "French Order." [The] Proofs Made at Metz. [The] System of Mesnil-Durand as It Was Executed at the Camp of Vaussieux. Examination of This System in All the Aspects of Its Detail   30

SECOND PART

Examination of the System of Mesnil-Durand in Its Fundamental Aspects and in Those of the Different Arms

1   The System of Mesnil-Durand: Is It Favorable to the Genius and the Character of the Nation?   61

2   The Deep Order, and Particularly the Species of Deep Order Proposed by Mesnil-Durand: May It or Must It be the Primitive and Habitual Order, in Preference to the Deployed Order?   65

3   The Column Considered in Two Aspects: One, as Means of March and Maneuver, and Two, as Attack Disposition. It May Only Ever Be the Momentary and Accidental Order   71

4   Examination of the System of Mesnil-Durand Relative to Cavalry   76

5   Examination of the System of Mesnil-Durand Relative to Artillery   86

BOOK 2

THIRD PART
Examination of the System of Mesnil-Durand Relative to Strategy, or the Tactics of Armies

1 If One Would Adopt the System of Mesnil-Durand, Would It Then Follow That One Would Be Able, as He Announces, to Re-Serry Positions, Camps, and Orders of Battle?   97

2 May Current Castrametation Change Form and Consequently Permit the Shortening of Positions?   99

3 Relationship of Positions to Subsistence. May One, Relative to Subsistence, Adopt the System of Shortening Positions?   102

4 Other Great Obstacles to the Re-serrying of Positions and Orders of Battle Drawn from the Nature of Operations and from the Circumstances to Which Armies Are Subjected   107

5 System of Mesnil-Durand Considered in Relation to Marches and March Orders   110

6 Examination of the System of Mesnil-Durand Relative to Grand Maneuvers and to Army Movements   113

7 [The] System of Mesnil-Durand Considered in Relation to Orders of Battle and to Battles   116

FOURTH PART
Résumé

1 The System of Mesnil-Durand Is Not Admissible in Any Respect. It Is a Matter of Holding to the One That Exists and Only Consolidating Our Constitution and Perfecting Ourselves in Modern Tactics   153

2 [The] Current System of War Examined in Relation to Politics and to the Administration. It Would Be Impossible and Even Disadvantageous to Change It   155

Appendix A: Diagram v: Vaussieux and Its Environs   177
Appendix B: The French Army in the Eighteenth Century   178
Appendix C: Glossary of Terms   189
Bibliography   192
Index   204

Acknowledgments

This book, like any research project, owes its existence to a large number of people who have helped with it, directly and indirectly.

My family, including my wife Melanie and my parents Jack and Rosemary Abel, has tolerated its existence and my incessant references to it. It would not exist without their love and support. My mother also assisted with the diagrams and answering spelling and grammar questions, as did Betty Sarratt with the latter.

Julia Osman originally gave me the idea to translate the *Defense of the System of Modern War* and persisted in requesting it for years. Nikki Dean has been an invaluable resource for both US Army doctrine and French issues. Lindsey Clark and Marie Martinez assisted with many inane spelling and grammar questions I put to them. Chloe Northrop has been an invaluable colleague, cheerleader, critic, and friend. Kelsa Pellettiere provided background research. Claudia Beltrame and Marjorie Galelli gave enormously useful help with Italian and French, respectively. Alex Burns remains a font of wisdom on all issues eighteenth-century military.

My colleagues at the US Army Command and General Staff College have all been helpful in some way; several deserve specific thanks. Bill Nance has been an always-insightful source of wisdom on US Army doctrine. Mike Bonura provided an excellent sounding board for many of the issues Guibert discusses; I also owe "linear but not contiguous" to him, and he gave valuable feedback on the introduction. Mark Gerges, Nate Jennings, and Dirk Ringgenberg assisted with questions related to tactics. Cameron Zinsou was kind enough to bring back papers from the French military archives at Vincennes. John Hosler and Mark Hull helped with advice and sourcing on affairs medieval and German, respectively. Ethan Rafuse allowed me to raid his bookshelf for sources on the American War of Independence. The staff at the Combined Arms Research Library, particularly Sierra Hochstatter and Wesley McVicker, have also performed heroic work answering my interlibrary loan requests, no matter how esoteric.

Figures

1. Diagram I 41
2. Diagram II 42
3. Diagram III 47
4. Diagram IV 48
5. Diagram VI 104
6. Diagram VII 140
7. Diagram VIII 142
8. Diagram IX 145
9. Diagram V 177
10. Prototypical Midcentury French Field Army Organization 188
11. Generalized Diagram of French Strategic Command and Control 188

On the Translation and Sourcing

The *Defense of the System of Modern War* was first published in 1779 in two volumes. Because it did not receive the *privilège*, the official right to be published in the kingdom, it was instead published in the Prussian exclave of Neuchâtel in modern Switzerland. Unlike Guibert's prior work, the *General Essay on Tactics*, it appears not to have been published in multiple additions or translations. It was included as Volumes 3 and 4 of his collected *Œuvres militaires*, produced by his widow in 1803. I consider this edition definitive and thus have used it for this translation.

French is not a difficult language to translate into English, for the most part. The two languages share a basic grammatical structure, and many words have passed from French into English. Sentences are generally constructed in the same way in both languages, with the single significant caveat that French is a subject-object-verb language, while English is a subject-verb-object language. French is also a gendered language, unlike English. Eighteenth-century French is largely identical to modern French, even allowing for centuries of use. This is chiefly the result of the governance of the Académie française and its strict enforcement of linguistic rules and continuity.

Perhaps the most notable difference between eighteenth-century and twenty-first-century writing is the predilection for lengthy sentences with several clauses and/or phrases, of which Guibert is demonstrably fond. These present a challenge to translate and to read, particularly when they nest within each other. In addition, contemporary writers located modifiers within sentences in places that do not read smoothly to the modern reader, particularly when the word or phrase being modified is followed by a list, as Guibert is fond of doing.

I have used several translation tools and resources in the process of making the translation. Google Translate and Wordreference are invaluable resources for anyone working in the digital age, particularly for clarifying odd turns of phrase and bygone idioms, respectively. Similarly useful is Cornélius de Witt Willcox's *French-English Military Technical Dictionary*, originally printed for American officers serving in the First World War. Finally, when another work failed, I turned to Etienne-Alexandre Bardin's *Dictionnaire de l'armée de terre*.

I believe in a literal translation style with little to no dynamic equivalence. There are several reasons for this, particularly in a work that is intended to be a technical manual and not a great work of literature. First, dynamic equivalence and other non-literal translation methods often replace the author's voice, and even intent, with the translator's; the task of the translator is to translate, not to write or opine on what the author intended, outside of footnotes. Second, dynamic equivalence often introduces anachronisms. This is particularly important in a work of technical military theory from a time when terms were being discussed and defined. An excellent example is the phrase "*état-major*." It is often translated as "staff," which is the closest modern analog to the early-modern usage and how the term is used in the modern French military. However, a modern military staff has personnel with assigned roles, special training, and documented procedures, while an early-modern *état-major* had none of those, rendering such a translation an anachronism. Third, many terms have changed in meaning since the mid-eighteenth century, such that modern equivalents simply would not do them justice. For example, "deploy" now has a general meaning of setting up or expanding, while it had a much more circumscribed and technical meaning to Guibert and his peers (moving men in a line into a column). The only occasions in which I have introduced some dynamic equivalence are the rare instances when Guibert uses a period idiom that simply does not make sense in modern English; there are fewer than five in the text. Otherwise, the translation is as literal a representation of Guibert's words as I can make it.

I have left several words and phrases in their original French (and, on one occasion, Greek). This is because the word or phrase does not have a suitable translation. An example is *toise*, which is a measure of around two yards, essentially a land fathom. I have also used English words that are identical to French words but have different meanings; for example, "place" or "place of war" in French denote a fortified position, usually a fortress. Both categories of words and phrases may be found in a glossary of terms in APPENDIX C.

There are four categories of changes I have introduced to the text in its translated form. First, I have de-gendered the language. This is relatively easy except on rare occasion when doing so would turn a single word into a longer phrase; for example, I have retained "*militaire*" rather than translating it as "a person engaged in military activities," for obvious stylistic reasons. Second, I have moved modifying phrases and clauses within sentences to clarify intent, almost all of them adverbial adjuncts. Third, I have adjusted the grammar of the original. In particular, colons, semicolons, and commas are used very differently today from how they were in the 1770s, and French uses a system of quotation marks that is different from modern English.

Finally, I have also changed Guibert's use of "barbarian" to refer to indigenous Americans. None of these changes has materially affected the intent or meaning of any passage, except to clarify it in the second instance.

A final word must be said on the nature of the work and its formatting. A large portion of the *Defense of the System of Modern War* consists of quotes from other works, particularly those of Mesnil-Durand. Quotations at the time did not work as they do today, in two major ways. First, quotations were not expected to be literal in their entirety, especially when they are included as part of a larger sentence. As a result, Guibert adds words or even paraphrases them in sections in order to fit his prose. I have not found an instance of his changing a quote's meaning or taking it out of its original context. He usually provides a citation of the work being quoted in or near the passage but not always, especially with the shorter quotes he uses throughout the text. Second and related, quotes do not always appear as and in quotes in Guibert's text, making it difficult to determine how to translate them into English. This is usually a choice between a paraphrase and a direct quotation. I have chosen to quote them as they would be in a modern English academic work, erring on the side of writing them as direct quotations in quotation marks. This has also required some small changes from the original, almost all involving moving non-quoted material outside of Guibert's quotation marks like changing "Mesnil-Durand says "that he believes ..."" to "Mesnil-Durand says that "he believes."" As the reader might notice, this still leaves a portion of the text that is not a quotation in quotation marks, which would be unacceptable in a modern academic work. I have chosen to leave these as they are written, because to write them according to modern standards would require a substantial revision of many passages, which would involve injecting my own style and voice into Guibert's text. I believe it remains obvious what is being quoted, and, as noted, Guibert provides citations for almost all of his quotations; those he has not, I have.

Beyond the above, I have chosen not to edit Guibert's citations for several reasons. First, almost all of them point the reader to the appropriate place in the source material even though they do not conform to modern citation practices, particularly in lacking specific page numbers in most cases. Second, Guibert cited works in French, and those reading a translation of a work from French into English would not benefit from exclusively Francophone citations. Third, Guibert's references usually correlate to a printed version of Mesnil-Durand's work, but not always, indicating that Guibert may have had access to other editions or even drafts of them, to which his citations may point. Finally, Guibert refers to diagrams in Mesnil-Durand's various texts on occasion. Digitized versions rarely include full diagrams, leaving the modern reader without them unless they come by a (usually very expensive) original edition. Given that there are few such references in the text and that the point of each passage remains even without the diagram for reference, I have left them in but not added citations for them.

Guibert includes several footnotes and citations in the text. I have rendered these as normal footnotes, and, as he often uses shorthand for the titles of works, I have provided the correct title of each work being cited if it is not clear from his note. He provides diagrams of exercises for the reader as well. In the original publications, these were printed on fold-out plates at the rear of the book, and readers of scanned digital books will be familiar with the frequent failure of archivists to expand and scan the full plate. I have digitized all of Guibert's diagrams and inserted them into the text where they are referenced so that the reader is not forced to flip back and forth, as a reader of the original would be forced to.

Finally, I have also included copious footnotes of my own; they are enclosed in brackets to distinguish them from Guibert's. Military authors of the period assumed a great deal of knowledge on the part of readers, particularly of military history and technical military affairs. Guibert is fond of peppering his text with references to campaigns and commanders ranging from Ancient Greece through the two wars being waged during the drafting of the book. He also favors dropping references to works of literature and mythology. My footnotes serve to provide clarity and context for these references. They also highlight Guibert's major themes and connect them to other military theorists and events from military history, particularly those that postdate the manuscript. I have provided few footnotes explaining the details of contemporary military practice, particularly at the tactical level, for two reasons. First, doing so would created a manuscript that would be much more footnote than text, and second, a reader of a military treatise from the 1770s requires a baseline of knowledge of contemporary military affairs in order to profit from it.

Anglophone sourcing for Guibert and the period is mixed. In general, given that this is a translation, I have endeavored to provide sourcing only in English, particularly for footnotes related to historical topics and references. However, sufficient sourcing does not always exist in English, leaving some of the references to point to works in French. Whenever possible, I have also attempted to confine sourcing to generalist or survey works on a topic so as to provide a tighter additional reading list for readers, particularly those not already well-versed in millennia of European military history.

Guibert's life is relatively well documented, both by contemporaries and by modern historians. Printed primary sources are plentiful, both his own works and those of his contemporaries. Secondary works range from biographies of him to works on the period in general and military theory and reform specifically.

Much of Guibert's work is available, albeit in French. His papers from his stints on the War Council in from 1775 to 1777 and again from 1787 to 1789 are housed in the "Guibert Papers," Service Historique–Armée de Terre 1M 1790–1794. Parts of his correspondence with salonnière Julie de Lespinasse are collected and printed, although she burnt the majority of his letters to her. His military works are contained in *Œuvres militaires*, printed by his widow Alexandrine-Louis Boutinon, née Hayes de Courcelles, in 1803. My translation of the *General Essay on Tactics* is the only modern translation of his magnum opus. Also in 1803, his friend François-Emmanuel Toulongeon published Guibert's *Journal d'un voyage en allemagne*, which includes a short biography of him. In 1822, Alexandrine also published a collection of Guibert's non-military works under the title *Œuvres dramatiques*. Aside from his own work, almost all of the important sources relative to his work were printed and published during or shortly after his lifetime, as the notes and bibliography illustrate. All the major theoretical works save the 1750s pamphlet of Chevalier Rostaing were printed and distributed during the period, if not published in multiple editions, as many were. The vast majority of these have been digitized, making them available to the average reader and historian. I have relied on digital sources with the exception of a printed edition of the *Œuvres militaires*, which is necessary for the full, intact plates.

My biography of Guibert is the only English-language source on his life. It owes a great debt to Toulongeon's essay, as well as those by Matti Lauerma, published in the 1950s, and Ethel Groffier, published in 2005, all in French. Guibert's work has been analyzed extensively, likely more than the work of any military theorist between that of Niccolò Machiavelli and Carl von Clausewitz. Perhaps the most significant assessment of his work is in Jean Colin's *L'education militaire de Napoleon* and *L'infanterie au XVIIIe siècle*, where he declares Guibert to be the prophet of Napoleon and Napoleonic warfare; this became the basis for all subsequent analyses of Guibert, including my own. Colin's argument appears largely wholesale in Robert Quimby's *The Background of Napoleonic Warfare*, making it accessible to Anglophone readers. Guibert's work is also addressed in Beatrice Heuser's *The Evolution of Strategy* and "Guibert: Prophet of Total War?;" Azar Gat's *A History of Military Thought*; and R.R. Palmer's "Frederick the Great, Guibert, Bülow," among others. My own "The Prophet Guibert" in *Napoleon and the Operational Art of War* and "Jacques-Antoine-Hippolyte, comte de Guibert," *Oxford Bibliographies Online*, provide further reading and elaboration of the above. Finally and significantly for the current translation, Julia Osman's "Guibert vs. Guibert" is the only modern Anglophone work to seriously examine the *Defense of the System of Modern War* in its own right.

General works on the period are relatively common in English, with a few notable gaps. Peter Wilson's *The Thirty Years War*, John Lynn's *The Wars of Louis XIV*, John Sutton's *The King's Cardinal*, M.S. Anderson's and Reed Browning's *The War of the Austrian Succession*, Franz Szabo's *The Seven Years War in Europe*, Dennis Showalter's *The Wars of Frederick the Great*, and John Ferling's *Almost a Miracle* cover the wars from 1618 until Guibert's time. Christopher Duffy's *The Military Experience in the Age of Reason*, Christy Pichichero's *The Military Enlightenment*, and Armstrong Starkey's *War in the Age of Enlightenment* provide an introduction to the issues of warfare in the period. Dorinda Outram's *The Enlightenment* and Daniel Roche's *France in the Enlightenment* are good surveys of the titular subject. Rafe Blaufarb's *The French Army*, Lee Kennett's *The French Armies in the Seven Years War*, and John Lynn's *Giant of the Grand Siècle* are excellent studies of the French army as an institution between 1650 and 1789. The various works of James Collins, William Doyle, John Hardman, Jay Smith, and Julian Swann provide background information and analyses of the French government and its institutions, especially as the Revolution neared.

Unfortunately, gaps exist in the modern Anglophone historiography of the period and the French army. Several of the above surveys are not written from the French perspective, leaving out important aspects of French warmaking. A few examples suffice to illustrate. Sutton's is the only modern Anglophone work on the War of the Polish Succession, and it is rapidly aging. Szabo's work is an effective survey of the titular conflict, but its vehement dislike of Friedrich II taints its utility. There are no omnibus accounts of French overseas conflicts during the eighteenth century, and few of the specific wars have any coverage either, especially outside of North America. The histories of international conflict about the period in English are almost exclusively about or written from the British perspective, making them of little use to a reader of French history beyond reporting basic facts. There are few Anglophone biographies of important decisionmakers during the period like Victor-François, duc de Broglie; Etienne-François, duc de Choiseul; Philippe-Henri, marquis de Ségur, and even Louis XV, much less more obscure people like Guibert's nemeses Jean-Charles, chevalier Folard, or François-Jean de Graindorge d'Orgeville, baron de Mesnil-Durand. There are few institutional histories of the French army during the period beyond those cited above.

Because of this deficit, I have relied on Francophone sourcing to fill it. Several works are key to this process. Louis-Hippolyte Bacquet's *L'infanterie au XVIIIe siècle* is the organizational counterpart to Colin's work. Albert Latreille's *L'œuvre militaire de la révolution* and the Thierry Sarmant-edited *Les ministres de la guerre 1570–1792* are invaluable surveys of the Ministry of War during the period. Michel Antoine's *Louis XV* remains the best deep account of the monarch's life. Jean Chagniot's *Le chevalier de Folard* is a fascinating biography of the subject and his military theories. Arnaud Guinier's *L'honneur du soldat* examines the soldiers of the contemporary French army.

Finally, two special technical notes. The Académie Française maintains the official dictionary of the French language and has done so since the publication of its First Edition in 1694. I have relied on it, specifically the Fourth Edition from 1762 as the closest to the publication of the *Defense of the System of Modern War*, for all definitions, unless otherwise noted. All biographical information is from Gabriel Michaud's *Biographie universelle ancienne et moderne*, published in the mid-nineteenth century, unless otherwise noted.

Introduction

Jonathan Abel

"It is on the formation of orders of battle that modern tactics has made, or, to speak more justly, is in the process of making, the most important and the most complete revolution." So says Jacques-Antoine-Hippolyte, comte de Guibert, in his second great work of military theory, the *Defense of the System of Modern War*. During his lifetime, it remained in the shadow of his first work, the *General Essay on Tactics*, which captivated readers and which they widely read and commented on, and it ultimately fell into obscurity. However, the *Defense of the System of Modern War* is no less worthy of reading or study than the *General Essay on Tactics*. It marks a significant shift in military theory and practice, as the quote intimates. It engages the reader in contemporary debates on those topics with Guibert's rival in military theory François de Graindorge d'Orgeville, baron de Mesnil-Durand. It also explains what took place at the Camp of Vaussieux, the most important event in the French army between 1763 and the end of the Old Regime. It marks the second half of his great work of theory, together with the *General Essay on Tactics*, and it anticipates the great theorists of the Napoleonic Era.

The Guibert family comes from the central part of southern France, around the town of Montauban. Its members likely followed the most common method of advancement by sending sons into the magistracy to build a fortune and then into the army to rise socially. Charles-Benoît and his son Jacques-Antoine-Hippolyte were the products of this effort. They probably belonged to the *anoblis*, the nebulous group of people who were on their way to joining the lower nobility but were not fully recognized as such.[1]

Charles-Benoît Guibert joined the army in the early eighteenth century and fought in the mid-century wars. He rose through the ranks to become what would now be called a staff officer attached to the powerful Broglie family. He was among the thousands of French soldiers taken prisoner after the disastrous Battle of Rossbach in 1757. He remained in the service of Marshal Victor-François, duc de Broglie, for the rest of the war. Between the Treaty of Paris 1763 and his death in the 1780s, he served in a variety of positions for the Ministry of War, including writing doctrine and as governor of the Invalides, a prestigious position, especially for someone of recent noble extraction.[2]

The French army for which Guibert senior fought was an institution faced with significant challenges in adapting to the new military philosophies and methods of the period. In a general sense, the rationalism and empiricism of the Military Enlightenment increasingly called into question the decentralized and amateurish traditions of the French army. In a more direct sense, the rise of Brandenburg-Prussia as a new paradigm of military professionalism and effectiveness threw the French army into increasingly stark relief.

Traditionally, the French army assembled in wartime from a series of disparate units, mostly regiments that were owned by their colonels, and around twenty percent of which were mercenary units imported from foreign countries like Switzerland. Units were mostly venal, granting their owners great latitude in how they were manned, trained, and equipped, especially during peacetime. The result was a patchwork of philosophies and experience levels that an army commander was expected to meld into a functional field army during the late winter and spring before embarking on the campaign season each year.[3]

During the reign of Louis XIV in the late seventeenth century, military bureaucrats, especially François-Michel le Tellier, marquis de Louvois, worked to professionalize and modernize the army by implementing reforms like appointing a Colonel General or inspector to oversee the training of individual branches like the infantry or dragoons, creating a quasi-national system of military supply, and erecting a prototypical general staff body. These reforms enabled the French government to use its vast resources more efficiently for war and represented a significant step towards professionalization and modernization, but they could not prevent the breakdown of the system and the army in both the War of the League of Augsburg in the 1690s and especially the War of the Spanish Succession in the 1700s and 1710s. Throughout the latter conflict, many generals with particularist ideas refused to cooperate with each other or train their troops

---

1 See Jonathan Abel, *Jacques-Antoine-Hippolyte, comte de Guibert: Father of Napoleon's Grande Armée* (Norman: University of Oklahoma Press, 2016), 34–38.

2 Ibid.

3 André Corvisier, *Armies and Societies in Europe 1494–1789*, trans. Abigail Siddall (Bloomington: Indiana University Press, 1979), provides an effective overview of the subject.

according to any standard doctrine, resulting in uneven performance, spectacular defeats, and a great cost in lives and money to the French state.[4]

In the *Defense of the System of Modern War*, Guibert provides a diagnosis of the French army's issues after 1700:

> Armies were neither divided nor constituted in a fashion to be able to be maneuvering. The different corps that composed them could move themselves individually only by movements [that were] slow [and] heavy and of which they did not even have the habit. General officers did not at all have the habit of handling troops. From this ignorance and from this general ill-address, as much on the part of the agents as on the part of the conductors, resulted that it took several hours to form an army *en bataille*, [and] that, once this army [was] *en bataille*, one dared not make the least change in its disposition for fear of confounding everything, of losing everything. In the end, [this] resulted in one always combining the order of march on the disposition that one wished to take.[5]

Contemporary armies engaged in linear warfare were naturally blocky, both at lower and higher levels, which made them difficult to command and especially to maneuver. Commanders lacked skill and training in moving units, especially large armies. The French army was, in a word, amateurish. This was the core of the problem that military theorists had to solve if France were to resume its position as the land-warfare hegemon in Europe that it had enjoyed in much of the prior century.

Throughout the period, a variety of ministers, generals, and reformers sought to rectify these issues, particularly during the long peace from 1715 to 1733. There were two major influences on this process. The first was the Military Enlightenment. Applying geometry and Newtonian mechanics to military affairs suited the Enlightenment mind, and many theorists like Jean-Charles, chevalier Folard, spilled a great deal of ink designing elaborate tactical and organizational systems known as "military constitutions" for doing exactly that.[6]

Another major influence was the rise of Brandenburg-Prussia and its new model of state militaries. Volumes have been written about the Prussian military model, but it may be summarized as quality over quantity achieved by emphasizing training, discipline, and professionalism; centralized control of what would now be called doctrine; breaking armies into higher-echelon formations like brigades and divisions; command by skilled generals capable of exercising informed judgment; and financial backing with a significant war chest capable of paying for the army's needs in specie.[7] As early as the 1720s, reform-minded French officers like Charles-Louis-Auguste, duc de Belle-Isle, looked to Prussia as the new paradigm army in Europe, a centralized and professional force, in contrast to France's. This received significant momentum from Prussia's performance in the War of the Austrian Succession, in which the Prussian army commanded by Friedrich II defeated the rival Austrians in a series of battles. Calls began for change to make the French army more professional and disciplined.[8]

These two trends culminated in the first great reform period in the 1750s. Secretary of State for War Marc-Pierre de Voyer de Paulmy, comte d'Argenson, promulgated a wave of army-wide doctrine designed to remake the French army along both Military-Enlightenment and Prussian-inspired lines. A series of regulations aimed at the level of petty tactics required deployment on three ranks and the same march cadence across the army.[9] At the same time, the government chartered the Ecole Royale Militaire, along with technical-branch academies, to educate and train future generations of officers.[10]

These bottom-up reforms set the precedent for the centralization and professionalization of the army. Most importantly, they illustrated the primacy of the War

---

4   John Lynn, *Giant of the Grand Siècle: The French Army 1610–1715* (New York: Cambridge University Press, 1997).
5   See 134.
6   See Azar Gat, *A History of Military Thought from the Enlightenment to the Cold War* (New York: Oxford University Press, 2001), 13–55; Christy Pichichero, *The Military Enlightenment* (Ithaca: Cornell University Press, 2017); and Armstrong Starkey, *War in the Age of Enlightenment, 1700–1789* (Westport, CT: Praeger, 2003).
7   Robert Citino, *The Germany Way of War from the Thirty Years War to the Third Reich* (Lawrence: University Press of Kansas, 2005), 1–103, provides an effective overview; see also Hamish Scott, *The Birth of a Great Power System, 1740–1815* (New York: Longman, 2008); and Peter Wilson, "The Origins of Prussian Militarism," *History Today* 51, no. 5 (2001): 22–27.
8   See Abel, *Guibert's General Essay on Tactics*, xvii-xxiii. See also Reed Browning, *The War of the Austrian Succession* (New York: St. Martin's, 1995); and Dennis Showalter, *The Wars of Frederick the Great* (New York: Longman, 1996), 1–134.
9   See Abel, *Guibert's General Essay on Tactics*, xxiii-xxiv. See also "Marc-Pierre de Voyer de Paulmy, comte d'Argenson, 1743–1757," *Les ministres de la guerre 1570–1792*, ed. Thierry Sarmant (Paris: Belin, 2007), 363–389.
10 Some of the technical schools predated this period by decades; they were brought into the burgeoning professional military education establishment in the 1750s. See Haroldo Guízar, *The Ecole Royale Militaire: Noble Education, Institutional Innovation, and Royal Charity, 1750–1788* (New York: Palgrave, 2020).

Ministry in issuing doctrine that the entire army followed rather than leaving training and execution to individual commanders. This represented the application of the principles of the Military Enlightenment and the adoption of the philosophy behind Prussia's military establishment. Collectively, the reforms of the 1750s were the first step in moving the French army from its feudal past to a more modern and professional force.

Guibert junior was born in 1743 and came of age in the midcentury reform process. He benefitted enormously from his father's position and upbringing. As he notes in the *General Essay on Tactics*, his father took the time to educate him in the theory of war, including a passage that may be one of the earliest references to a modern wargame.[11] When Guibert had finished his basic education, he went to war alongside his father in the Seven Years War. According to a contemporary, he was noted for his discernment in altering an order he was conveying at the 1759 Battle of Minden because it had become obsolete when he arrived to deliver it.[12] He was fifteen years old.

Like the War of the Spanish Succession, the Seven Years War was a wrenching event for the French army. It performed poorly, both because it lacked effective leaders and because its doctrine remained deficient compared to its opponents'. Its defeat at the 1757 Battle of Rossbach may have been one of the most spectacular of the period, and one of the most illustrative. A Franco-Imperial army launched an attack on a Prussian position commanded by Friedrich II; the attack took so long to deploy and move that Friedrich had enough time to eat lunch, mobilize his forces, and crush the enemy attack columns, inflicting over 10,000 casualties to less than 1,000 of his own. Perhaps more telling was the inability of the French to overcome the Prussia-assisted Hanoverian army of Ferdinand, prince of Brunswick-Lüneburg, for much of the rest of the war.[13]

The Seven Years War thus inaugurated another long period of reform, lasting from the early 1760s until around 1780. Subsequent Secretaries of State for War continued to make changes to the army's organization and manning systems, including working to eliminate the last vestiges of venality within units. They also strove to reduce costs, given the burgeoning state bankruptcy that would eventually consume the Old Regime. Doctrine remained paramount as well, although several problems remained outstanding in the ongoing transition from decentralized, tactical warfare to centralized, higher-echelon warfare.

All of the problems with linear formations noted above remained. Although the cadenced step, along with the regularization of army sizes and minimum standards for promotion promulgated in the 1760s, aided in solving them, they were only a few building blocks in the process. Armies were still required to assemble their units into massive march columns and then ponderously deploy them on the square into battle order, which could take hours, like it had at Rossbach. Organizational challenges also persisted, as the regiment continued to be the largest permanent echelon in the French army, stymieing efforts to develop the levels of war above the petty tactical.

The obvious solution was to break the formation into sections that operated autonomously within the larger battle plan, a system referred to as "mission command" in the modern United States Army, and one that would eventually be reached by the French armies of the Revolutionary and Napoleonic Wars.[14] However, this was impossible in Guibert's period for a variety of reasons. For one, communication was conducted entirely by courier, which presented obvious problems on a chaotic battlefield covered by smoke, rendering coordination extremely difficult. For another, mission-command systems require a baseline of competence, and intensive education, of the officers implementing it. Most French officers in the late 1770s had little formal military education, as the Ecole Royale Militaire, the first professional military education institution in France, was opened only in 1751, as noted. It also catered to the lower nobility, particularly the members of that class who could not afford the traditional educational institutions of the upper nobility like page schools, resulting in an officer corps bifurcated by both social extraction and education. During wartime, officers "interned" by joining militaries at the age of twelve or thirteen and learned the trade, usually from their fathers, including participating in combat. They were thus inculcated into the culture of martial bravery and leadership from the front that traditionally characterized the French nobility. However, this guaranteed neither competence nor skill in the basic handling of a unit, much less the

---

11 Abel, *Guibert's General Essay on Tactics*, 238–239.
12 See Abel, *Jacques-Antoine-Hippolyte, comte de Guibert*, 37.
13 No account of the Seven Years War in English serves as a history of the war from a French perspective; see Lee Kennett, *The French Armies in the Seven Years War: A Study in Military Organization and Administration* (Durham: Duke University Pres, 1967); and Franz Szabo, *The Seven Years War in Europe 1756–1763* (New York: Routledge, 2013).

14 See ADP 6–0 *Mission Command* (2019); Rafe Blaufarb, *The French Army 1750–1820: Careers, Talent, Merit* (Manchester: Manchester University Press, 2002); and John Elting, *Swords Around a Throne: Napoleon's Grande Armée* (New York: Free Press, 1988).

kind of high-level skill and discretion required to conduct a mission-command-style battle.[15]

The temptation for the modern reader is to assume contemporary *militaires* were blinkered or even stupid. However, their projects were not the products of either prejudice or stupidity; they were efforts to solve the exact problems Guibert spent his life and career helping solve: how to fight effectively with armies of up to 120,000 men arranged into block formations, carrying muskets with bayonets; supported by cavalry, artillery, and engineers; and having little time or money to engage in large-scale training exercises in peacetime. Armies simply had to deploy and fight in linear formations because of extant technology. Previous generations' solution to this was to develop the kinds of processional warfare that was slow, unresponsive to conditions, and largely dependent on the skill of the army commander and his subordinates to function. Hence they created simple linear formations that did not greatly stress soldiers' or officers' abilities. A French army of 80,000 might be broken into two march columns of 40,000 each; these would become the first and second battle lines when they found the enemy. Moving from march to battle order would require the entire army to maneuver itself in front of the enemy, a process that could take hours or even days. As a result, large-scale battles were infrequent, and taking an enemy by surprise was essentially unheard of.

Even at the lower level of war, change was hampered by practicalities of linear warfare. Deployment on the square remained the norm because it allowed commanders to select a specific point on the terrain, called a point of view, on which to align their unit and their march direction. This concept was borrowed from Prussian practice and brought to France by Johann Ernst, baron Pirch. Any deployment method other than on the square all but eliminated the use of points of view, making maneuvers much more difficult, especially for junior officers.[16] Thus, Guibert and his contemporaries could not simply jump from the system they had inherited to one that looked like a Napoleonic army, which could deploy on the square, on obliques, or by any suitable method. Their task was to provide the bridge between the two.

Even taking this into consideration, the post-war period seemed to illustrate a failure of imagination among French military theorists and practitioners alike. Almost all remained stubbornly attached to solutions only at the lowest level of war. Writers focused a great deal of their work on the petty tactical level and simply scaled this to the higher levels of war. It appears that contemporary theorists simply could not imagine a large army broken into articulated blocks that functioned as an analog to the subordinate units of smaller echelons; this kind of fractal organization seemed beyond them. Instead, they imagined either petty tactics at higher scales, or tiny armies fighting independently, like the legions of Chevalier Rostaing or Maurice de Saxe.[17] In addition, many favored rigid adherence to a strict system of tactics, maneuvers, and marches, whether in *l'ordre profond*, deep order emphasizing shock columns, or *l'ordre mince*, thin order maximizing firepower. Several of these were drawn from Greek or Roman examples, including reviving obsolete weapons systems like the pike. There were also many questions on how exactly to integrate the other arms with the infantry, whether light or heavy cavalry, or newer specialties like field artillery and combat engineers. These often degenerated into petty squabbles over system and amour-propre rather than genuine efforts at practical reform, which the French army desperately needed.[18]

Mesnil-Durand, the most prominent mid-century theorist, falls into these traps. His system was constantly evolving throughout the period, but the core principle was a series of large, deep attack columns that functioned largely independently of each other. Instead of connecting the tactical level of war to higher levels, his system sought to win battles at the lowest possible level, desynchronizing the columns from each other and disintegrating the levels of war.[19]

Guibert saw further and more deeply than his contemporaries. After the war, he assisted his father in working on the many regulations implemented by Secretary of State for War Etienne-François, duc de Choiseul, in the 1760s. The Guiberts developed a prototypical maneuver unit called the Guibert Column that would break large march columns into smaller units that could maneuver however necessary from march to battle order. Late in that decade, Guibert junior found service in Corsica as the French fought to conquer their new possession from indigenous

---

15 Blaufarb, *The French Army*, 12–45; and Rafe Blaufarb, "Noble Privilege and Absolutist State Building: French Military Administration after the Seven Years War," *French Historical Studies* 24 (2001): 223–246.

16 Colin, *L'infanterie au XVIIIᵉ siècle*, 73–134.

17 See Maurice de Saxe, *The Art of War: Reveries and Memoirs* (London: Davis, 1811); and "Mémoire concernant l'essai de la legions, la tactique et les évolutions," Service Historique-Armée de Terre 1M 1707.

18 See Abel, *Guibert's General Essay on Tactics*, xviii–xxxii.; see also Robert Quimby, *The Background of Napoleonic Warfare: The Theory of Military Tactics in Eighteenth-Century France* (New York: Columbia University Press, 1957), especially 26–105.

19 See Quimby, *The Background of Napoleonic Warfare*, 62–79 and 210–232 for an analysis of Mesnil-Durand's ideas.

forces. He remained there for a few years as Colonel-Commandant of the Corsican Legion, affording him the time to draft the *General Essay on Tactics*.[20]

The *General Essay on Tactics* was Guibert's magnum opus, and it is the primary reason his life, career, and works are remembered and studied. It has two major sections corresponding to its two major themes. Its Preliminary Discourse is a fiery criticism of the reigning political systems in contemporary Europe. Guibert concludes that they all lack proper foundation, spirit, and inspiration of their citizenry. In an oft-quoted passage, he speculates that a better form of government, with an army of citizen-soldiers, might one day appear and sweep away the Old Regime "like the north wind bending the reeds."[21]

The second theme relates to the Guibert Column. Perhaps the closest Guibert comes to providing a thesis statement in this regard occurs in its second book: "the troops arrive by the shortest route on the points that they go to occupy, and in war, method must not shackle; it must not degenerate into routine."[22] A Guibert Column was simply a small column that was able to maneuver however it was necessary to move from position in a march column to position *en bataille*, in the battle formation. The Guiberts' work in the 1760s provided the technical specifications for how this was to be done. However, breaking the unitary march column into smaller echelons presented a wide array of technical problems that remained. The *General Essay on Tactics* is mostly dedicated to solving several of these. In particular, Guibert provides detail for how these maneuvers might take place, especially by moving units on oblique lines rather than on the square, as was the accepted practice. He also explores how larger echelons might function on campaign and in battle. Portions of the text are dedicated to what he calls "march-maneuvers," actions that larger units took when within range of the enemy.

By providing guidance for these larger-scale maneuvers separate from those for smaller echelons, he uncoupled the two from each other, just as Guibert Columns had liberated march from battle order. While Guibert would not have recognized the term, he was working on the origins of operational-level warfare by liberating the higher levels of war from petty tactics, which none of his French contemporaries had envisioned. This would provide an army capable of more flexible and mobile warfare, like the Prussian army of the period. He had imagined an army deployed on a formation that was still linear, but it was no longer contiguous.[23]

The *General Essay on Tactics* was wildly popular, being printed in multiple languages and distributed around the world in the early 1770s. Its fiery critique of current affairs opened the doors of the prestigious Parisian salons to him, and he became "the strategist of the enlightened."[24] The next few years were a whirlwind for Guibert. He returned to the mainland and "pursued glory by all routes: receiving the applause of armies, the theatre, and women."[25] He attended the leading salons, including that of Julie de Lespinasse, with whom he carried on a relationship. He also had an affair with Jeanne Thiroux de Montsauge, the wife of a financier, who aided his burgeoning career. He was noted for his eidetic memory and his charming if passionate conversation. He used these connections to aid his literary aspirations, nearly winning the 1775 essay contest sponsored by the *Académie française*, and writing a play, the *Connétable de Bourbon*. The latter drew the attention of Queen Marie Antoinette, who arranged two showings of it at Versailles in 1775; both were disasters. Not long after, he married Alexandrine-Louise Boutinon des Hayes de Courcelles, who brought a significant dowry and income.[26]

Guibert was also appointed to the Council of War under Secretary of State for War Claude-Louis, comte de Saint-Germain, who entered the office with a mandate to enact sweeping changes to the French army. For the next eighteen months, the War Council worked to meet that mandate, in particular by reducing costs within the army. Much of its work focused on the ongoing elimination of the *Maison militaire du roi*, the king's household units;

---

20 See Abel, *Jacques-Antoine-Hippolyte, comte de Guibert*, 41–54. See also Jean Colin, *L'infanterie au XVIIIe siècle*, 73–134; Samuel Gibiat, "Etienne-François, duc de Choiseul, 1761–1770," *Les ministres de la guerre*, 407–436; and Albert Latreille, *L'oeuvre militaire de la révolution: l'armee et la nation à la fin de l'ancien régime: les derniers ministres de la guerre de la monarchie* (Paris: Chapelot, 1914), 1–25.

21 Abel, *Guibert's General Essay on Tactics*, 7.

22 Ibid., 234.

23 See Jonathan Abel, "The Prophet Guibert," *Napoleon and the Operational Art of War: Essays in Honor of Donald D. Horward*, ed. Michael Leggiere (Leiden: Brill, 2021), 8–38; and Quimby, *The Background of Napoleonic Warfare*, which is drawn in turn from the various works of Jean Colin.

24 Ethel Groffier, *Le stratège des lumières: le comte de Guibert (1743–1790)* (Paris: Champion, 2005).

25 Voltaire to Friedrich II, quoted in Abel, *Jacques-Antoine-Hippolyte, comte de Guibert*, 96–97. Guibert likely drew on Prussian and Austrian inspiration for these suggestions; see Alexander Burns, "Writing for Pleasure: Christopher Duffy's Historiographical Legacy," *The Changing Face of Old-Regime Warfare: Essays in Honor of Christopher Duffy*, ed. Alexander Burns (Warwick: Helion, 2022), 37–41; and Christopher Duffy, *By Force of Arms: The Austrian Army in the Seven Years War* II (Chicago: The Emperor's Press, 2008), 129–145.

26 Ibid., 77–96.

reforming military discipline; writing a new tactics manual; eliminating the *Ecole Royale Militaire*, the officers' school, in favor of regional officers' academies; and eliminating the remaining vestiges of venality. These were necessary to continue building on the foundation laid in the 1750s and 1760s of professionalizing the French army, but they occasioned significant criticism. Saint-Germain resigned in 1777, and Guibert lost his official position.[27]

Guibert had little time to reflect on his failures over the next year due to looming War of American Independence and the most important exercise conducted in France between 1763 and the end of the Old Regime. By the time of Saint-Germain's fall, the American Patriots had succeeded in not being overrun by the English, opening an opportunity for France to join the war. Louis XVI opted to declare war on England in early 1778, which meant mobilizing at least a portion of the army. In order to do so, the crown ordained a massive training camp be held in Normandy around Bayeux. This Camp of Vaussieux would finally put to rest the lingering debates over thin and deep orders, and it presented the leading theorists like Guibert and Mesnil-Durand an opportunity to hash out their differences with actual troops. The camp's commander, Marshal Broglie, was a partisan of Mesnil-Durand's system, particularly its use of many small attack columns. Most of the rest of the army had already decided against the functionality of that system, so Broglie intended the camp to put the issue to rest. Over several weeks, Broglie divided the army in half and commanded one against the other, commanded by Rochambeau. Rochambeau repeatedly defeated Broglie in exercises, illustrating the failure of Mesnil-Durand's system, and those based on the deep order.[28]

Vaussieux was a watershed for the French army, and for Guibert. It finally put to rest the tactical disputes that had raged since Folard's first works were published; the thin order emphasizing firepower was the only functional tactical system. More specifically, it demonstrated that a system like Mesnil-Durand's, which remained focused on petty tactics and perverted the Guibert Column into a series of small attack columns deploying on the center, simply did not function.

Guibert would not be sent to America, much to his disappointment, but he continued his career and service. He wrote more plays and essays, including the *Defense of the System of Modern War*, among other works on military affairs. He spent much of the following decade travelling around the country inspecting the garrisons attached to his father's Invalides command. He continued to attend salons, including perhaps having an affair with Anna-Louise-Germaine, baroness de Staël, née Necker. He also won election to the Académie Française in 1785. When the Revolution came, he ran for a seat in the Estates-General but was denied, leading him to publish his final work, *On the Public Force*, examining civil-military relations. He died in 1790, swearing "I will be known! I will have justice!"[29]

The majority of historical analysis of Guibert's work naturally focuses on his magnum opus, the *General Essay on Tactics*. Its clarion denunciations of contemporary governments and the armies they produced resonated with many in French society, and his military reforms promised to untangle difficult issues that had not yet found solutions among *militaires*. The work served as his introduction to military Europe and marked him as a leading military philosophe. It also likely won him a seat in the Académie Française and two separate stints on the Council of War.

The primacy of the *General Essay on Tactics* continues in analysis of Guibert, and of militaries of the period. It is likely the most-analyzed work of military theory written between 1750 and 1789, and perhaps even between the works of Niccolò Machiavelli and Antoine-Henri, baron Jomini. In particular, historians have written volumes analyzing its Preliminary Discourse, which contains most of its incendiary political rhetoric and apparent predictions of the Revolution and its mass armies. Others have noted its importance in shifting away from the tactics of stolid linear deployments to more dynamic formations deployed at the commander's will.[30] The *General Essay on Tactics* serves as a convenient encapsulation of the debates and reforms of the period, a bridge between Old Regime and the Revolutionary and Napoleonic periods. Unfortunately, as a result, it is often the only work of theory from the early modern period with which many are familiar.

The *Defense of the System of Modern War* suffers by comparison, both as a work encapsulating Guibert's thought and as a microcosm of any particular era or school of thought. When it was written, the tactical dispute between Mesnil-Durand and Guibert, and their supporters, was a pressing issue for the French military, but the issue was settled at the Camp of Vaussieux, and Mesnil-Durand quickly faded into obscurity. His name was removed from the title of the work in the definitive edition published

---

27 Ibid., 98–117.
28 See Quimby, *The Background of Napoleonic Warfare*, 233–248. Another smaller camp was held contemporaneously near Paramé that confirmed the results of Vaussieux but with much less fanfare or consternation.
29 Abel, *Jacques-Antoine-Hippolyte, comte de Guibert*, 156–174.
30 Jonathan Abel, "Jacques-Antoine-Hippolyte, comte de Guibert," *Oxford Bibliographies Online* (2014), https://www.oxfordbibliographies.com/display/document/obo-9780199791279/obo-9780199791279-0037.xml, provides an overview of Guibertian historiography on both counts.

with Napoleon's assent in the early 1800s. As a result, the bulk of the work, which is a refutation of Mesnil-Durand's ideas, appears relevant only to the arcanities of tactical systems in the 1770s. Further, Guibert places his political analysis at the end of the work, not the beginning, as he did in the *General Essay on Tactics*. Much of it is a repetition of the ideas presented in his first work. Finally, Guibert disavows the more contentious claims he made in the *General Essay on Tactics*, noting that the fervor of youth had led him to false conclusions about societies and the militaries they produced.

As a result, analysts and even contemporaries seem to have either ignored or offered apologies for the *Defense of the System of Modern War*. R.R. Palmer refers to it as "the conservative military technique of 1779 ... unfortunately for his reputation as a prophet."[31] Azar Gat's analysis of Guibert in *A History of Military Thought* does not even mention it.[32] Robert Quimby describes it as "a frankly controversial work," and he notes "inconsistencies" in Guibert's thought across both works.[33] Jean Colin dedicates few pages of his *Infantry of the Eighteenth Century*, a work long on analyses of contemporary treatises, to it.[34] Only Julia Osman's "Guibert vs. Guibert" addresses the *Defense of the System of Modern War* on its own merits by arguing that it deserves to be seen both as a continuation and an evolution of Guibert's ideas.[35]

The *Defense of the System of Modern War* serves two stated purposes. The first, as suggested by the work's full name, is to respond to the system created by Mesnil-Durand, and to proponents of the deep order in general. The stated is to expand and update the ideas Guibert presented in his first work, the *General Essay on Tactics*. A third theme emerges from the text, one especially useful to scholars of the period: an analysis of the great Camp of Vaussieux, the only major camp held between the end of the Seven Years War and the beginning of the Revolution in the late 1780s.

Guibert dedicates over half of the *Defense of the System of Modern War* to an exhaustive refutation of Mesnil-Durand's system and its principle of deploying an army exclusively in small attack columns formed on the center. He begins with Mesnil-Durand's inspiration, Folard, and shows in great detail how Mesnil-Durand's columns are neither his own invention nor functional. In this analysis, an important theme emerges: Guibert's distinction between "cabinet war" and war in reality. The former constitutes plans drawn up in a sterile environment, armies laid out on paper on battlefields that are entirely flat and devoid of any difficulty. This contrasts with the realities of war, according to Guibert, which present an almost limitless variety of circumstances that hinder plans and systems. Throughout the work, he castigates Mesnil-Durand for not taking practicalities into account in the development of his system, particularly terrain that might disrupt the use of his columns. Readers familiar with Carl von Clausewitz's *On War* might recognize Guibert's argument as a possible antecedent to Clausewitz's concept of friction, which he defines as "the only concept that more or less corresponds to the factors that distinguish real war from war on paper."[36]

A related theme of the *Defense of the System of Modern War* is to illustrate the "inadmissibility" of Mesnil-Durand's system via the example of the Camp of Vaussieux. Building on the previous theme, Guibert uses examples from the exercises conducted there to show how Mesnil-Durand's columns repeatedly failed when they were "transported from the cabinet to the battlefield."[37] Although his argument involves a great deal of technical analysis, it is important in two regards. First, no complete account of the camp and its exercises exists, so Guibert's is a valuable record of the activities of the most important exercise undertaken during the period. Second, Guibert illustrates the necessity of training officers with real troops instead of simply educating them in a schoolhouse despite the cost of training camps.

The most important theme of the *Defense of the System of Modern War* is Guibert's continuation of his recommendations for further reform of the army. As noted, Guibert elaborated a system that would allow French armies to maneuver and deploy in a simpler and easier fashion via the Guibert Column, producing a formation that was linear but not contiguous. This had not been fully accepted by the establishment, particularly as the pendulum had swung to favor Prussian-influenced thin orders deploying on rigid squares. The *Defense of the System of Modern War* is a continuation of his effort to build "systems that do not shackle."[38] He elaborates further on his system of march-maneuvers, illustrating how they can be used to ease the burden of march, deployment, and fighting. He also notes the importance of combined arms and how a system that is less rigid in its application allows for better integration of the arms. Finally,

---

31 R.R. Palmer, "Frederick, Guibert, Bülow," 111–112.
32 Azar Gat, *A History of Military Thought*, 45–55.
33 Quimby, *The Background of Napoleonic Warfare*, 249–268. Quimby also defends the work, noting it demonstrates consistency in Guibert's core philosophy with the *General Essay on Tactics*.
34 Colin, *L'infanterie au XVIIIᵉ siècle*, 185–245.
35 Osman, "Guibert vs. Guibert."
36 Carl von Clausewitz, *On War*, 119–121.
37 See 30.
38 See XVIII.

he highlights the importance of educated and skilled leadership in commanding contemporary armies.

This was the mid-point between the linear armies of the past and the articulated Napoleonic armies of the future. His technical reforms were aimed at this goal, although he never quite reached the point of seeing beyond the unitary army, as R.R. Palmer notes.[39] He also recognizes the importance of officers in this system. He notes that tactics were "a facile instrument that await[ed] only to be employed by the genius ... to find great success ... this is why today a skillful general may, in making positions, extend himself, separate himself, [and] finally hazard more than one dared to do then."[40]

Finally, one of the more interesting themes in the *Defense of the System of Modern War* is a refutation of some of the parts of the *General Essay on Tactics*, particularly its political analysis. Most importantly, Guibert denounces the "vapors of modern philosophy [that] aroused [his] mind and obfuscated [his] judgment" and led him to condemn all contemporary political systems.[41] Older and wiser, he recognizes that the governments that exist are not ideal, but they are natural products of the societies and people of each country and that they cannot be easily changed. He disavows the citizen armies of the prior work, preferring instead the professionals of his own day as less destructive to public order. Following from this, he also distances himself from the desire to completely rewrite French doctrine, to himself become a maker of systems. Instead, he is fully invested in the current system, as the title suggests. His new stance is to improve on the extant system rather than tear it down.

These changes have vexed readers since Guibert originally wrote them, as noted. Much of the criticism relates to the about-face on citizen armies, which seems to be a retrograde opinion given the looming French Revolution and its mass armies. However, Julia Osman, "Guibert vs. Guibert," provides a succinct and insightful solution to this conundrum: in the *Defense of the System of Modern War*, "Guibert is not contradicting, but expanding or continuing his ideas ... the transition from the *General Essay on Tactics* to the *Defense of the System of Modern War* is not a strange problem to solve but an acceptable progression in thinking."[42] Thus, the *Defense of the System of Modern War* is a valuable addition to the Guibert canon, the second half of a great work begun in the *General Essay on Tactics*. They are the most important works of eighteenth-century military theory, marking the transition from the rigid linear armies of the Old Regime to the distributed, linear-but-not-contiguous armies of the Napoleonic period. They also anticipate the arguments of great theorists like Jomini and Clausewitz by a generation, encouraging readers of nineteenth-century history and theory to delve more deeply into the past.

---

39 See Palmer, "Frederick, Guibert, Bülow."
40 See 58.
41 See 155.

42 Osman, "Guibert vs. Guibert," 64.

Avant-Propos

Never has there been elevated a question in the art of war [that is] more interesting, as much in substance as in circumstances. It is no longer an obscure polemic between tactics writers. The question was brought into plain sight. The proofs were made in a considerable camp under the eyes of the premier man of war that we have, the one whom the choice of the king and the wish of the nation called in concert to the command of the army.[1]

The opinion of Marshal Victor-François, duc de Broglie, in favor of the system of François-Jean de Graindorge d'Orgeville, baron de Mesnil-Durand, the weight of his reputation, [and] the immense support that he gave to this system: all make me sense how it is hazardous to enter into the lists, but my love for my métier, my attachment to my country, [and] the commitment that I imposed on myself to vow to its service the few faculties and [little] knowledge that I may have speak to me louder still. The Marshal is too generous to not esteem my motives. When one has as many means as he has of influencing opinions, one is above being bound by them.

I will thus dare to treat the question in all its extent, or to say it better, I wish to place all the pieces of this great process before the eyes of the public.

In every discussion, impartiality is the condition that one promises the most and to which one is commonly the least faithful. But, if one may flatter oneself in accomplishing it, it is doubtlessly when one is not led by any personal interest. But what genre of passion may animate me here? I am not the creator of any system.[2] In my *General Essay on Tactics*, I only extended and wrote about known ideas. I did not have any part in the Maneuver Ordinances [that have been] promulgated since the Treaty of Paris 1763.[3]

In the end, if in this work I demonstrate that the project of Mesnil-Durand is inadmissible, I pretend to draw from this success neither prize nor glory, because I will have only obtained it via a collection of the opinions of the greater part of the army and the principles of Friedrich II, King of Prussia.[4] My ambition will be fulfilled if I pass for a good spirit who has observed and conceived well, and, above all, for a frank and courageous man whom no consideration arrested in his research and in his exposition of the truth.

After impartiality, that to which I will attach myself to carrying the most in the discussion that I undertake is method and clarity. For too long has this question agitated without being deepened. For too long have large volumes, vague conversations, [and] superfluous forms of geometry and metaphysics spread ennui and obscurity over it; it must be treated for once so that it would be read, studied, and judged definitively. I do not at all write for France alone; I also address myself to the foreign armies that practice while we discuss. It is in war that one senses the value of the simple and the true, and it is where it [war] is made that military problems above all must find arbitrators and judges.

At first, I was only counting on making a pure and simple refutation of the system of Mesnil-Durand. The

---

1 [The Camp of Vaussieux.]
2 [In the parlance of contemporary military theorists, "system" denoted a work whose author expected it to be adopted wholesale from the page into the official Regulations; these were frequently referred to as "military constitutions." Mesnil-Durand's work fit this definition, as did that of his mentor Jean-Charles, chevalier Folard.]
3 [Two major periods of army reform took place between 1763 and the late 1770s, both of which involved Guibert to some degree. The first took place under Etienne-François, duc de Choiseul, in the 1760s and regularized the army's units and practices, including eliminating venality of companies, at least in theory. The second occurred under successive Secretaries of State for War in the 1770s, culminating in the ministry of Claude-Louis, comte de Saint-Germain, from 1775 to 1777; it continued the Choiseul reforms and eliminated all remaining venality, again at least in theory. Despite issuing several official Regulations and Ordinances related to the tactical dispute between thin and deep orders, the issue was not settled, in large part because thin orders were still too processional and deep orders were vulnerable to enemy fire. Brent Nosworthy, *The Anatomy of Victory: Battle Tactics 1689–1763* (New York: Hippocrene Books, 1990), 350–352; and Robert Quimby, *The Background of Napoleonic Warfare: The Theory of Military Tactics in Eighteenth-Century France* (New York: Columbia University Press), provide effective summaries in English. See also Louis-Hippolyte Bacquet, *L'infanterie au XVIIIe siècle. L'organisation* (Paris: Berger-Levrault, 1907), 73–201; Jean Colin, *L'infanterie au XVIIIe siècle. La tactique* (Paris: Berger-Levrault, 1907), 73–245; Albert Latreille, *L'œuvre militaire de la révolution: l'armée et la nation à la fin de l'ancien régime; les derniers ministres de la guerre de la monarchie* (Paris: Chapelot, 1914), 1–134; and *Les ministres de la guerre 1570–1792*, ed. Thierry Sarmant (Paris: Belin, 2007), 407–467.]
4 [Friedrich II, popularly known as Frederick the Great, was King of Prussia from 1740 until 1786. He started three wars, the War of the Austrian Succession, the Seven Years War, and the War of the Bavarian Succession, the first two of which resulted in the acquisitions of Silesia and Glatz for Prussia. Unlike his contemporary monarchs, Friedrich led his armies from the front and proved to be a military genius, winning the Seven Years War against a coalition of superpowers, albeit with a generous helping of good fortune. As the text proves, Friedrich is one of Guibert's chief inspirations, and he claims throughout to simply have adopted Friedrich's ideas for the French army. See Christopher Duffy, *The Military Life of Frederick the Great* (New York: Atheneum, 1986); and Patrick Shrier, "Frederick the Great," *Oxford Bibliographies Online* (2013), https://www.oxfordbibliographies.com/display/document/obo-9780199791279/obo-9780199791279-0094.xml.]

material that was spread before me, the interest and the importance of the subject bound me; I saw that one could only respond well to the attacks made by Mesnil-Durand against the modern system by developing this system, that there remained parts that were not deepened enough or that were not heard, and that this was what had been able to induce errors in some good spirits. I thus will work not only on the refutation of the system of Mesnil-Durand but also on the defense of the system of modern war, and I have given to my work a title relative to this double goal.[5]

Another motive, I must confess, carries me to giving my work more extent and more importance. If I were to bound myself simply to the discussion of the system of Mesnil-Durand, this polemic would have perished with it; already it excites only a feeble interest; the public has cooled, and that which formed spirits in a so-great fermentation three months ago is regarded at present as void. I desire that my work, in presenting the question in the broadest possible extent, would arouse attention, would draw an attention independent of the moment, and would survive the system of Mesnil-Durand.

Several people asked why I would write against a system that was condemned by the opinion of the army and by the current silence of the public. The complaint of the army against the system of Mesnil-Durand was almost universal, but Marshal Broglie's vote remained entirely [for it], and this one alone balances all [others]. The army wished to judge the system of Mesnil-Durand, but the reasons that were the foundation of the judgement of the army must be developed by adding to them new ones, and perhaps brand new ones.[6] There are people who, suspended by a great authority, still hesitate in their opinion. There are those who, in condemning the maneuvers of Mesnil-Durand, [still] approve of the foundation of his system. There are those, as I said above, who have not studied the modern system enough, or for whom this system has not been sufficiently developed. The greater part of the French military [and] of foreign militaries, among which I also search for judges, did not at all assist in the Camp of Vaussieux and may be able to make an opinion only by the reports [of it that are] vague and are always suspected of passion. The public, it is true, does not speak any more of the question that will agitate me, but of what does the public, and above all the public of the capital, speak about a month after the event? *Militaires* think about it, and it is for them that I write. In every species of science, it is to the people of the art that one must address oneself, then to those who advise the public, and the public follows in their tracks. Finally, as it is important to fight the system of Mesnil-Durand, to destroy it and to prevent it from being reproduced, it is a matter of opposing it with a corpus of reasons and doctrine that enlightens the mass of the public and places the truth under its safeguard.[7] It is always, in the long run, the general voice that dictates the laws, and even governments are governed by them.[8]

Among the aid that has been furnished to me in all parts from the discussions, the views, [and] the enlightenment of a great number of *militaires*, my recognition must cite the most direct and most positive aid that that I drew from a memoire of comte de la Chapelle, which began, during the proofs of Metz,[9] to give account of these proofs to the late Marshal Louis-Nicolas-Victor de Félix d'Ollières, comte du Muy, a memoir full of good, healthy, and solid reason;[10] from a manuscript of François-Jean de

---

5 [As noted, the editor of the 1803 edition abridged the title, rendering this passage confusing for readers unfamiliar with the original.]
6 [The expression Guibert uses here, "*de nouvelles et de neuves*," is a layered colloquialism that does not translate. It literally means "new ones and new ones," but "*neuves*" carries the sense of renewal, of a new start, and/or of a change that has been made very recently. He is essentially arguing that his work exists both to clean house of obsolete theories and to take into account the most recent developments.]
7 [In French, both in Guibert's day and at present, "doctrine" generally carries a religious or philosophical meaning. However, the modern English meaning of a set of military rules and regulations was used at the time; see La Fontaine, *La doctrine militaire ou le parfait général d'armée* (Paris: Loyson, 1671), for example.]
8 [Guibert here demonstrates his solidarity with the constitutional party of Charles-Louis-de Secondat, baron de la Brède et de Montesquieu, and against the absolutist, divine-right theories promulgated in support of Louis XIV by writers like Jacques-Bénigne Bossuet. A massive corpus of literature exists on the political theory of the French Enlightenment, of which Montesquieu is perhaps the central figure; Dorinda Outram, *The Enlightenment* (New York: Cambridge University Press, 2019), 26–42; and Daniel Roche, *France in the Enlightenment*, trans. Arthur Goldhammer (Cambridge: Harvard University Press, 1998), 251–484, provide an overview. See also Catherine Volpilhac-Auger, "Montesquieu," *Oxford Bibliographies Online* (2020), https://www.oxfordbibliographies.com/display/document/obo-9780195396577/obo-9780195396577-0275.xml.]
9 [Probably Alexandre-François-Marie le Filleul, comte de la Chapelle. Metz housed the most important frontier garrison in the kingdom, serving two purposes for the French army: it held the nucleus of units around which the main field army would be built in case of war, and its active units performed regular exercises to test new tactics, systems, and doctrine. As a result, throughout the century, peacetime command of Metz was given to the most prestigious field commander, who would have expected to command the field army in case of war. A garrison exercise was held at Metz in 1775, which favored the deep order and served as a prelude to Vaussieux, according to Colin, *L'infanterie au XVIIIᵉ siècle*, 185–245.]
10 [Louis-Nicolas-Victor de Félix, comte du Muy, was from a Provençal family of old noble and military extraction. He served in the three mid-century wars, repeatedly demonstrating personal

Beauvoir, marquis de Chastellux, who made it at the end of the Camp of Vaussieux, which he destined for printing and with which his amity was good enough to enrich me;[11] [and] from a memoir of comte de Surgères containing excellent observations on the details of the system of Mesnil-Durand, observations precious because they are the result of his practice at the head of one of the best-instructed regiments in the army.[12] Finally, it remains to me to cite my father, Charles-Benoît Guibert, above all, whose opinion on this occasion has fortified mine all the more; inviolably attached to Marshal Broglie, he gave it against the prejudices of his spirit and the sentiments of his heart.[13]

I will commence this work by placing the plan by which I conceived it at its head. The reader and the author both gain by this method: the author, in making his plan before his work, [despite] not always achieving it, better accomplishes it in going straighter to their target, and, if their plan is well conceived, it inspires for them an advantageous prejudice, [and] the reader embraces with a coup-d'œil the goal and the ensemble of the work that is presented to them; prepared by this program, then the execution follows with more interest and facility.[14]

---

courage and command skill. Despite this, he was seriously defeated at the Battle of Warburg in 1760, and only his status as a client of Louis, Dauphin of France, saved his career. After Choiseul's fall, he refused the position of Secretary of State for War before accepting it in 1774 after the death of Louis XV; he served in office for only a short time before dying in late 1775. During his tenure, he ordered exercises of the infantry regulations in force, including the aforementioned 1775 Metz maneuvers. See Guillaume Lasconjarias, "Louis-Nicolas-Victor de Félix, comte du Muy," *Les ministres de la guerre*, 450–456.]

11 [François-Jean de Beauvoir, marquis de Chastellux, came from a military family and spent his life in the family trade. He also wrote extensively, winning election to the Académie Française in 1775. He is best known in America for his service in the French army during the American War of Independence; see Chastellux, *Travels in North America in the Years 1780, 1781, and 1782* (London: Robinson, 1787).]

12 [Probably Charles-Henri de Granges de Surgères, marquis de Puyguyon et la Flocellère, listed in André Corvisier, *Les contrôles de troupes de l'ancien régime*, 2 Vols. (Paris: Etat-Major de L'Armée de Terre, 1970), II:478, as colonel of the First Battalion of the Bourgogne Regiment in 1775. See also Etienne Pattou, "Maison de Maingot de Surgères et Granges de Surgères," *Racines Histoire* (2022), http://racineshistoire.free.fr/LGN/PDF/Maingot_de_Surgeres.pdf.]

13 [Charles-Benoît Guibert served in the mid-century wars, including being taken prisoner after Rossbach. He worked closely with the Ministry of War for the remainder of his life and career, including becoming governor of Perpignan and the Invalides. Guibert and his father shared military service but differed in many other ways. Guibert senior preferred to remain out of the public eye and debates, dedicating himself to what would now be called staff work as a client of the Broglie family. He disapproved of his son's public career, particularly his literary pretensions. Nevertheless, Guibert junior credits him with his military upbringing, and Guibert senior undoubtedly helped create Guibert junior's system, particularly the mobile columns that broke up the linear blocks of past practice. See Jonathan Abel, *Guibert's General Essay on Tactics* (Leiden: Brill, 2022), 238–239; and *Jacques-Antoine-Hippolyte, comte de Guibert: Father of Napoleon's Grande Armée* (Norman: University of Oklahoma Press, 2016).]

14 [Guibert speaks of the French custom, including to the present, of placing the table of contents at the end of the work rather than at the beginning, which is customary in Anglophone works.]

BOOK 1

∴

FIRST PART

CHAPTER 1

[The] System of Mesnil-Durand, Originally Drawn from That of Folard. Who Folard Was. Exposition of His System

When Jean-Charles, chevalier Folard, imagined the column, or rather brought it back to light, he did not dare to propose it as the primitive and habitual ordinance of the infantry despite his having the heart of a father for it. He gave it only as an accidental disposition destined on one hand to reinforce and to support an order of battle, and on the other to make efforts on the enemy and to penetrate them. The Disciple [Mesnil-Durand] went further than the Master [Folard], that is to say that he outdid him in prejudice and enthusiasm. It is somewhat the same in all nascent doctrines. The first sectarians always exaggerate the opinions of the sect founders.[1] Not being able to pretend to the merit of its discovery, they rack their brains to add to it. If they succeed, if they comment on and develop some points, if, above all, they believe themselves to have redressed some errors of the Master, they identify themselves with the system, or perhaps they identify the system as themselves; this is at what Mesnil-Durand arrived. "In searching," we learn in one of his prefaces,[2] "the debris of all the military systems, he found the Folard Column; this raw diamond was misunderstood and rejected; he took it and implemented it." Was this a discovery so precious that this column, and the system that Mesnil-Durand drew from it in pretending to perfect it, is better? This is what I will examine.

Before speaking of the Folard Column, let me be permitted to say a word on Folard himself; this digression will not at all be foreign to my subject. Many people, faithful to the prejudices of their education, still have a great respect for Folard; it is good to make them appreciate who Folard was and if his name is, in effect, a great authority.

Folard studied war more than he made it; he served only in the subaltern grades, and he consequently did not have the practice of command, of circumstances, or of men.[3]

He much studied military antiquity, and he saw everything in the Ancients, but he did not reflect on the fact that that the constitutions, the arms, the customs, and even the men were different. Such was his blindness for everything that came from them that he maintained that the effects of their missile weapons were superior to our artillery.[4]

His passion for antiquity was further augmented in him by the discontent that he had for his century and his country.[5] He found himself mistreated by the service, and he was; he only reached a simple commission as colonel, and he was never employed actively in this grade. The government was doubtlessly guilty, because it was required to furnish him with opportunities; the recompense of men who have acquired knowledge of their profession must be that it at least be put to the test. Folard had also received from nature a character full of morosity and sourness, which contributed often to shrinking of spirit and to falsification of judgment. The same foundation of character rendered Antoine de Pas, marquis de Feuquières, the Aristarchus of all the generals, but Feuquières had genius, and his criticisms are immortal lessons.[6] Folard had none,

---

1 [Guibert perhaps takes a jab at Folard here, as Folard was a member, and even a leader, of a radical sect of Jansenist convulsionaries who gathered at the Saint-Médard cemetery in Paris around 1730 until their official dispersal by the government, including Folard's arrest. Jansenism, a belief system that resembled Protestantism but claimed to be Catholic, had been popular in France as a locus of resistance to centralized, absolutist royal rule, but the convulsionaries offended most French subjects, leading the movement to become less religious and more political in future decades. See William Doyle, *Jansenism: Catholic Resistance to Authority from the Reformation to the French Revolution* (New York: St. Martin's, 2000). After the incident, Folard spent most of the rest of his life out of the public eye; see Jean Chagniot, *Le chevalier de Folard: la stratégie de l'incertitude* (Paris: Editions du Rocher, 1997), 233–258.]
2 "Preliminary Discourse," *Fragments de tactique*, 15.
   [François-Jean de Graindorge d'Orgeville, baron de Mesnil-Durand, *Fragments de tactique ou six mémoires* (Paris: Jombert, 1774), 15]

3 [Guibert is correct that Folard did not serve as a general officer, although he did have extensive experience as a junior officer serving in Italy during the War of the Spanish Succession; see Chagniot, *Le chevalier de Folard*, 31–56.]
4 [See, for example, Jean-Charles, chevalier Folard, *Nouvelle découvertes sur la guerre* (Paris: Josse and Labottière, 1724), 125–127: "the catapult and the ballista may serve in war today … ; they made the same effect as our cannon loaded with cartridge" despite being cheaper, lighter, and easier to use, according to Folard.]
5 [Guibert rightly places Folard within the *Querelle des anciens et modernes* (Quarrel of the Ancients and the Moderns), a wide-ranging debate culminating in the late seventeenth century about whether Classical Greek and Roman or modern cultures were superior. One of the chief "moderns" was Charles Perrault, redactor of fairy tales and military writer; Folard was clearly an "ancient." See Joan DeJean, *Ancients Against Moderns: Culture Wars and the Making of a Fin de Siècle* (Chicago: University of Chicago Press, 1997).]
6 [Antoine de Pas, marquis de Feuquières, was a general during the reign of Lous XIV. More importantly, he was the author of *Mémoires*

and his works have only the merit of a vast erudition; he is the Scholastic, the Dom Antoine Calmet of military authors, except that he did not know Greek, and it was the Benedictine Vincent Thuillier who furnished him his translations, which, as Karl Gottleib Guichard proved, caused him to fall into strange blunders.[7] All that Folard compiled, all that he drew from others, instructs and interests; all that he added to it and that he drew from himself is a mass of ennui and errors.

As soon as he discovered, or believed he discovered, his column, he lived only for it; he proposed only it. His commentary on Polybius, his research on the Ancients, his [commentaries] on modern wars: everything brought him back to his column. In antiquity, he searched for facts and examples to support it. He analyzed the battles of our days, then gave them back in his own account and in his own manner, the result always being that, if the vanquished party had made use of columns, it would not have lost. This manner of reasoning, which proves more erudition and passion than healthy logic, passed a little to his successors.[8]

We come to his column and to the employment that he pretended of it in his tactics. To fight Mesnil-Durand on an even footing, we must return to the source from where he drew [his system]. Besides, it is curious to see the analogy and the difference that are found between the principles of the disciple and those of the master.

"The column," as Folard defines it,[9] "is a corps of infantry that is serried and compressed, that is to say a corps ranged on a long square where the frontage is much less than the depth. The ranks and the files must be so condensed that the soldiers preserve only as much space between them as they need to be able to march and to make use of their weapons."

It may be composed of one battalion or as many as six and formed of more or fewer files and ranks according to the countryside where it may find itself obliged to act and to fight.

Folard nevertheless fixes the proportions at twenty, twenty-four, or at most thirty files in free terrain. He adds that, in terrain that is not, it may maintain itself in its strength from as many as thirty or thirty-four files, or as few as sixteen. However, he is not at all attached to the even number, which he says is not necessary for evolutions for him.

Folard divides his column into three sections that do not leave any interval between them at the moment of combat. He calls the wings of the ranks or the flanks "faces," because the term "flanks" refers to the feeble sides of a battalion, [and] there is no such feebleness in a column, according to him. [A] strange blindness made him believe that his column would no longer have flanks if he would call them "faces."

Folard always separates the grenadier companies from his column; they serve him as supports and as reserves, and he consequently places them at the tail or on each side of the last section.

The officers and subalterns are always placed at the head, at the tail, and on the two sides of the column.

Folard supposes battalions of five-hundred men, or four-hundred fusiliers and one-hundred men carrying partisans, not counting the grenadiers, officers, and sergeants.[10]

His column is divided into two "manches," one named "the manche of the right" and the other "the manche of the left." Each manche is then subdivided from five files into five files.[11] The three of the right are named "the divisions of the right" and the three on the left "the divisions of the left."

---

contenants ses maximes sur la guerre et l'application des exemples aux maximes, 4 Vols. (London: Dunoyer, 1736), which were a standard reference for *militaires* in the eighteenth century, as Guibert says. See John Lynn, *The Wars of Louis XIV 1667–1714* (New York: Palgrave, 1999).

Aristarchus of Samos was one of the leading scientists of the Hellenistic period; he probably championed heliocentrism and began the process of calculating the sizes of the Sun, the Moon, and the Earth, and their distances from each other. See Thomas Heath, *Aristarchus of Samos: A History of Greek Astronomy to Aristarchus* (New York: Cambridge University Press, 2013).]

7 [Antoine Calmet was a Benedictine in the Congregation of Saint-Vannes in the early eighteenth century and a prolific writer, especially of history and religious studies.

Vincent Thuillier was a Benedictine in the Congregation of Saint-Maur in the mid-eighteenth century and a scholar of Classical Greek. Folard relied on him to translate Polybius, as Folard did not read Greek; the idea was that Thuillier's language and Folard's military expertise would make the work better than a simple translation. However, this opened Folard up to criticism for errors in the translation, which Karl-Gottleib Guichard, *Mémoires militaires sur les Grecs et les Romains*, 2 Vols. (Den Haag: Hondt, 1758), seized upon; see Chagniot, *Le chevalier de Folard*, 79–100.]

8 [Chagniot, *Le chevalier de Folard*, defends Folard against most critiques of him, but even it agrees that Folard often argues his Classical examples to a fault, supporting Guibert's argument.]

---

9 See *Histoire de Polybe*, I, "Treatise on the Column."
   [Jean-Charles, chevalier Folard, *Histoire de Polybe*, 7 Vols. (Various, 1753), I: LIV.
10 [The term both men use, "*pertuisaniers*," last appears in the 2nd edition of the Academie Française's dictionary, published in 1718, reflecting the obsolescence of the weapon and the men who carried it by that time.]
11 It is then formed on five ranks.

Folard counts much on the division and subdivision of his column, as much to fall on the flanks of the enemy line after having pierced it as to maneuver by what he calls the faces of his column and, in every sense, against the enemy that would seek to envelop it. This is also the great advantage that Mesnil-Durand pretends to draw from the organization of his own.

Folard reputes his column thus formed invincible; he finds in it all the advantages: "solidity, lightness, [and] security of the sides," because, for the flanks, one recalls that he proved that the column no longer had them by naming them "faces." No circumstance, no terrain can and will not hinder it. It even has, according to him, the ability to advantageously serve itself with its fire. He works to demonstrate this; what fire is this? "It is fire by tranches or by ranks in such a manner that each rank, after having fired, kneels with nose almost lowered to the ground."[12] But it is above all in fights of the *arme blanche* and in shock actions that his column must triumph. There, his expressions no longer have measure. He attributes all of his column's strength to its weight, and this weight he believes is born of the density and the pressing of ranks, as if it would act with the adherence of physical bodies. "If the column," he says gravely, "falls with all its weight on another disposition, it will carry it and go straight through it, as a ram knocks down a section of a wall."[13] Elsewhere he compares it to "the rock that Polyphemus threw with the force of a giant at Odysseus's ships."[14] Later, he employs an entire chapter in proving that eight battalions in column must defeat thirty-two battalions in the customary order [three-deep lines].[15] A quadruple superiority is still only a game for him, because he advances soon after that "it is morally and physically impossible" that a column would ever be able to be broken. No cavalry, however brave, however numerous that it may be, would dare to abandon itself on it. "Yes, my column," he adds, "has nothing feeble, [so] it may be make face to all sides and reform itself easily. It is a bundle of thorns that no one will know from which side to take it, and its shock, its solidity, its weight, [and] its strength are so violent that there is nothing that would be able to refuse its passage, nothing that it would not open and would not penetrate. Quite far from shaking it, there is no battalion that it does not break. It would even disappear when faced with its fire, and against the forest of partisans and sponsons of the officers and the halberds of its sergeants that find themselves placed near it," etc.[16] If you do not wish to believe in this mass of dreams written in the style of the Apocalypse, he treats you as "absurd, ignorant, [and] stubborn," and he finishes in saying that "there is nothing to say to you except what Ajax said to Aphrodite: "go; war is not your métier; involve yourself in giving birth to it.""[17] We apparently cannot speak of the column with more moderation, as we have seen Mesnil-Durand, in re-dressing it under the name "*plésion*" in his project of tactics, vaunt it and defend it quite differently still.

Folard would reclaim long arms;[18] he would regard them as absolutely necessary for infantry, but he proposes, in lieu of the pike, a sort of partisan of twelve feet, which, in effect, would be worth more. He would have them be a fifth of a battalion.[19] In his column, he would mingle the pikemen alternatively with the fusiliers in the first ranks of each section and in the first two files of the wings, that is to say that he would place a man with a partisan between two fusiliers.

The Folard Column would form itself by movements of the files such that, its battalion being five deep, he would triple the files. This movement would make itself in a manner too curious not to report here. The manche of the center of the battalion would return on that of theright, the first rank behind the first, the second behind the second, and thus the others. At the same time, the manche of the left would return on its two manches joined together, the first rank behind the first of the center manche, the

---

12   "Treatise on the Column"
    [See Folard, *Histoire de Polybe*, I:XVC.]
13   "Treatise on the Column," 18.
    [See Folard, *Histoire de Polybe*, I:LX.]
14   "Treatise on the Column," 23.
    [Folard, *Histoire de Polybe*, I:LXIII. The myth referenced is from Book IX of Homer, *Odyssey*, https://www.perseus.tufts.edu/hopper/text?doc=Perseus:text:1999.01.0136. Odysseus and his men escape from Polyphemus, a giant cyclops, culminating in his throwing a large rock at Odysseus's ship. Odysseus taunts Polyphemus by revealing his name to the giant, leading to the extension of his journey home by a decade.
15   "Treatise on the Column," Chapter 4.
    [Folard, *Histoire de Polybe*, I:LXXVII.]
16   "Treatise on the Column," 46–47.
    [See Folard, *Histoire de Polybe*, I:LXXVII.]
17   "Treatise on the Column," 14.
    [Folard, *Histoire de Polybe*, I:LVII. The story being referenced here is from Book V of Homer, *Illiad*, https://www.perseus.tufts.edu/hopper/text?doc=Perseus:text:1999.01.0134, although Folard replaces Diomedes, who wounds Aphrodite during the Trojan War in the original story, with Ajax, another prominent character in the myth. A popular contemporary translation, Homer, *L'iliade*, trans. Anne Dacier (Paris: 1699), 92, does not make Folard's error, which Guibert repeats. The specific reference is to the myth of the origin of the Trojan War, which stemmed from a competition between Aphrodite, Athena, and Hera.]
18   ["Long arms" refers to spear-like weapons, including pikes, partisans, halberds, etc.]
19   [The second edition of the Académie Française's dictionary defines a partisan as a long arm "approaching a halberd," and a pike as a long arm with a "flat and pointed iron head."]

second behind the second, and thus the rest, in such a way that each battalion would find itself fifteen deep. Folard supposes a battalion of four-hundred and fifty fusiliers, not counting the grenadiers; this is, according to him, the most-perfect number, and five deep in its habitual order, which is, according to him, the least depth that may be given to an infantry troop. In taking this calculation, his battalion finds itself ranged on a frontage of thirty, and fifteen deep. It must be recalled that a battalion in this order is only a section of his column, which he supposes must be of two battalions at least, of three in its perfection, and of four, five, and up to six when he wishes to make support masses for the wings of his order of battle.

Folard also speaks of sometimes forming columns of only one battalion; then, he ranges them eight deep and makes them triple the files in the same way; this gives it twenty-four files of depth, [a] proportion somewhat parallel to the *plésions* of Mesnil-Durand.

It must be agreed that there is nothing in the world worse than this organization of the column and this manner off forming it, because, if Folard would have contented himself with placing the three battalion manches one behind the other, then they would pass, but he inserts the ranks, he mixes them, [and] he decomposes everything. It is the same in all the maneuvers that Folard makes for his column and in all the movements that he makes the armies formed in his system execute. Everything in it feels like the infancy in which tactics was then. Everywhere we see men without talents, without resources, and incapable of drawing the science [of tactics] from the barbarism where they found it.

We pass to the use that Folard makes of his column in armies. It is the least bad part of his system. It is only ever an accidental and momentary disposition that he takes with one or several battalions to reinforce one's line and support one's order of battle.[20] He wishes that they also be interlaced between two brigades on the points on which one wishes to make effort. He wishes further that they be placed on the flanks and at the center of the order of battle, and there he proposes three or four battalions at least.

Employed thus, but with address and intelligence when the terrain and circumstances permit, and without becoming a habitual order, columns may be advantageous; this is what we have said in the *General Essay on Tactics*, and this is what we will repeat in the course of this work.[21] But the idea did not at all begin with Folard; Gustav Adolf employed them thus at the Battles of Breitenfeld and Lützen. He intermingled his order, with several columns forming bastions [and] his line eight-deep and behind his columns, forming, to speak properly, the curtain wall.[22]

Folard makes no case for cavalry; he almost always regards it as an embarrassment, and often as useless, and his favorite proof is that the Romans knew how to do without it. As it is nevertheless necessary to obey our prejudices, which are not those of the Romans in this regard, here is how he proposes to employ it.

First, he intermingles the squadrons with infantry platoons composed of twenty-five picked grenadiers or fusiliers; these platoons must charge at the same time as the squadrons, and, to this end, "make their discharge at close range, then flow between the intervals and charge the flank of the enemy squadrons with bayonets fixed."[23] A host of citations, as many Greek and Roman as modern, follow, according to his usage, supporting this ridiculous mélange.

With regard to the rest of the cavalry, he intermingles it by demi-brigades or by entire brigades between infantry brigades, and, so that this chaos be yet more complete and more dangerous, he does not miss to recommend that each cavalry brigade of the first line find itself supported by a second line of infantry and the infantry of the first line by a second line of cavalry. Here is the tactician whom our young people have studied for forty years; here is one of the masters consecrated again among us by routine and by ignorance!

---

20 [See Abel, *Guibert's General Essay on Tactics*, 53–54: "here is the résumé of my discussion: 'the primitive, fundamental, and habitual ordinance of the infantry will be on three ranks of depth; the momentary and accidental ordinance will be in column.'"]

21 [Abel, *Guibert's General Essay on Tactics*, 88–96.]

22 [Gustav II Adolf, popularly known as "Gustavus Adolphus," was king of Sweden from 1594 until his death in at the latter battle in 1632. He led Sweden into the Thirty Years War, championing the Protestant cause and bringing several adaptions, particularly the use of combined arms, to contemporary armies. He joined the canon of great captains via these reforms and his military genius, and Guibert will have frequent recourse to him as an example and a paragon. The 1631 Battle of Breitenfeld was the first major Protestant victory in the Thirty Years War. Gustav's six-deep formations were more nimble than his opponents' deeper ones, allowing him to make better use of his combined-arms and more-disciplined force.

The Battle of Lützen took place the following year as the Catholic forces attempted to retake Northern Germany. The battle was a bloody draw, but its most important consequence was that Gustav Adolf was killed during it, as noted. According to Peter Wilson, *The Thirty Years War: Europe's Tragedy*, (Cambridge: Harvard University Press, 2011), 472–476 and 507–511, Guibert is correct in ascribing tactical flexibility to Gustaf Adolf at Breitenfeld but incorrect in doing so at Lützen, which he calls an "unimaginative frontal assault" by the Swede. See also Geoffrey Parker, *The Thirty Years War* (New York: Barnes & Noble, 1987), 125–132; and Michael Roberts, *Gustavus Adolphus* (London: Routledge, 2016).]

23 [Folard, *Histoire de Polybe*, I:LXXV–LXXXI.]

Folard is, in general, not much of a partisan of second lines. He believes that the order that would conform best to a French army, whose first approach, following his expressions, "is everything that one may find to be the most redoubtable, the strongest, the most lively, and the most terrible," would be to range itself on a single line by small intervals.[24] This doubtlessly is what gives Mesnil-Durand, in his French Order, the idea of inserting his *plésions* of the second line into those of the first to charge the enemy all together and on a single line.

As to artillery and to the objections that it may furnish against deep orders, Folard contents himself with responding that "he does not take any account of it, that to get rid of it is not black magic, [and] that there is only to close with the enemy."[25] It is true that, [being] more reasonable, he then formally advances that he must only form in column with the goal of marching on the enemy, and, at the moment when he decides to march on them, he says, "I would be able to appear in the presence of the enemy, my battalions on a front as large as those that oppose me, up to forty or fifty paces from them; then, the scene changes, the thin battalions disappear in an instant, [and] their files double, triple, and become columns. This movement is so light, so sudden, [and] so simple that one would hardly have time to perceive how it was done."[26] Here the master and the disciple fall, as one sees, into a manifest dissension, as the master is quite far from wishing that the column be an habitual order, and he wishes that it would be regarded only as an accidental and momentary disposition that he pretends to form only within fifty paces of the enemy. The maneuver that he proposes to this end is doubtlessly absurd, but it evidently demonstrates what his principle is.

This is, in short, a faithful exposé of Folard's system. However bad it was at its foundation, however maladroit and imperfect it was in its means, it had its partisans. It had for it all the people [who were] amorous of times past and frondeurs against their own times; it had for it many people who let themselves be imposed on by the mass of erudition that accompanied it. Indeed, the means, unless one has a spirit superior to prejudices and capable of more profound [thought], of not letting oneself go to the opinions of a man who ceaselessly supports his opinions indiscriminately, it is true, [with] the names and pretend examples of all the great captains, ancient and modern!

But what he had going even more for him was the ignorance and the imperfection of tactics that existed at the time. He attacked our armies broadly: their slowness, their weight, [and] their inadequacy of maneuver, and he doubtlessly did it well. The ingenious creator, the man who had to remedy all these faults, lightening armies by discipline and by the art of handling them, enlightening military Europe by his writings and astonishing it by his victories: Friedrich had not appeared.

Some critics presented themselves to fight Folard, but among them, one need only cite the four letters of a Dutch general officer, known under the name *Sentiments of a Man of War*.[27] They appeared successively over time, and they are dissertations that, although a little long-winded, contain excellent objections. They agree with Folard on the vices of modern tactics, but, at the same time, they completely ruin his column and his system. Sensing the inconveniences and the defaults of the routine used then was neither difficult nor rare. All the generals, all the *militaires* of the times complained of them, but remedying them, making happen what Friedrich has made happen since: here is what could only have been done by him, and this is what seemed to await him.

Folard tried to respond to the second letter of the Dutch general officer, and this earned him a reply in the third letter, which is the best and most decisive. In it, he took the side of saying that "he was criticized by people who had only seen war in a painting, and from over the mountains,"[28] allowing this controversy to be taken up by his students and passing the rest of his life following the assemblies of convulsionaries and continuing his indefatigable commentaries on antiquity.

He was even less fortunate relative to the revolution that he had hoped to instigate. He never had the satisfaction of seeing his system being tried. In 1710, our armies being at the height of dishonor and misfortune, Douai

---

24 [See Folard, *Histoire de Polybe*, I:XCIII.]
25 "Treatise on the Column," 72.
 [See Folard, *Histoire de Polybe*, I:LXXVIII.]
26 "Folard's Response to the Criticisms Published against his System by Two Dutch Officers," *Histoire de Polybe*, VII.
 [Folard, *Histoire de Polybe*, VII:239–273.]

27 This general officer was named Savornin and was a French refugee. His letters are printed in the suite of *Histoire de Polybe* (Amsterdam: 1753), VII.
 [See Folard, *Histoire de Polybe* (Amsterdam, 1753) VII:79–238, probably referencing Johannes van Savornin. Guibert touches on the crux of the dilemma of military reform in the Old Regime, particularly in the first half of the eighteenth century: small, incremental changes were required before large-scale reforms could be made, including the development of operational-level warfare. This is discussed in the introduction to Abel, *Guibert's General Essay on Tactics*.]
28 "Folard's Last Response," VII.
 [Folard, *Histoire de Polybe*, VII:177. "Over the mountains" is a half-idiomatic expression that denotes matters that occur in distant lands and thus beyond the care of the speaker, as it suggests; it is similar to "cabinet war," a favorite phrase of Guibert's directed at Mesnil-Durand throughout the text.]

being besieged, France being open and at bay, Folard was always saying and printing that it was the fault of our tactics; the government resembling all those desperately ill people who listen to all the *empiriques*,[29] Folard was made to go to propose his system to Marshal-General Claude-Louis-Hector, duc de Villars,[30] who, with a superior army, was in range of being able to deliver Douai by attacking Prince Eugene-Francis of Savoy, who covered the siege.[31] Never would a better occasion be presented, never would the enemies better display the thin order in all its feebleness: Eugene's position covered a league and a half, with his right anchored on the Bernières Swamp and his left on the scarpe; no ravine, no stream, no obstacle covered the front; he was only defended by some redoubts, and, in truth, by a numerous artillery, although less numerous than that of an army of the same strength that would occupy a similar position today. On many points, Prince Eugene had only a single line of infantry. It was the case of "going and penetrating;" it was the case of the double oblique, the famous order perpendicular to one of the wings, or, even better, on the enemy center. Folard proposed to attack on these principles: "the infantry by columns of two and of three battalions between the intervals of the infantry brigades, the cavalry supporting it on two lines, the squadrons interlaced with infantry platoons, the large battalions on the wings ten-deep, and some others spread along all of the front of the first line."[32] A war council assembled; it examined Folard's project and rejected it with a common voice.

Folard's partisans have much cited the amity that united him to Marshal-General Herman-Maurice, comte de Saxe, and the esteem that he [Saxe] appeared to have for his [Folard's] works in his favor.[33] I avow that I have seen no part of this opinion enunciated in the writings that are attributed to the Marshal-General. He speaks in them of the inconveniences of the thin order and of the difficulty of moving our modern orders of battle. He says in them that the science of marches and movements is in its infancy and that the art is to create it. This proves that, among many others, he saw its faults, but, as I have already said, seeing the faults is far from foreseeing the means of remedying them, and foreseeing them [is] further still from posing principles and reducing them to examples. What the Marshal-General positively states at least is his disdain for the column when he says that "it is the heaviest and the worst machine that he knows."[34] With regard to the amity that he may have had for Folard, I do not contest it, but it proves nothing; it was as simple as the Marshal-General, then comte de Saxe and a general officer distant from command, not minding conciliating Folard, who wrote and who was acting on the opinion of the mob, and he was above all somewhat grateful to him for having put

---

29 [An *empirique* was a naturopath or other fraudulent physician.]

30 [Claude-Louis-Hector, duc de Villars, was the last great marshal of Louis XIV's wars. He served under the great commanders during those wars in the seventeenth century before winning his marshal's baton but running afoul of court politics early in the War of the Spanish Succession. He commanded the forces that brutally repressed the Camisard Revolt in southeastern France and fought the British to a bloody standstill at the Battle of Malplaquet in 1709. The following year, he defeated Eugene at the Battle of Denain, reversing years of French losses and ensuring that the war would not be an abject humiliation. He ended his career, and his life, as Marshal-General of France and commander of French forces in the War of the Polish Succession. See W. Gregory Monahan, *Let God Arise: The War and Rebellion of the Camisards* (New York: Oxford University Press, 2014); and Claude Sturgill, *Marshal Villars and the War of the Spanish Succession* (Lexington: University of Kentucky Press, 1965).]

31 [Prince Eugene-Francis of Savoy was Villars's contemporary and frequent opponent. He grew up in France but was denied a position in the French army, leading him to Imperial service. He proved to be one of the great captains of the era, as Guibert regularly notes. He oversaw the great Imperial campaigns against the Ottoman Empire that retook huge swaths of territory in Hungary and the Balkans in the late seventeenth and early eighteenth centuries. Like Villars, he finished his service and his life in the Polish Succession. See Caleb Karges, "Prince Eugene of Savoy," *Oxford Bibliographies Online* (2023), https://www.oxfordbibliographies.com/display/document/obo-9780199791279/obo-9780199791279-0238.xml.

The Siege of Douai opened the 1710 campaign and saw the armies of Eugene and John Churchill, duke of Marlborough, lay siege to the fortress to continue to open the fortress belts that guarded northeastern France. Villars moved an army to raise the siege but demurred from attacking, and the fortress fell. See Chagniot, *Le chevalier de Folard*, 31–56; and John Lynn, *The Wars of Louis XIV 1667–1714* (New York: Longman, 1999), 337–354.]

32 "Treatise on the Column," Chapter 11.
   [Folard, *Histoire de Polybe*, I:XCIV–XCVI.]

33 [Herman-Maurice, comte de Saxe, was the best French general of the early eighteenth century. He was the bastard son of Augustus II, Elector of Saxony and King of the Polish-Lithuanian Commonwealth. He served in the Imperial forces as a junior officer in the War of the Spanish Succession and Eugene's campaigns against the Ottomans before decamping for France in the 1720s. He received his first significant commands in the War of the Polish Succession and made his reputation in the War of the Austrian Succession, taking Prague in 1741 and almost single-handedly winning the war with his great campaigns from 1745 to 1748, of which Guibert makes frequent reference. He also authored a work of military theory in his youth, *Mes rêveries* (Amsterdam: Arkstée et Merkus, 1751), which entered the canon when it was published after his death in 1750. See Herman-Maurice, comte de Saxe, *The Art of War: Reveries and Memoirs* (London: Davis, 1811); and John White, *Marshal of France: The Life and Times of Maurice, comte de Saxe, 1696–1750* (London: Hamilton, 1760).]

34 *Reveries*, Chapter on the Column.
   [Saxe, *The Art of War*, 41–43. Saxe provides a systematic debunking of Folard's core claims about the utility and science of columns.]

forward, with the dogmatic tone that was his gift, that "he saw in the comte de Saxe the germ of one of the greatest generals that Europe had ever produced."

After Folard's death, it was even less of a question of his system than it was during his lifetime. Two great wars were made without any sovereign, any general, any nation having attempted to adopt them.[35] Some proselytes collected the ruins and worked to reproduce them in diverse forms; their voice losing itself in the desert, they took the part "of groaning about the fate of France, and on the blindness of the nation." Mesnil-Durand was the most ardent of them; he did not recoil; he bound a great constituency to himself, and, supported by it, he became a formidable adversary.[36]

---

35   [Guibert mentions "two great wars" since Folard's death, but Folard died in 1752, and only the Seven Years War would seem to qualify as a great war between that date and the writing of this passage. Guibert is likely mistaken about Folard's date of death and includes the War of the Austrian Succession as the other "great war."]

36   [As noted, the "great constituency" was Marshal Broglie.]

CHAPTER 2

[The] System of Mesnil Durand Enunciated in His Diverse Works. [The] Form by Which I Propose to Analyze It

It is not light work to follow the system of Mesnil-Durand in all its variations and in all the works that contain them. A volume entitled *Project of Tactics*, or *Treatise on* Plésions; a *Supplement* to the aforementioned *Project*; *Observations on Cannon and on the Column*; *Fragments of Tactics*, containing six memoirs; other *Fragments* containing three memoirs, all in the same format; [and] finally, three successive editions of a *Project of Maneuver Regulations*, with variants on variants, not counting a number of small polemical writings dropped haphazardly, whether in journals or in brief pieces: here is what I had to read to respond to him.[1] I took my time, [with] patience and care. Before this, I worked to forget my previous opinions and to make my judgement a tabula rasa. I demand that my readers dispose of their prejudices in the same way. Here, there must be neither friends or enemies; there must be judges.

So that my readers not be frightened, it is not a comprehensive and detailed analysis of these numerous works that I undertake here. It is the system of the author to which I will expose them, [and] above all, [to] the spirit of this system and the tableau of the consequences that result from it. What I doubtlessly owe to the author, and that which I will observe with all the loyalty of our profession, is that he will not be able to argue infidelity in my citations, and, to this end, I will never make any without indicating the work that furnished it to me. But what I also must do, what I owe to the cause that I defend, is to not lose myself to the abyss into which almost all military works fall [and] to make my work readable until its end, because the premier necessity, when one wishes not to be judged haphazardly or by lassitude, is to not put one's judges to sleep.

Mesnil-Durand takes the same base as Folard for the establishment of his system. He regards the extended order of battalions and the suppression of the pike as the enfeebling of infantry and the degradation of tactics; the number of cavalry introduced to our armies as useless and ruinous; the mélange of arms and the shortening of orders of battle as fundamental principles; shock action or combat of the *arme blanche* as the principle and decisive action; fire action, on the contrary, as the accessory action; [and] finally fire in itself, whether musketry or artillery, as of little consideration in the determination of the order of battle that one must take and as having much less effect and influence than one [normally] attributes to it.

It seems that I would naturally be obligated to commence by discussing this base [and] by analyzing which of these principles are true when they are reduced or mitigated and false when they are absolute, but this march would take me away from that of the plan that I have sketched, and I believe [that plan] to be more synthetic and more sure, the state of the question necessarily needing to be asked before coming to the discussion. Thus, I will first expose the system of Mesnil-Durand with its variations, from its origin under the name of *"plésions"* up to and including the state in which it was tested at the Camp of Vaussieux; I will then examine it in all its aspects, whether particular or general, in the order and with the method that I announced by my division [of this work].

---

1 [François-Jean de Graindorge d'Orgeville, baron de Mesnil-Durand, *Fragments de tactique* [mémoires 7–9] (Paris: Jombert, 1776); *Fragments de tactique; Observations sur le canon par rapport à l'infanterie en général et à la colonne en particulier, suives de quelques extraits de l'essai sur l'usage de l'artillerie* (Paris: Jombert, 1772); *Projet d'un ordre français en tactique* (Paris : Boudet, 1755); *Réflexions sur l'ordre et les manœuvres de l'infanterie: extraites d'un mémoire écrit en 1776* (Paris: Nicolle, 1778), which was originally published as the ninth memoir in *Fragments de tactique* (1776); and *Suite du projet d'un ordre français n tactique pour servir de supplément à cet ouvrage et preparer à en faire usage pour le service du roi* (Paris: Jombert, 1758).]

CHAPTER 3

[The] System of Mesnil-Durand as It Is in His First Work, Titled *Projet d'un ordre français*

It is in the form and under the name of "*plésions*" that Mesnil-Durand first reproduced the Folard Column; he was then quite young and freshly imbued with the study of military antiquity; he consequently took a part of the nomenclature of his new tactics from it. From this [results] the terms "*plésion*," "phalanx," "maniple," "centurion," [and] "decurion," etc. The pompous names of these celebrated militaries, [having] the names of "manche," "manchette," "*plésionette*," "tranche," [and] "*tiroir*," etc., which were of his creation, were a so-bizarre assortment, and, whatever Mesnil-Durand may say in his *Memoir on Military Language*, formed a ridiculous jargon for the mob, and at least [one] foreign to enlightened people.[1]

La plésion, or I believe instead *le plésion*, signified for the Greeks an order of four fronts and was not, properly speaking, a disposition of the phalanx when it made face on four sides.[2] This is what undoubtedly determined Mesnil-Durand to adopt it. His pretention was, like that of Folard, effectively [to have] a column that did not have any flanks and whose sides were all faces. *Plésion*, among the Greeks, drew its etymology from the word Πλίνθος [*plinthos*], which means "brick." The Greeks, who liked images, wished to express by this the form, the density, and the solidity of the phalanx in this disposition. It is as such doubtless that Mesnil-Durand, after having compared a line in the deployed order "to a ribbon that frays," says that "on the contrary, his column, in the different movements that one may make it make, and in the different positions that one may give to it, experiences no more derangement and alteration in the individuals who compose it than the respective parts of a brick that one turns in every way experience." And elsewhere that "the faces of his column are walls and that the exterior files of officers that he places there are its facings."[3] I assuredly much honor the Greeks, but I am pleased that the poverty of our language, or perhaps its just severity, do not at all admit such metaphors.

Folard, as we saw in the preceding chapter, only proposes his column as an accidental order. Mesnil-Durand establishes his *plésion* as [the] primitive and habitual order of the infantry for his premier principle. His *plésion* thus takes the place of our battalion. As to the rest, he composes and organizes it in the following manner:

> The *plésion* is seven-hundred sixty-eight men ranged on a frontage of twenty-four and thirty-two deep. Divided perpendicularly from the head to the tail, the two halves are named "manches;" they next cut themselves parallelly to the front in four "sections," which are consequently each of a frontage of twenty-four men and eight deep. Finally, they divide themselves into two "*plésionettes*," each formed of two sections joined together. To these three divisions must be added two others: each manche cut in half gives the "manchettes" of a frontage of six and thirty-two deep, and the *plésion* cut crosswise gives four "maniples," each of them of a frontage of twelve and sixteen deep.[4]

I will not at all stop myself here to examine this organization. In time, we will return to all the vices of the column in the last edition, which was executed at the Camp of Vaussieux, and it is there that I will analyze them.

I do not have need of speaking here of the division of *plésions* into companies, companies into "*cinquantaines*," *cinquantaines* into "tranches," [and] tranches into "decuries;" of "tribunes," "centurions," "decurions," "captains of arms;" [or] of the formation of *plésions* into regiments, etc., etc. It is the *plésion* that forms the base of the system, and [it is] of little import today that Mesnil-Durand

---

1 [Mesnil-Durand, "Sur le langage de la tactique française," in *Fragments de tactique* [mémoires 7–9], 39–46, in which Mesnil-Durand pleads for the simplification of military terminology and the proper use of terms by eliminating some in contemporary use and adding others.]

2 [French is a gendered language, and almost all nouns carry a gender that their articles must reflect; Guibert is thus being petty by suggesting that Mesnil-Durand made a grammatical error in the use of an article for a word that did not exist in contemporary French. The distinction Guibert draws between "an order of four fronts" and "the phalanx when it made face on four sides" is a very fine one, perhaps also in the realm of pettiness. See Louis Rawlings, "War and Warfare in Ancient Greece," *The Oxford Handbook of Warfare in the Classical World* (New York: Oxford University Press, 2013), 3–28.]

3 "Reflections on the order and the maneuvers of the infantry," published at Bayeux, 3,5, and 17.

4 "*Projet d'un ordre français*," 44.
 [See Mesnil-Durand, *Projet d'un ordre français*, 44–45; and *Suite du projet d'un ordre français*, 10–12.]

greatly wished to bend his column to the constitution of our regiments to know how he then wished to bend our constitution to his system.

The *plésion* has three manners of forming itself: one, which Mesnil-Durand calls "*en bataille*," consists of serrying the ranks in each section, leaving two or three paces of interval between them and double [that] between the second and third. The second manner, which he calls "in phalanx order," is when all the sections are serried one on the other to create mass. Finally, the third is when the *plésion* has all ranks open.

We see, following Mesnil-Durand, the objective of these three formations; it is he that I copy:[5]

> The *plésion* will be *en bataille* all the times that it will arrive *on the field*, and, after having maneuvered, it will reform before returning. This will be the habitual state. It is again in this state, and no other, that it will march at the redoubled pace.[6]
>
> It will form in phalanx order at the moment of the charge and only a few paces from the enemy.
>
> It will only have open ranks when marching far from the enemy or *while running*.[7]

These three manners have a quite-precious advantage in the eyes of Mesnil-Durand: their conformity with the three formations of the ancients: *ordinati, densati,* [and] *constipati*.[8]

Moreover, Mesnil-Durand makes the same usage with his manches and his *plésionnettes* that Folard makes with his manches and his sections. When his *plésion* has opened the enemy line, "which," he says, "is always infallible," it separates itself by manche or by *plésionnette* to fall on the enemy flanks and achieve their destruction; this is what Mesnil-Durand names "embellishing the victory."[9]

Mesnil-Durand continues:

> The division of manches and of manchettes will take place in all the divisions of the battalion. I have just indicated the use of the *plésionnettes*. In my ordinance, the sections establish the greatest neatness, facilitating rallying and maneuvers, and, above all, absolutely prevent depth from opposing itself to lightness. When the *plésion* changes front and separates itself by *plésionnettes*, *all the divisions changing front also change in use*, but in such a manner that the *plésionnettes* preserve all the properties and all the maneuvers of the entire *plésion*. The sections of the *plésion* become their manchettes, the manchettes their sections, [and] the maniples their *plésionnettes*. A *plésionnette en bataille* is thus serried by manchette, as the *plésion en bataille* is serried by section, and thus the rest.

Mesnil-Durand makes here a small civility to the reader on this foreign jargon. "I hope," he says, "that this detail will appear quite clear and quite easy to those who will give it a little attention, and it is quite sure that the troop that would wish to learn it would find it much easier yet."[10]

The opinion of Mesnil-Durand on long arms and their employment is conformed to that of his master. He wishes only, in lieu of partisans, for pikes of seven and a half feet. He gives them to all the officers and sergeants, and eleven more per company. He then places them in the first two ranks of each section and in the first two files of each flank, mixing them alternatively with a fusilier, as Folard does.

Independently of the eight fusiliers companies, each of a hundred men counting the officers, that form the base of the *plésion*, Mesnil-Durand adds to each a company of foot grenadiers, one of light arms, and one of horse grenadiers, all three of fifty men. These companies are the backstops, the supports, and the accessories of his column in every way.

This company of horse grenadiers holds, as one sees, to the principle of the mélange of arms that Mesnil-Durand borrows from Folard, but it is an extension of it, as Folard only proposes that the infantry platoons interlace themselves with the squadrons. Mesnil-Durand goes further, following his custom, and he wishes the reciprocal mélange. As it happens, in joining the cavalry to his *plésions*, always faithful to the disdain that he has for cavalry, he hardly counts on it, as he adds that, "if the *plésion* be

---

5   *Suite du projet d'un ordre français*, 17.
6   [Guibert's italics.]
7   [Guibert's italics.]
8   [Probably a reference to Æneas Tacticus, *On the Defense of Fortified Positions* (London: Loeb, 1928), 267–271. Although Æneas wrote in Greek, a Latin translation from 1524 and of the type likely to have been referenced by Guibert and Mesnil-Durand includes the three terms; see https://books.google.com/books?id=Mwt1kDuAN9sC&dq. See also "L'influence de la pensée militaire antique dans la réforme oranienne: entre appel au passé et recherche de solutions nouvelles," *La revue d'histoire militaire* (2022), https://larevuedhistoiremilitaire.fr/2022/05/25/linfluence-de-la-pensee-militaire-antique-dans-la-reforme-oranienne-entre-appel-au-passe-et-recherche-de-solutions-nouvelles/.]
9   *Suite du projet d'un ordre français*, 12.
    [Guibert paraphrases Mesnil-Durand in the first part of this quote; the original reads that *plésions* "would be quite sure of beating the battalions that they would charge."

10 [This and the previous paragraph are from *Suite d'un projet d'un ordre français*, 16–17.]

without horse grenadiers, its victories would be perhaps a little less complete, but they will not be less difficult."[11]

This is the formation of the *plésion* in the first works of Mesnil-Durand, which are a *Project of Tactics* and the *Supplement* to this project.

With regard to his maneuvers, I will report succinctly, and quite succinctly, their principles. Extracting them faithfully and delivering them without commentary and without reflection to the judgement of the reader: this is assuredly not a harsh critique, and it is, unfortunately for Mesnil-Durand, the most annoying [thing] that one can do. One well observes that, in the course of this extract, that which is in quotation marks is the literal text of Mesnil-Durand. The rest is what I have added to draw the materials together and to bind them.

The object of the *plésion* being always to march, to charge, and to penetrate, almost all his maneuvers are relative to this.

The front movements of the *plésion* consist only of its carrying itself forward; I have nothing to say about them. It is those of the flanks or the faces that, according to Mesnil-Durand, are the strength of his system and to which he consequently attaches himself with the most care.

One recalls the use that Folard makes of manches in his column for taking the enemy line that it penetrated in the flank. Mesnil-Durand adopts this maneuver for his *plésion* and calls it "going by manches." "The right manche," he says, "makes a right, [and] the left makes a left, then both march, distancing themselves from each other." We follow this march; it will be curious.

> One sees with what promptitude these two manches will be on two enemy battalions and how it is impossible for each of them to resist, charged by a small battalion on a frontage of thirty-two [and] a depth of sixteen. Each manche will reverse its own [enemy battalion] at so little cost that it will still be in a condition to beat the next [battalion] and will go thus to the end of the line if the enemy does not find the means to arrest it. But what will this means be? These manches move with so much vivacity! because, from the moment that they make their movement, that is to say a simple right, they take up the chase; their front, a little more extended than that of the *plésion*, is not enough to remove this lightness from them … I would that the battalion of the second enemy line that is behind advance itself to arrive on the flank of this manche, but this second line is at three-hundred paces; while it traverses this distance, the *plésion* will do six-hundred, since it runs. Thus, when it will arrive, it will have made a useless voyage; it will already be quite far from the point where it [the manche] penetrated the line; it will be six-hundred paces distant and will have already carried away this part [of the formation]. If the enemy then wishes to stop it, this is not the way it is done; it must be done as in the case of a violent fire: without losing time to throw water on a house that is impossible to save, one lets it burn as long as one works to level the next [house] to stop the flames from travelling to others; in the same way, some battalions must be allowed to flee, because they cannot be stopped. It will thus be a distant battalion that one will seek to support.

I ask that my readers not be put off, as I prune yet more to arrive [at the point]. He resumes:

> Finally, suppose that a battalion of the second enemy line arrives on the flank of the manche to charge it when it will pass before it; then, the manche may play a pleasant trick on this battalion. When it will be ready to pass along its front, it will make a right and will march as if it would wish to go to the second line. When it will be at the height of the battalion, it will then reform itself by a left and will go to charge its flank. This has the air of a pleasantry, but one seriously searches if the battalion may make some maneuvers in time to avoid this wrong-footing.[12] But when one would succeed in charging the flank of my manche, I do not know what would arrive. Taken in this sense, it is a petite column of a frontage of twelve and thirty-two deep. Its head is no less than a feeble flank. I very much agree that it is a little too thin, as we do not at all admit any under sixteen, but we have a remedy for everything. Thus, when the manche will see, at twenty-five or thirty paces, a body that will charge its flank, the sixteen first files will continue to march twelve paces, serrying then vigorously, and the sixteen rear [ranks] will stand firm. Then the first will stop themselves and make face, [and] the others will carry themselves alongside them to form a false *plésionnette* that, having a frontage of twenty-four and a depth of sixteen, will be in a state of piercing the enemy battalion, etc. Finally, when the enemy will have amassed too much strength, or when the manche will be fatigued, and either will only arrive

---

11 [*Suite d'un projet d'un ordre français*, 21–22.]

12 [Mesnil-Durand uses "*croc-en-jambe*," which is a phrase from wrestling that denotes a maneuver that forces the opponent to lose footing via the foot carrying weight.]

when it has done much ill to the [enemy] line, it will retire triumphant and without disorder.[13]

But these movements of the *plésion* by manches, as formidable as they have been presented, are nothing yet. Then arrive the movements by *plésionnettes*; Mesnil-Durand claims the honor of them and places them well above the movements by manches imagined by Folard. I wish I were able to extract them, but they comprise eight large pages, all of the same strength and logic as those that I have cited. The *plésionnettes* separate themselves from the *plésion* like the manches, then always march, run, cut down, and penetrate all that presents itself to them. "The *plésionnettes*," says Mesnil-Durand, "may in a moment decide a battle. There are neither forces nor maneuvers that can arrest, nor even retard, their ravages; they must continue to reverse all that they will find before them in line." This is demonstrated to excess by a supposition accompanied by plans in which three *plésions* alone "*in the view of the entire army that needs only a moment of good countenance* win a quite-prompt, quite-complete, and quite-bloodless victory.[14] In this great battle, only one enemy battalion was attacked, and it was by quadruple forces; all the rest is only pure rout. In the battles won by *plésions*," concludes Mesnil-Durand, "one may see truly, to the letter, the words of Marshal Camille d'Hostun de la Baume, duc de Tallard: win more flags than one loses soldiers."[15]

Folard said that his column had, by the smallness of its front, the facility of detaching a first broken section, which would go rally itself at the tail, while the rest would be firm. Mesnil-Durand defends and adopts this maneuver; he has preserved it in the French Order, under the name "substituting." See how he defends it; this logical sample is yet more curious:

This movement will however be quite rare, because a column will never find resistance capable of disarranging its head; however, the troops must learn it, if only so that they know this maneuver and do not take it for a flight, if one finds oneself by chance in the case of having recourse to it. I will not at all amuse myself with making its use and its facility seen, which present themselves so naturally; I well expect that difficulties will be found there, but it would take too long to smooth them out. Each will think of this movement as pleases them. If it be impracticable, it is only to not use it; this will never be a default in the *plésion*, compared to a battalion, which is not capable of a similar maneuver; this will only be one less advantage that it [the *plésion*] will have over it [the battalion]. I demand only of those who do not have a taste for the movement in question the permission for it to serve me when I wish as long as I were not pressed by the enemy; I will re-present to them also, counting what I may say to justify it, that it is nothing new; that it is the precisely the same [maneuver] from which a column makes the *feu de chaussée*; that the turmæ of the ancients always made it, and sometimes better; [and] that the Indians employed it against Pedro Gutiérrez de Valdivia, Governor of Chile.[16] Their maneuver was quite different from ours. Their column was 15,000 men, consequently much larger and longer than a *plésion*; it was thus much longer for the first section to unmask the second; it took it much more time to regain the tail. During the entire time, it pushed strongly, because it was cavalry that attacked this Indian column; with all this, the Indians made way ten times. The Spanish, seeing that, by this maneuver, the battle was not at all finished, took the part of the retreat, but the Indians had provided for this, so they [the Spanish] all perished.[17] Without flattering ourselves too much, we may thus hope to execute a maneuver that was not too difficult for the Chileans and to not fear, after this example, that all the troop will go to disorder when we make a place for the first section. I account the same that, by means of a small

---

13   *Projet d'un ordre français*, Chapter 3, Article 2.
      [*Projet d'un ordre français*, 76–79]
14   [*Projet d'un ordre français*, 83–84. Guibert's italics.]
15   *Projet d'un ordre français*, Chapter 3.
      [Ibid. The reference is to Folard, *Histoire de Polybe* I:117, which quotes a letter from Tallard to Louis XIV as saying "we have taken more flags and standards than your majesty has lost soldiers."
      Camille d'Hostun de la Baume, duc de Tallard, was a career soldier who served in Louis XIV's wars along with a stint as ambassador to England. He is most famous for having seized Alsace early in the War of the Spanish Succession, from which came the quote and his marshal's baton, and then having lost the Battle of Blenheim in 1704, resulting in his imprisonment in England for nearly a decade.]

16   [Pedro Gutiérrez de Valdivia was a sixteenth-century military commander in the service of the Habsburg crown. He was present at the 1527 Sack of Rome before departing for the Spanish colonies in the Americas, where he established several important settlements in Chile, including the eponymous city, before his death.]
17   [Mesnil-Durand references the 1553 Battle of Tucapel in modern Chile, where Valdivia's force of around fifty Spanish and several thousand native auxiliaries were exterminated by the Mapuche. Mesnil-Durand's exact source for the detail of the battle is unknown, but a contemporary one like Alonso de Ovalle, *An Historical Relation of the Kingdom of Chile* (London: Churchill, 1703), 144, provides a brief description of the battle.]

Roman bagatelle that would be good for the *plésion*, there will not be a single man of the second section who follows the first and who profits from the occasion to flee.[18]

This "small Roman bagatelle" is yet to come, and I will not at all attach myself to divining it. But what [an] apology! examples taken from Chile! Chileans in column! This recalls Folard, who, to support his opinion against cavalry, cited the example of King David, who hamstrung all his horses.[19] I confess that, king for king, I like better, in favor of cavalry, the example of King Friedrich, who perfected the art of usefully employing the hamstrings of his own.[20]

We go to the employment that Mesnil-Durand wishes to make of the *plésion* in fire action.

He spares us the pretention that Folard has of drawing fire from his column, and he confesses that the column and the *plésion* in their natural state are quite improper for musketry. Here then [are] the principles that he establishes on this subject:

1. One must never, and the *plésion* will never forget this principle, amuse oneself with musketry unless it is impossible to employ the *arme blanche*.
2. If the *plésion* cannot charge, finding itself totally separated from the enemy by an obstacle that it cannot cross, the enemy may not charge it [either].
3. It may thus take whatever disposition that it will wish, however ridiculous it appears; it will always be quite good if it furnishes much fire.[21]

Here now is the extract of the means by which Mesnil-Durand remains quite faithful to this third principle:

The first means will be to develop oneself by sections in full line, and thus the *plésion* will be *deux de jeu* with the battalion;[22] it will be, in truth, eight deep, but with the last ranks loading the fusils and passing them to the first, the fire will be more lively than that of a battalion.

If one does not wish this, but [instead] only a line of musketry three deep, one need only draw new platoons from the tail of the *plésion*, to which one will join the foot grenadiers and light soldiers to form the line in advance of the shortened *plésion*.

One may then make the *plésion* fire by tranches; the first, as soon as it has fired its volley, passes to the tail to unmask the second, and thus the others.

There are a thousand other means of making the *plésion* fire, [such as] *en tenaille*, *en tenaille renversée*, *en scie*, [etc.]."[23]

The author much wishes to spare us all the movements of the *plésion* to form itself *en festons* and *en découpures*. As for me, to critique [it], I have always only to expose it faithfully, and to remain quiet.[24]

In his *Suite du projet d'un ordre français*, Mesnil-Durand further extends his fire methods.

First, he no longer develops his *plésion* by sections, but on a thin and elongated line like our battalions, that is to say three deep. This is where he employs his famous development on the center that then plays so principal a role in his *Fragments of Tactics* and in his maneuver regulations. As great discoveries do not have all their perfection at their origin, one sees that he grasps for it and that it is not yet well founded. Regardless, this maneuver, which he calls "developing the *plésion* by fifties to make fire in line," is, in effect, with some details of execution excepted, the same movement by which he currently deploys his column and contains the germ of all the central organization that is now the base of his system.[25]

But is this a new means that Mesnil-Durand has found, as he pretends? And does the glory of this discovery, if

---

18   *Projet d'un ordre français*, 87–88.
19   [See Folard, *Histoire de Polybe*, IV:XIV. The story being referenced is in 2 Samuel 8:4, in which King David defeats a series of enemies, captures "one-thousand seven-hundred charioteers," and hamstrings all the chariot horses. David was the second king of the Jews in the Jewish and Christian scriptures. Argentero Brézé, *Observations historiques et critiques sur les commentaires de Folard et sur la cavalerie*, 2 Vols. (Torino: Reycend, 1772), 1:33–39, points out the inanity of Folard's example, given that David had other horses at his disposal in the story, per Mosaic law.]
20   [Guibert doubtlessly references, among other cavalry actions, the 1757 Battle of Rossbach, in which Prussian cavalry under Friedrich-Wilhelm Freiherr von Seydlitz aided in the rout of the Franco-Imperial army attacking in large columns, inflicting over 10,000 casualties on it, including the capture of his father. The battle was a humiliation for the French army, which spent the rest of the war trying to reclaim its glory. See Christopher Duffy, *Prussia's Glory: Rossbach & Leuthen 1757* (Rosemont, IL: Emperor's Press, 2004), and Franz Szabo, *The Seven Years War in Europe 1756–1763* (New York: Routledge, 2013), 96–99.]
21   [*Suite du projet d'un ordre français*, 33–34.]
22   ["*Deux de jeu*" is a draw in a game in which two points remain until the victory, like a deuce in a tennis game. It is not a full stalemate, but it has elements of one.]
23   [*Projet d'un ordre français*, 89–92.]
24   [See "Tenaille," *Merriam-Webster's Dictionary*, https://www.merriam-webster.com/dictionary/tenaille: "an outwork in the main ditch between two bastions of a fortification." "*Scie*" is a saw. "*Feston*" is a palisade or barrier made from tree branches. "*Decoupures*" means "cut" or "divided." Mesnil-Durand proposes a series of deployments based on the objects or actions that the base words denote; they are likely derived from Vegetius, *Epitome of Military Science*, 93–119.]
25   [See *Suite du projet d'un ordre français*, 52–55.]

there is any glory in a discovery as thin in the base and as dangerous by the application that he makes of it, belong to him, in effect? I have only to oppose this pretention with a single fact to destroy it.

Before Mesnil-Durand would have considered developing his *plésion* by the center, that is to say on its head, the Infantry Exercise Ordinance formed the attack column on the center of two battalions and then reformed *en bataille* by the contrary movement. This means of re-folding the two wings of a troop on the center to form most promptly in columns and then to develop it on its head to reform it in line, was it [not] then known? And it is from it [the Ordinance] that Mesnil-Durand borrows the lynchpin and the universal mechanism of his system[?] We prove this by dates.

The *Projet d'un ordre français* is from 1755, and there is no mention of the development on the center in it. This maneuver "by fifties" of which I spoke above exists only in the *Suite du projet d'un ordre français*; this *Suite* was not printed until 1758.

However, the ordinance of infantry exercise in which the attack column was formed by the center is from 1753, and this column [of Mesnil-Durand] thus appears to be nothing new [and] nothing marvelous.[26]

It would be malicious to push this extract further, to speak of a certain "manchette fire" against which the author pretends "that a battalion line would never be able to hold," and of ten other maneuvers of the same strength. He has abandoned almost all of them, and analyzing those that he preserves in ceaselessly correcting them and modifying them will be returned to in their place. We pass to his principles and maneuvers of grand tactics.

Like Folard, Mesnil-Durand thinks that the most advantageous order of battle is on a single line, that almost never does it arrive that a battle lost by the first [line] would be reestablished by the second [line], [and] that, consequently, one must carry, as much as one is able, all one's forces to the first line and render one's shock decisive.

As such, Mesnil-Durand would that an army of *plésions* range itself on a single line with spaces between them that are double their frontage. This is his habitual order. It diminishes its intervals at need, which gathers yet more forces in a yet smaller space. His principle is always to shorten; never does he fear being disordered; it is [only] for our feeble lines that this pusillanimous prejudice exists.

Sometimes, however, he will arrive at forming *plésions* on two or three lines, but this will be because the terrain absolutely will require it or to reunite yet more troops on a point, but then these lines will only be twenty-five *toises* apart; they will be both full and empty,[27] and, at the moment of the shock, they will insert themselves [between each other] to make a single full line or to penetrate successively to renew their efforts. But we listen to Mesnil-Durand himself and, to this end, we always transcribe literally his principal résumés.

> One may oppose as many lines as one will wish to the *plésions*. These lines may be arranged full [without intervals], or both full and empty; in the end, we will not take notice of what the enemy will wish for, and it will hardly cost us more to beat twelve [lines] as to beat a single. This is why we do not have need of a second line; it would be better to have one that, fighting the enemies with all possible advantages, will dispatch them very quickly, and all the others soon after. We will thus only ever form one, whatever number that it pleases the enemy to have, and we will always hope that they multiply theirs. Our victory will be no less sure and much more complete. It may only arrive on us sometimes to double the line in certain parts for some particular reason. We may even make two [or] three lines when having a large army, and it will see itself serried, us having troops that do not know what to do.
>
> In the case where we will have several lines, we will leave only twenty-five *toises* of interval between them, and, at other times, we will bring them closer yet. Three lines of *plésions* thus closed make properly only one [line], which has all the benefits of plurality without having the deficits.
>
> By the facility that several lines of *plésions* will thus have to penetrate, there may arrive no disorder or misfortune that would not be immediately repaired. Suppose, for example, that the first line of the *plésion* finds a resistance to which it is not accustomed, would appear bored of the fight; to relieve it, one advances and charges [with] the second, [either] to then reform the first and thus successively, or to

---

26 [*Ordonnance du roi portant règlement sur le service de l'infanterie en campagne* (1753). See also Colin, *L'infanterie au XVIIIe siècle*, 27–72; and Quimby, *The Background of Napoleonic Warfare*, 81–84.]

27 ["Both full and empty (*tant pleine que vide*)" can have several meanings, all evoking alternating mass and space. In architecture, it refers to a construction like a colonnade, with alternating columns and empty space, or a building with alternating wings and courtyards. In a military formation, it might be translated as a quincunx, although that term is not always an apt description, especially when speaking of eighteenth-century armies deployed on long, thin lines.]

make the two charge at the same time, forming a single doubled phalanx cut by quite-small intervals.

One will perhaps object that, the second line being so near, [it] will suffer the enemy fire. It will hardly suffer, because the dispute will not be long. It will thus be masked by the first.

To abridge and not repeat, I will hardly say that, even on paper, an order comparable in strength to that of a corps of *plésions* on two or three lines, both full and empty, separated by twenty-five *toises* from each other is never seen. No one at all tells me here that this prodigiously shortens the army's front; I speak of this disposition in itself and do not pretend that it must be employed on the army front and on all occasions, although, to speak truly, there would be no danger, as the flanks fear nothing.[28]

By what means does Mesnil-Durand pretend to "assure its flanks and to allow it to be outflanked as much as one will wish without relenting or deranging its victory for a moment?"[29] It is in placing four *plésions* with their platoons and four squadrons on the wings of his army. These troops must range themselves there by echelons and embrace the enemy flank when they will believe to envelop them: "thus," says Mesnil-Durand, "did Gaius Julius Caesar at Pharsalus, with a reserve of six cohorts that covered his right. If this protection sufficed on this memorable day to guarantee uncovered and outflanked flanks, one may believe that the flanks of the *plésions*, without this recourse, having nothing to fear, will be doubly tranquil."[30] As to the rest, Mesnil-Durand hastens to add that, "with an army of *plésions*, there will not be much to do, as, yet again, an army of *plésions* never fears for its flanks; it always goes forward; it only has to the enemy ahead of it; everywhere where we will change front, we will easily [defeat]the enemy. We thus [defeat] them everywhere where we encounter them, inferior or superior."[31] What logic, good God!

In addition, who may believe that this is not at all a default of logic, or of absolute knowledge of the manner in which armies move themselves, that Mesnil-Durand supposes that the enemy army can only outflank him by curling itself around his flanks by quarter-conversions; that thus, him seeing it coming, [he] will go at that moment to meet it and will fall on its flank; [and] that, as such, he consequently employs six great pages in calculating to the foot, to the inch, and to the minute the length and the inconvenience of this conversion movement? Would a well-commanded modern army depart from its order of battle and parallel lines spread before him to outflank him? Would it not turn him by its march? Would it not debouch by his flank at the same time that it would menace his front, as Friedrich did at Leuthen [and] Ferdinand did at Krefeld, etc.?[32] Would the countryside not almost

---

28 *Projet d'un ordre français*, Chapter 11.
   [See Mesnil-Durand, *Projet d'un ordre français*, 199–216.]

29 [See Mesnil-Durand, *Projet d'un ordre français*, 53–54, and *Suite du projet d'un ordre français*, 24–25.]

30 [*Projet d'un ordre français*, 263.
   Gaius Julius Caesar was a Roman politician and military leader who played a key role in the collapse of the Roman Republic and the transition to the Roman Empire. He conducted several notable campaigns, including the Gallic Wars, about which he wrote; his memoir of them was required reading for contemporary *militaires*, and he was considered a prototypical military genius, as Guibert will frequently intimate. See Gaius Julius Caesar, *The War for Gaul*, trans. James O'Donnell (Princeton: Princeton University Press, 2019).
   The Battle of Pharsalus was the 48 BCE culminating event of one of Caesar's wars, a civil war against his political partner and rival Sextus Pompeius, known as Pompey. Broadly speaking, Pompey enjoyed the support of the elites of the Roman political world, known as the optimates, while Caesar drew his support from the masses, known as the populares. Pompey engineered Caesar's recall to Rome from Gaul, which Caesar responded to by bringing his army to Rome ("crossing the Rubicon"), which caused Pompey in his turn to flee to Greece. Caesar pursued, and the two conducted a campaign of maneuver before meeting at Pharsalus. Despite being outnumbered, Caesar defeated Pompey with a hidden reserve, as Mesnil-Durand intimates, although he had cavalry to cover his flanks. Pompey fled to Egypt after the battle and was assassinated.
   A cohort was the main tactical unit of the Roman army of the late Republic and early Empire; it comprised six centuries of around eighty men each. See Adrian Goldsworthy, *Caesar: Life of a Colossus* (New Haven: Yale University Press, 2006); and *The Roman Army at War 100 BC – AD 200* (New York: Oxford University Press, 2009); and Patricia Southern, *The Roman Army: A History 753 BC – AD 476* (Stroud: Amberley, 2014), especially 120–124.]

31 *Projet d'un ordre français*, Chapter 11, 270
   [*Projet d'un ordre français*, 270.]

32 [The Battle of Leuthen was one of Friedrich's signal victories in the Seven Years War. Barely a month after his crushing defeat of the Franco-Imperial army at Rossbach in 1757, Friedrich confronted the Austrians in Silesia. Despite being outnumbered nearly two-to-one, Friedrich feinted at the Austrian right before attacking the left, winning a decisive victory. The battle became a lesson, for Guibert and his contemporaries of the "oblique order," as the text shows, and for modern analysts of Friedrich's operational art. See Duffy, *Prussia's Glory*; see also Robert Citino, *The German Way of War: From the Thirty Years War to the Third Reich* (Lawrence: University Press of Kansas, 2005), 63–104; and Claus Telp, *The Evolution of Operational Art, 1740–1813* (New York: Frank Cass, 2005), 5–18.
   The Battle of Krefeld took place in the summer of 1758. Ferdinand of Brunswick found Louis de Bourbon-Condé, comte de Clermont-en-Argonne, entrenched in a defensive position and awaiting reinforcements from another French army. Like Friedrich at Leuthen, Ferdinand attacked Clermont despite being outnumbered. Unlike Friedrich, Ferdinand did not win a decisive or instructive victory; instead, his five attack columns struggled

always favor these sorts of movements? The master and the disciple, full of antiquity, only ever see the plains of Pharsalus and Gaugamela.[33] In effect, these plains much resemble blank paper on which they make their supposition. I stop myself, as yet again it is not to all here that I wish to respond; I wish only to render account and extract here.

But how to accomplish this task for that which concerns the orders of battle proposed by Mesnil-Durand? These are parallel orders of three or four species, simple obliques, double obliques, [and] orders that are perpendicular or by separated divisions, all dividing already-formed lines without any relation to march orders and without [taking the location into account]. The enemy with which he engages is always spread out, counted, aligned, [and] passive. If they oppose some maneuvers to the maladroit movements of the *plésions*, they are maneuvers that are yet more maladroit. In the end, they are barbarians against barbarians. Mesnil-Durand must not be accused of this; he employs the knowledge that they had at the time. In the epoch when he wrote, they did not know better. The resources of modern tactics were in the head of a single man [Friedrich], and they were still secret, even to the enemies that he beat in battle. Nevertheless, we continue to extract the results that Mesnil-Durand promises himself in these foreign tactics.

Mesnil-Durand says [that]

> until now, we have seen the *plésion* [be] superior to all infantry or cavalry corps [formed] in the current order, but it is in ranged battles that it must be seen; it is there that it is in all its glory. An army of *plésions*, possessing at large all the properties of a single one, is sure, by its strength, to defeat all that it charges frontally. By the rapidity and the lightness of its movements, it is assured that the enemy will never reach engaging the fight by its flanks. Consequently assured of fighting only when it is at its greatest advantage, it vanquishes quite easily all the times that it will fight, inferior or superior [to the enemy].

> And when the enemy will be able to attack our flanks, we will be disquieted little; they are as strong as the front. When they [the flanks] would not be safe from any accident and the corps that protects them would be beaten, it would not matter; the other *plésions* surviving, the enemy would always find someone to speak with; their success would only be our shrinking [our front] without throwing us into disorder; our line would touch their front and terminate the affair quite quickly.

> This advantage, of not at all fearing for our flanks, means that we do not have need of good posts. Our order of battle is an excellent post that we carry everywhere. It will never arrive on us to be attacked in the flanks and beaten, as it does not fail to arrive on a superior army that would fight *en plaine* in the ordinary order; as it often arrived on equal armies, and even superior [ones]; [and] finally as it arrives on well-posted armies that, losing or gaining terrain, could not preserve this advantage. We cannot be taken by such attacks, and they would be quite useless against us.[34]

But we continue, this becoming more and more curious.

> The variety of *plésions*, their facility, and the promptitude with which they change order when they wish suffice to give them continual victories. They are susceptible to all the forms and all the dispositions imaginable. Taking them and quitting them is a badinage for us. In a hundred years of war, we were able to fight in the same fashion [only] twice. In a word, all that is called "grand maneuver" is so simple and so easy for *plésions* that, employing an ordinance so convenient, I was not at pains, my indignant tactician, to render the oblique order, [which is] so vaunted but so difficult for any other ordinance, more prompt, more facile, and more sure, and to invent a usage [that is] yet more facile, extended, and advantageous [for] the perpendicular order.[35] It is by it that an army in my

---

against Clermont's positions before finally outflanking him and forcing him from the position. See Szabo, *The Seven Years War in Europe*, 144–147.]

33 [The 331 BCE Battle of Gaugamela was Alexander III's third great victory over the Achaemenid Persians of Darius III, after which the latter was assassinated by his satraps. As Guibert indicates, terrain played only minor roles at both Pharsalus and Gaugamela. See Peter Green, *Alexander of Macedon, 356–323 BC: A Historical Biography* (Berkeley: University of California Press, 1991), 285–297. See also Ian Worthington, *Philip II, Alexander the Great, and the Rise and Fall of the Macedonian Empire* (New York: Oxford University Press, 2016).]

34 *Projet d'un ordre français*, 438–439.
    [Mesnil-Durand, *Projet d'un ordre français*, 436–438.]

35 [The "oblique order" was drawn from Flavius Vegetius Renatus, *Epitome of Military Science*, trans. N.P. Milner (Liverpool: Liverpool University Press, 2001), 104–105; in its most basic form, it required refusing one flank of an army to reinforce the other. Guibert and his contemporaries fetishized Vegetius and his work, including the "oblique order," which they imagined to be a battle-winning tactic employed by commanders across the millennia, including Friedrich; see Abel, *Guibert's General Essay on Tactics*, 17–18 and 194–198. Much of Guibert's analysis is drawn from or patterned after Vegetius's work, and he was not alone

system will reach the enemy, will charge them with the *arme blanche* even when they will be covered in obstacles [that make] ninety-nine percent of their front inaccessible, and will be sure, no matter how inferior, of beating them in so advantageous a post. It is this same order that, employed in affairs of posts, will render them short, little bloody, and decisive. It is it that, employed in the defense, will render posts impregnable, or at least unable to be held when they will be taken. Finally, it is by this order employed *en plaine*, in three or four parts of the line, that one may form one's battle divisions under the enemy's nose, which will pierce them [the enemy] in many places without the rest of their army being able to take part in the fight.

Today, winning a battle is losing many men and killing a few more, pushing the enemy some leagues back, [but] not always; for us, a battle or a victory, which will always be synonymous, will consist of seeing the enemy, running to them, losing some hundreds of men, and destroying their army in less time than is needed to read half this chapter.[36]

After having proved, and by good and solid reasoning, as one sees, that there is no battle that must not be won by his system, this would seem too little yet for Mesnil-Durand. He works to demonstrate the universality of the superiority of *plésions* in all cases and in all ways. He thus successively places a *plésion* against infantry and then cavalry, and it is victorious everywhere. Then, he commands it in all the operations that war may offer. Attacks on army flanks, ambushes, rear-guard attacks, attacks on the march, army surprises, river passages, descents, mountain warfare, attacks and defenses of entrenchments, sieges: a chapter is employed in each of these operations, and everywhere the *plésion* is "the best, the easiest, the surest, and the most formidable ordinance that has ever existed."[37] This enthusiasm recalls that of Vegetius when he says at the end of his work, in speaking of the Romans, "a god inspired the legion," but Vegetius's enthusiasm was excusable: the legion was not his creation, and it had vanquished the universe.[38]

Two or three citations remain to complete this extract; they are drawn from a chapter destined to prove that the arrangement of the *plésion* gives valor and discipline in some fashion.[39]

> The same man will always be braver, or at least will comport himself better, in the *plésion* than in the battalion …
>
> Suppose in the *plésion* fifty militia members who had taken the billet that morning placed in several ranks and files on all sides: they believe themselves invulnerable and will not be entirely wrong.[40] The noise will astonish them a little at first, but there is no means for them to flee, [and] it will finish by animating them. One runs; they will believe that one pursues.
>
> In the end, it is not possible to flee in the *plésion*. It would be, if one wished, in the rearmost ranks. But they have so small a part of the danger that the desire to do so will not take them. For the rest of the troop, the first ranks above all, they are too well supported to be able to recoil. There would only be one [direction] for them to go: by the side! But this is not at all possible for those in the center. Many people would have to be deranged. Those of the flanks would have more facility. But the majority of them are officers or sergeants, [who are] at least good, sure men. Moreover, this is a too-reasonable flight. The only movement natural to fear is to turn around and to distance oneself from the danger by the shortest route. Despite that, I would that someone will go

---

in that among his contemporaries; see Christopher Duffy, *The Military Experience in the Age of Reason* (New York: Atheneum, 1988), 53: "[Vegetius's ideas] were absorbed so completely by the Age of Reason that he became effectively an eighteenth-century author."]

36 [Mesnil-Durand, *Projet d'un ordre français*, 436–438, for this and the preceding paragraph.]

37 [*Projet d'un ordre français*, 315–385. A descent was an amphibious operation that was designed to be either a raid or an occupation of a fortified position; English descents on French coastal areas were ubiquitous throughout the wars of the period.]

38 [Vegetius, *Epitome of Military Science*, 55: "It was not by human counsel alone but by divine inspiration as well, in my opinion, that the Romans organized the legions." Guibert cleverly identifies himself with Vegetius here, as he has already said that his ideas are not his own but rather derived from Friedrich's; he also displays the prejudices of the times, as Vegetius clearly identifies himself as a Christian and would thus not attribute the legion to "a god."]

39 *Projet d'un ordre français*, Chapter 1, Article 3.
[See Mesnil-Durand, *Projet d'un ordre français*, 52–56.]

40 [Contemporary France had a militia system in which young men drew lots in their village to determine service. It was designed solely for self-defense, but it often ended up being used as a manpower reserve for the field armies, usually illegally. A comprehensive study of the French militia does not exist in English; see Jacques Gebelin, *Histoire des milices provinciales (1688–1791): le tirage au sort sous l'ancien régime* (Paris: Hachette, 1882); Lee Kennett, *The French Army in the Seven Years War: A Study in Military Organization and Administration* (Durham: Duke University Press, 1967), 78–87 and 141; Lynn, *Giant of the Grand Siècle*, 371–379; and especially Julia Osman, *Citizen Soldiers and the Key to the Bastille* (New York: Palgrave, 2015).]

from the head of the *plésion* along the side. Where will they go? Either they will file along the *plésion* and quote close [to it], getting themselves knocked out, as this cannot fail to happen; the *plésion* is interested in punishing this cowardice, and the officers spread everywhere will take care of this execution, or they will go in front of the foot grenadiers, who make the same operation, or the horse grenadiers, who will not treat them better. Thus in a *plésion*, flight will be much more dangerous than the fight, and, as one will have taken care in instructing the troop that it must thus be necessary to reason to find the means of flight, there is assuredly no one who would not make a quite-simple rationalization, [which] is that, of the two dangers, one must hold to that which is both the lesser and the more honest.

Surely nothing better proves that the *plésion* is proper for everything as [the fact that] we just saw here that it is the order that suits cowardice. And in twenty other passages, Mesnil-Durand advances that it suits valor and audacity par excellence, and it is on this that he principally founds himself to propose it to the nation.

This was the system of *plésions* of Mesnil-Durand in its primitive state. We will now see, in the following chapters, what modifications it passed through, up to the moment of the great test made at the Camps of Vaussieux and Saint-Malo.

CHAPTER 4

[The] System of Mesnil-Durand Accommodated to Our Constitution and Named [the] "French Order"

The system of *plésions* that promised victories [that are] so prompt, so infallible, and so little bloody, appearing in the middle of the first two campaigns of the Seven Years War, was made to be welcomed. That of Folard had similarly found a moment of credit in the misfortunes of the Succession War.[1] The times much resembled each other: the troops complained about the generals, the generals did not pay the troops, [and] people who did not wish to discontent anyone said that our misfortunes were the fault of tactics, as if these tactics had not been those with which we had beaten the enemies. Some officers, imbued with the principles draw from Folard and Marshal Jacques-François de Chastenet, marquis de Puységur, [who] were then [the authors] of the only classical works, demanded the deep order and long arms.[2] Marshal Charles-Louis-Auguste Fouquet, duc de Belle-Isle, then War Minister, had a taste for the system of *plésions*, and he was at the cusp of forming a regiment on the author's plan.[3] This test was to be made for the army. His death unfortunately prevented this proof, as it would have dispensed us of the refutation that we have seen today. Marshal Broglie became army commander; he sought to organize it on the principles of the King of Prussia, and he succeeded in some regards; he at least replaced disorder with discipline; in the end, he rendered honor to our arms, he won battles, and it was not a question of *plésions*.[4]

The system of *plésions* remained drowsy until 1774, and I confess that, after the reflective study that I made [the *General Essay on Tactics*], I believe that it was an eternal sleep. But Mesnil-Durand, faithful to the sermon that he had recorded in his works, "to never abandon the cause of the deep order," had worked in silence and published that year a new [work] titled *Fragments of Tactics* containing six memoirs preceded by a preliminary discourse.

> The first memoir on chasseurs and on the charge.
> The second on infantry maneuver.
> The third on the column and on principles of tactics.
> The fourth on marches.
> The fifth on orders of battle.

The honor of the sixth concerns me.[5] It is a long and lively critique of the *General Essay on Tactics*. I did not respond at the time, and I will continue not to respond here, because I flatter myself that this refutation will not be regarded as a response, although it sometimes necessitates me to repeat the principles established in the *General Essay on Tactics*. There is an essential difference between Mesnil-Durand and me that must render my amour-propre less susceptible and less ardent to responding: it is that he defends his system and I a system that I did not create. I write for the defense of the art, and he for his own.

---

1 [Guibert likely refers to Folard's advocacy for the deep order during the War of the Spanish Succession, not the first publication of his works in the 1720s.]

2 [Jacques-François de Chastenet, marquis de Puységur, was a commander in the wars of Louis XIV and then a leading member of the Council of War, receiving the marshal's baton in 1734 during the War of the Polish Succession. His posthumous *Art de la guerre par principes et par règles*, 2 Vols. (Paris: 1747), marked him as a leading proponent of the deep order.]

3 [Charles-Louis-Auguste Fouquet, duc de Belle-Isle, was one of the most important *militaires* of eighteenth-century France. Grandson of the disgraced finance minister Nicolas Fouquet, he joined the military and fought in the Wars of Spanish Succession, the Quadruple Alliance, Polish Succession, and Austrian Succession before becoming Secretary of State for War in 1758, a post he held until his death in 1761. He was one of the most forward-thinking generals in French service, overseeing many of the training camps held early in the century and pushing for military reform along Prussian lines as early as the 1720s. He also headed the anti-Habsburg camp at court, pushing France into alliance with Prussia during the Austrian Succession. Unfortunately, there is no modern scholarly biography of him in English; see Alix de Rohan Chabot, *Le maréchal de Belle-Isle ou la revanche de Foucquet* (Paris: Perrin, 2005). See also Benjamin Mercier, "Charles-Louis-Auguste Fouquet, duc de Belle-Isle, 1758–1761," *Les ministres de la guerre*, 396–406.]

4 [Broglie became the leading French field commander in late 1759, commanding the main army until his disgrace in 1761. As Guibert references, Broglie organized the army along Prussian lines, including creating units that might be termed divisions. See Jonathan Abel, "An Aspect of the Military Experience in the Age of Reason: The Evolution of the Combined-Arms Division in Old-Regime France," *The Changing Face of Old-Regime Warfare: Essays in Honor of Christopher Duffy*, ed. Alexander Burns (Warwick: Helion, 2022), 140–160.]

5 [Mesnil-Durand, *Fragments de tactique*.]

Following these first *Fragments*, a new one appeared, containing three other memoirs: the first "On Artillery," the second "On Military Language," and the third entitled "Project of an Instruction for Maneuvering Infantry."[6]

It is this mass of memoirs that composes in some way the second edition of the system of Mesnil-Durand, that is to say the system of *plésions* adapted to battalions. "There, seeming to condescend to the prejudices of our century and sensing (these are his expressions) that care must be taken for prejudice when it is strong and general at a certain point, *he much wished* for some time to renounce *plésions* and take battalions to the point where he finds them to give them *plésionnique* maneuvers and dispositions, that is to say the advantages and the properties of their rivals the *plésions*. By this," he adds, "he works himself to perfect his current system and the manner of employing it to try to knock out the reasons that made it be rejected; finally, he draws together and identifies the methods most opposed [to him] so much that they become one, and, reaching this method thus composed and modified, the partisans of the current system will be able to believe nothing at all has changed, with as much reason as he believes he gave them in his."[7]

After this confession stripped of artifice, we thus see how Mesnil-Durand operates this marvelous amalgam. On one hand, he gives to the battalion the organization of his *plésion* by giving the former the honor, or perhaps the bad joke, of leaving it its name. He then proposes the column as the primitive and habitual order; he holds to all of his principles of grand tactics like the shortening of orders of battle, a different employment of cavalry, etc., etc. On the other hand, he appropriates all that he finds good in modern tactics. Perfection in the details; means of maneuvers; even maneuvers, both large and small; in the end, the Prussian tactics that he destroys so much; our exercise ordinance; [and] myself: he puts all to work to draw his system from the state of barbarity. We do not at all anticipate the judgement that we believe will be made of this bizarre assemblage; a profound analysis must precede it and serve as its base.

The names drawn from antiquity did not at all act on spirits enough [for him]. Mesnil-Durand formally titles his new system the "French Order" to oppose, he says, the extended order that he names the "Prussian Order." Thus he calls national prejudices to his aid. He reawakens all the clichés of audacity and French valor, of the impossibility that our character gives us to attain a certain perfection of maneuver.[8] He turns the variations [and] the work of our troops since 1763 to the detriment of the current system, as if it were quite simple to grope for what one is ignorant of, as if the Prussian armies themselves had not spent twenty years in school, and truly, consequently, in work, in uncertainties, and in faults. [He claims that] the tactics that he will substitute for these tactics [that he says are are] foreign, anti-national, [and] destructive to our genius require neither study nor fatigue on the part of the troops; they must above all lighten and soften the fate of particular officers on whom we have weighed with so much vexation since 1763 and that we would wish to assimilate to the "foreign officers, who are automatons without any affair, idea, fortune, or domicile other than their platoons."[9] With these words, which sound agreeable to the ears of the fool, one tries to prepare votes [for the system], or at least partisans [of it].

Despite this new form and these means, Mesnil-Durand's system nevertheless gained no favor when the support of Marshal Broglie suddenly made it the greatest and the most important affair that could be elevated in the military. First, he put it to the test at Metz with the Limousin and De La Couronne Regiments. Then, named last summer as commandant of the Breton and Norman camps, he made the proofs at large that he had made at Metz two years prior with only four battalions and by all the troops under his orders.

In the name of Marshal Broglie; in considering his glory, his experience, the preponderance of every genre that accompanies him; in thinking that I had been elevated in his school, that my father is one of his oldest and most faithful servants, the pen falls from my hands, but when I reflect that it is not my opinion that I take the liberty of placing alongside his, that I am only the organ of that which is the greater part of military Europe, that the system that I defend is that of the King of Prussia, that is to say of the greatest man of war who has appeared since Caesar,

---

6 [Mesnil-Durand, *Fragments de tactique* [memoirs 7–9].]
7 "Preliminary Discourse," *Fragments de tactique*, 51–52.
 [Mesnil-Durand, *Fragments de tactique*, li-lii. Guibert's italics]

8 [Mesnil-Durand, *Fragments de tactique*, xl-xlv. Debates over national character were ubiquitous at the time; Matthew d'Auria, *The Shaping of French National Identity: Narrating the Nation's Past, 1715–1830* (New York: Cambridge University Press, 2020), 1–248, provides an excellent analysis. The debate rose to the level of a *Querelle* during the mid-century tactics discussions, one that may be termed the *Querelle des français et des prussiens*.]
9 "Reflections on the Order and the Maneuvers of the Infantry," 51.
 [This appears to be a reference to a work that was either not printed or has not survived.]

and the general of generals, when I believe above all (and not by stubbornness and pride, since there is only the thin merit of the redaction for me here, but with the purest disinterest) that the adoption of the system of Mesnil-Durand would have the most destructive consequences for the nation and for the army, I dare to reanimate myself and pursue that which I have begun. Eh! Why should I in my turn not have the right to be read by the marshal, as Mesnil-Durand did? Why would he refuse to throw his eyes on the defense of a system that has been badly developed or disfigured? Why, in a word, would I believe that he, descending from his place, would take part in a process of whom he is the judge?[10]

10 [Given that Broglie commanded forces himself at Vaussieux, this may be interpreted as a criticism of the marshal.]

CHAPTER 5

New Variations of the "French Order." [The] Proofs Made at Metz. [The] System of Mesnil-Durand as It Was Executed at the Camp of Vaussieux. Examination of This System in All the Aspects of Its Detail

The chapter that I work here would become a volume if I wished to subject myself to rendering account of all the variations in the details of Mesnil-Durand's system that have arrived since the new form that he gave it in his *Fragments of Tactics*. Each month, each year has seen writing on writing, memoir on memoir hatched. In the Metz proofs, there were new variants each day. It was the same in the cantonments that preceded the Camp of Vaussieux and in the camp [itself]; the reason was simple: Mesnil-Durand had calculated them all in his cabinet and on paper.[1] Transported to the terrain, his maneuvers suffered a thousand inconveniences; he had to modify, palliate, and re-found them at each step. In many maneuvers, the author's text disappeared under the corrections.

As one must always depart from a base, I will begin the examination that I will make with the project of the regulations printed for the instruction of troops of the camp, according to which these troops were formed for the maneuvers that they executed.

The vices and inconveniences remarked on in the execution of these regulations have, as I have said above, forced a departure from it on many points.

These changes were of two species: one [set], and [examples of it] were the greater number, [comprised] the details of execution, which we wished to be simplified or perfected; the other [set comprised] all the important points and appeared to be the modifications that the marshal wished to carry to the system of Mesnil-Durand; that [latter] is interesting to put under the eyes of readers, [as] one sees in it the marshal often in contradiction to the principles of Mesnil-Durand, [and] often disavowing them, rejecting them, or at least modifying them. And, [if] we will be permitted to say, we would have seen yet more of this if there had been proofs that [were] more multiplied, more followed, more exposed to the liberty of discussion, proofs made on all sorts of terrains and in all sorts of circumstances, in the end proofs of war, if one may do so in peacetime, as it is impossible that the truth may remain problematic for a long time for a great talent and that the chimeras of a false theory do not extinguish themselves before him when they are practiced and performed.

To thus render a faithful account of the system of Mesnil-Durand as it was executed at the Camp of Vaussieux, I will divide the analysis that I will give after this into two parts. One, under the title "Text," will contain the literal extract of the maneuver regulations that served as the instruction to the camp troops. The other part will contain my reflections or objections as well as the principal changes that were made in their execution, under the title "Observations."

I must everywhere alert that I will pass rapidly over the details of the maneuvers as well as the means of [their] execution and that I will only attach myself to major objections that hold to the base of the system. It is not at all by [its] accessories that a grand system must be judged. If the system is good in itself, Mesnil-Durand or others will easily correct the vices or the imperfections of detail, and then my critique would soon be false. If the system is bad, it will perish entirely; I thus do not need to waste my time to beat the branches when I wish to attack the roots.

Preliminary Note

I have divided the following text into paragraphs and numbered them so that the observations that I will make correspond to the numerals of the paragraphs to which they refer.

The maneuver regulations of Mesnil-Durand relate only to infantry; thus, his principles relative to cavalry and artillery must be found in his other works; I have done this analysis in the second part of this work in examining his system in these two respects.

[The] System of Mesnil-Durand, as it was Executed at the Camp of Vaussieux

---

1 ["Cabinet" has two meanings in eighteenth-century French: as a "place of retreat for working" or "the most-hidden secrets [and] the mysteries of the Court." When Guibert uses the phrase "in cabinet," he intends it to describe the process of imagining a formation, a tactic, or a system in a sterile theoretical environment; it may be thought of as a synonym for "in theory" and thus an antonym for "in practice."]

Text

Formation

I

The divisions of the army, the brigades of the division, the companies of the battalion, in a word, all the troops large or small, will be placed between them in numerical order by the center, the odd numbers to the right.

Applying this rule to the order of battalions results:

1. In a regiment alone, the first battalion will be to the right.
2. In a brigade alone, the first regiment will go to the right, the second to the left; the first two battalions to their rear will go to the ordinary places, the first to the right, but in the first regiment, the first battalion will go to the left to be near the center of the brigade.
3. In a division having an odd number of brigades, the brigade of the center will be arranged as if it were alone, but in all the brigades of the left, the first regiment will go to the right, and in each regiment the first battalion will then go to the right; on the contrary, in the brigades of the right, the first regiment will go to the left, and in each regiment, the first battalion will then go to the left, because in these brigades of the left, the left side is quite near the center of the division, and the division is the whole, of which the regiments and the battalions are the parts.

Note: The divisions that are spoken of here are the three great divisions of the infantry of an army, which are to the brigades what the brigades are to the battalions and each of which, in the army's march, habitually forms its column.[2]

Observations

Formation

This formation is not an easy thing to hear, and brains must assuredly be wracked to imagine it, but it was necessary to reverse all that existed; novelty had to be given, and when one is not on one's guard, one falls from the useless to the bizarre and from the combined into the complicated.

One must see how it is contrary to the important rules of *simplicity* and of *unity of principles* to adopt a formation that ceaselessly varies, first according to whether the battalion is first or second and in this or that regiment, and then on the place that the regiment takes in the brigade and the brigade in the division. This is nothing yet, as Mesnil-Durand might respond that we are subject to a part of these combinations in our current formation; in his system, it is yet another complication. As all his movements are made, and may only ever be made, by the center, if a brigade is detached from its division, it must change the individual formation of all the others. And if a regiment or a battalion is detached, this derangement is greater still: one of the two "twins" becomes lame and unequal.[3] The battalion or the regiment that remains alone finds itself coupled in the formation to the column of a battalion of another regiment or to another regiment, etc., etc.

Mesnil-Durand, in thus making all his movements on the center, in making the center the post of honor and the principal point, wished to be consistent with his principle, which is to always form columns by the center of the battalions, and successively by those of the regiments, brigades, [and] divisions; to act always by the center; to attack by preference by the center; [and], above all, to no longer regard the wings as active and principal in the order of battle. We will prove, in grand tactics and in treating orders of battle, that this revolution may never take place; that it is one of the chimeras of his system; that the facts, the circumstances, [and] the grand rules of war ceaselessly contradict this principle; [and] that the wings of an army on the offensive will always necessarily be its active parts, and the wings of an army on the defensive its exposed parts, etc.

Doubtlessly struck by these inconveniences, the marshal did not wish to entirely adopt the formation of the regulation. Thus, the formation on the center took place only within each brigade individually and not in the totality of divisions, [an] insufficient modification, and [one] that brought another inconvenience, which is that the divisions may only be able to be formed of an even number of brigades and that every odd number would derange the general organization necessary for the central formation of Mesnil-Durand. Consequently, although we had more troops than were required, we only ever formed divisions of two brigades.

The excess troops were camped outside the line and never entered into the division maneuvers, altogether or

---

2 [Throughout most of the Old Regime, brigades and divisions did not exist as permanent units in the French army, although both were used to varying degrees. Brigades were probably formed when field armies were assembled for war as early as the mid-seventeenth century; they were mentioned in regulations during Guibert's period and were clearly in common use, as his text indicates. Divisions came into use after 1760; the earliest clear organization of them was by Broglie in his instructions to his army in that year, but they were not made statutory until 1788. Guibert's explanatory note indicates that divisions were not widely known, even by around 1780. See Abel, "An Aspect of the Military Experience in the Age of Reason."]

3 [Mesnil-Durand's system forms "twins" by placing units next to each other in formation.]

in part. I will return to this subject in the course of these observations.

Text

[*The*] *Division of the Battalion* [*and*] *Position of Its Parts*

I

A battalion will divide itself into *two manches*, right and left; [each of] *four companies* [and] *eight platoons*; in its column order, it will divide itself again into *four sections*.

II

In the deployed battalion, the order of the companies from right to left will be third, first, second, and fourth.

In the companies of the right manche, the first platoons will go to the left, and in those of the left manche, the first platoons will go to the right.

III

The right manche will be thus composed of the first and third company [and] the left manche of the second and fourth. In the first battalion, the first company will be the colonel's; in the second, it will be the lieutenant-colonel's.

IV

The four sections of the battalion in column will be placed one before the other, the first composed of the first platoons of the two first companies, one alongside the other, [and] the second of the second platoons of the last two; finally, the fourth section [will be composed] of the second platoons of these same last companies.

V

The platoon will always be on six ranks in the battalion in column so that it will be called the "formed" platoon; it will divide itself by the center perpendicularly to its front in two "tranches," right and left; it will also subdivide itself parallel to its front in two *tiroirs*, each of three ranks and which will find itself one alongside the other in the deployed order.

VI

One sees by this that the head of the battalion in column will be composed of the two platoons of the center of the deployed battalion and that the two manches will find themselves in the column alongside each other, each having its four platoons one ahead of the other.

Observations

[*The*] *Division of the Battalion* [*and*] *Position of its Parts*

Here is what Mesnil-Durand calls his column; here is what is his primitive and habitual order. This formation is not, as one sees, anything other than the *plésion* wearing the name "French," with words like "tranches" and "*tiroirs*," which are Welsh at least.[4]

The great perfection of this column, according to Mesnil-Durand, resides in its organization, in the simplicity and the facility of its divisions and subdivisions, in the advantage that it has to be able to re-serry itself, to open itself, [and] to move itself in every sense. "You admire," I said one day to a disciple of Mesnil-Durand in the language of the master, "the interior game of this column; it extends itself, it closes itself, it dilates itself, it re-serries itself, it separates itself, it reunites. A machine does not have movements that are more regular and more sure."

But first, is this multiplicity of divisions and subdivisions to infinity an advantage? It results [from it] that the column of Mesnil-Durand, including the grenadiers and chasseurs, is formed of forty parts, and, because of this, it becomes a machine with too many parts. When one multiplies parts too much, when one reduces them by this to subdivisions that are too feeble, as those of the tranches in Mesnil-Durand's column assuredly are, everything becomes necessarily too complicated. Add to this that this multiplication of subdivisions requires a too-great nomenclature [and] that the soldier, whose intelligence must always be supposed to be limited, must necessarily lose themselves there. We see all that it is that a soldier must retain to find their rank and file: first, it is which platoon and which section; this is simple, but independently of this, which "*tiroir*," which "tranche," which "manche," etc.

In the end, is it a property exclusively attached to the column of Mesnil-Durand that allows it to open itself, re-serry itself, march, and act in every sense? Does it not belong to every species of column? Does it not belong by name to the column of a battalion that is trained in the current infantry ordinance? To this end, we compare, in that regard and in that of organization, this column with the column of Mesnil-Durand.

---

4 [Guibert makes a curious statement here, as both "tranche" and "*tiroir*" are of French etymology, not Welsh. He is perhaps making a joke that references the Welsh historian and theorist Henry Lloyd, *The History of the Late War in Germany between the King of Prussia and the Empress of Germany and her Allies* (London, 1766). Lloyd's work is often compared to Guibert's; see Azar Gat, *A History of Military Thought from the Enlightenment to the Cold War* (New York: Oxford University Press, 2001), 27–55; and Patrick Speelman, *Henry Lloyd and the Military Enlightenment of Eighteenth-Century Europe* (Westport, CT: Greenwood Press, 2002). Speelman may perhaps be credited with coining the term "Military Enlightenment" in print.]

Formed by platoons, which is its almost-habitual formation, the ordinance column is composed, like that of Mesnil-Durand, of twenty-four ranks; the officers who are at the center of the platoons divide it perpendicularly from the head to the tail in such a way that the sections of the right represent the right manche and the sections of the left the left manche; the platoons respond *aux tiroirs*; thus, [this] is no less than the subdivision of the manches and tranches, which modern tacticians fortunately have not imagined. If the column of the ordinance must be separated, opened, re-serried, [and] made to march in every way, it is susceptible to it like Mesnil-Durand's, but by divisions [that are] less broken and consequently simpler and more military.

Moreover, we observe that this interior game, carried as far and as minutely as Mesnil-Durand does, is a puerile thing and has no useful application in war. A column only has need of composing and decomposing itself by parts of a reasonable proportion, whether by divisions, which must be its greatest front, [or] by platoons or by sections, which must be its smallest. The inferior subdivisions enter into the movements by files. Similarly, a column only has need of opening and re-serrying itself by the three following manners, which correspond to all possible cases: *at whole distances*, to be able to form *en bataille*; *at half-distances*, to shorten itself when one has the certainty of being able to form oneself only on the march front; [and] *at serried distances*, when one wishes to maneuver *en masse*, deploy, or charge in column. In this last case, one must again well observe to always leave at least three paces of interval between each division of the column in such a manner that each division has the officers to command and contain it; the advantage of the order in column for the attack and its pretend force of shock does not consist of, as we have said in the *General Essay on Tactics*, and as we will be in the case of repeating in the second part of this work in examining the order in column as the attack order, and consequently as the accidental order, as I said, the exact pressure of the ranks and the files, but in the continual succession of efforts that is furnished by several divisions of troops ranged one behind the other.[5]

Enough about the column of Mesnil-Durand considered relative to its organization. We will easily examine it relative to the pretend advantages that it draws from its formation and from its development on the center.

---

5 [Abel, *Guibert's General Essay on Tactics*, 53–55.]

Text

Grenadiers and Chasseurs

I

The grenadier company, in the order of battle, will always be on three ranks and separated into two platoons, the first placed on the right flank of the first battalion ([which is] supposed to have the right), [and] the second on the left flank of the second battalion.

II

The chasseur company, also on three ranks and separated in the same way, will send its first platoon to the left of the first battalion (same supposition) and its second to the right of the second battalion.

III

If the first battalion is to the left, this order will be inverted in such a way that the grenadiers will always be on the exterior flanks of the regiment.

IV

The battalion being in column, the grenadiers and chasseurs will align themselves on its front, leaving intervals of four paces between them and it, and often more, to place cannon there.

V

But if it must form itself in march order and not to fight or to maneuver, the two platoons of grenadiers and chasseurs will place themselves on the front of their battalion, one alongside the other and each of them on six ranks, serried three on three, or by *tiroirs*.

Observations

Grenadiers and Chasseurs

One sees how Mesnil-Durand separates the grenadiers and the chasseurs from the battalion. He destines them to act independently of it. They must form the famous curtain of musketry, behind which he pretends to shield his columns and that we will analyze in [the right] time and place.

As to the rest, these grenadier and chasseur companies in the maneuvers of Mesnil-Durand are always moving; they fly ceaselessly from the head to the flanks, and always running, because Mesnil-Durand poses as a principle that they will have no other pace.

This strange employment relative to the grenadiers above all, this perpetual agitation, this necessity of always maneuvering at the run, absolutely contrary to all possibility when it will be done in war, and [a] thousand other inconveniences too long and of too-little importance to be recapitulated here, elevated a complaint so widespread in the Camp that Marshal Broglie, from the first moment, changed this part of the instruction.

The grenadiers were ordered to follow the movements of the battalion as if they were part of it, and in the proofs made by the De La Couronne Regiment at the end of the camp, it was a question of placing them at the center of the battalion to always give them the head of the column. We do not take the pain of discussing here this change that, doing nothing for the base of maneuvers nor the organization of the column, does not render them better. Thus, there were only the chasseurs destined to maneuver and to run in advance and on the flanks of the columns, which diminished the inconvenience by half but also greatly thinned the famous curtain [of musketry]. Also, Mesnil-Durand groaned at this change, as well as [at] all the modifications that were made to his system, and he did not cease to say that it was disfigured and that it was not adopted entirely, [which] was detrimental to it. We are far from thinking like him, as we regard all these changes and all that may be made as [being] in the same genre: variants [that are] quite insignificant in themselves and which, being the best possible, would nevertheless leave us entirely in our opinion on the base of the system.

Text

Places of Officers

I

The first captain, the first lieutenant, and the first *sous-lieutenant* of each fusilier company will attach [themselves to] and place themselves in the first platoon [and] the three other officers in the second; the sergeants will place themselves between the two. The officers thus divided will place themselves on the exterior flanks of the column in such a manner that there is one outside each file.[6]

---

6   This is the habitual order of officers, since the habitual order of the battalion is to be in column. Mesnil-Durand enters into the greatest details to indicate the variations that these positionings must prove relative to the different circumstances in which the battalion might find itself, like in case of fire, etc. These positionings find themselves yet more varied in the detail of the maneuvers, but I make mention here only that the habitual disposition of the officers is, as one sees, entirely outside of the column. I pass over the place of superior officers in the same way.

Observations

Places of Officers

Once the base is established, there are bizarre ideas as there are simple ideas in it; they succeed each other and enchain each other. Thus, having named the faces of his column "curtain walls," Mesnil-Durand, to complete the analogy, pretended that the officers and *bas-officiers* that he places all along the exterior files are its "facing stones."

These figures not being truths, they do not convince. It was found with a common voice that the officers were placed in a manner [that was] little intelligent and little military, that they did not accomplish the objective of marking and separating the divisions of his column, that they were not at all within range of containing and directing their troops, [and] that the soldier remained abandoned to himself, etc., etc. These objections even struck the partisans of the system, as, in the tests that were made in the last days of the camp in the De La Couronne Regiment to try to correct the Regulations, the places of the officers were changed to return to the principles of the ordinance.

Text

Places of the Flags

I

The flag of each battalion will be to the left and in the second rank of the first company.

II

There will always be two pennants [each] carried by a corporal on the front of the battalion in column; they will place themselves in advance of the two exterior files and will serve to fix the alignments in the march and in the maneuver.

Assembly of the Companies and of the Battalion

I

To be able to carry the precision necessary in the detail of the maneuvers, suppose companies of ninety-six men under arms, and consequently platoons of forty-eight, without counting the officers, sergeants, [and] drummers, forming sixteen files on three ranks.

II

In assembling the battalion, we will count on the files of each company to carry them to the proportion fixed above; those that exceed it will furnish them to those that lack them, and, if in the totality of the battalion there remain supernumeraries, we will form them in a platoon behind the battalion commanded by an officer or a sergeant according to its strength.

III

The companies will form by size rank.

Observations

Assembly of the Companies and of the Battalion

Mesnil-Durand supposes here his column habitually formed on a frontage of sixteen files and on twenty-four deep. This proportion is relative to the principles of Folard, who defined the column [as] a long square being one-third deeper than its frontage.[7]

Attached to this proportion, he would that, when all the companies of the battalions will have been equalized and fixed at thirty-two files or ninety-six men, the excess files form a supernumerary platoon placed behind the battalion. Thus composed, his column is of three-hundred eighty-four men, not counting the grenadiers and chasseurs, which never take part in the column and which are only independent and accessory pieces.

This is quite good for peacetime and with the current strength of our companies, which tallies more or less with this supposition today.

But when war arrives, I demand of Mesnil-Durand: how will he form his column?

We will surely not go to war with battalions of four-hundred men. In all the foreign regiments,[8] the footing of battalions is at least eight-hundred men, and some of them [have] 1,000. The one of our eventual constitution in times of war carries the four fusilier companies that make up the battalion, [making] seven-hundred twenty-four men. Thus, to preserve his favorite proportion in his column, this leaves three-hundred forty supernumeraries behind the battalion? I ask: what is the order that leaves a part of the battalion thus as an hors d'œuvre and outside of being able to fight? [What if] they entered the column? Then it would find itself on a frontage of almost twenty-four files and twenty-four deep and consequently a perfect square formed essentially contrary to the fundamental principle of the column and that effectively renders it too heavy and too [difficult] to handle.

"But," Mesnil-Durand will respond, "if my system is admitted, the constitution will bend to it, and then we will have battalions of only five-hundred men." Quite good, but then I expect the opposite inconvenience.

These battalions of five-hundred men will find themselves, in the midst [or] at the end of the campaign, [or] after an action, so reduced that they may not be able to furnish the complete number of files that the column of Mesnil-Durand requires. He was able to judge this at the Camp of Vaussieux. Our battalions are five-hundred forty men today, there was no wartime service, and, in the midst of the camp, some of the line battalions did not have their complete files.

What will Mesnil-Durand do? Will he diminish the frontage of his column? Then, it will lose the proportion of its principles; in the opposite inconvenience, it was a mass; here, it will become a needle. Will he diminish the depth of the platoons, as he did at the Camp of Vaussieux? Then, what will the *tiroirs* be when it must deploy! and what will the line of musketry be that will result [when] opposed to the enemy line!

Here is the abyss into which the spirit of the system throws [itself] when experience, when judgment, [and] when habit, reflecting on all the circumstances that war may offer, do not stop it and do not enlighten it.

In reflecting on what the touchstone of all military systems is, and above all in transporting it to war, Mesnil-Durand would have foreseen a crowd of objections that remain to be made to him. I will cite only some here.

I admit his battalion as calculated and his complete column: we depart from the camp, and, if we demand on the march a detachment of fifty, sixty, eighty, [or] one-hundred men, the files must be recounted, etc. This operation done, another detachment will return; must they be recounted again? And if it is a war march, or if this march is made at night in a country of difficult roads, will all these combinations of the files be as easily done?

And if, in lieu of mingled detachments, we detach one or two companies from the battalion to occupy a post, the head of a defile! etc., and if, for the same objective, we detach a battalion from the regiment, a regiment from the brigade, or a brigade from the division! here is the entire column upset, the manches disunited, the twins lamed, in the end, the entire ingenious mechanism at least quite confused.

And if, in an action, a column finds itself beaten in the flank by a violent fire, and if the loss strikes one manche more than another, what will become of this column

---

7 [See 10.].
8 [The French army maintained several units known as the "foreign regiments" that were raised and manned by men who were not French subjects, at least in theory. The most famous of them was the Swiss Guard that defended the Tuileries Palace when it was stormed by a mob on 10 August 1792, resulting in its massacre. Foreign units were expected to introduce new ideas to the French army, particularly those of German extraction; see Abel, *Guibert's General Essay on Tactics*, 57 and 73. See also Jeremy Popkin, *A New World Begins: The History of the French Revolution* (New York: Basic Books, 2019), 278–284.]

organization, [which is] entirely founded on files [that are] complete [and] equalized, and then divided and subdivided into equal fractions?

And so, after having sustained a musketry action that will remove many people from combat and that will have carried more to one part of the battalion than to another, the march column must form itself; how will dispersed and unequal platoons form this column?

Will Mesnil-Durand pretend that these inconveniences exist equally for the battalion? Assuredly, they do not exist. One counts, one equalizes the files of the battalion when one is on the exercise terrain itself, but this is not at all of absolute necessity. [It is of] little importance to the battalion if one of its platoons has two or three files of more or fewer [men]; [it is consequently of] little importance if one makes or absorbs detachments on the march. The column of the ordinance does not at all do so by combined and complicated movements; it does not at all have a determined number of files; it is not at all composed of fractions divided and subdivided to infinity. If one detaches a company from the battalion, whether *en bataille* or in column, this does not disorganize it, [and] it does not require shrinking; it rests entirely on what remains to it, and it fights for what will preserve its front. If it loses everyone in an action, it will only be able to re-serry itself and occupy a very small front, but its ranks and its files will always preserve their primitive order, etc. On these essential differences I appeal to all educated *militaires*, above all to all *militaires* who, having seen the column of Mesnil-Durand, had to reflect on the complication of its organization. Let them compare, and let them judge.

Text

Detail Maneuvers

I

They will consist of:
1. Deploying and reforming the platoon, that is to say making it pass from the order on six, which is its habitual order, to that which will be called "the platoon formed in the order on three," which is the deployed order.
2. Making the platoon double and redouble, that is to say forming "by tranches," and reforming in platoons.⁹

II

The grenadiers and chasseurs will pass from the order on three ranks to the order on two ranks. We will see elsewhere to what this maneuver is relative.

III

The officers, *bas-officiers*, and soldiers will never have bayonets fixed if it is not a moment for an infantry charge or to receive a cavalry charge. We will remove the bayonet as soon as it will not be one of these cases, but only [one] of marches or maneuvers in column, or of deploying for musketry.

Observations

Detail Maneuvers

I do not at all stop myself on the maneuvers contained in this article, their object only being elementary and insignificant to the base of the system.

I demand only of Mesnil-Durand why the habitual order of his platoons is on six ranks when in no case do infantry fight in this order? This uselessly elongates his maneuvers in a preliminary movement, that of forming on six ranks; this procured him, in truth, the novelty of *tiroirs*, which have never had either utility or purpose.¹⁰

Text

March in Column: Definitions [and] Distances

I

The column of a battalion that will be employed alone in battle order and, when the terrain will permit, also in march order, will be simply named "column," or sometimes, for greater clarity and precision, "simple column."

II

When the terrain will not permit marching on this front, which will be by sections, we will form the column by platoons. When the terrain will not permit the front of the column even by platoons, we will form it by tranches.

[With] the terrain opening, we will be able to return to the column successively by platoons and then in simple column.

---

9   I will not enter here into the detail of these maneuvers; I will extract from them only two essential articles that Mesnil-Durand establishes in principle. One is that a platoon should never form itself or deploy on the march, [and] the other is that any doubling in depth for a troop of the right (and vice-versa for a troop of the left) will be done by advancing the left part over a quantity of terrain equal to that which it occupies in depth, and in making the part of the right double behind it, which will march by its left for this, and that any doubling of the front will be done by the last troops that will carry themselves by the right of the first, which will not budge.

10 The two principles reported in this note are important for the inconveniences that result from them in marches, [which] is what we will see below.

III

[With] several columns marching in a line behind each other "in simple column," if the terrain works in such a manner as to permit a quite-great frontage for a long time, we will form them "in double column," that is to say in two simple columns, one alongside the other. These two columns, which will be named "twins," will always have an avenue of some distance between them. The right twin will be composed of all the troops that, in line, must have the right and the left twin those that must have the left.

IV

The simple column will be called "serried" when it will have ranks of each section serried and interlaced. The battalion will habitually be in this state in the fight and in maneuver.

V

However, in this case, we may open the distances to two paces between the *tiroirs* of each platoon to march more easily, but we always then serry them before making any other command.

VI

When we will wish to give the march yet more ease, we will march the column at the route step.

VII

The simple or double column will be called "assembled" when the sections will be serried in such a manner as to have only one pace of distance between them.

VIII

The column by platoons and by tranches only taking place for the march, there are hardly any occasions to assemble them.

IX

The column by platoons having double the depth of the simple column, the doubling to pass one to the other will be done successively and will retard the tail; this is why, until it will be achieved, the head will march at the maneuver pace.

X

However, we may make this doubling at the same time along all the length of the column, having first taken the necessary distances.

XI

We may also close the column by platoons before returning to the simple column so that there are few things to do when it will be formed to regain the distances.

XII

We may even be able to hold the column by platoons in the length determined for the simple column when the defile will last for only a moment, there being only a quite-small space to cover with such ease.

XIII

All that is above on lengths and distances is clarification rather than precept and always subordinate to the general principle to never elongate the columns more than is necessary for the ease of the march and to never fear shortening them.

XVI

The simple column must be regarded as composed of two manches or two united columns; when the one on the left [has] the head, the other is on the right.

Observations

March in Column: Definitions [and] Distances

This entire chapter wants to be read with attention; it contains one of the most important parts of the Regulation, since it acts as the function and the mechanism of the column of Mesnil-Durand relative to marches.

I will not at all stop myself here to remark on the complication of names, principles, and means that reign here; there is no *militaire* who cannot sense the default in a simple reading, and it is much more apparent yet when one sees this strange formation on the terrain.

We bound ourselves here to demonstrating these inconveniences in a column of a single battalion; the analysis of the Regulations that we will make below will develop these inconveniences yet further still when it will [be a question of] a column of more than one battalion, and finally of a column of an army division.

If one examines the formation of the column of Mesnil-Durand, that is to say of that which he calls his "simple column" (see paragraph 1), relative to a single battalion, his formation makes itself by the center of the deployed battalion; [there is] nothing simpler than this formation, but [there is also] nothing less new, because, as I said above, Mesnil-Durand took this column from the Infantry Exercise Ordinance of 1753, and it exists in our current Ordinance.[11] Employed as it is in this latter ordinance above all, it is applied to its true objective: it is the maneuver column, [and] it makes itself while standing still and when one has the certainty of deploying it in the same place where it was formed. Further, one may, and the Ordinance does not exclude it, [although] it may perhaps have better indicated it, employ it as the attack column; and finally, all the times that one has before one a free terrain, one foresees having

---

11 ["Our current Ordinance" is probably *Ordonnance du roi pour régler l'exercice de ses troupes d'infanterie du 1ᵉʳ juin 1776*, which was written during Guibert's first term serving on the Council of War.]

to deploy by the center. But making this central formation a universal and exclusive principle, applying it to march orders and thus also adopting the central development as the unique means, is to lose and confound everything in believing to have simplified everything and in wishing to generalize everything.

1. The column formed by the center is advantageous only when the debouche by which one forms oneself in march order, and that by which one arrives on the terrain that one goes to occupy, is found precisely at the center of the formed line and the line to form.
2. It requires, without which result grand inconveniences, that the march be open in such a manner as to never be in the case of diminishing the extent of the front by which one marches.
3. It becomes quite embarrassing if one is in the case of forming oneself *en bataille* on the new flank.

We prove these diverse inconveniences by the example of a column of a single battalion forming itself, placing itself in march order, and then marching according to the principles of Mesnil-Durand.

First, we distinguish a march from a maneuver. A maneuver ordinarily makes itself on a circumscribed terrain and relative to a given objective; one foresees the point where one will arrive and maneuvers there successively. Thus, when a battalion wishes to carry itself in column in a free and open countryside to occupy a position parallel to its old front in a countryside equally free and open, it may, without inconvenience and even with advantage, form in column on the center, since it is the master of directing itself against the center of its new position and of developing itself there by the center. A march, on the contrary, ordinarily takes place in a large space, and it goes to places that one has not reconnoitered. One does not foresee where one will be obliged to form oneself, whether making the route or arriving at the end of the march. Forming oneself in march column by the center is thus an inappropriately exclusive method, since it is possible that the debouche not be opposite the center of the old front and that the opening of the march does not correspond to the new center. [For every] unique case where the debouche departs from the center and leads to the center, there are two where the debouche may depart from the wings and lead to the wings without counting those where the debouches may be found between the wings and the center, but when the debouche would be found opposite the center of the old front, this would still not be a reason to form oneself in march column by the center, as one is not sure if one will be able to arrive by the center of one's new position, and it is always a two-to-one bet that one will arrive by the wings. Finally, if one is forced to develop oneself unexpectedly on the route, it is advantageous to find oneself formed in such a manner as to place oneself *en bataille* without preparation, without fumbling, and at the point where one finds oneself; this is what one cannot do with the column of Mesnil-Durand, as we will prove below.

We again take up the supposition of a column of a battalion forming itself, forming itself in march order, and marching in the system of Mesnil-Durand, and, to render this supposition more striking, we oppose to it here a column of a battalion forming itself, forming itself in march order, and marching according to the means of the Ordinance.

First, the formation of the column is a true maneuver for the battalion of Mesnil-Durand: it requires calculations and the equalization of files, then a formation of platoons to form itself on six, [and] then a combined maneuver of the two wings towards the center; in the end, [it is] a maneuver commanded by voice, subjected to a certain precision, and that requires free terrain in advance of the front. How circumstances, and circumstances frequent in war, may render these preliminaries to marching uncomfortable and difficult! Suppose a night march or a front full of obstacles such as is often found in camps or in positions of passage. Suppose [a] column of several battalions, of several brigades, and then it is another embarrassment, but I wish not to anticipate, and I hold myself here to speaking only of a single battalion.

We now go to the Ordinance battalion. Its formation in column is not at all a maneuver; it requires no preparation. Day, night, in all sorts of terrains, in the midst of any species of embarrassment, it may form itself in march order; it need only detach one of its wings; it does not even need a command for this: the platoon, the section, [and] the division of the wing form themselves in movement, and all the rest of the battalion follows. The line being composed of several battalions [or] of several brigades brings neither lengthening nor embarrassment; all break in the same movement, all march, and the column is in route at the same time as [it] forms.

Here are columns formed from either side, but, if that of Mesnil-Durand does not have its debouche exactly before its center, it is then obliged to maneuver to go to find it. Suppose this debouche [is on] its wings or between its wings and its center, [or] suppose [it is] behind its wings: even worse. For the Ordinance battalion, all is equal: whether the debouche be in advance of it, on its flank, [or] behind it, once broken and formed in column, it bends itself, it turns itself, it re-turns itself as it wishes; it does not have to maneuver at all; its movements, in all sorts of directions, are only a simple march in which the soldiers may first carry their arms at will and [then] march at their free and natural pace.

Finally, I would that the column of Mesnil-Durand enter in the debouche of its march; this debouche, as it arrives only too often in war, is no longer found on the same front as when it [the column] departed. It must diminish its front. See how Mesnil-Durand proceeds in this situation.

Suppose the column forms in march order according to the principles of the "simple column," that is to say by sections.

One commands "column by platoons." Then, the second company makes halt to wait on its place in the column, and then for the entire battalion. By this doubling (see Paragraph IX), one thus necessarily retards the march of the column. [If] the terrain closes more, one commands "column by tranches," then [follows] same movement of the platoon to the tail of the column, and consequently, the same retardation.

Now suppose the column of Mesnil-Durand thus formed by platoons, and, for a stronger reason, by tranches, obliged to form itself *en bataille* on its flank by the unforeseen appearance of the enemy. Everything is confounded, everything is mixed up; no officer, no *bas-officier* will find himself a place to command and to contain [it]. In this moment, [there will hopefully] be some shots [or] some local difficulties that may draw it from this inextricable confusion!

But suppose that the enemy presents themselves only and simply on its [the column's] front [and] that it has a position to occupy, an important point that it must support or prevent [the enemy from attacking]: it does not have an entire troop to oppose them, [and] it is obliged to wait until it has re-formed by successive doublings from the column by tranches to the column by platoons, and from the column by platoons to the state of [the] simple column, which is the only one in which it may maneuver. Before it will be able to, time will be lost, the position missed, and the enemy on it.

This necessity of always returning to the state of [the] simple column to be able to maneuver is found in many of the maneuvers of Mesnil-Durand and is one of the most destructive results of the complication of his primitive order. This alone, in my opinion, renders his system, relative to interior details, absolutely defective and inadmissible [in] war.

Now place the ordinance column in the same suppositions, and we will see it face all without difficulties, without delay, [and] without embarrassments. It is formed by divisions, which correspond to the simple column of Mesnil-Durand. [If] the terrain closes, it forms itself by platoons.

This is not at all a maneuver for it; it is a movement that it makes without stopping, without relenting in its march, [and] without general commands: the head of the column indicates to it this movement, and it follows. [If] the terrain closes yet further, it forms itself by sections. [If] the terrain closes even further, it marches by six files, [or even] by three. It thus always elongates itself without stopping, without breaking, without fractions that so confound and so disunite it. At the head of each of its fractions, until it reduces itself to files, are always found an officer to command it [and] officers on the flanks to observe the distance and the point of view as well as serry the files to maintain order. What if it is attacked on its flank? It may form *en bataille*; it has its distances to make face to it. What if they are on its front? It may immediately oppose a troop [to the enemy], occupy a point, [or] support its wing, which is an important objective in war. The first troop of the column, not needing to wait for the troops that follow, forms itself, and the others arrive to support it.

The inevitable chaining of objections [and] the difficulty of dispersing that which is made to be tied [together] has made me anticipate observations relative to other articles here. The regulations of Mesnil-Durand are so poorly worded, they have so little order in their materials, that to analyze them, I am, despite myself, forced to renounce following them step by step. But [of] what importance [is] my march, provided my objective is attained!

Text

Order of the Troops in Columns

I

Whether the companies march two-by-two in simple column or one after the other in columns of much smaller front, they always follow in their numerical order; those that have the center in the deployed order take the head of the column, excepting the grenadiers and chasseurs, which will march in advance of the others.

II

The deployed battalion will never break itself by its last companies, which are its flanks, or at least this will arrive only in the case of a flank march, decided as such by the objective of carrying itself to the right or the left to the point, [and], having arrived there, of making front on the same side on which it did before marching.

III

In the same way, when one division of several brigades will form a column, they will follow in their numerical order according to which they were placed in line by the center of the division.

Observations

Order of the Troops in Columns

This article explains the order and the rank that the companies, the battalions, the regiments, and finally the brigades will take in the march columns. The consequences of the general method adopted in this regard by Mesnil-Durand are curious when a march column of several battalions must be formed. To give a just idea to our readers, we cite an example.

[Suppose] there is a body of twelve battalions or of three brigades camped or formed in line; this corps will be, following the principles of Mesnil-Durand, ranged in the following order: the oldest brigade to the center, the first regiment having the right and the second the left [and] the first battalion of the first regiment having the left and the first battalion of the second regiment the right in such a manner that these first two battalions have the center of the brigade; the second brigade to the right, the first regiment of this brigade having the left and the second regiment the right, and, in each regiment, the first battalion again having the left; the third brigade to the left, the first regiment having the right, and, in each regiment, the first battalion then having the right. When it results that these brigades are, I suppose, composed of three brigade-command regiments, Picardy, Champagne, and Navarre, which would have brigaded the Aquitaine, Anjou, and Nivernais Regiments, their order of battle would conform to figures 1, 2, and 3, Diagram I.[12] [This] arrangement [is], as one sees, quite complicated, [an] arrangement that must change if it has one brigade more or one brigade less, etc. See what I have said in this regard in my observations on Paragraph I, at the commencement of this text.

Now suppose this corps is obliged to form itself in march order on a single column: it will form itself, according to the principle of Mesnil-Durand, in double column. We thus see the inconveniences of this formation. Here, it is only a question of the order and the rank of the troops in the column.

The double column formed by the center of the division will find itself thus composed of what is presented in Figure 1, Diagram II. The first battalions of each brigade find themselves coupled *en jumelles* and followed by their second battalions in the same order.

Now [if] the double column [will be] obliged by the nature of the route to form in simple column, the brigades will be obliged to intercalate: the brigade of the center, which is that of Picardie, passes the first; then the brigade of the right, which is that of Champagne; then the brigade of the left, which is that of Navarre. But this is not all. In the Picardie Brigade, which is that of the center, the first battalion of the Picardie Regiment will pass the first, then the second of the Picardie Regiment, then the first of the Aquitaine Regiment, and then the second of the Aquitaine Regiment; from this results that, in this simple column, the first battalion of the Aquitaine Regiment finds itself separated from the first of the Picardie Regiment, alongside which it finds itself in the order of battle, by the second of the Picardie Regiment, and that the brigade of the left of the division is separated from the brigade of the center, alongside which it must be in the order of battle, by the brigade of the right that immediately follows that of the center. See Figure 2, Diagram II.[13]

If one then examines with attention the interior organization of this column in following the interior details of its march movements in the Regulations, one will see that, independently of the alternating mélange of brigades of the right and brigades of the left, it similarly makes a mélange of companies of the right and companies of the left in each battalion at the instant when the debouche reduces it to the frontage of the column by platoons, and that this mélange always subsists when the debouche reduces it to the frontage of the column by tranches. One will see that the interior mélange of each battalion only ceases at the moment when, in leaving the debouche, the column may pass successively from the state of [the] column by tranches to that of [the] column by platoons and the column by platoons to that of [the] simple column, and that this mélange of brigades of the right and the left dissipates only at the moment when the twin column may re-form itself. Above all, one will see, and one will observe as a major vice of this entire machine, that all its movements to intercalate itself and then return to the state of the double column are only able to be executed by continually stopping all parts of the column that find themselves behind the fraction that must change form. Now, as

---

12 [As Guibert indicates, French army units were ranked by precedence, usually by date of creation, which dictated where they were placed in line and which regiment would command a brigade formed of multiple regiments.]

13 This mélange was so extraordinary in the *Fragments of Tactics*, because, following the principles that are established there, the simple column composes itself in this manner: the first battalion of the Picardie Regiment, then the first of the Aquitaine Regiment, then the second of the Picardie Regiment, and then the second of the Aquitaine Regiment, etc. From this would result that, in this simple column, the regiments would be intermixed battalion by battalion, [a] strange variegation from which we were at great pains to draw Mesnil-Durand; what is substituted is a little less complicated, but it is still in an unheard-of manner, and nothing will change [regardless], because this complication is the destructive result of his central formation.

NEW VARIATIONS OF THE "FRENCH ORDER." [THE] PROOFS MADE AT METZ

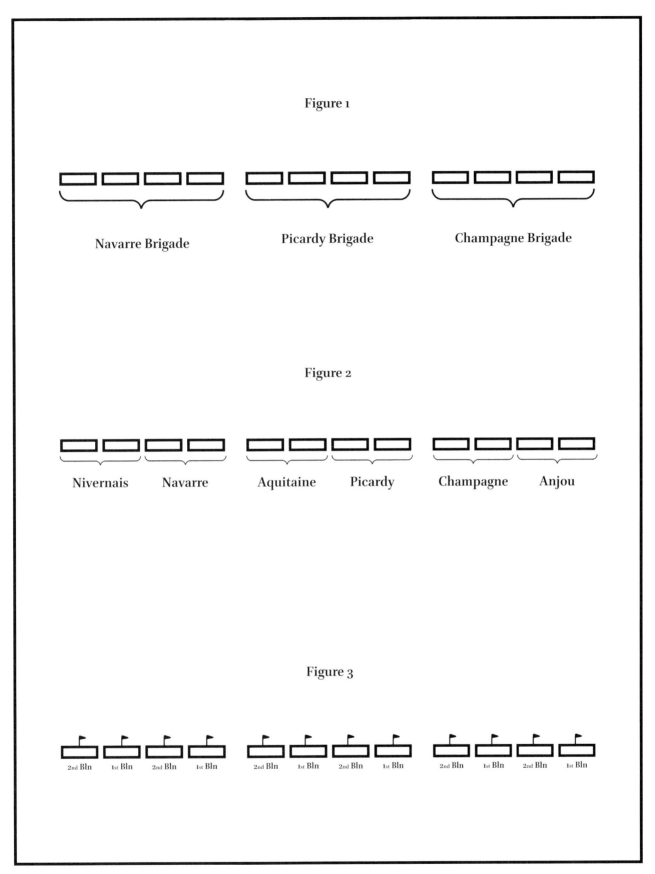

FIGURE 1   Diagram 1

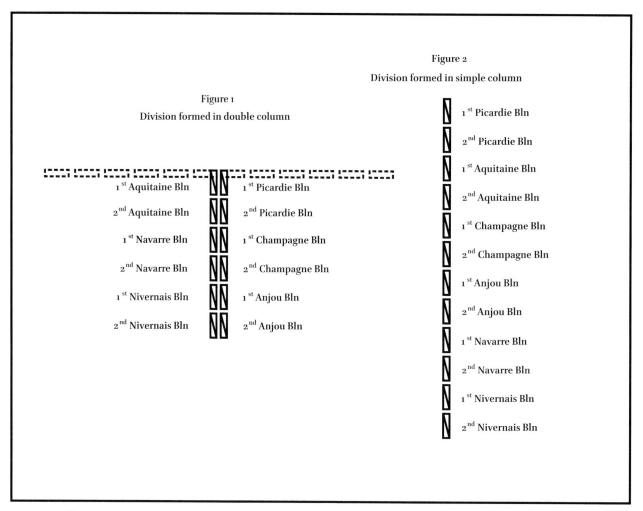

FIGURE 2 Diagram II

long as columns have marched in war, fatigues have occasioned to the troops in the tail every time the head stops, without counting the slowness and the loss of time that results from it.

I will dispense myself from giving a diagram for the comprehension of these last observations. The complication of these movements, even on paper, frightens me and arrests me. The exposé that I have just made will suffice to make them understood.

In the same way, I will dispense myself from adding any reflection. To judge, it suffices here to read.

Text

Specific Movements of a Battalion

I

When the battalion will be required to maneuver, it will always be *en bataille* in its column order and never deployed.

II

All the movements of the battalion will be done at the maneuver pace and those of the grenadiers and chasseurs at the run.

Observations

Specific Maneuvers of a Battalion

I

This exclusion is, as one sees, quite positive.

II

I will raise this strange principle of Mesnil-Durand elsewhere. In war, and in army movements above all, one does not at all march at the maneuver step, [and] one runs even less; one marches at a free and natural pace that allows it [the army] to sustain itself for a long time and without fatigue.[14]

---

14 [See Abel, *Guibert's General Essay on Tactics*, 186.]

Text

First Maneuver
Flank and Tranche Marches

The battalion will march by its flank in several manners:

1. The entire battalion by a right, all the parts of the battalion marching in the state where they find themselves without opening.
2. By manches, the two manches observing six paces of distance between them.
3. By tranches, the tranches observing three paces of distance between them.

To form itself on its first front, the battalion will only have to stop itself and serry its distances.

Second Maneuver
Change of Direction

I

The battalion will change direction in two manners: standing still or on the march.

II

To change direction on the march, suppose to the right, the first section will turn to the right, and [then] the others successively.

III

If one wishes to make this movement standing still, all the sections will make a right at the same time; the battalion will then have made its change of direction, but the sections will be in echelons and will no longer have their distances. Thus, the last sections must then make a left to carry themselves behind the first and then serry so that they can re-take their distance.

Third Maneuver
Changing Front to the Right

I

If the battalion is in movement, this will be a simple change of direction, the four sections successively making their conversion movement.

II

Any column will change the front of its march in the same way: all the divisions successively turning at the same point, [and] the pivots not stopping them but [rather] describing an arc less grand and maintaining the ordinary step through the totality of the column, by means of which its march will not at all be retarded.

III

The means for changing front while standing still are not at all given because there is no case in which this maneuver may be necessary for the battalion in column.

Fourth Maneuver
Changing Front to the Rear

This is done in the same way: by successive quarter-conversions, each section marching four paces forward, then turning a second time to the right.

Fifth Maneuver
Substituting

This is done [via] the two companies of the column's making a right and a left [respectively] and demarcating the section that they [vacated], which may in turn make [a] place for the two following sections, etc.

Sixth Maneuver
Deploying and Reforming the Battalion in Column[15]

I

[This] deployment will only take place when we will wish to form the battalion on three ranks to make use of musketry.

II

It will always be [done] on the center and by *tiroirs*, etc.

III

If this deployment is made within range of musketry, at the beginning, we will command the files that will extend themselves from the center to the right and the left to fire as the *tiroirs* will be deployed and aligned.

IV

A battalion will never deploy otherwise, and this central maneuver will always be possible, because, at the moment of deploying the battalions, each of them will already be in line between two intervals.

V

If, in some case, a battalion, having deployed, would be forced to arrive on its terrain by the left, this would not hinder the same maneuver; only before deploying, it would carry itself to the center of its terrain marching by the right, and this movement of twenty-five *toises* joined to a deployment of twenty-five *toises* would not exceed the length of a deployment of fifty *toises*.

VI

To reform the deployed battalion in column, one will commence by forming the platoons, that is to say by forming

---

15 [Contemporary *militaires* usually used the term "deploy" in its technical sense, meaning to move from column to line, rather than its more generic sense, which was and is "to spread out, utilize, or arrange for a deliberate purpose;" see "Deploy," https://www.merriam-webster.com/dictionary/deploy.]

them on six, [and] then the column will form itself in advance by the center, etc.

This maneuver is the only one that the deployed battalion employs to form itself in column.

VII

If it only has a debouche in advance of its right or of its left, it will nevertheless employ this central formation, after which, marching by the right, it will carry itself to its debouche.

VIII

If it is too close to a stream so that the column may not advance thirty paces in its formation, but only fifteen, this will not hinder the employment of the same means. The column will form itself without intervals between the sections, and it does not have need of them for the moment, because it wishes to only march first by the flank.

IX

If we do not have these fifteen paces before us, there will still be no embarrassment, and the platoons in their flank march can press their left or their right [in order] to form the sections behind the first, which does not budge.

Eighth Maneuver[16]
Forming *En Bataille* by Company

This maneuver is for forming four small columns of each battalion in lieu of only one [column].

Ninth Maneuver
Forming by Companies in Sections, etc.
    Maneuvers of Several Battalions
    Forming *En Bataille*
    Dispositions for Forming *En Bataille*

I

When a column will approach the terrain where it must develop itself, it will direct itself on the center of the line that it must form.

II

If the debouche by which it arrives there is not directly behind the center in departing from the debouche, it will carry itself there by the shortest route by means of a small change of direction in its march.

III

The column of several battalions approaching the terrain where it must form itself *en bataille* will commence by doubling and shortening to form itself in double column, if it is not already.

IV

The double column thus [being] formed and prepared, before proceeding with its development, we will occupy ourselves in establishing its front in the alignment determined by the points of view indicated.[17]

V

At the same time that the battalions will establish themselves on the line of direction and that the rest of the double column will follow this movement, the commander will assemble the column.

VI

In all cases, to form ourselves *en bataille*, we will begin from the state of "assembled double column."

Differences in the Formations En Bataille

I

Forming one or several regiments *en bataille* is to present the battalions in line, having intervals between them and each in its simple-column order serried by section.

II

Forming a line on three ranks is deploying the line.

III

We fix the intervals between the deployed battalions at six *toises*, but between the battalions *en bataille*, they will vary according to the extent of the terrain, the quantity of troops, and the objective that we will propose.

IV

To establish something to fix, at least preliminarily, we will suppose, as it often will arrive, that two battalions *en bataille* will hold the front of a deployed battalion so that [there will be] an infantry corps equal in front to an enemy of the same strength that would be deployed on two lines. This is thus how we will form *en bataille* all the times that there will not be a contrary order.

V

If we wish to re-serry in front of a deployed battalion, not just two battalions, but three or even four, we will sound the warning at the same time as the commands necessary for it to form itself *en bataille*.

VI

In the intervals thus re-serried, or in advance of them, there will not be enough space for [both] the grenadiers and chasseurs, only for the latter. The grenadiers will thus form in advance of the battalions' fronts and the chasseurs in two troops on the flanks.

VII

We will remark that, as [is] generally [the case] in important dispositions, the parts of the line destined to act and that must decide the victory will also be *en bataille* with intervals less than in the primitive disposition. This will

---

16   [There is no Seventh Maneuver listed; Guibert either omitted it, or he or Mesnil-Durand made an arithmetic error.]

17   [Points of view were landmarks selected by officers on which to dress the formation as it marched and maneuvered; for example, see Abel, *Guibert's General Essay on Tactics*, 66.]

hardly ever take place, at least in the totality of the line, except for the first order of battle at the head of the camp.[18]

Observations

First, Second, Third, and Fourth Maneuvers

I will not at all arrest myself on all these specific maneuvers. I would have many defaults of detail to raise in them. But, once more, I am indifferent to the details all the times that they are not drawn from the base of the system.

Fifth Maneuver

Substituting

This is the maneuver that Mesnil-Durand borrowed from Chile. See chapter 3, page 20. It does not succeed on our continent, and even its partisans proscribe it with one voice.

Sixth Maneuver

Deploying and Reforming the Battalion in Column

I will return to this in treating deployments in greater detail below in the large article that concerns them.

Eighth Maneuver

Forming *En Bataille* by Company

One could never conceive the objective of this maneuver. I have heard the partisans of Mesnil-Durand say that this order corresponds to that of the Roman maniples and that it may be good for attacking several points at once with a single battalion. Regardless, it was generally proscribed at the Camp.

Ninth Maneuver

Forming by Company in Sections, etc.

[This] had the same fate as the preceding maneuver.

Maneuvers of Several Battalions

Forming *En Bataille*

Disposition for Forming *En Bataille*

I will gather here all my observations on what relates to the central deployment; it is the important and principal maneuver of Mesnil-Durand, that which he believes [to be] the most advantageous and consequently that which must be fought.

I have already said, in Chapter Three page 22, [that] this development on the center was not at all invented by Mesnil-Durand. It existed before he attributed it to himself under the name "development by fifty," and it existed in the Infantry Exercise Ordinance of 1753. The current Ordinance, in adopting it and employing it, as well as the central formation, in the maneuver of passage of lines, thus did not plagiarize him, as Mesnil-Durand pretends.[19] It [the Ordinance] took its property where it found it; it served itself with a maneuver know from old ordinances, and it perfected the details and the means of execution of them, whereas Mesnil-Durand, in appropriating them for himself, arranged them quite poorly.

But it is no longer a question here of examining to whom the central development belongs in its origin. It is [a] question of examining the maneuver in itself, as I did for the formation of the column by the center.

In refuting this formation, I have already [listed] the reasons that oppose themselves to adopting the movements by the center as unique and exclusive means, and these reasons being common to the central deployment as well as to the formation, I refer the reader to them.

Thus we come to the two great advantages that Mesnil-Durand attributes to this deployment. One is, he pretends, that of promptitude, [and] the other [is] that of being covered during its execution.

It is beyond doubt that, if one supposes a battalion column formed by the center and arriving directly on its terrain by the center, the central deployment would not be much shorter or more covered than any other species of deployment.

I also repeat what I have already said in speaking of the formation of the column on the center: that, without contradiction, it must be preferred when one is sure of being able to arrive on the terrain of the new position by the center; also the Ordinance employed it quite appropriately in movements when halted, like the passage of lines where one has the certainty of deploying oneself at the same place and by the contrary movements; also I will go even further than the Ordinance, and I will believe that it will be even better to employ in many cases as the attack column and all the times that, having before one a free terrain, one foresees being able to deploy oneself by the center.

But, as I then proved, this formation and this development by the center may not be the exclusive and universal methods. Above all, they may not be applied to army marches. In marches, one does not know where one will end up; one cannot foresee the point where one may be obliged to develop oneself. In [every] unique case in which one may arrive by the center of one's new position, there are two in which one arrives by the wings, without

---

18   Here, the Regulations enter into long details on the interior means for forming *en bataille*, whether forward or to the rear, [or] to the right or to the left. My objective not being to discuss all their details, I will pass them in silence.

19   [See Colin, *L'infanterie au XVIIIe siècle*, 27–72.]

counting all the directions that are found between the center and the wings, etc. But let us avoid the inconvenience of conviction, which is to abound in its sense and in repeating itself sometimes; let us pass to new reasons.

[Even] in agreeing that the central deployment is a little shorter and a little more covered than any other species of deployment, in the supposition that the column arrives immediately on its new terrain by the center, this advantage reduces itself to one, so-light difference by comparison to the deployment on the division of the center, as it is done in the Ordinance, that it is hardly calculable.

In effect, if one compares the two maneuvers relative to promptitude, the deployment makes itself equally in both, by two parts of the battalion at once. A division of the battalion finds itself established on the new line of front equally in both.

There is only a single advantageous difference [in] Mesnil-Durand's deployment: the movement makes itself on the two sides in advance and on a fixed point, which is the division of the head of the column; instead, in the deployment of the Ordinance, the division of the center of the column, which is the division of alignment, is obliged to carry itself forward until [it is] on the new front line, the others successively going to reunite themselves with it, a movement [that is] a little more complicated [and] a little slower and that [results in] the difference of several seconds more in its execution.

As to the difference between the two maneuvers relative to the objective's being more or less covered, here is what it is reduced to. In the deployment of Mesnil-Durand, the division of the head of the column may make fire from the first moment, and it is from that that this deployment is, in effect, protected from its commencement; instead, in the deployment of the Ordinance on the center, this division may not fire until it has arrived on the new front line, or, if the deployment is made standing still, until it has been unmasked by the divisions that will be in front of it.

But it is not a matter here of considering the central deployment [only] relative to a column of a single battalion; it must be applied to larger columns, to army columns, and to all the varieties of terrain and circumstances that war may offer; one will then see that it is not a column as numerous as a column of a single battalion; that this former, under the form of [the] double column, becomes a machine [that is] quite heavy, quite embarrassing, [and] quite little susceptible to bending itself to certain combinations of circumstances and terrains; [and] finally, that the central deployment is quite inferior to the deployments of the Ordinance. This is too important a point for me not to search to enlighten on it as much as possible.

I will thus give a diagram for the intelligibility of my observations.

There is a corps of twelve battalions; I suppose it to be composed of the same brigades as in the diagram, being formed in march column, that is to say in double column, marching for some time in this order; then encountering a defile in advance of the prolongation of the right of its old position (see Figures 1 and 2, Diagram III); passing this defile and testing there (see Figure 3) all the modifications from the double column to the simple column, from the simple column to the column by platoons, and [from the column by platoons] to the column by tranches; then reforming itself successively into double column when it has entered into the plain in order to arrive in twin column on the center of the position that borders the stream (see Figure 4).

Arriving there, the deployment of each twin makes itself by the right in each right twin [and] by the left in each left twin, each battalion carrying itself *en masse* to the center of the terrain for which it is destined (see Figures 5 and 6).

We follow this deployment. We will remark first that all the battalions of the right carry themselves uselessly towards the center to then deploy by their right and then re-cover the same route that they have taken too far. The battalion of the center of the line and the battalions of the left, if they must deploy themselves from the march column only to remain in simple column, do not have more of a route than they must use, but, if the disposition that one must take is the deployed order (this is what is indicated by the nature of the terrain [and] by the principles of Mesnil-Durand, since the position has a stream before it), all the right manches of the left battalions and all the left manches of the right battalions cross twice for demi-battalion frontage, a maneuver that is surely defective when all the parts of the troops that execute it do not at all reach the goal of the maneuver by the shortest route and by covering the least space possible. One will see below that the deployment of the Ordinance in the case presented above fulfills exactly this condition.

We now examine how this central deployment finds itself covered, and we will see that this pretended advantage dissipates when it is a question of several battalions and consequently of departing from deploying the formation in double column, following the system of Mesnil-Durand.

At the instant when the battalion of the head of the right twin and that of the head of the left twin arrive on the center of their terrain, they halt and are able to commence their specific deployment, but the second battalion of each of these twins commences to arrive at the instant when the deployment of its first battalion finishes,

NEW VARIATIONS OF THE "FRENCH ORDER." [THE] PROOFS MADE AT METZ

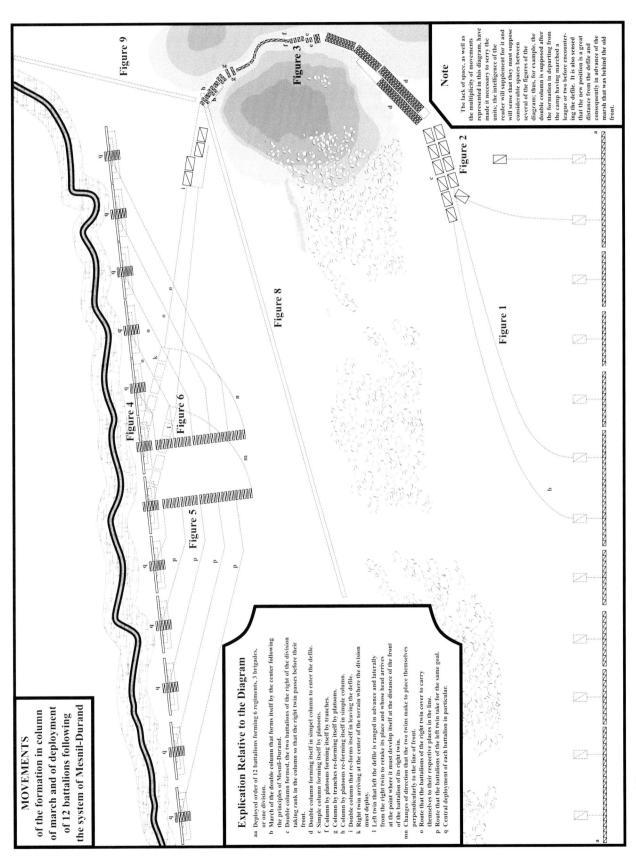

FIGURE 3 Diagram III

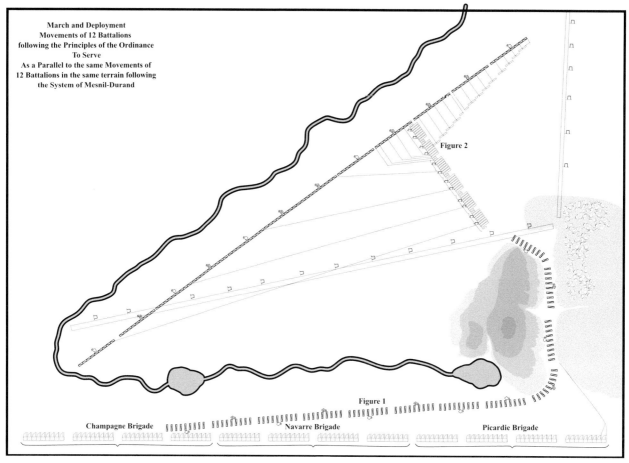

FIGURE 4 Diagram IV

covering the extent of a demi-battalion frontage uncovered [in order] to arrive at the center of their terrain where they must commence their specific deployment. This inconvenience repeats for all the other battalions of the right and the left.

It is thus necessary that the deployment of each battalion be covered in the deployment of the double column as it is in the individual deployment of each battalion once arrived in simple column on the terrain, and the inconvenience of this first deployment, if there is one, lasts for quite a longer time than in the deployment of the Ordinance.

I raise this circumstance of marching uncovered during a part of the deployment only to make known that in no regard does the central deployment have any advantage over that of the Ordinance, as I do not fundamentally attach much inconvenience to this pretended disadvantage [of marching uncovered]. Never has a troop, and, for a stronger reason, an army column, unless there is a surprise that could only be destructive, found itself in the case of deploying under the musketry fire of the enemy.[20] Thus [it is of] little importance that one exposes the flank [for] some seconds in deploying, because the enemy is outside of range of profiting from it. Artillery fire will be objected to me; to this I will respond [that] it is true that this is departing from another principle than Mesnil-Durand; that, in counting artillery fire for something, I will only quite rarely attempt to deploy a column under a lively and murderous artillery fire; and that, in addition, if I arrived within range of this fire in column, it is hardly more inconvenient to lend to it the flank than [it is] the front since, if my flank presents to it a side with a greater prolongation, it offers to it another side of lesser depth than a column that it beats from the front and the reverse.

This small digression distances me a little from the analysis of the maneuvers of twelve battalions, but, after having commenced by proving that the central deployment applied to several battalions is not covered as much as Mesnil-Durand would pretend, I did not wish to leave behind me the error that made him attach importance to

---

20 [See Abel, *Guibert's General Essay on Tactics*, 80: "Every evolution under fire ... is impossible to make with troops who are not at all warlike, and delicate with the troops who are, especially if the enemy is in range to advance on them before the end of their movement."]

this pretended advantage without fighting it. I return to my objective.

Now compare the one seen above with the march and the deployment of twelve battalions following the means of the Ordinance and in the same hypothesized terrain and circumstances (see Diagram IV).

First, we see (Figure 1) that the entire column will already be in movement and in open march, while the battalions of the line of Mesnil-Durand are still working to form themselves in simple column in advance of their front.

We see that the battalion of the right will already be in the debouche, while the battalion of the center, following the formation of Mesnil-Durand, will still have to cover the frontage of the six battalions of the right. We see that, whatever be the doublings and re-doublings that may be occasioned by the greater or lesser width of the defile, the column will always advance, the brigades, the regiments, the battalions, [and] the companies always preserving their primitive order; finally, each troop, whatever frontage it takes, will always be preceded or followed by the same troops that it had to its right or to its left in the order of battle.

As to deployment, we see that here one is not at all subjected, as in the other formation, to carrying oneself to the center of the position where one is to deploy oneself, that the head of the column carries itself right in advance of the debouche, [and] that, arriving there, three battalions deploy by their right and nine by their left, from which results that the line is formed on the same front and that it supports all the same points as in the preceding maneuver.

What we see next, in examining the details of this deployment and in comparing them to the deployment of the double column, is that each battalion [and] each portion of the battalion in the former does not make a step that does not bring it closer to the end of its movement, that is to say to the point that it must occupy in the new position; that the six battalions of the right are deployed there at the instant when the central column of Mesnil-Durand will commence its deployment; that, the six battalions of the left commencing their deployment at the same time as the left twin commences its own, there will not be a moment of delay for them; [and] that, each battalion commencing its deployment to the right or the left of the terrain that it will occupy, the demi-rank in the central formation that twice covers the extent of its front is deployed here at the instant when this same battalion, in the system of Mesnil-Durand, will only be commencing its deployment in the center of its terrain.

Finally, we see that the central deployment that was announced to be covered is effectively much less so than [said], since each battalion marches uncovered [for] half of the extent of its front, while in the maneuver of the Ordinance, it is uncovered only for the three battalions of the right, the nine other battalions always maneuvering covered behind the last formed troop.

The maneuver in Diagram III only presents the column of Mesnil-Durand in the most favorable case [or] in the unique case when it may arrive on its terrain by the center. But suppose other circumstances that war and the countryside may quite frequently offer.

Suppose that the column may not be able to gain the center of its terrain because it would find intermediary obstacles between the center and it, as in Figure 7, Diagram III.

Suppose that it be necessary to form oneself in departing from the debouche and to occupy the wooded heights that are to the right of the defile to support one's right (see Figure 8).

Suppose that the enemy demonstrates on the flank of the march; it is necessary to form *en bataille*, the right on the defile and the left towards the stream (see Figure 9).

These suppositions, which the column of the Ordinance would face without any confusion [or] slowing and with the greatest simplicity, would become for that [the column] of Mesnil-Durand veritable problems to solve, and these problems would be able to be resolved only by quite-slow and quite-complicated means. I will not at all arrest myself here to give these solutions and to refute them; I have said enough to get one started. It is to relieve my readers and myself to abandon the rest to their intelligence.

Text

Forming **En Bataille** *on Two Lines*

I

When the line *en bataille* will find itself at the moment and in position of making use of its musketry, all the battalions will deploy, etc.

II

If the line be *en bataille* holding two battalions in the extent of a single deployed one, before deploying, we will retire behind those of the second line, but for the little that we will be pressed into making use of our fire, we will instead retire the last sections of all the battalions, and we will ordinarily deploy the first.

Observations

Forming **En Bataille** *on Two Lines*

I and II

One sees in these paragraphs the confirmation of the principle of Mesnil-Durand to only fight ordinarily on a [single] line. He forms only on two lines for musketry action. It is in the chapters on Grand Tactics, in treating orders of battle, that I will re-examine this dangerous part of his system.

Text

March En Bataille

I

This march, infinitely difficult, if not to say impossible, with deployed battalions, will be quite easy for a line formed *en bataille* after the principles of this instruction, and it will indifferently permit all species of step; the line will march *en bataille* at the maneuver step as well as at the ordinary step.

II

We may, with the same facility, change direction, march in retreat, and march by our front, etc.

III

All the times that the line will be deployed, it will not at all march forward, since it will only have to deploy on the occasion of an obstacle that, covering its front, reduces it to musketry combat.

IV

However, if it would have to march by its flank, for example to file by its right along a stream that it would border and on which the enemy would extend on its side by the left, in this case, we would form the platoons, then break to the right by platoons and arrive on the terrain where we would wish to make front, reforming in line by quarter-conversion by platoons and thus, in making the platoons deploy, in the fire order.

Observations

March En Bataille

I

We have seen in the Camp how this assertion is denuded of foundation. The march *en bataille* of a line of columns is at least as slow as that of a line of battalions, and it is much more difficult. This extreme slowness comes from the difficulty of observing one's intervals by the right and by the left at the same time, as one is obliged in a line of columns. Also, all the times that the columns of Mesnil-Durand marched in line, we were obliged at each instant to stop to redress them and to make flank movements. With regard to the celerity that Mesnil-Durand attributes to his columns, we then saw that they did not march more quickly than the battalions in line in the proof of comparison made one day, in the presence of the Marshal, between the Bassigny Brigade executing the maneuvers of the Ordinance and an army brigade maneuvering according to the system of Mesnil-Durand. The two brigades were placed in concurrence, one alongside the other, for the march *en bataille*; they were made to cross spaces of at least three- or four-hundred *toises* at the maneuver step, and the advantage was only a few paces for the brigade in columns. But it must be observed:

1. That the Bassigny Brigade had just maneuvered for two hours without rest in the presence of the Marshal and that that the other brigade was made to leave its camp for this comparison; from this resulted [a fact] that doubtlessly merits some consideration: a fresh troop struggled against an exhausted troop.
2. That, after marching thus, the battalions found themselves always perfectly formed and in a state of fighting, while the columns had so poorly observed their intervals that it would be impossible to deploy them if the circumstances required it.
3. That the columns had thus taken all possible facilities to march rapidly and that consequently, whether involuntarily or [because] it had been commanded, the *tiroirs* [and] the sections marched with intervals, which was contrary to the principles of the Regulations of Mesnil-Durand and drew his column closer to the principles of the Ordinance on this point.
4. That, finally in this genre of proof, this species of struggle may not, no matter the result, signify or prove anything, because the partisans of the modern tactics have never pretended that it is not easier to make a long-winded[21] movement in columns than [it is] in a line of battalions. This is so true that, in these tactics, all grand army movements are made by columns, that never and in no case did the King of Prussia attempt to move his army in line, and that he holds it in columns, in whole or in part, until the moment when his order of battle is determined. This will be more amply developed in treating orders of battle.

Is the objective of the march *en bataille*, that is to say the march of battalions in line, thus so poorly understood by Mesnil-Durand when he seems to regard this march as one of our means of grand movements that he always consequently cheers himself with the inconveniences of lines

---

21 [The phrase I have translated as "long-winded," "*de longue haleine*," has two contemporary meanings: working hard, and "to place in a state of uncertainty, mixing hope and fear." While the former is intended in this passage, the latter could apply in a combat situation. See Abel, *Guibert's General Essay on Tactics*, 206n5.]

[that are] "thin and trailing" and to which he opposes his movements in columns? Like him and before him, we were making our movements in column; like him, we arrive in all our orders of battle and all our dispositions by columns; like him, we use them for traversing great spaces and for making grand maneuvers; like him, we use them at need for assembling more forces on a point; finally, like him, we employ them in our orders of battle and in actions, but this will not be indifferently and in all species of terrains and circumstances; this will be when we wish to form them protected from enemy fire or approaching them from cover; this will be when, by a superior artillery fire, we will extinguish, or at least diminish, theirs; this will be, in a word, when the attack will be reduced to entrenched points that must be carried by a succession of efforts, etc. These are, relative to columns, the principles of modern tactics well-understood and well-employed. Here now are also their true principles relative to the march *en bataille*.

The march *en bataille* must only be employed for covering quite inconsiderable spaces; it is thus that the Ordinance formally establishes that *one form in column all the times that a grand movement will be required.*[22]

The march *en bataille* must only ever be considered relative to the portions of the line, because an army does not at all break, act, or attack at once and with the same movement. In its habitual organization, it is already divided into divisions, and, in an action in war, these divisions are necessarily more subdivided by the nature of the terrain and by that of circumstances; suppose a division charged with a point of attack: it never acts all at once and on a contiguous line; it has parts that attack the front, others that search to embrace the flanks, [and] others that support or that are *en panne*.[23] Thus, one never sees long lines marching *en bataille* in war. If the King of Prussia, in his peacetime camps, makes some march like this with eighteen or twenty battalions covering quite-great spaces, it is because he wishes to see the astounding result of the instruction of his troops and because he knows quite well that, having formed the most difficult movements in peacetime, what he will demand of them in war being the simplest and least exaggerated, they will then be familiar with and skilled in it.

The march *en bataille* is indispensable in an infinity of circumstances:

1. For charging the enemy in deployed order, as we are far and quite far from thinking that it must always attack in column, and when we will examine the column as the ordinance of attack in the second part of this work, we will distinguish and detail the only cases in which we believe that it may be employed.
2. For acting in rough terrain, where there is need to alternatingly fire and march.
3. For traversing uncovered spaces [that are] beaten by a great fire and for arriving more surely on the enemy.
4. For embracing points of attack, for enveloping flanks, for supporting columns in attacks on posts, and for occupying, when they will have been pierced, which is never made without much loss and disorder, the post carried away by a line of musketry.
5. For intermingling, if one judges it appropriate, the battalions with the columns in making this attack.[24]
6. For making the troops that are in reserve advance to the support of troops that are engaged in action and so that they are not maladroitly crushed by enemy artillery before they enter into action themselves. Here, it is not a question of marching rapidly and of joining the enemy; they must advance step by step and following the progress of the corps that attacks; [they] must alternatively march and halt themselves, holding themselves always within range of sustaining and refreshing at need.

I did not believe this digression on the march *en bataille* [to be] insignificant; it is a point of modern tactics that has need of being developed, as much for its critics as for its partisans.

II

Marshal Broglie had so well-sensed that deployed battalions would be able to be in the case of marching in this

---

22 [Guibert's italics. *Ordonnance du roi pour régler l'exercice de ses troupes d'infanterie du 1ᵉʳ juin 1776*, the Regulations in force when Guibert wrote, do not contain this passage, but they do contain a chapter on marching *en bataille*; Guibert perhaps references an ordinance used during the Camp of Vaussieux.]

23 [See Etienne-Alexandre, baron Bardin, "En panne," *Dictionnaire de l'armée de terre ou recherches historiques sur l'art et les usages militaires des anciens et modernes*, 17 Vols. (Paris: Corréard, 1841–1851), VII:2092: "Several authors and Napoleon, in his memoirs, borrowed the term "to be *en panne*" from the language of the Marine to signify the state of immobility in which one leaves a troop exposed to enemy fire;" and Cornélis de Witt Willcox, "En panne," *A French-English Military Technical Dictionary* (Washington, DC, 1917), 306: "to be exposed to enemy fire without being able to return it."]

24 [This passage demonstrates the fallacy of a formation called "mixed order" or "*ordre mixte*," which is sometimes argued to have been a compromise between the thin and deep orders used during the French Wars of 1792 to 1815. As Guibert indicates, the point of reform was to give commanders options for their deployments and attacks, not chain them to a specific formation. See Paddy Griffith, *The Art of War of Revolutionary France 1789–1802* (Mechanicsburg, PA: Stackpole Books, 1998), 219–222, where the author attempts to clarify the point but still gives the impression of a "mixed order" as a specific formation.]

order that he did not at all adopt, in this regard, the exclusive principle posed by the Regulations in this paragraph, and that, in several maneuvers, he arrived at ordering the deployed battalions to march forward himself.

III

In the Ordinance, we accomplish this objective with a single quite-simple movement: it requires only breaking the battalion by platoons to the right or making it march by its flank. Here, instead of adopting one of the two means that are assuredly the shortest, we see all that Mesnil-Durand has substituted for them. First, he forms the platoon for it to form itself on six ranks, then break; then, arriving on the point where it wishes to make face, it must reform itself in line by quarter-conversions and then in fire order, in making the platoons deploy. This is thus what Mesnil-Durand uses almost everywhere. He always puts the compound in the place of the simple, and he calls this "perfecting."

Text

Forming a Line in Column for the March

I

The entire line, or [the] part of the line that must form itself in march column, will form itself in double column, the first two battalions forming the head of the column into which all the others will successively enter, etc.

II

Marching thus in double column, if the terrain requires it, we will re-serry its avenue; if it re-serries any more, we will then form ourselves in simple column, or even in column by platoons and by tranches.[25]

---

25   Then come, with the greatest detail, all the different manners of forming oneself in march order, like [the] march forward, the debouche being before the center; [the] march forward, the debouche being before the wings; [the] march in retreat; [the] march taking the deployed order; [the] march to the rear; [the] front right march; [the] front march to the wings, etc. This entire text is not susceptible to extracts, but, on the other hand, it would first require a commentary on each article to clarify what the author wished to say and then a long discussion to combat it; all appears useless to me, because, once again, it is not at all by the details that one's system must be judged, and, as I have already observed, if the system be good in itself, all the maneuvers would be redone.

To prove what I advance, I will content myself with exposing the first two cases of march, as they are in these Regulations.

Observations

Forming a Line in Column for the March

I have said enough on this subject in speaking of the formation of the column. I return my readers to the same text. It carries its [own] critique with[in] it. I demand that we only speak of the two foreign maneuvers that I reported there: the one for forming the line in column in advance, the debouche being before the right of the line, and the other for forming the line in march column in retreat. However, I cannot prevent myself from observing in relation to this latter maneuver that it will be quite embarrassing, if not to say impossible, in a camp where the front would be embarrassed with obstacles, because then the means of making all the movements, half in advance and half to the rear, are prescribed in this maneuver! It may then often arrive that the clearing of a march must be done via the rear of the camp. This will first arrive for all marches to the rear, but also for many flank marches. It is from this, and from [a] thousand other inconveniences that the local and accidental circumstances would have given birth to at each step, that it would only be necessary, to confound the system of Mesnil-Durand relative to all its mechanical and interior parts, for the army to execute three or four marches, whether by day and by night, in diverse [circumstances] and in countryside that would be a little rough, the army's being obliged, by the appearance of the enemy, to take an order of battle relative to circumstances in which it would find itself.

Text

Forward March, the Debouche being Before the Right of the Line

If the debouche is in advance of the right and quite near, so that the column, going from the center, may easily carry itself to it by a simple change of direction, we will command on the march "double column on the right, march." At this command, repeated by all the superior officers, those only of the two battalions of the center will add "forward;" then, at the command "march," which will only be repeated by them, all these battalions will march eighty paces. (If the terrain would only permit fifty, all the right, which has not yet budged, would march thirty to the rear).

Then, the superior officer of the first battalion, followed by those of the left, will command "to the right, march." At this command, all the battalions will march by their right until, the first two having arrived facing the debouche, we will command them "to the left, march." All those that would follow will do the same at the same point where the first of the left made "front" and will march behind it, forming the left twin.

As to those of the right, they will not at all [receive] a general command, but when the first of the right and those of the left, carrying themselves forward, have made "to the right," the second of the right, at the command of its superior officer, will march forty paces forward, then, making the same "to the right," will march to the height of the first, so that, when it [the first] will arrive at the debouche, the second, making front at the same time, will find itself behind it [the first] and ready to follow it.

As soon as the second battalion of the right will have passed the third, it will take the same forty paces forward, then march to the right behind and to the height of the first of the left.

When it will arrive at the debouche, it will make front at the same point where the second did so in order to march behind it in the right twin, and thus the others.

Retreat March

To march in retreat in reversed column, the commander will command "double column in retreat," unless he prefers to send this order only to the two superior officers of the last battalions of the right and the left. At this command, the other battalions not yet moving, their superior officers will command "half-turn to the right" and "march." After having taken forty-five paces, those of the right battalion will command "to the right, march" and arrive behind the battalion that was to its left in line; "to the left, march," then the last battalion will make a half-turn to the right, etc., and both, having marched forty-five paces to the rear [and] then by the flank, will follow the third in the same way, and thus the others, those of the left maneuvering in the same way, marching forty-five paces in retreat, then seventy-five by the left to form themselves behind the one to their right, until, all having arrived behind the first two battalions [at the] center of the line, these will make [a] "half-turn to the right" and will march behind the double column.

The grenadiers and chasseurs will follow on the flanks of their battalions as in the retreat march *en bataille*, and, as these battalions will enter into the column arriving behind those that precede them, the grenadiers and chasseurs will place themselves behind the first sections that have become the last [sections].

Passage of the Defile[26]
Passage of Lines

If, the first line being deployed, we wish to replace it with the second, which is not, we will march the second until it will have carried its pennants into alignment [with the first] and it will have entered into the small intervals of the first. This being done and the pennants aligned, we will deploy all the battalions of the second line, while all those of the first will form the retreat column, and, when the second will be entirely deployed, the first, entirely reployed, will carry itself one-hundred fifty paces to the rear.

Observations

Passage of the Defile

I have spoken of its inconveniences in my observations on the article titled "Order of Troops in the March Columns."[27] Errors of which to detail the relief would be left to me, but I wish to abbreviate.

Passage of Lines

This maneuver does not have need of observations; it can only take place, following the system of Mesnil-Durand, in the case of a combat reduced to fire action, since it is only in this case that he forms more than one line. I will content myself with demanding of him only what he pretends to with a line passively formed in column at seventy-five *toises* from the first, supposedly engaged in a musketry combat, and consequently the recipient of enemy fire.

Text

Changes of Position

I

The change of position of a line for each particular battalion is not at all a maneuver but only a march that it makes in its ordinary order, carrying itself to the place where it is destined to be in its new direction, etc.

II

All oblique changes of position do not have need of being commanded, and it will suffice that they be indicated by the change of direction of the pennants of the alignment battalion.

---

26 I will dispense myself here of making the extract of the diverse manners that the Regulations give for the passage of the defile marching in battle order. I may only refer to the preceding note in this regard.

27 [Presumably 45–49.]

III

All changes of position of this species are nothing more than a change of direction of the line on the march and [are] consequently made by means of a new direction that the alignment battalion takes.

IV

Perpendicular changes of position may be made by two means:

1. We may make all the battalions change front at the same time, suppose to the right; then, if the new position is behind the first, the first battalion counting from the right will extend itself there, marching by the flank. All the others will follow and will make a right on the same point. If, on the contrary, the new position is in advance of the right of the first, the entire line, becoming a column, will approach on the battalion of its right, which is at the head; then will develop by its left, maneuvering as left twin.
2. We may take it there by another way: carrying each battalion of the first position to its place in the second by the shortest route and making its change of front on the march.

v

The perpendicular and central change[s] of position will be done the same as above, one of the two parts of the line maneuvering behind and by the last ranks of the battalions.

VI

The great usage of perpendicular changes of position will find itself in the changes of the order of battle and other grand maneuvers in army corps when the parts of the lines will pass from parallel to perpendicular; the changes of this species will be much simpler than the preceding, since the battalions will not have to change front but only to march [for] some time by the right or by the left, then reform themselves on front to march in perpendicular line behind an indicated battalion. The effect of this means to vary the disposition even when arriving on the enemy, reinforcing parts of the lines and refusing others, evading too-difficult or too-defended terrain, and itself attaching to suitable points will give to the line a grand facility for forming all the arms in action and will accommodate itself all species of terrain without effort.

Observations

Changes of Position

It is in the maneuvers of changes of front and of position that Mesnil-Durand pretends to have a great superiority over modern tactics, and notably over the Ordinance. We examine this pretended superiority, and we see what it reduces itself to.

First, it is null for corps of troops [that are] a little considerable, and for armies (as I will prove in treating the great maneuvers and movements of armies) that all changes of front or of [the] position of an army or an army corps are never executed by evolutions and that they necessarily [belong] to the class of marches.

Thus it is only in the assembly of several battalions at most that this is a question to consider, since it is only in this case that they may be regarded as maneuvers and be executed by evolutions.

In the maneuver regulations of Mesnil-Durand, all the changes of front and position execute themselves in column by battalion, and the battalions, in arriving on the new position, thus find themselves always in their habitual and primitive order. While these movements by masses may not be absolutely exempt from inconveniences because of the difficulty that they have in moving themselves and in turning on themselves, it must be agreed that these changes of front present an ensemble of surety and solidity [that is] more imposing than those of the ordinance. But let us see what is drawn from them and if it follows that the means of the ordinance are not the best possible relative to the base from where it departs.

The deployed order being our primitive and habitual order, almost all changes of front or of position come from the deployed order and lead there. This is what necessarily renders our changes of front and of position longer to reach their last term than those of Mesnil-Durand. We have two more movements to execute them, the one of the deployed order for us to form in column, and the other to then, in arriving on the new position, re-pass from the state of column to that of the deployed order. Add to this that, our front being always more extended and our principle being always to leave between our ordinary columns the interval necessary for them to deploy themselves, the terrain that we have to cover is always double or three times that covered by Mesnil-Durand, who does not at all depart from the same principle and who re-serries his columns without ever embarrassing himself with the little terrain that may remain between them for deploying.

There is thus no term of comparison between the maneuvers of the two systems because they depart from a different base and arrive at a different result. Thus, wishing to compare their respective lengths and to applaud oneself, as Mesnil-Durand does that his change of front is executed rather than ours, is to claim that one covers a league faster than one covers two; this is to delude oneself or work to delude others.

Mesnil-Durand will fall back to saying that it is one of the advantages of his system to have only a single disposition that serves it for both maneuvering and fighting and to consequently find oneself always formed for maneuvering when maneuvering is required and always formed for fighting when the maneuver is done, while we, departing from the deployed order, are obliged to form ourselves in column to maneuver and then, arriving on the terrain of the new position, form ourselves *en bataille* to retake the deployed order. But, as I will prove in the course of this work, infantry is much more in the case of fighting in deployed order than in columns, and, from that and for a thousand other reasons, its primitive and habitual disposition must be the deployed order, [the result of which is that] the pretend advantage of Mesnil-Durand is null and purely illusory, that his order in column may only be accidentally serve it as combat disposition, and that thus, when his maneuvers always depart from this order or always lead to it, he makes false hypotheses, and [these] circumstances are almost never realized.

We now go to the means, that is to say to the evolutions by which the changes of front or of position of the Ordinance are executed. We will see how their variety is susceptible to conforming to all terrains [and] to all cases, and how modern tactics are, in this regard, superior to those of Mesnil-Durand.

If it is a question of an army or of a corps of more than a brigade or two brigades at most, I have established in principle (and I will discuss in the grand tactics [section] the reasons for this principle) that all the changes of front or of position will then [be] in the class of marches. We thus now bound ourselves once again to speaking only of those of some battalions.

If a single battalion must execute a change of front or of position, it executes it by platoons, marching by their flanks after having broken, etc. It may not be denied that, of all the manners of carrying a deployed battalion from the position that it occupies to another position that it must occupy in the same order, this would certainly be the promptest and the shortest.

If several battalions must execute a change of front or of position, then there is only the single battalion by which passes the new front line, and, if I may express myself thus, the battalion is the home of the movement that changes front by platoons. All the others carry themselves in column by battalion until [they are] on the terrain of the new position, and it is only there that they maneuver by platoons to place themselves and to form themselves in the deployed order. This change of front is thus as sure [and] as united as that of Mesnil-Durand, and one does not see in it, as he said on page forty-one in the brochure that he published at the Camp of Vaussieux, "five-hundred platoons carry themselves on a broken line, marching by the flank and flowing behind the captains who, at the same time, range the points of view," etc. When one criticizes, one must be exact, [and] one must not exaggerate. Yet, there is never, in the Ordinance's changes of front, a single battalion that, to use the expression of Mesnil-Durand, "breaks itself" thus by platoons; all the others maneuver entirely and *en masse* until [they are] on the terrain of the new position, and the movements that they then make by platoons to enter into the line to form themselves on the points of view and to form themselves *en bataille* are surely the most prompt and the most exact possible for occupying a position subject to the given points.

This is a manner of executing changes of front, but the Ordinance does not at all exclude [them], and it even indicates [one] of executing them by deployments, [a] manner [that is] doubtlessly a little longer in that it requires, after being broken into column [and] serrying *en masse*, whether in advance or behind and consequently covering two sides of the square, but which may be advantageous in some circumstances, because it is yet more assembled, more sure, and more defensive than the preceding.

Finally, there remains a manner of changing position, also indicated by the Ordinance, which is simpler and easier than the two manners above in that it is as much a march as [it is] an evolution: after having broken to form in column, directing the column in advance or behind, diagonally or perpendicularly, to arrive at the new position; elongate itself; and reform itself *en bataille*. Such is the simplicity and the commodity of this movement, above all departing from a line *en bataille* to reform oneself in line on another position, that one may carry oneself by it and establish oneself in all possible directions and that, excepting the unique case when the new position finds itself exactly parallel to the old [one] and where it is consequently shorter and more advantageous to form oneself there by deployments, there is not at all a manner [that is] easier and more advantageous to go to occupy all the positions that are diagonal or oblique from the position that one quits and, for a stronger reason, those that are on one's prolong.

By these three manners (although all three lead to the same result, [they] are nevertheless by no means *synonyms* to the eyes of the skillful and maneuvering tactician), changes of front or of position relative to all the possible varieties of terrains and circumstances may be executed.

Thus, if he wishes to change front or position by a maneuver on the terrain that he occupies, and the enemy would be outside of range of being able to attack before his movement would be finished, he will be able, without inconvenience, to employ the first manner, which is at once the most regular, the shortest, and the most certain for moving him between the given points.

If the enemy would be in range of him, if he would fear being attacked before the end of his movement, and he would be forced to change front or position, he will prefer the second manner, which, although lengthier, is the least hazardous and least delicate.

Finally, if he would have a considerable corps to move, if his change of front or of position would require carrying him far from his old position, if he consequently would make it in a great space and enter by it into the class of marches, he will employ the third manner, which is the simplest and the easiest.

Such are the relationships under which the maneuvers of the Ordinance must be considered, studied, and employed. I believed that this commentary was not useless to its [the Ordinance's] apology, as, for want of having grasped its spirit well, many people critique it or execute it without hearing them [the relationships], which is yet more unfortunate. I will terminate this long observation by a reflection that is not foreign to it.

In his critiques on the maneuvers of the ordinance, Mesnil-Durand ceaselessly advances that such a maneuver has no value, because it is not covered, [and] for another [reason], because it disunites the parts of a troop, and that, in these two cases, one would not find oneself on defense if the enemy would attack the troop that maneuvers while it executes its movement.

Nothing is more vague and more denuded of truth than this manner of analyzing and judging maneuvers. Permit me to oppose to it what I have said in this regard in my *General Essay on Tactics*. I do not have the silliness of citing myself as an authority; I repeat myself, because, having already spoken on the same subject, I have nothing better to say:

"Every evolution under fire, and under a lively enemy fire, is impossible to make with troops who are not at all warlike, and delicate with the troops who are, especially if the enemy is within range to advance on them before the end of their movement.

No evolution of any kind is impossible or imprudent in the presence of the enemy if it can be executed before they can traverse [the distance] and if, having good troops, a great number are formed to resist their first efforts and cover the end of the movement.

It is on the species of troops that [often] depends the possibility or the impossibility of a movement. [If] they are bad, either by fault of nerve or discipline, only a more-or-less soft fight, standing or in posts, must be expected of them. [If] they are brave and maneuverable, much can be done, because then the manner that they know how to move can be calculated, as can the result of their movements.

The enemy being … six-hundred paces from me, I will dare to deploy, [change position, and] execute before them whatever evolution that I wish, [however disunified this evolution may even be], when I will have already speculated that this evolution will be finished and that I will be in a state to receive them; stirring in the first instant of my movement to profit by it, they must not be able to cover the six-hundred paces that separate us. […]

Thus, there is no evolution that is properly dangerous in and of itself. Everything depends on the circumstance in which it is applied, and this properly consists of the most precise and surest combination that will be employed to make one's movement with that which will be employed by the enemy to come trouble it, [a] combination that can only be perfectly affirmed by the habit of moving the troops of the two arms in all sorts of terrains, and mostly in war, which produces many more circumstances than peacetime exercises [do]."[28]

These principles adopt themselves perfectly to those that I have said above, as one sees, and it results from their application to our maneuver Ordinance that what constitutes its health is the variety of its means, the resource[s] that it offers to officers who know how to draw them out, and finally, whatever Mesnil-Durand may say, what I regard as the greatest of advantages: its susceptibility to conforming itself to all terrains and all circumstances.

Text

Fire

I

We will never make fire on the march other than that of the grenadiers and chasseurs.

II

Deployed battalions will only know fire by files.[29]

Column against Cavalry[30]

---

28 [Abel, *Guibert's General Essay on Tactics*, 79–80. Guibert lightly edited and abridged the quote, as the brackets denote.]

29 The Regulations here enter into the detail of some changes of positions of feet and hands that are worth neither being extracted nor being analyzed.

30 This is the last maneuver of the Regulations; it consists of making the column's front on four sides, then in forming six paces of interval between each manche.

    The battalion thus arranged (says the Regulations), if it is charged by cavalry, will make fire by column, employed on this sole occasion, and also the sole one that is made having the bayonet [fixed].

    This fire will be of front by the first *tiroirs* or first three ranks, of the tail by the last, [and] of each side by the rest of each tranche.

Observations

Fire

I will not at all make observations on this article; Mesnil-Durand formally announces that the battalions will only ever make fire behind an obstacle or only by means of its curtain wall of grenadiers and chasseurs. Marshal Broglie, in this as on many other points, did not appear to wish to adopt the exclusive principles of Mesnil-Durand in all their extent. There was not at all any maneuver where the battalions did not deploy and make much fire despite not at all having an obstacle before them.

We also saw the Marshal, in an attack that he commanded himself on the day of the passage of the Seulle against the infantry of Jean-Baptiste Donatien de Vimeur, comte de Rochambeau, posted on the heights of Villiers-le-Sec, stopping his columns, engaging the fight by musketry, and marching on the enemy only after having beaten them for a half-hour with a lively fire.[31] This was not at all the system of Mesnil-Durand; this was the victor of Bergen and Sandershausen bending this system to his talent and leading the troops with the principles that made his glory.[32]

Column against Cavalry

I will have nothing to say on this maneuver; that of the Ordinance accomplishes the same objective, and it is less complicated, although it is not exactly an example of this default.

Résumé

It results from the examination above, and this result was the almost-unanimous example of the camp:

1. That the column of Mesnil-Durand, with an illusory appearance of perfection and simplicity, is maladroit, complicated, massive, favorable to disorder and to indiscipline, subject to a thousand inconveniences in practice, and, above all, a veritable *pièce de cabinet*.[33]

2. That his formation and his development by the center, proposed as unique and exclusive methods, enchain, embarrass, [and] elongate almost all movements, [and] that they are above all full of inconveniences relative to what troops must do the most frequently and with the greatest facility: to march and to pass promptly from their march disposition to their combat disposition.

3. That almost all the maneuvers of Mesnil-Durand are deprived of simplicity and plausibility, [and] that, in wishing to always return to the unique principle of acting by the center that is at their base, they almost always arrive at their goal by the longest route and by the most difficult means.

4. That it is not that these maneuvers have not been much changed, corrected, [and] modified, that all the means of execution in the Prussian tactics and in the Ordinance have not been adapted to them as much as possible, but that the only result of this amalgam that must, according to Mesnil-Durand, reconcile the two

---

Two, four, or whatever number of battalions ranging themselves the same way always form two twin columns.

31 [Jean-Baptiste Donatien de Vimeur, comte de Rochambeau, came from a military family that was a client of the Orléans branch of the royal family. He served in the mid-century wars, distinguishing himself by his personal bravery and command skill in battle and his attention to detail and interest in theory in garrison. He served with Guibert on the War Council under Saint-Germain in the late 1770s, and, as Guibert indicates, he commanded the force fighting in thin order against Broglie at Vaussieux, and his skill contributed to the final defeat of Mesnil-Durand's deep order. From Vaussieux, he was given command of the French army in the American War of Independence, which he held until the defeat of the British. He returned to France a hero and remained active in the military, including presiding over the Camp of Saint Omer in the late 1780s and receiving the marshal's baton. He was involved in the Revolution both as a political figure and as a military commander; his record in the early French Revolutionary Wars was not as distinguished as his American campaigns. He was nearly guillotined during the Reign of Terror, but he escaped and was later feted by Napoleon at the behest of his chief of staff, Louis-Alexandre Berthier, who had served under Rochambeau in America. His memoirs, *Mémoires militaires, historiques, et politiques*, 2 Vols. (Paris: Fain, 1809), serve as an important source for history of the events of Rochambeau's life, including Guibert's period and the Camp of Vaussieux.]

32 [The Battle of Sandershausen took place in May 1758. A French army under Charles de Rohan, prince de Soubise, overran Hesse-Cassel, prompting Ferdinand of Brunswick to detach a small force to link up with local militia units, forming a corps of around 6,000 to oppose it. Broglie, commanding the advanced guard of around 7,000 men, attacked the Hessian force and won a bloody fight that cost over 4,000 combined casualties. The battle enabled the conquest of Hesse-Cassel by the French.

The Battle of Bergen was fought in April 1759 between Ferdinand and Broglie. Broglie, operating with under 30,000 men as an auxiliary of the main French army near Wesel under Louis-Georges-Erasme, marquis de Contades, positioned himself in Frankfurt, which he had captured the prior summer. Ferdinand, with roughly similar numbers, determined to maneuver Ferdinand out of the Free City before Contades roused his army from winter quarters. After weeks of maneuvering, Broglie dug his army in at Bergen, where he successfully pushed back Ferdinand's attacks.

Sandershausen demonstrated Broglie's ability to win a smaller fight, and Bergen was Broglie's first significant victory. Both marked him as one of the few competent French generals in the Seven Years War, as Guibert intimates. See Szabo, *The Seven Years War in Europe*, 180–181 and 215–218.]

33 [See 30.]

systems, is a monstrous assemblage, so that today it is difficult to pronounce which is worse: the maneuvers of Mesnil-Durand in their primitive barbarism or the state of pretend perfection to which the changes that have been made have brought them.

5. That the maneuvers of the Ordinance appeared, in one voice, [to be] infinitely superior, simpler, more military, more favorable to order and discipline, [and] more applicable to all species of terrains and circumstances. It is true that Mesnil-Durand, in the diatribe that he published during the Camp of Vaussieux against the Ordinance of 1776, marked a profound contempt for those bounded spirits who, speaking always of "case" and "circumstances," cannot at all elevate themselves to the high combinations of a unique method and an exclusive system.[34] It is true that, with regard to this almost-general voice against his maneuvers and in favor of the maneuvers of the Ordinance, [a] voice that was so strong that it was only able to be muffled by the profound veneration that [people] had for Marshal Broglie and that elevated from the tents of soldiers, Mesnil-Durand had the gift of foreseeing it [this voice] and of declaiming against it in advance by printing in one of his prefaces that "it took twenty oppositions to make the currency of a vote; that, if his system had the tenth part of the voices, this would be [a] plurality; and that, if he had a quarter, he would regard it as admitted by acclamation."[35]

That these maneuvers were so simple and so facile that there was not a regiment that could not learn them in eight days was put forth a great deal, and this was one of the baits by which Mesnil-Durand searched to conciliate the votes of particular officers. The example[s] of the Limousin and De La Couronne Regiments, which had learned them at Metz in this length of time, were cited. The fact is that the majority of the regiments that camped at Vaussieux exercised them for more than three weeks, often twice per day, and several hours each time. Now, three weeks thus employed [is] the equivalent to the time that a regiment, well-mounted and -commanded in modern principles like those prescribed in the Ordinance, gives to its exercises for an entire year.

It was not missed by the opposition to say in advance that the infantry maneuver Ordinance was impracticable for regiments that were not exercised at length [and] that this was one of the principal vices of modern tactics. But a contrary fact, which had the entire Camp of Vaussieux for its witness and for its judge, is that the Médoc and Bassigny Regiments, which composed the brigade that executed the maneuvers of the Ordinance, had only been assembled two years prior; that they had commenced to practice the Ordinance maneuvers, in regiment[s] and in [the] brigade, at the same time that the other regiments of the army commenced to learn the maneuvers of Mesnil-Durand; that they learned these latter maneuvers at the same time; that they had thus a double instruction, quite likely to overload them; and that, [even] with this, in the proofs of the comparison that were made in the presence of Marshal Broglie, they maneuvered with a celerity, an intelligence, [and] an ensemble beyond which it is perhaps useless to search to attain.

I would that the limits of this work, [which is] perhaps already overloaded with details, permit me to render account of the superior manner that Rochambeau, who commanded this brigade, made it maneuver before Marshal Broglie. He made seen, by the most intelligent exposition of all the maneuvers of the Ordinance, that modern tactics are susceptible to all, conform to all, [and] employ columns at need, and columns simpler than those of Mesnil-Durand; they combine, they intermingle with the deployed battalions and support a line, etc.; [and] that, in the end, they [modern tactics] are a facile instrument that await only to be employed by the genius of the marshal [to find] great success.

---

34 [François-Jean de Graindorge d'Orgeville, baron de Mesnil-Durand, "Réflexions sur l'ordre et les manœuvres de l'infanterie (extraites d'un mémoire écrit en 1776 et déjà imprimées en 1778)," *Collection de diverses pièces et mémoires*, 2 Vols. (Amsterdam, 1780), 11:101–171.]

35 "Avant-propos," *Suite du projet d'un ordre français*, 8.

SECOND PART

Examination of the System of Mesnil-Durand in Its Fundamental Aspects and in Those of the Different Arms

∴

Until now, I have fought the system of Mesnil-Durand only relative to its interior details, that is to say, in relation to elementary tactics, and I believe I have proven that it is quite inferior to the modern system in this regard.

But it is in arriving at grand tactics that these proofs multiply and become much more important, as, having demonstrated that the organization of the column and the maneuvers of Mesnil-Durand are defective, it would be to have nothing done against his system if it remained that the base and the principles on which it rests are good in themselves (in effect, this is what some of his partisans have retrenched themselves in today), since they would have nothing easier than to change its organization and its maneuvers and substitute better ones for them, work that would finally, after seven or eight successive editions, come to the goal of Mesnil-Durand and his cooperators.

My objective will thus be to prove, in the course of this work, that the base and the principles, both fundamental and general, of the system of Mesnil-Durand are yet more defective than its interior means [and] that the system is evidently contrary to all the great principles of war; to the primitive and habitual order that it agrees to adopt; to the species of arms in use today, and, whatever effort Mesnil-Durand makes, he will not return them [ancient weapons] to Europe; to the use that must be made of cavalry and to the tactics of this arm that must amalgamate itself with those of the infantry; to the true principles of castrametation [and] to those of the science of positions, of marches, and of orders of battle; [and] finally, to all those that constitute and compose strategy, or the tactics of armies.[1]

Before passing from these important discussions, I wish to fight Mesnil-Durand on another point [that is] no less important in that it contains the principal cause that determined Folard and all the French Tacticians (those who profess [that] foreign tactics [are] unworthy of being used here) to propose to the nation the system of depth.

---

1 [The term Guibert uses for strategy, "*stratégique*," is a new one in French, and it would not appear in the official dictionary until the 1835 Sixth Edition (it was removed in the current edition). He is likely drawing on Paul-Gédéon Joly de Maïzeroy, *Institutions militaires de l'empereur Léon le Philosophe*, 2 Vols. (Paris: Jombert, 1771), 1:5–8, which defines *"stratégique"* as "the art of commanding, of employing properly and with skill all the means that the general has in hand to make all the parts that are subordinated to him move and to dispose them for success," or, more concisely, "the science of the general." Guibert, in his first work, Abel, *Guibert's General Essay on Tactics*, 252, refers to "the science and the habit of moving all the arms that enter into the composition of an army," which may have been influenced by Joly de Maïzeroy's work, or even vice-versa. See Jonathan Abel, *Jacques-Antoine-Hippolyte, comte de Guibert: Father of Napoleon's Grande Armée* (Norman: University of Oklahoma Press, 2016), 70. See also Alexandre David, *Joly de Maïzeroy: l'inventeur de la stratégie* (Paris: Ecole de Guerre, 2018); Ethel Groffier, *Le stratège des lumières: le comte de Guibert, (1743–1790)* (Paris: Champion, 2005); Beatrice Heuser, *The Strategy Makers: Thoughts on War and Society from Machiavelli to Clausewitz* (Santa Barbara, CA: Praeger, 2010); and especially Ami-Jacques Rapin, "The Invention of Strategy at the Turn of the 18th to 19th Centuries" (Unpublished, 2023).]

CHAPTER 1

The System of Mesnil-Durand: Is It Favorable to the Genius and the Character of the Nation?

This chapter will respond to all the authors of the systems given on the deep order at once, since they have all begun from the same principle to arrive at the same result. It is just that I always address myself by preference to Mesnil-Durand. Among all the tacticians who have professed the deep order, it is he who has not ceased to cry with one indefatigable voice that it is the order par excellence, the order exclusively suited to the genius of the nation, and who, consequently, has most generously renounced all his antique nomenclature to give us his system under the name "French Order."

Here is how Mesnil-Durand reasons in this regard. I will summarize here, in some articles, the true and sometimes literal sense that he spreads over several volumes.

"The audacity, the valor, the impetuosity of the shock, *the fury of the first moment*, are what particularly characterize the French nation. It is, by its qualities and in these regards, superior to all the other nations; thus, the system of tactics that suits it must always have for its objective to attack.

There are two manners of attacking: one by fire, the other by shock. Foreigners are superior to us in fire action, because it requires more sangfroid, more phlegm, [and] more discipline, and they are inferior to us in shock action, because they have no movement, impulsion, or the hardiness that distinguishes us; thus, we must always attack by shock and never by fire.

Whatever effort that we make, French troops will never reach, and are not even made for reaching, the same point of discipline and order as foreign troops. Our lightness, our constitution, [and] our customs all refuse them. We may pretend by them only to bastardize the genius of the nation, to extinguish its gaiety, to chill its courage, to render, in a word, *the soldiers as machines and the officers as automatons*; thus we must abandon to the foreigners tactics that we have maladroitly borrowed from them and make ourselves *national* [tactics]. The order in *plésions*, or said otherwise, in columns: this is what suits us; by this order *heads are electrified* [and] courage ignited; the old soldier, the recruit, the lazy even, are equally swept along; *misfortune to the phlegmatic battalions that fall under the hand of fanatical* plésions![1] To teach these new tactics to an entire army would require [only] some weeks; the majority of the regiments that camped at Vaussieux did not study them for any longer; several of them were able to exercise them for only fifteen days, and they were as advanced as the others. All the small details, all the research, the minutiae of perfection of the Prussian tactics extinguish themselves in an order in which, to vanquish, it is only a question of marching to the enemy and engaging them."

One cannot be more completely opposed than I am to part of the assertions above, and to all the results that Mesnil-Durand draws from them.

It is assuredly not on French valor and audacity that I am tempted to challenge him, but, without being a bad citizen, may I not represent to him that its perhaps very badly serving his nation to ceaselessly go on exalting it beyond measure and denigrating other peoples, [and] that such remarks are good to make, albeit soberly, without which they miss their goal, when one speaks to the troops, but in the calm of reflection and in the silence of the cabinet, when it is a matter of enlightening spirits and not inflaming heads, when one wishes to become a legislator and to found one's new legislation on the genius and character of a nation, one must depart from prejudices and consult facts?

In studying history, one unfortunately sees many events that dispel these fumes of national vanity a little; that French troops doubtlessly had many of the traits of audacity and courage but that these qualities are not exclusively their share; that each nation more or less also has glorious epochs to cite; that, if we have for us Menorca [and] Bergen-op-Zoom,[2] the Russians have Ochakov [and]

---

1 *Suite du projet d'un ordre français en tactique.*
    [See Mesnil-Durand, *Fragments de tactique*, XXX.]

2 [The Invasion of Menorca was the immediate cause for the outbreak of the Seven Years War between England and France. In April 1756, a French fleet under Roland-Michel Barrin, marquis de la Galissonnière, landed an army under Louis-François-Armand Vignerot du Plessis, duc de Richelieu, which quickly conquered the British-held island while la Galisonnière defeated the British fleet sent to relieve the island. The French held the island until the peace, in which it became an important bargaining chip. See Szabo, *The Seven Years War in Europe*, 16 and 348–349.

    The Siege of Bergen-op-Zoom took place in the latter half of 1747. Maurice de Saxe commanded the main French army in the Low Countries aimed at Maastricht while he detached a corps under Ulrich Frédéric Woldemar, comte de Löwendahl, to seize opportunity elsewhere, a favorite strategy of Maurice's. Löwendahl lay siege to Bergen-op-Zoom while Maurice fought a great battle at Lauffeld, a siege that dragged into the late summer. In mid-September,

Bender,[3] the Austrians Schweidnitz,[4] the English Havana,[5] etc.; [and] that, without speaking of those memorable days where our indiscipline and our chivalric ignorance broke us against foreign phlegm like Crécy, Poitiers, [and] Azincourt[6] (examples that would give leave for Mesnil-Durand to respond that they prove nothing in favor of foreigners, since they were on the defensive, which he pretends to be exclusively their genre), there are twenty occasions when these same foreigners beat us *à la Française*, that is to say, in attacking: they beat us thus at Blenheim[7] and Torino, among others; at Torino alone, 6,000 Prussians commanded by Anhalt carried our entrenchments sword in hand, which commenced their reputation;[8] [and] at Minden, ten English and Hanoverian battalions came *in line* and not *in column* to present themselves on a plain in view of the seventy-two squadrons of our cavalry, whose successive efforts they endured and repulsed, certainly lacking neither audacity nor courage, etc.[9] I cite with bitterness these dolorous epochs, but this is not about making illusion; it is about searching for the truth and modifying exaggerated and dangerous assertions via the conclusions that one is able to draw from them.

What I have seen, above all in history, that must be taken as a guide when one wishes to speak on the genius and the character of nations is that, if the French nation is more capable than any other of the first effort, none can

---

a French force stormed the fortress walls, and the defense evaporated, giving them the city. What followed was a sack of the city that horrified Europe, although Löwendahl won his marshal's baton as a result. See MS Anderson, *The War of the Austrian Succession 1740–1748* (New York: Longman, 1995), 173–174; and Reed Browning, *The War of the Austrian Succession* (New York: St. Martin's, 1995), 319–321.

Both operations are examples of audacity, which fit the contemporary definition of French national character.]

3 [The Siege of Ochakov took place in 1737. Russian forces took the city by storm and then sacked it, foreshadowing Bergen-op-Zoom. The Russians surrendered the fortress the following year and would not regain it until the 1790s. The seizure of Bender, a key fortress in Moldavia, took place in 1770 as Russian forces overran Ottoman defenses in the region; it was not a particularly notable action, contre Guibert's intimation. See Virginia Aksan, *Ottoman Wars 1700–1870: An Empire Besieged* (New York: Pearson, 2007), 107–110; and David Stone, *A Military History of Russia from Ivan the Terrible to the War in Chechnya* (Westport, CT: Praeger, 2006), 66 and 80–81.]

4 [The Siege of Schweidnitz took place in late 1757 as an Austrian army moved into Silesia to contest Prussian control of it. It fell to the Austrians shortly after the Franco-Imperial disaster at Rossbach, partially easing the pain of that defeat, although the subsequent Prussian victory in the Battle of Leuthen ended the year on the positive side for the Prussians. See Szabo, *The Seven Years War in Europe*, 101–104.]

5 [The Siege of Havana took place in 1762 and was an important victory for the British, who had long coveted the key to Spanish Cuba. A British force took the city, and the Spanish fleet intact, putting England in a commanding position for the peace talks that concluded the following year. See Daniel Baugh, *The Global Seven Years War 1754–1763* (New York: Routledge, 2014), 559–620; and David Syrett, "The British Landing at Havana: An Example of an Eighteenth-Century Combined Operation," *Mariner's Mirror* 55, no. 3 (1969): 325–331.]

6 [Guibert names three infamous French defeats from the Hundred Years War. At Crécy in 1436, Poitiers in 1356, and Azincourt in 1415, French armies were routed by English forces, particularly archers. Poitiers was especially devastating, as the English captured King Jean II during it. See Juliet Barker, *Conquest: The English Kingdom of France, 1417–1450* (Cambridge: Harvard University Press, 2013); 72–86; and Jonathan Sumption, *The Hundred Years War*, 5 Vols. (Philadelphia: University of Pennsylvania Press, 1990–2015), I:489–534 and IV:431–467. Guibert makes the same argument about the three battles in Abel, *Guibert's General Essay on Tactics*, 43–44. The three battles are regularly portrayed as a contest between outmoded French chivalric heavy cavalry charging senselessly into massed English longbow fire; while this characterization has been moderated in recent decades, the core of the narrative remains true, and the French learned to adopt a more combined-arms approach after both Poitiers and Azincourt, resulting in their eventual victory in the war; see Kelly DeVries, "Catapults are not Atomic Bombs: Towards a Redefinition of 'Effectiveness' in Premodern Military Technology," *War in History* 4, no. 4 (1997): 454–470; and Clifford Rogers, "The Efficacy of the English Longbow: A Reply to Kelly DeVries," *War in History* 5, no. 2 (1998): 233–242, for an overview of the debate.]

7 [The Battle of Blenheim took place during the War of the Spanish Succession and marked Marlborough's and Eugene's first great victory in the war. Their Allied army of around 56,000 attacked a dug-in Franco-Bavarian force under Ferdinand, comte de Marsin; Bavarian Elector Maximilian II; and Tallard of around 60,000. The French commanders refused to cooperate and positioned their troops poorly, allowing the English commander to win a decisive victory and "establish [his] classical tactic of threatening the flanks of a foe and then smashing through a weakened center," according to Lynn, *The Wars of Louis XIV*, 290–294, thus proving Guibert's point.]

8 [The Siege of Torino took place in 1706 as a Franco-Spanish force of around 40,000 under Louis d'Aubusson de la Feuillade, duc de Roannais; Marsin; and Philippe, duc d'Orléans, opened the siege in the summer of 1706. A relief army of around 30,000 under Eugene and Vittorio Amadeo II, Duke of Savoy, arrived in August and pinned the Franco-Spanish army against the city. A series of attacks from both sides ensued, culminating in Eugene's victory and significant defeat for the French in early September. See Lynn, *The Wars of Louis XIV*, 309–310. Guibert's argument about the Prussian force commanded by Leopold, Prince of Anhalt-Dessau, is contrary to traditional narrative, which places the rise of Prussian military prowess in the prior century at the 1675 Battle of Fehrbellin, what Citino, *The German Way of War*, 14–22, calls "the true birthday of the Prussian army" and "the Prussian army's 'creation myth.'"]

9 [Guibert's italics. The Battle of Minden took place in the summer of 1759 as a sequel to the Battle of Bergen, which gave Contades control of much of the Weser region with around 54,000 men, including Broglie. Ferdinand maneuvered to counter, and Contades positioned himself in a defensive position at Minden. Ferdinand attacked the position on 1 August, which resulted in another French defeat and retreat. Ferdinand's attack included the action Guibert notes, an advance of nine, not ten, Allied battalions that were repeatedly attacked by the cavalry of Charles, duc de Fitz-James, which they repulsed with heavy French losses. See Szabo, *The Seven Years War in Europe*, 257–263.]

be repelled more easily, none more promptly communicates its impressions of every genre, and thus, like [how] a word of energy, an example of courage, or a great man makes an army of heroes in an instant, in the same way, and with the same rapidity, a word of discouragement, an example of laxity, a leader without talent, throws the same army into abasement.

What I have also seen in history is that no nation has lost more battles by indiscipline, nor has one lost them as completely, [and] that, in almost all these lost battles, our audacity, our first movement always commenced in giving us the advantage, and then this advantage escaped us for want of order and of maneuvers.

From all these facts, I draw the following reflections and consequences:

That it is much less necessary to give to a nation an order that favors the advantages of its character than [it is] to give it an order that counterbalances its faults, above all when the misfortunes that arrived on it by its faults were more frequent and more decisive than the successes that it had by its pretended advantages.

That, in thus consulting the genius of nations and in admitting that the French were born for the offensive and that foreign nations were only proper for the defensive, it would thus be the latter and not our [nation] that would be forced to adopt an order that would give them the qualities that they lack, [and] that such was the principle of the ancients in their military legislation, and one finds a trace of it in the details of their tactics, [details] that appear to be most insignificant. Thus, for example, the Spartans being natural impetuous, their generals took care to march on the enemy with the sound of the flute rather than the resounding sound of the trumpet, says Thucydides, so as to suspend the too-boiling courage of the young Spartans and oblige them to preserve their ranks.[10]

That it is, moreover, illusory to think that there was an order that gave valor and audacity; that these qualities were passing, momentary, and belonged to all nations when they were warlike, and, above all, well commanded; that these qualities similarly sometimes depend on circumstances, incidents, [or] causes that one cannot account for, so that the best troops sometimes have unfortunate days and that the worst sometimes have moments of courage and energy; finally, so that the same troops, the same nations, experience the alternative. Witness the French at Blenheim or at Steenkerque,[11] the Russians at Narva or Poltava,[12] the Turks in the times of Suleiman I and Bayezid, or those of Khotyn and Bender, etc.[13]

That, if valor and audacity are not permanent qualities and depend above all on the condition of being in column rather than being in battalion, it is in return well demonstrated that modern tactics are more favorable to discipline than those Mesnil-Durand wishes to substitute for them; that the column, and above all his own, is more subject to floating and to tumult than a battalion; that the solder in [the column] is less under the hand and under the eye of the officer; [and] that all the impressions that may result from indiscipline, fear, [and] disorder communicate themselves more to a troop of men *en masse* than in line, and their ill effect[s] are repaired in [a column] more slowly and with more difficulty, etc. I do not wish to repeat here what I have already said or anticipate what will more naturally find its place later.

That these inconveniences [that are] already apparent in relation to a single mass will become yet more in an army composed of a great number of similar masses; that, if, unfortunately, contrary to the infallible assurance of victory given by Mesnil Durand, some of them are beaten, trouble and confusion will soon expand to others; [and] that then, reduced to defending in lieu of attacking,

---

10 [See *The Landmark Thucydides: A Comprehensive Guide to the Peloponnesian War*, ed. Richard Strassler (New York: Free Press, 1996), 343: "... the Argives and their allies advance[ed] with haste and fury [and] the Spartans slowly and to the music of many flute players—a standing institution in their army that has nothing to do with religion but is meant to make them advance evenly, stepping in time without breaking their order as large armies are apt to do in the moment of engaging."]

11 [The Battle of Steenkerque took place in August 1692 as part of the War of the League of Augsburg. The main French and Allied field armies met in an encounter battle that was hard-fought and ended in a draw with heavy casualties. See Lynn, *The Wars of Louis XIV*, 226–227.

12 [The Battles of Narva and Poltava took place during the Great Northern War. At Narva, the Swedish army led by King Karl XII defeated a much larger Russian army that lay siege to the fortress. This was an "utter humiliation for Russia and for Tsar Pyotr I personally" that was avenged in 1709 at Poltava, when Pyotr destroyed the Swedish army and sent Karl into exile in the Ottoman Empire; see Stone, *A Military History of Russia*, 50–56.]

13 [Suleiman I, called "the Magnificent," was Ottoman Emperor during the height of Ottoman power from 1520 to 1566 as it stretched from Hungary to Persia and the Pontic Steppe to the Maghreb. "Bayezid" is probably Sultan Bayezid I, who ruled the Ottoman Empire from 1389 until 1402. He defeated a Crusader army at Nicopolis in 1396, ensuring continued Ottoman growth in Europe, but he was in turn defeated and taken captive by Timur in 1402. See Caroline Finkel, *Osman's Dream: The History of the Ottoman Empire* (New York: Basic Books, 2005), 22–47 and 115–151; and Colin Imber, *The Ottoman Empire, 1300–1650: The Structures of Power* (New York: Palgrave, 2009), 6–46 and 263–283; see also Rhoads Murphey, *Ottoman Warfare, 1500–1700* (New Brunswick: Rutgers University Press, 1999). "Khotyn" is probably the Battle of Khotyn, another bloody draw fought in 1621 between the Polish-Lithuanian Commonwealth and the Ottoman Empire; see Imber, *The Ottoman Empire*, 66–86.]

crushed by enemy artillery, embraced by their flanks, not having in their primitive order the intervals necessary to deploy themselves or, for a stronger reason, having many fewer in the course of an action (this would perhaps be a greater danger, in having too-considerable [intervals]), they will form only either a vast mass of men or a corps [that is] scattered and without support, in both cases at the mercy of the vanquishers.

"The battalions," Mesnil-Durand will say, "the long serpentine lines, these ribbons that fray, will they play a better role if they are pierced?" Doubtlessly not a line of battalions; again, the distant parts will have time to re-fold themselves and take positions. But this is not the way that the order of battle in an army in our principles must be represented. It will have a second line, reserves, intervals in every sense, [and] points of support; its extension will even preserve it from a complete rout. Never is it engaged along all of its front; never have both wings been embraced at the same time; on one side or the other always remain resources, points of retreat, and, at worst, great debris that, gathering themselves, repairing themselves, growing in good positions, will become new armies.

That, with the character and the genius of the nation, what is to be feared above all is [a system of] tactics that favors our natural faults in lieu of counterbalancing them and that exposes us to only losing battles ruinously and completely. This last consideration is important, as winning a battle is often for us only the vain honor of the triumph, [while] defeat makes us evacuate provinces and may shake the kingdom.

My point will not be mistaken, I hope. I did not write this chapter to give hard truths to my nation. Ah! If between Mesnil-Durand and me, someone likes it [the nation] and likes it usefully, it is the one who spares nothing to try to prevent its eyes from being fascinated [or] from being drunk with chimeras, and, from lauding it with exaggeration, does not precipitate it into an error that may lead it to great misfortunes.

CHAPTER 2

The Deep Order, and Particularly the Species of Deep Order Proposed by Mesnil-Durand: May It or Must It be the Primitive and Habitual Order, in Preference to the Deployed Order?

The solution to this question would perhaps be the only response that must be made to the system of Mesnil-Durand, because in proving the negative, one entirely collapses his system. But it is a complete refutation that I promised, and Mesnil-Durand would not miss taking action [if] I did not respond in all regards. Although a single demonstration that I made for myself a long time ago suffices for me to judge this system, nevertheless, all the other proofs having only supported my opinion, it does not follow that my readers must be equally persuaded. One may say that I have judged lightly; one may believe that I have some prejudice; I thus owe to the public, become my judge in its turn, an exact account of this system envisaged in all its branches. I am obliged to say all, to expose all, and finally to discuss that which I demonstrated to myself as if I would still doubt it.

In the observations that I made on the interior details of the system of Mesnil-Durand, I could only sketch this question, because it essentially drew from the grand parts of tactics on which it was not yet time to speak.

I place here as a problem if the deep order, and particularly the species of deep order proposed by Mesnil-Durand, may and must be the primitive and habitual order in preference to that which we follow.

To go step by step, we commence by defining. It is in questions where definitions pose principles and consequently become bases.

The "primitive and habitual" order of a troop is the order in which a troop forms itself primitively and habitually, [an] abstraction [being] made of all local or accidental circumstances.

This order must be that in which a troop, by the nature of its arms or circumstances, is most frequently in the case of ranging itself.

It must first be calculated on the species of arms that will oppose it and then on the diverse circumstances in which it may find itself forced to make face.

It must derive from the primitive organization of this troop and preserve it in all its integrity.

It must be the simplest and least complicated possible so that it may be taken with the greatest promptitude and so that the soldier, day or night, in the tumult of the action and even in the "alarm" of a defeat, may easily find his rank and his file.

It must be proper to both the attack and the defense, but it must be particularly and above all to the defense, because the state of defense is the primitive state, and that of the attack may only ever be accidental. This important principle, by which, above all, I believe that I will solve the question, has need of being developed, and it will be in its [proper] place.[1]

It must never be contrary or a hindrance to the evolutions and maneuvers of elementary tactics, which must all depart from it and return to it.

For a stronger reason, it must accomplish the views of grand tactics in all their aspects. Finally, the great parts of war ostensibly foreign to tactics like encamping, positions, [and] subsistence draw essentially on it, and it directly influences them.

It will be said that I wish everything in this primitive and habitual order, but in effect everything is there, or, to speak more justly, everything derives from it; it is the first link in the chain and the base of all tactics.

Thus it is not (as many people who have only ever touched the question believe) a simple dispute of words and of vain honors between the deep order and the deployed order. By the change that would make the deployed order the accidental order and the deep order the primitive and habitual order, the entire modern military system would be [in a state of] upheaval, and it would have to fight, march, camp, subsist, [and], in the end, make war on absolutely different principles.

The idea of this absolute upheaval does not appear to me to be a reason to reject the system of Mesnil-Durand if it had demonstrated that it was more advantageous

---

1 [This passage is notable as the introduction of a major theme in the *Defense of the System of Modern War*: the primacy of the defensive, which Guibert will develop from this point. Readers familiar with contemporary military theory might recognize that theme from Carl von Clausewitz, *On War*, ed. and trans. Michael Howard and Peter Paret (Princeton: Princeton University Press, 1989), 84. Clausewitz may perhaps have been inspired by Guibert, although the idea was certainly not unique to the French theorist at the time; see Chagniot, *Le chevalier de Folard*, especially 276–281.]

than ours. In fact, in subjects of so major an importance, it is not changes that must arrest them, and, in the fact of changes, I will always be for not making [only] partial and modifying ones and, when one admits an evidently good system, [be] for establishing it in all its branches, but I hope to prove by this work that the principles, means, [and] consequences in the system of Mesnil-Durand are all false, defective, and destructive.

The deployed order unites all the conditions that I have exposed above [as being] the necessary properties and attributes of *the primitive and habitual order*. The deep order, on the contrary, substituted for this usage, would fulfill none; it is this that it is a question of demonstrating.

1 First Demonstration

1.1 *The Deployed Order Is Analogous to the Arms in Use Today. The Deep Order Is Absolutely Contrary to them*

To develop this demonstration, a short discussion on the species of our arms is necessary. This discussion will expand on the other articles to which it relates.

We seem to agree today on the superiority of our firearms as missile weapons over the missile weapons of the ancients. Folard, in his delirium in favor of antiquity, never dared to claim superiority for javelins, arrows, darts, or other weapons thrown by hand, but he pretended to formally establish machines like catapults or ballistæ in our artillery. He made several small proofs on this whose results he gave as positive.[2] This pretention appeared to have been abandoned by his sectarians. At least Mesnil-Durand evaded treating this subject, and he contented himself with trying to prove that the effect of artillery was much more to be feared for the battalion than for the column.

If it is demonstrated that our missile weapons are superior to those of the ancients, it must also follow that the ancients had weapons superior to ours for shock. The Greeks had the pike, and the Romans were much more redoubtable yet with the pilum and the sword.[3] The legionary soldier, armed with his sword in the right hand and covered by his shield that he held in the left hand, was able to abandon himself to the run and to strike in the mêlée. The pike and the fusil, on the contrary, have a disadvantage for shock: they must be held in two hands, and the [result] of this is that the body is necessarily opened and in an attitude contrary to the rapidity of the march.

The fusil, superior without any doubt as a firearm but perhaps inferior as a shock weapon even though it is armed with its bayonet, armed with this same bayonet, unites in a single weapon the properties fire and shock, although it possesses the latter less perfectly than the former. In this double title, it thus had to obtain the preference [over other weapons systems], and it is without contradiction the most redoubtable weapon that has ever existed.

The ancients had defensive arms that protected them from the effects of the majority of their missile weapons. On the contrary, we have been forced to abandon defensive arms because of the uselessness that they had if they were light and the impossibility of carrying them if they were proof against musketry alone. From this essential difference in the manner of being armed necessarily results that the ancients had to count on missile weapons for little in the attack and the defense and that we instead count on ours for much.

The shock action thus, by the nature of the ancients' weapons, being their principal action, and their defensive arms sheltering them from the effects of missile weapons, it follows that, for them, the attack had all the advantages if the enemy took the part of waiting, and, as a consequence of reciprocally conserving all the effects of their weapons, the attacker and the attacked fought in the same manner, which was by shock and by approaching each other.

Today, the attacker has no means drawn from the nature of their arms against the missile weapons that may oppose them other than to make use of their own, and these same weapons in their hands lose the greater part of their effect by the impossibility of marching and firing at the same time, these two operations only being able to take place at the expense of the other. In the hands of the attacked, on the contrary, missile weapons acquire, by the state of immobility and consequently the defensive, the greatest effect that they can have. The result is that a great part of the advantages that were once found on the side of the attacker have today passed to the side of the attacked.

Thus the ancients were founded in reason and in principle when they took the deep order for their primitive and habitual order. It was favorable to the species of their arms; it was analogous to the sole species of action to which they attached importance.

Thus, in the sixteenth and seventeenth centuries, we had reason to form ourselves six and eight deep, because the firearms, and above all the manner of making use of

---

2 [Folard, *Histoire de Polybe*, III:42–44.]
3 [Guibert illustrates the simple efficacy of combined arms in this example. The Greek heavy infantryman could only deliver shock, while the Roman soldier, armed with pila for throwing and a sword and shield, could engage in both shock and fire actions. See Randall Howarth, "War and Warfare in Ancient Rome," *The Oxford Handbook of Warfare in the Classical World*, 29–45; and Rawlings, "War and Warfare in Ancient Greece."]

them, were not perfected as they are today, [and] because a part of the battalions was still armed with pikes and partisans, and we consequently held to the ideas of shock. It is thus good to observe, and one may consult all the contemporary memoirs on this, that, despite this order of depth, we rarely charged. The little poor and maladroit musketry that existed then already rendered fire action predominant and almost habitual; quite rarely did we lower [our] pikes. This is what tacticians have done in vain: they may wish to prescribe laws as they please, [but] instinct and the first movement will always carry the day. But it is in both of them to render to one's enemy the ill that one receives from them as much as one can and to believe, rightly or wrongly, that the danger augments in approaching the place from where the rounds depart.

Thus, since troops have no more than firearms; since the perfection of these weapons and our skill in making them serve us has made great progress, although we are still far from the goal on this latter point; [and] since artillery, of which we have not yet spoken, has become so numerous, so adroit, and so mobile, we have reasonably and consequently acted to take the order on three ranks as the primitive and habitual order because it is the most analogous to the species of our weapons.

In forming ourselves on three ranks, we have taken a just middle [ground] between too-great density and too-great feebleness: we have sufficient consistency to march with lightness and with order, we place all our forces in action, we expose to enemy blows only individuals who may act and give fire in their turn, [and] finally, we offer to our artillery only the absolutely indispensable prize.

This would perhaps be the place to discuss the strange assertion of Mesnil-Durand's that artillery fire is not as redoubtable for the deep order as it is for the deployed order, but, destining a specific chapter to the examination of his system relative to artillery, I will return to this discussion.

2 Second Demonstration

2.1 The Deployed Order Is That in Which Infantry Is the Most Often in the Case of Ranging Itself

We have seen that the deployed order necessarily derives from the nature of our arms, and it is the best analog to them; it is now a matter of proving here that this order is that which the infantry is the most frequently obliged to take.

The nature of our arms' passing all the advantages that used to be on the side of the attacker to the side of the attacked, as we have seen by the preceding demonstration,

occasioned another change that is quite important to develop.

It used to be that infantry, putting all its strength into shock, not only did not search for rough terrain and advantageous positions, but also it avoided them as obstacles that would deprive it of its principal advantage. From this one sees that, in the accounts of ancient battles, there is almost no mention made of any topographic detail; there are always armies in flat plains.[4] The depth, and consequently the closing, of their order permitted them to find nude and open battlefields almost anywhere. The system of the Romans was so good in this regard that, when Hannibal penetrated into Italy, it was neither in the mountains nor in the difficult countryside that is their debouches that he waited for them; it was in the plains of the Trebbia, the Ticinus, [and] Cannae that they successively lost battles, and, in these plains, it was not the rivers that they sought to defend.[5] "But the ancients fortified themselves," it will be objected to us; "never did they encamp without enclosing themselves in entrenchments." Doubtlessly yes, but these entrenchments were for placing them out of the range of surprises, to give them a depot for their subsistence, sometimes to refuse to fight, or to be a refuge in case of misfortune. But if they ever did wish to resort to arms, they never missed departing from them [the camps], and it was to the plain that they sought to go.

Today, on the contrary, the infantry, having more advantage in defending than in attacking by the nature of its arms, seeks posts and avoids plains. It is almost never in the case of fighting in open country, because, if it is superior to the enemy, either the enemy abandons it to go wait in a covered position, or they entrench themselves there; this makes its position then enter into the nature of defensive positions. If it is inferior to them, it acts the same in its turn.

Now if we reflect that almost everything becomes a post for infantry by means of the prodigious fire by which it [the

---

4 [Here, Guibert largely repeats a passage from Abel, *Guibert's General Essay on Tactics*, 252. While he may be correct in saying that his sources did not include topographical detail in descriptions of ancient battles, topography did play a significant role in many important Greek and Roman battles like Cynoscephalae and Plataea, as I noted in the footnote to the aforementioned passage; see Herodotus, *Histories*, IX; and Polybius, *Histories*, XVIII.]

5 [Guibert names three battles fought between the Carthaginians of Hannibal Barca and the Romans during the Second Punic War. Hannibal, a scion of the powerful Barcid family, led an invasion of Italy from modern Spain and fought several battles along the way, including the Trebbia and Ticinus in 218 and Cannae in 216. Each was a Roman defeat, and the last virtually annihilated the sole remaining Roman field army; it also became a synonym for a decisive tactical victory. See Adrian Goldsworthy, *The Punic Wars* (London: Cassel, 2000), 167–219.]

infantry] may defend it [the position]; that a village, a wood, a ravine, a fosse, a height, [or] a simple commanding position garnished with artillery suffices for them to form in a state of resisting a superior enemy; [and] that it does not need these obstacles to reign over the entire army front, but only over some points of this front, thus forming counterforts or salient parts of the position that oblige the enemy to carry them before going beyond them; if one then wishes to consult the history of all modern wars and observe that, for a century, in one-hundred infantry combats, there were at least ninety that were given in posts or in advantageous positions, one will agree that the deployed order is that in which the infantry has been in the case of making use most often until the present. Mesnil-Durand flatters himself that his tactics will operate a revolution in this regard; we will discuss this possibility in examining his system relative to the positions and the grand operations of war.

3   Third Demonstration

3.1   *The Deployed Order Is the Simplest and the Most Facile Formation. That of Mesnil-Durand Unites All Opposing Inconveniences*

Our battalions' deployed order is, in formation, the simplest and the least complicated that it can possibly be. It is a facile organization which divides the battalion from right to left into two demi-ranks, four divisions, [and] eight platoons, [with] the platoons separated into two sections. This formation never varies; it adapts the battalions to the regiment, whatever the number of battalions that compose it; the regiments to the brigade, whatever the number of regiments; [and] the brigade to the division, whatever the number of brigades.

From the deployed order, which is the primitive and habitual order in the modern system, what if one wishes to pass to the order in column, which is our accidental order? The companies, or the fractions of the column, such as they are, always have the troops that were to their right or to their left in the primitive order before them or behind them. Thus, no difficulty [exists] at all for them to rally themselves if they are broken, [and] no embarrassment [exists] at all for them to form themselves in their place or in their rank if they must take up arms unexpectedly, whether day or night. A soldier always promptly finds his rank and his file when we are only formed three deep; he is quite well in the hand and under the eye of his officers and *bas-officiers*; he may not be negligent, speak, or move without being seen.

Will Mesnil-Durand pretend that his column, which is the primitive and habitual order of his system, would be a formation as simple and as facile as that of the deployed battalion?

Will he pretend that his complication of divisions and subdivisions, which he nevertheless regards as a chef-d'œuvre of organization; his parallel and perpendicular sections; his nomenclature that never ends; his varieties of formation and place that must be observed according to whether one finds oneself to be a grenadier, a chasseur, [or] a fusilier of this or that manche, this or that tranche, [and] this or that *tiroir*; his diverse distances, all a number of counted paces, all leading to different definitions and denominations; finally, all his mass of distinctions, of names and of precepts, would be comparable to the truly military simplicity of the organization of the battalion?

Will he pretend that his changing the formation and the place of the battalions in the regiments, the regiments in the brigades, [and] the brigades in the divisions according to their number, so that following the variations that this number will experience, variations that arrive ceaselessly in war via the detachments that one is obliged to make requiring the battalions, the regiments, [and] the brigades to ceaselessly change place and formation, would not be a great inconvenience? I have need only of recalling here these inconveniences; I gave details of them in rendering account of the system of Mesnil-Durand as it was executed at the Camp of Vaussieux.

Will he pretend that it would not be a great vice of his formation to not be able to pass from the state of the column to that of the deployed battalion (that is to say from his primitive and habitual order to that which he wishes to regard only as [the] accidental order and that will nevertheless be, despite him, that in which he will fight the most frequently) without disrupting his formation, the companies that, in his column, find themselves alongside each other separate themselves by their deployment to only rejoin when the battalion will reform itself in column, [and] that this is contrary to the fundamental principle, so sagely observed in the current system, that the formation never varies regardless of whether the battalion forms itself in deployed order or in column, and thus the companies, divisions, platoons, or sections will always be in the column preceded or followed by the same troops that are to their right or to their left in the deployed order?

The faults that I have recalled above, particularly [those that] belong to the central formation of Mesnil-Durand, may yet not prove anything against the system of depth, because Mesnil-Durand would surely be able to employ the best means [of them]. But decisive inconveniences remain that belong to both the system of Mesnil-Durand and to the deep order in general, whatever the formation that would be adopted. They are: to be in the greatest inconvenience when arms must be taken up, day or night, at the head of the camp; to be sometimes difficult to take in [restrictive] terrains; to be always longer to take than the deployed order; to not be able to maintain order and silence with facility; [and] to not at all be easily susceptible to rallying after a defeat and in the tumult of an action, inconveniences that, taken alone, render impractical that the deep order may ever be the primitive and habitual order.

4 Fourth Demonstration

4.1 *The Deployed Order Must Be the Habitual Order, Because It Is Proper Both to the Attack and to the Defense, and because It Is Principally [Proper] to the Defense, Which Must Be the Primitive State of a Troops, While the State of the Attack May Only be Accidental*

I have demonstrated in the preceding articles how fire action, which is the defensive action of infantry by the nature of our arms and by the continual influence that the supports that are born from the terrain, as much as entrenchments and artillery, have in infantry combats today, would become the principal and most frequent action, and how it would consequently follow that the defensive disposition would necessarily become the primitive and habitual disposition today. What I will say below will accumulate new proofs in favor of this opinion.

It is on a grand scale in war as it is on a small scale in fencing. Before delivering a blow, one must be on guard; before thinking of attacking, one must consider one's defense. One knows when one wishes to attack, but one is ignorant of when one will be attacked. Whenever one may be able to be, whenever one occupies a position, one is tranquil in a camp, and the state of repose must also be a defensive state. The defensive order must thus be the primitive and habitual order; it must serve as the base; it is from it that one must depart to act and to attack. While the deployed order would thus not be the order in which one would wish to attack, it would at least be the primitive and habitual order. But I am yet again far from agreeing that it must be included as the attack order; this is what I will discuss in the following chapter.

Now, to terminate this demonstration, let us see if the column of Mesnil-Durand may at any time have the pretention to be considered as [a] defensive order.

It will not be by fire that Mesnil-Durand will advance that it [his order] may be defensive. The opinion that he established in his *Projet d'un ordre français en tactique*, in support of which he imagined all [kinds] of strange fire by tranches, manchettes, saw, [and] pincer, he formally abandoned in his subsequent works. In them, he posed in principle that the column must never fire and that it would pass to the deployed order whenever it must fight by musketry.[6]

"But," Mesnil-Durand will say, and in this, he will only repeat what he advanced in his *Projet d'un ordre français en tactique*, "a column is truly and par excellence the defensive order, because it is strong everywhere, it has no flanks, and it may not be attacked with advantage on any side, but," he will add, "it will attack the enemy as soon as it will see them coming towards it. What is a better and more sure manner of defending than attacking?" And then, supporting these arguments, he will add the invincibility of his column; the certainty that it has of winning everywhere, even over an inferior force; and all the other marvelous properties that he attributes to it.

Eh! Truly, it is good to be strong in the rear and on one's flanks, that is to say where one will not be attacked! It is a question of being [strong] on one's front to be able to garnish and defend the position that one occupies. Mesnil-Durand, in pressing this property that the column has of being an order on four fronts at need, seems to always suppose infantry [that is] isolated and without points of support, but, as we have already objected and as we will yet again object at the risk of repeating ourselves, infantry almost never finds itself in this situation, at least when it is not maladroitly commanded, or when it has not been removed from a post.

[Now] we respond to the second objection. All infantry that is on the defensive, ordinarily occupying an advantageous position, whether by the nature of the terrain, by the obstacles that art adds to it, or by the support of the other arms, will never quit this position to attack the enemy. Garnishing and defending it: this is the objective that it must accomplish, and it is by the deployed order that it accomplishes it.

As the deployed order is thus habitually the defensive order, it does not follow that one must always, on all occasions, deploy one's troops in the position that one wishes to defend and that it must only ever be defended by deployed troops. This is where the modern system does not at all show itself to be exclusive. This is where talent and circumstances may modify the general principle. But we do not at all anticipate here the exceptions that will find their place in the course of this work. It is

---

6 [Mesnil-Durand, *Projet d'un ordre français*, especially 75–95; and *Suite d'un projet d'un ordre français*, 33: "the column is not at all proper for musketry."]

the general principle that we have wished to discuss in this chapter, and we believe that we have demonstrably established it.

New proofs yet remain to us to furnish [in order] to determine the preference that would be suitable to give to the deployed order as the primitive and habitual order when we will examine the connection that this order essentially has with all the great parts of war, with orders of march and of battle, with castrametation, with the science of positions, [and] with subsistence. But each of these objects requiring a particular chapter, we are forced to send our readers there.

CHAPTER 3

The Column Considered in Two Aspects: One, as Means of March and Maneuver, and Two, as Attack Disposition. It May Only Ever Be the Momentary and Accidental Order

Considered in all aspects of the means of march and of maneuver, it is well proven, I believe, that the column belongs to the system of Mesnil-Durand no more than it does to modern tactics. Armies have always maneuvered and marched in column. The King of Prussia, in perfecting tactics, knew more than anyone the resources and the options that one could draw from the mechanism and the handling of columns. It is by this mechanism that he is the first modern [person] who knew how to facilely move numerous armies and give, if I may express myself thus, maneuvering battles. Mesnil-Durand assuredly taught us nothing [new when he wrote] that one must march and maneuver in column. People of war thus judge, in examining the analysis of his column adapted to the marches and maneuvers of armies that I have made in the first part of this work, if the ordinance column and all the maneuvers that derive from it are not infinitely superior, relative to these great subjects.

Consequently, I have only to examine the column in relation to the attack disposition here; this examination merits to be deepened.

From the demonstration established in the preceding chapter, that the primitive and habitual order must be the deployed order, because this order is essentially the defensive order of infantry and that which it is consequently in the case of taking most often, it then necessarily follows that the order in column, considered as [an] attack disposition, may only ever be the momentary and accidental order. This is also the place to which it is assigned in modern tactics. But admitting the column as an advantageous attack disposition requires yet more clarifications, modifications, and exceptions.

The advantage of the order in column does not at all consist, as Folard believed and as Mesnil-Durand also appears to think (although he pronounces on this subject less positively than his master), of the shock force produced by the exact pressure of ranks and files; this exact pressure may not take place between active and thinking individuals to the point of forming a body without interstices and capable of acquiring a force equal to the combination of the quantity of force and movement.[1]

This advantage consists of the continual succession of efforts made by troops ranged one behind the other and succeeding each other rapidly in carrying themselves to a point of attack such that, covered by the troops that precede them, they neither see obstacles nor directly sustain blows.

It consists of [the fact that] that, the column having a small front, one may carry it to the salient parts [of a defensive position] without it having to much suffer from [incoming fire]. Compare the direction that a battalion formed in column follows to go to attack the angle of an entrenchment to that which a deployed battalion would follow for the same attack. The former advances on the capital of this angle and is only exposed to a small amount of frontal fire, all the rest being indirect or distant. The latter would be beaten by so great a quantity of fire that, in admitting that it had enough courage to go up to the foot of the entrenchment, it would arrive there too diminished and too lightened to seize it.

Finally, it consists of [the fact that] this order gives confidence to the assailant and intimidates the attacked. It gives confidence to the assailant because they sense themselves either sustained or preceded, and it intimidates the attacked because the soldier does not reason [and] because they only see with the eyes of the machine and, via this illusory organ, they are carried to exaggerating the efforts of the order [that is] the thickest and that assembles the greatest number of men in the smallest space.

These are the advantages of the column, but it also doubtlessly has some inconveniences. It is subject to floating, to tumult, and to disorder. If its flanks would be beaten by a lively fire, if the first effort would not surmount the obstacles that it encounters, the distances re-serry

---

1 [Guibert provides a simple application of Newton's Second Law of Motion, which may be summarized as force equals mass times acceleration.]

themselves, the solders press on themselves, the ranks confound themselves, the officers are no longer heard, [and] the mass swirls, disperses, and may rally itself only at a quite-far distance; naturally it will never again rally itself in column, because, as we have said above, rallying is only ever possible in a thin and extended order because a troop in disorder is only ever rallied by its officers [and], the voice, the example, the gesture being able to make an impression, the officers must be able to draw each solder under their eyes and in their hand in some way.[2]

Another inconvenience of the column is that, in attacking and even in carrying the post that it attacks, it often arrives that it serries itself and suppresses itself, a sort of herd and mechanical instinct carries the soldier to his neighbor's support at the approach of danger, as much to search for shelter as for protection, and, from this, master of the post that it carried, it is at pains to sustain itself there for want of being able to maneuver to deploy itself and to extend itself. Thus, if the enemy has fresh troops within range, they march on it, as it is still in the confusion of its success, [and] reverse it, and it [must] recommence at new expense. Thus pass the majority of attacks on posts in column in the confession[s] of the majority of old officers. The details of the Battle of Neerwinden in [the memoirs of] Feuquières must be read on this subject; he was an eyewitness and commanded a part of the attack. We carried the village of Neerwinden seven times, and we were chased from it as many, always because our columns, after having carried it, found themselves too much in disorder to establish themselves at the head of the village and to retain it.[3]

One remedies these inconveniences of the column, or at least much diminishes them, when one gives it a simple organization analogous to the formation of troops in the deployed order, derived from this order in the end and returning to it quite facilely, such that, in a word, the companies preserve in the order in column the same rank that they had in the deployed order and such that each of them is preceded or followed by the troop that is immediately beside them in the deployed order. Above all, one remedies it in placing officers and *bas-officiers* with intelligence both on the flanks and at the head, [and] at the center and in *serre-file* of the divisions, to contain and command the soldier. Finally, one remedies it in leaving intervals between whatever fractions compose the column, intervals that must never be less than three paces, even at the moment of the attack, so that the divisions may not at all intermingle and confound themselves, and, in the case of [an] advantage, it may deploy itself at need to occupy and to retain the post that it will have carried.

I leave now to those of my readers who have read with some attention the parallel of the column of Mesnil-Durand to that of the Ordinance in the first part of this work to judge which of the two better accomplishes the objectives exposed above. We resume that which concerns the column in general.

The order in column, as we have seen previously, having advantages [that are] as much real as of opinion and inconveniences [that are] able to be diminished or prevented when one gives a well-trained formation to the column and when one then knows how to employ and to command it, it then follows, and there is not a partisan of modern tactics who would be tempted to deny it, that this order is quite appropriate to attacks, and particularly attacks on posts, [and] that the troops must consequently be frequently exercised in passing from the deployed order to the order in column and repassing from the order in column to the deployed order. The one is their primitive and habitual order; the other is their momentary and accidental order. Both essentially compose their tactics, and neither of the two may supplant or exclude the other.

We will not dissimulate (the impartiality that we profess makes it our duty) that our last Maneuver Ordinances, and above all those of 1776, have neglected a little too much to speak of the column with regard to it as the attack order. It perhaps did not suffice to perfect in them, as was done, all the movements in column; it did not suffice to indicate there a column by battalion formed by the center in applying it solely to the maneuver of passage of lines.[4] It must expressly articulate that one may serve oneself with the same column as the attack column, that one even would prefer it only in all the cases that one would see before one the certainty of being able to deploy at need by the contrary movement and without being obliged to make flank movements to gain the center of one's terrain. Finally, it must consecrate an entire chapter (and it would be well employed) to treating the attack in column. It must

---

2 [Guibert's somewhat confusing prose here means that officers must be able to be heard in order to command the unit, which is more difficult in column than it is in deployed order.]

3 [The Battle of Neerwinden took place in 1793 during the War of the League of Augsburg. The French army under François-Henri de Montmorency-Bouteville, duc de Piney-Luxembourg, including Feuquières, lured the Allied army under Willem Hendrick, Prince of Orange and future King of England, into attacking it near Liège. Heavy fighting produced many casualties and a victory for the French, resulting in the nickname "upholsterer of Notre Dame" for Luxembourg. See Lynn, *The Wars of Louis XIV*, 233–235. Feuquières, *Mémoires*, III: 291–306, contains the passage Guibert references; see also Abel, *Guibert's General Essay on Tactics*, 91.]

4 [*Ordonnance du roi pour régler l'exercice de ses troupes d'infanterie en campagne* (1776), 167–180.]

consign in this chapter *that one will march to the enemy all the times that one will have reasonable hope of closing with them* as a fundamental principle. For want of this, we have been given to thinking that we would exclude the attack in column [and] that we would adopt the deployed order as the unique order, and we furnish arms to Mesnil-Durand.

The principle above would doubtlessly appear vague to Mesnil-Durand, but it would not be able to be announced more formally and more positively without inconvenience. One must sense that it is to circumstances to determine the moment when one must march on the enemy. Establishing as an axiom that we will march on the enemy all the times that we will not be separated from them by an obstacle, as Mesnil-Durand does, is to pose the most false and the most dangerous precept.

Without doubt, [one] must march on the enemy without any preliminary fire if the enemy is in a flat plain and without support; one must march on them if one extinguishes the fire of their artillery with a superior artillery [fire], if one shakes them with one's fire, [and] if one sees them floating and uncertain, but, if they are in an advantageous situation, if they bristle with a formidable artillery, if their position necessarily reduces the attack to salient point, one must maneuver before them; one must work either to turn them or to engage them in [weakening] some part [of their position]; one must beat the fires of their points of defense with superior fire; in the end, one must only march to them when there is a true probability that one may [do so] with success. What if one is audacious, if one has better troops than the enemy, [and] if one senses, if one sees, in the people who follow one, the will, the elan that promises great efforts and that presages victory? One may then dare more; one may hazard that which would appear to be, and that would be, impossible in another circumstance. With the French, more than with any other nation, there doubtlessly exist these fortunate moments that a man of talent may seize and that he even may give birth to, if to [his] talent is joined a certain moral fiber, but to conclude from these moments, which are always quite rare, and to infer from them, as an infallible and general principle, that one must always march on the enemy all the times that it is not absolutely impossible [to do so] is to assuredly not have reflected on either the variety of circumstances or on the human heart.

Marching on the enemy and charging them with the bayonet, as Mesnil-Durand wishes, is an always-delicate maneuver, and it must be hazarded only in decisive moments for a simple reason: a charge of this species is as decisive for the troop that makes it as for that which receives it, and, if it misses its objective, it has no more resource to rest on. Mesnil-Durand thus acts in vain; he thus promises victory to those who make use of it, as one kills oneself without meeting them [the enemy], [and], as it is natural to immediately return the blows that one receives and to believe them more redoubtable the closer that they approach, shock and the *arme blanche* will only ever be the momentary and accidental action.

I sense that it is a long way from these modifications to all the great effects that Mesnil-Durand promises from the shock of his column, as it must not only march on the enemy, but also, according to him, marching is too little; it must run, [as] the run is its natural pace. Permit me to cite here Mesnil-Durand himself, speaking on the running of his column. This is drawn from one of his most recent works, his *Fragments of Tactics*, in his Memoir on the Column.[5]

"The column elongates on the run, but it also shortens itself at each instant. In approaching the enemy, it will partially serry and will even achieve being [serried] in time, which will bring the greatest effort of pressure that the depth will be capable of on contact. The first objection that was made of me on the running is that the last ranks would throw the first on their bellies. Not quite; they will only throw them on the enemy. One may doubtlessly make endless arguments about this. There is only one response to this: the same one Zeno made to those who deny movement.[6]

The run, like depth, has more moral force than physical; it does not multiply the mass by the speed but [rather] audacity by euphoria and fear by terror …

When one will wish to test the true run, one will first see that it is quite facile, [and] moreover, that the soldiers, heated or perhaps enflamed by this run, will carry forward in such a manner that each individual, even despite themselves, would be caught up in the torrent. One will see, even in the exercise, the troop, as attentive and master

---

5   Pages 79–80.
    [Mesnil-Durand, *Fragments de tactique*, 79–80. The portion after the ellipsis is contained in a note on 80.]
6   [Zeno of Elea was a Greek philosopher who lived in the fifth century BCE and was famous for his paradoxes. He belonged to a sect known as the Eleatics who denied the reality of motion. Mesnil-Durand's reference is likely to Pierre Bayle, "Zeno," *Dictionnaire historique et critique*, 4 Vols. (Basle: Brandmuller, 1738), IV:544n1: "I know quite well that, among the people, it was a paradox almost as strange to deny vacuum as to deny movement," which makes the idea Bayle's, not Zeno's; see also John Wright, "Skepticism and Incomprehensibility in Bayle and Hume, https://philarchive.org/archive/WRISAI-2, 138. Pierre Bayle was a radical skeptical rationalist and one of the most important figures of the Enlightenment. He is thus the subject of a voluminous historiography; see Michael Hickson, "Pierre Bayle," *Oxford Bibliographies Online* (2022), https://www.oxfordbibliographies.com/display/document/obo-9780195399301/obo-9780195399301-0482.xml.]

of itself in running in as-good order as it would in marching, being so ardent and so gay that it will always be ready to bound, wishing for enemies with risible good faith and sparkling eyes, and, if one does not silence it, walking with great cries like a pack of dogs. It would even not be easy to contain these cries in arriving on the enemy. Eh! Why contain them? If it is not to manage one's breath and to be able to throw the thunderclap at thirty paces with more ensemble and strength, [then command] "lower arms." This note will perhaps make some readers laugh, but the representation would not at all make enemies laugh."

It remains to me to examine in what circumstances attack columns must be made use of and if the order in column must be exclusively the order destined to attack.

We have already seen the modifications that I established above on the general principle of Mesnil-Durand in demonstrating that there are many circumstances in which one may not be able to march to the enemy despite there being no physical impossibility [of doing so]. In these circumstances, the fight must necessarily be engaged with fire, and this fire may then have several objectives: to occupy the enemy while one turns them and attacks them more decisively on another point; to beat them and to dislodge them with a superior fire, if they have an advantage over one in this regard; or finally to lighten them and to put them in disorder to then march on them, when one sees them enfeebled and shaking. These are already [some] circumstances, and they are quite frequent, in which the nature of the attack requires the deployed order.

But they are not the only ones, as there are attacks in which it is appropriate to mix deployed battalions with columns to march together and in concert, the deployed battalions thus having for their objective to embrace the faces and the curtain walls and to occupy or to extinguish their fire while the columns march on the salient parts. There are other attack dispositions in which one may support the columns with deployed battalions, the columns thus having for [their] objective to take the point of attack and the deployed battalions to establish themselves there immediately after, to garnish them and to defend them against efforts that the enemy may take to retake them. Finally, there are occasions in which one may march on the enemy [with] the first line deployed [and] the second supporting it in columns.

What reflection and experience teaches is that this is not at all a general and exclusive method. Columns are quite proper for attacking; they are above all proper when the enemy is behind an entrenchment or in some other post whose natural or artificial flanks necessarily reduce [one] to attacking the salients and to not presenting [oneself] on the faces; they are proper when, being able to debouch on the enemy only by a point, one is forced to assemble one's troops on this point and to arrive by it; finally, they are proper when, in an entrenchment or a closed place, one wishes to make a sortie on the attacking enemy [that] is already in disorder by the ill-success of their attack, or even more so when one must immediately re-attack the post that they [the enemy] have just taken and where they have not yet had time to establish themselves.

But deployed battalions also have their advantages for an attack. They are proper for embracing a flank; they are proper for being combined in a general disposition with columns, whether to march to the same height and in concert with them, to support them, [or] to be supported by them. There are even cases in which, without cooperation, without support, without mixing with columns, I will charge the enemy in line if they are in the same order: for example, in a position in which the terrain will not give them any advantage over me, as then we play an equal game with regard to our ordinance, and it suffices that I will be superior to them, whether in number, maneuver, or courage. Suppose another circumstance: if I have sustained a musketry combat with the enemy for some time, and I see them in disorder or tottering? If I see their line or their position pierced on collateral points? Then I will certainly not form myself in column to march on them. This would be a bad maneuver to make under their fire; this would expose me to being beaten if they would charge me during my movement. I will thus shake out my battalions, fully deployed as they will be, and I will carry them to the enemy, not at the run, as Mesnil-Durand wishes, but at the maneuver step, which will gradually accelerate by the united effects of the instruments of war, movement, and circumstance.

In the end, modern tactics are so distant from [being] general and exclusive methods that they do not even exclude those that are the most opposed to their habitual principles. Thus, although the usage of lines both full and empty is proscribed, although our deployed battalions constantly form in contiguous line, or at least with quite-small intervals, the King of Prussia nevertheless makes use of the order *en échiquier* in some circumstances; the battalions thus sustain and replace themselves without embarrassment and without confusion to enter into an attack or to make a rear-guard. I saw this maneuver employed several years ago at the Camp of Neiss in Silesia.[7] I doubtless do not cite it as one of those in which he has confidence, but [rather] at least as a proof of the opinion of this great man that good tactics must be quite varied in their

---

7 [Jacques-Antoine-Hippolyte, comte de Guibert, *Journal d'un voyage en allemagne*, 2 Vols. (Paris: Treuttel et Würtz, 1803), II:141–188. See also Abel, *Guibert*, 85–89.]

means, because there is nothing so varied as terrains and circumstances.

In seeing me thus pose these principles that are not exclusive in the least and do not solely proscribe the column as a means of attack, but also in recommending their usage, Mesnil-Durand will not miss repeating that "[this] is a manner of eluding the defeat of the thin order [and] that these modifications signal only, in good French, that one well wishes to take his method provided that it not be said that one took it [and] provided that, not taking it all of a piece, one may dismember and disguise it a little in making some breaches in it that will be covered with some scraps of modern tactics."[8]

But I confess that I cannot conceive on what Mesnil-Durand founded [his] pretention that we search to rob and to modify his system to adopt it without agreeing [to it]. This work has already proven so far (and I hope that it will prove more and more) that the two systems are absolutely different. They are different in their principles, in their means, and in their results at the same time; would he levy this accusation against us because modern tactics make use of columns and because they are our almost-universal instrument of maneuver? But columns belonged to us before he thought of his, and the King of Prussia moved 100,000 men in columns, truly organized differently from his, without having read his works. Would he [Mesnil-Durand] believe that it was he who forced us to conceive that the order in column might be advantageous for the attack? But before him, and always, we attacked posts in column, and we supported attacked posts in column. Before him, Marshal Broglie gave us his wise disposition for the defense of the village of Bergen, a grand lesson in the utile mélange of the two orders.[9] Finally, for that which concerns me, if Mesnil-Durand wishes to convince himself that he has neither shaken me nor caused me to vary and that my opinion, as I give it here, modified and anti-exclusive, is what it always was, he only has to take the pain of reading the chapters of the *General Essay on Tactics* in which I treat the column envisaged in different aspects.[10] Having made this work in my early youth, I have the rare pleasure, ten years later, of not being obligated to return to the principles that I exposed there. Mesnil-Durand has varied a little more in his own; it is true that he pretended to the honor of having created a system and that I humbly preferred to make myself the pupil of a great man.

---

8 *Reflections on the Maneuvers of the Ordinance*, published at the Camp of Vaussieux, 115–116.

9 [See Appendix A, 177.]

10 [Abel, *Guibert's General Essay on Tactics*, 88–96 and especially 207–237. This section begins Guibert's refutation of some of the ideas presented in that book.]

CHAPTER 4

Examination of the System of Mesnil-Durand Relative to Cavalry

Here again [is] a relationship under which it is quite important to examine the system of Mesnil-Durand. The usage and the employment of cavalry are entirely changed by this system. One believes not only to be able to diminish their number by this system but also that one could even go as far as to not have them at need. This last assertion, positively announced in the *Treatise on* Plésions, was a little mitigated by Mesnil-Durand in his later works, but it remains at least that, in his current system, cavalry is counted for almost nothing and that it is only employed as an arm [that is] secondary, passive, and entirely subordinated to the infantry, [a] destination absolutely opposed to that which it has in modern tactics.[1]

Mesnil-Durand has much varied in the [use] that he wishes to make of cavalry. First faithful to the principle of the mélange of the arms and outstripping Folard in this regard, he wished a company of horse grenadiers in each *plésion*. Then, he appeared to have renounced this formation and adhered to having horse troops separated from the infantry, but at the same time, he did not at all wish cavalry on the wings and employed it all in the second line behind the intervals of his *plésions*. Finally, having apparently reflected on the inconvenience of having no cavalry support on the wings of his infantry and perhaps commencing to suspect that his columns, despite [being] "without flanks," despite [being] "invincible," might find themselves a little isolated and uncovered, but, not wishing at the same time to fall into stereotypes, he imagined a completely new manner of placing cavalry: posting half on a line two- or three-hundred *toises* behind the infantry flanks and the other half behind this infantry to be able to sustain its columns by passing via their intervals at need. This is the disposition that we believe to be at least the current "ultimatum" of Mesnil-Durand, since it is what we employed the small number of horse troops in at the Camp of Vaussieux in several maneuvers. So that I will not be misunderstood, for the rest, I will respond successively to the different versions that he adopted in his system.

I will not at all literally repeat here the reasons that determine Mesnil-Durand to give to cavalry a destination so opposed to what it has today; a literal extract of Mesnil-Durand always carries too far. I will content myself with collecting the best sense that I will be able to of his numerous writings and in what I have heard his partisans say.

One of Mesnil-Durand's premier reasons is, as one may believe, the example of the ancients. They intermingled the arms, [and] they had little cavalry; they made little use of it, [and] they regarded it, Mesnil-Durand says, as the arm of the barbarous and undisciplined nations.[2]

His other reasons are founded on the inconvenience of extended orders of battle; on the uselessness of second lines; on the intrinsic strength of infantry ranged in his system, [a] strength that renders it equally susceptible to attacking and defending itself without means foreign to it; on the value of cavalry; on the difficulty of making it subsist; and on the augmentation of infantry that one may procure it in proportion to [how much] one would reduce it [cavalry].

"Finally," say the partisans of Mesnil-Durand, "it is relative to cavalry that his system is important and useful to adopt." The situation in which this part of our army is, the continental war that menaces us: everything militates, according to them, in favor of his system.[3] They say [that]

---

1 [See Mesnil-Durand, *Fragments de tactique*, 272–287; *Projet d'un ordre français*, 230–248; and *Suite du projet d'un ordre français*, 19, where he amusingly accuses a contemporary of designing a system that has "spared itself too much of cavalry."]

2 [Ibid. Cavalry in ancient Greece and Rome is a contentious topic, particularly given that the period spans a millennium. The stereotypical armies of Classical Greece and Republican Rome did not have large formal cavalry contingents, although armies from both were often accompanied by auxiliary or allied cavalry. Some Greek or quasi-Greek polities like the Thessalians were noted for their cavalry, and Imperial Roman armies often did contain large cavalry contingents. See Ann Hyland, "War and the Horse," *The Oxford Handbook of Warfare in the Classical World*, 493–526.]

3 [Guibert probably refers to the American War of Independence, which France had formally joined. Alternatively, "continental war" may mean the War of the Bavarian Succession, a conflict fought between Prussia and Austria in 1778 and 1779. Austria sought to annex Bavaria, which Prussia sought to prevent; the war ended with minor territorial gains for Austria but an independent Bavaria. The war is notable as having been waged without any major battles, giving it the derisive name of "Potato War." France was designated a guarantor of German peace and liberties in the 1648 Peace of Westphalia, giving it the right to intervene in German affairs, although it did not in the Bavarian Succession. Guibert will reference the conflict several times in the remainder of the text. See Orville Murphy, *Charles Gravier, comte de Vergennes: French Diplomacy in the Age of Revolution 1719–1787* (Albany: State University of New York Press, 1982); and Dennis Showalter, *The Wars of Frederick the Great* (New York: Longman, 1996), 337–352.]

France does not at all have cavalry, or at least what it has is quite inferior and quite insufficient compared to that of the other great military powers. If we had to incessantly face a land war, we would not be able to make cavalry either at the cost of effort or at the cost of money. We must thus regard a system that forms [us] in a state of making war advantageously with the little cavalry that we have as the salvation of the army [and] of the common good.

Before passing from this examination of the diverse manners in which Mesnil-Durand proposes to employ cavalry, I will discuss the reasons alleged above, both by him and by his partisans, in favor of the base of his system.

It is certain that the ancients (only considering among them the Greeks and the Romans; all the other peoples may be reputed barbarous with regard to the military science) generally had less cavalry than modern nations and that they counted on it much less than [they did] on their infantry. But what does this prove? That the Greeks and Romans had infinitely neglected this arm and that they were themselves almost barbarous in this part of war. To convince, it suffices to see the formation of their cavalry: among the Greeks, it formed itself in trapezoids, [and] among the Romans in *turmæ*, that is to say among both in deep order and consequently with the incapacity of moving itself and of having the premier properties of cavalry, which are the speed of shock and rapidity of movements. It suffices to recall that, among the Greek cavalry, the only [contingent] that had some reputation was the Thessalian, [a] species of cavalry that fought armed with axes on extremely fast horses and without forming themselves into squadrons, and that the Roman cavalry could not hold the campaign against the Numidian, Spanish, [or] Carthaginian cavalry, etc., which, despite [being] without order and without discipline, at least had speed [going] for it.[4]

However little-formidable were the Greek and Roman cavalry, it must nevertheless not be concluded that they did not often and decisively influence battles. Without pretending to make [an] assault on the erudition of Mesnil-Durand, I will recall to him Epaminondas's commencing the Battle of Mantinea by beating the left wing of the enemy cavalry with the cavalry of his right wing, [and], having uncovered the flank of the Athenian infantry, it did not stand against the attack of his own;[5] Alexander III's making great use of cavalry and always fighting at its head;[6] Hannibal's almost always [being] victorious by his own;[7] Xanthippus's beating Marcus Atilius Regulus, who had had none and who believed he could do without;[8] Caesar's employing all the resources of art and genius to counterbalance the inferiority that he sensed by the superiority Pompey had in cavalry at Pharsalus, etc. Mesnil-Durand accused me in one of his works of "having lightly studied antiquity."[9] I confess that I have not studied it to enrich my memory and to make it weigh on my readers but [rather] to enlighten my judgment and form me as a result.

Cavalry was not nearly as necessary to the ancients, given their genre of war, than it has become to us today,

---

4 [See Hyland, "The Horse in War;" and Southern, *The Roman Army*, 71–117.]
5 [Epaminondas was a Greek general who helped create the army of Thebes that decisively defeated the Spartans at the Battles of Leuctra and Mantinea 371 and 361 BCE, ending Sparta's paramount position in land warfare, although he died in the latter battle. His favored formation and tactic was to refuse one of his wings and heavily reinforce the other, occasionally up to fifty lines deep. As Guibert indicates, cavalry were important in these battles to clear the way for the infantry to make the decisive blow. His formation became the basis for the "oblique order" of Vegetius and Guibert. See Abel, *Guibert's General Essay on Tactics*, 27–28; and John Buckler, "Epaminondas at Leuctra, 371 BC," *The Oxford Handbook of Warfare in the Classical World*, 657–670; see also Kevin Daly, "Ancient Thebes," *Oxford Bibliographies Online* (2021), https://www.oxfordbibliographies.com /display/document/obo-9780195389661/obo-9780195389661-0362 .xml.]
6 [Alexander III, often called Alexander the Great, was King of Macedonia and founder of the Hellenistic Empire in the fourth century BCE. His combined-arms armies conquered the Achaemenid Persian empire and laid the foundation for the spread of Greek culture throughout the Ancient Near East. His position in battle was often at the head of the Companion Cavalry, an elite heavy cavalry unit that usually charged directly at the enemy commander in an effort to decapitate the enemy army and create maximum consternation in the enemy force. See Green, *Alexander of Macedon*, especially 172–181, 226–235, and 288–296; and JE Lendon, *Soldiers and Ghosts: A History of Battle in Classical Antiquity*, 115–139.]
7 [Hannibal experienced significant battlefield success with the aid of his cavalry, particularly the contingents from Gaul, modern France, and Numidia, in western North Africa. Only when Rome induced the Numidians to switch sides did a Roman army defeat Hannibal, at the 202 BCE Battle of Zama, ending the Second Punic War in Rome's favor. See Goldsworthy, *The Punic Wars*, 143–330.]
8 [Guibert speaks of the 255 BCE Battle of Tunis, which was fought during the First Punic War. A Roman army under Marcus Atilius Regulus conducted several amphibious raids on the Carthaginian homeland in modern Tunisia before landing and defeating the unprepared Carthaginians at Adys before capturing Tunis. The Carthaginian leadership, including the Barcids, hired the Spartiate Xanthippus to train their army to drive the Romans out of Carthage. In the ensuing battle, Carthaginian cavalry, including elephants, routed the small Roman cavalry and then inflicted a significant defeat on Regulus, whose infantry was ineffectual against the Carthaginian cavalry, especially the elephants. See Abel, *Guibert's General Essay on Tactics*, 27–28; and Goldsworthy, *The Punic Wars*, 256–257.]
9 [Mesnil-Durand, *Fragments de tactique*, lvi-lvii.]

given ours. They generally had less-numerous armies. (I speak of the Greeks and the Romans in their good years). They maneuvered on small fronts; they camped in small spaces and always entrenched; they had fewer embarrassments and less equipment; they were thus, on one hand, easier to make subsist, and on another, they were certainly more sober. Consequently, they did not embrace, and were not in the necessity of embracing, large [parts of] the countryside with their operations and with their positions, [requirements] that today impose the obligation of having a cavalry sufficient to control the campaign. Mesnil-Durand would, in truth, return us to this genre of war, but it is a chimera, as we will demonstrate, whether to him or to the public at least, that we must renounce.[10]

The art of war that we believe, whatever Mesnil-Durand may say, [to be] infinitely superior today to that of the ancients, is, among other points, above all infinitely perfected with regard to cavalry. Particularly over the last twenty years, the progress has been immense, and it is again to the King of Prussia that we owe it.

The proof of this progress is that today, we no longer agitate [ourselves] over the useless question of the preeminence of the two arms. A wiser theory [and] more-healthy reflections have placed each of them in its place. Thus cavalry and infantry no longer either have the pretention to be exclusive. In enlightening themselves, they have ceased to be jealous of each other. The infantry is proper to work, to sieges, to fights, [and] to all [types of terrain], and [it] doubtlessly is always the principal arm; [it] would, at need [and] in certain circumstances, suffice by itself. But without cavalry, it would only advance at a tortuous pace; it would be ceaselessly harassed, ceaselessly exposed to losing its subsistence; it would never complete its success; it would [suffer] the greatest reverses; in the end, it would do nothing rapidly. Cavalry in its turn often decides or re-establishes fights; it makes courses, advanced guards, [and] expeditions, but without infantry, it would do nothing decisive, [and] it would be able to establish itself nowhere.[11] The least post, the least obstacle would arrest it. At night, it would tremble for its surety. These properties and this utility are well known on both sides, today making these two arms be, and regard themselves as, an army; they are the members of a well-organized corps, the parts that constitute the whole and that may not separate and pass from each other without weakening themselves.[12]

Today, the cavalry, in acquiring the speed that it lacked and in combining it with the order and the discipline that it lacked even more, has become a formidable arm and the greatest resource in the hands of the general who knows how to handle it. By it, the inconveniences of the extended order may be remedied in great part because by it, one may support weak parts, carry rapidly to the aid of distant parts, [and] embrace a great extent of the countryside and consequently procure much subsistence and [many] commodities. By it, one may re-establish a desperate fight and complete a victory in the blink of an eye. The great blows, the audacious blows, the blows of genius must be struck by cavalry. Thus the victory of Freiburg was due to the hardiness of a Prussian dragoon regiment; that of Rossbach to a decisive charge by General Friedrich-Wilhelm Freiherr von Seydlitz; that of Kolin, already almost gained by the King of Prussia, to two regiments of Austrian and Saxon dragoons and light horsemen; [and] that of Kunersdorf to Marshal Loudon, who, like an eagle, swooped down on the Prussian infantry, relentless in pressing their success and fatigued from vanquishing.[13]

---

10 [Guibert repeats a mistake that he made in Abel, *Guibert's General Essay on Tactics*, 27–28, of assuming that Greek and Roman armies were smaller than contemporary ones. In reality, they were often of similar size; for example, the combined total of the armies at the 479 BCE Battle of Plataea and the 1757 Battle of Leuthen was probably around 100,000 each; the combined total of the armies at the 301 BCE Battle of Ipsus and the 1708 Battle of Oudenaarde, perhaps the largest of the century before 1792, was probably around 160,000–170,000. See Peter Green, *The Greco-Persian Wars* (Berkeley: University of California Press, 1996), 247–271; Lynn, *The Wars of Louis XIV*, 319–320; and Robin Waterfield, *Dividing the Spoils: The War for Alexander the Great's Empire* (New York: Oxford University Press, 2011), 153–154.]

11 [The term Guibert uses, "courses," is borrowed from naval warfare and denotes a raid or a swift attack by a ship or squadron. See Abel, *General Essay on Tactics*, 241.]

12 [The notion of combined arms is perhaps as old as warfare, but it was not institutionalized in the French army of the period. In theory, separate infantry, cavalry, artillery, and other units would be united in a combined-arms force when they were assembled and trained in winter and spring camps before campaign, but the result was not always a force that operated efficiently or effectively. Theorists like Maurice de Saxe and Chevalier Rostaing proposed combined-arms formations in the early part of the century; by Guibert's period, they were the subject of serious study, but they would not be implemented in practice until the combined-arms divisions of the Wars of the French Revolution. See Saxe, *Mes rêveries*; and Chevalier Rostaing, "Mémoire concernant l'essai de la légion, la tactique, et les évolutions," SHAT 1M 1707 54, which were clearly inspired by Classical examples. See also Abel, "An Aspect of the Military Experience in the Age of Reason;" and Quimby, *The Background of Napoleonic Warfare*, 300–344.]

13 [The Battle of Freiburg was one of the last actions of the Seven Years War. A Prussian army of 30,000 under Prince Heinrich, Friedrich's brother, attacked an Austrian army of around 21,000 under Friedrich-Karl, prince of Stolberg-Gerden, and Andreas graf Hadik von Futak and drove them away from Freiburg, which he captured.

But, it must be confessed, this grand manner, this decisive manner of employing cavalry, is known to us only [secondhand]. We have an example of what a man of talent may do with it seen in the last war [Seven Years War], [which] is to defeat the rear-guard of Karl-Wilhelm-Ferdinand, Hereditary Prince of Brunswick, at Grünberg; this homage will not appear suspicious; I pay it to the memory of a general officer who is no longer: baron Clausen. The enemy rear-guard, composed of seven or eight battalions, was in retreat column. It debouched in his view. An ordinary man, a man [who was] only courageous, would have attacked the tail of this rear-guard, [as] it was the closest to him. Clausen wished to deliver a more decisive blow; he went alongside the column with around three- or four-hundred cavalrymen; then, when he was around the height of its center, he closed, fell on it, separated it into two, made all who were from the center to the tail lower their arms, then would have visited the same fate on the rest of the column if it had not already been covered by the difficulties of the countryside.[14]

I will respond elsewhere to the reasons that Mesnil-Durand draws from the extension of our orders of battle to support the novelty of his cavalry principles in examining if this extension is a vice and if it is possible to remedy it. We now pass to the reasons that he pretends to draw from the costs of maintaining cavalry. My response will be short because, in proving that one cannot do without it, I have nothing to add to justify the expenses that it occasions. He may remain debating the amount that it is convenient to have at most, and my ideas on this subject are again quite opposed to the opinions of Mesnil-Durand.

It seems to me that the amount of cavalry maintained today by the two premier military powers in Europe, the King of Prussia and the Emperor, is not at all directly relative to the footing of their infantry. They have around 35,000 or 40,000 cavalrymen for 180,000 infantrymen. This proportion is outside of that which was established in principle by all the classical authors. Montecuccoli and Feuquières, who hold the first rank among them, fix it at one-fifth of infantry.[15] Louis XIV maintained even more. We saw up to two-hundred squadrons in his Army of Flanders, and the squadrons were then one-hundred and sixty men.[16]

Not having as few cavalry and pretending, as Mesnil-Durand pretends, to be able to compensate for it by means of a relative augmentation of infantry would be, without operating a great economy, forming oneself outside the state of being able to fight equally against enemies that are constituted on another principle. Because, whatever Mesnil-Durand may say, infantry, however good, however numerous it be (at least if one does not make war in a

---

The Battle of Kolin was fought on 18 June 1757 between around 40,000 Prussians under Friedrich and around 55,000 Austrians under Leopold-Josef-Maria, Reichsgraf von und zu Daun. Daun dug his army in to a prepared defensive position, and Friedrich tried to turn his flank. Daun countered ably, but the Prussian attack almost succeeded; it was ultimately turned back by Austrian cavalry, including a regiment of Walloon dragoons. The battle was Friedrich's first defeat in the war and marked a significant blow to his reputation as a military genius.

The Battle of Kunersdorf took place on 12 August 1759. Friedrich took an army of around 50,000 to meet the advance of a Russo-Austrian army of almost 80,000 men under Count Pyotr Semyonovich Saltykov and Ernst-Gideon Freiherr von Laudon in modern Poland. Friedrich executed a flanking maneuver followed by an oblique attack with a refused flank that foundered against Allied superiority in numbers and especially artillery. Loudon's counterattack shattered the Prussian army and completed Friedrich's most comprehensive defeat. See Szabo, *The Seven Years War in Europe*, 60–65, 234–239, and 414–415.]

14 [Guibert describes an action fought between the armies of Broglie and Ferdinand in early 1761 on the Ohm River. The two armies faced each other, and Clausen attacked the Allied right commanded by the Hereditary Prince as they withdrew, in the manner Guibert indicates. See Richard Waddington, *La guerre de sept ans*, 5 Vols. (Paris: Firmin Didot, 1899–1914), IV:318–319.]

15 [Raimondo Montecuccoli was an officer who served the Empire during much of the seventeenth century, including against the Ottomans and as a rival to the great French general Henri de la Tour d'Auvergne, vicomte de Turenne. His *Mémoires*, 3 Vols. (Paris: 1712), were an important source of military theory and maxims of the period, including for Guibert, as will become evident. Both he and Feuquières seemed to be in favor of a greater percentage of cavalry than Guibert says in their printed works. Feuquières, *Mémoires*, I:174–178, discusses the creation of an army without the noted proportion. Montecuccoli, *Mémoires*, 46–47 gives an example of an army that is around one-third cavalry, while 82 argues that "infantry is good for sieges [and] cavalry for battles," and 227 says of fighting against the Ottomans that "cavalry must weigh at least half as much as the infantry …" John Lynn, *Giant of the Grand Siècle: The French Army 1610–1715* (New York: Cambridge University Press, 1997), 527–530, notes that the cavalry to infantry ratio throughout the period from 1660 to 1715 was around one to three. Both make a special note that armies must be raised and composed relative to the conflict they are to be used in, not set at a fixed proportion. Guibert is perhaps drawing from unpublished or archival materials for his references.]

16 [Louis XIV was the longest-reigning monarch of a large state in European history. He ruled from 1743 until his death in 1715, a period often identified as the "Grand Siècle," or Great Century. Much of his reign was spent in war as he sought to conquer land on his frontiers, particularly the Rhine. While he succeeded in doing so, and in placing his grandson on the Spanish throne, his policies led to the deaths of hundreds of thousands and the virtual bankruptcy of the state. Lynn, *Giant of the Grand Siècle*, 32–64, discusses the problem of determining the exact sizes of the armies Louis XIV fielded that has vexed historians since the mid-twentieth century.]

mountainous country) will not be able to compensate for [not having] cavalry.

But never, in no case, augmenting the proportion that the masters of the art fixed at a fifth of the infantry at its highest point; reducing oneself, in peacetime, to another proportion so that the eventual augmentation in case of war would only ever be a fifth of each squadron at most; [and] ensuring at the same time that this cavalry would always be well mounted, well equipped, well maneuvering, and saving no pain, care, [or] money to this end: here is what the wise system would be, the midpoint between the two extremes, and, in the end, the indispensable part.

As to the arguments that I heard said to be decisive and peremptory in favor of the system of Mesnil-Durand on the current situation of our cavalry, on the state of feebleness to which it is reduced, on the impossibility of carrying it to a wartime footing by augmentations that would be sudden and forced without noticeably deteriorating it and rendering it quite inferior to that which enemies may oppose us with, [and] on the embarrassment that this augmentation, and then the maintenance that would follow it, would throw the kingdom's finances into, I confess that I am at pains to conceive of them. What! Cavalry is necessary! The Emperor [and] the King of Prussia have a formidable one, and the king of France will not be able to form his own to the same point! And we will be forced to search for a supplement [that is] at least uncertain and in all likelihood dangerous, in a system that has all the great principles of war, the officer, the soldier, [and], in the end, all the traditions and the customs of all of military Europe against it! We do not at all have cavalry, and we will adopt tactics that will lose the little that we have and that will prevent it from ever raising itself again!

Ah! Instead say, instead ceaselessly repeat that the king has no cavalry at all; that, without cavalry, we have no army; [and] that, without [an] army, we have no glory, consideration, base for our negotiations, security for the future, or peace. Let it strike his ears, his imagination; let us speak the truth every day, at every moment; a truth of this importance may never become trivial, and it would even be a question of, if it were necessary, daring to render it importunate. Let it be done, and soon the king will have a cavalry. It is an enterprise that is neither as difficult nor as expensive as is liked to be exaggerated. The germ exists. Our [cavalry] regiments are almost null, but we have the discipline and the instruction. We have some general and superior officers who have been stealing the secrets of this arm from among foreigners who possess the theory and have the talents to wait only for great occasions to join it to practice.

We go to the variants of Mesnil-Durand on the manner in which he employs cavalry in his system.

In his first version, he wished to attach a seventy-five-man company of horse grenadiers to each *plésion*. He took this idea from the Roman legions, and this example apparently seemed decisive to him without [any] other examination, yet, for the little that he wished to reflect, he saw that it was almost useless to maintain ten- or twelve-thousand cavalrymen. I say "almost useless" because these companies, already too weak to fight alone and in squadrons, would only ever have formed bad cavalry fighting in large corps and in line. We can assume what the amalgamation of all these little troops, accustomed to an absolutely opposite manner of fighting and not having either any knowledge or any practice of line maneuvers, would be. Mesnil-Durand will object [that] our foot grenadier companies, assembled in diverse regiments, form battalions and corps well, but Mesnil-Durand does not understand that the grenadiers always maneuver in our battalions as part of the battalion and that the maneuver of the battalion and the line is familiar to them; [in contrast], a small squadron, habituated to maneuvering alone, may not take any idea of maneuvering in the corps and in the line of its arm. Thus in the cavalry, it is the habit of spaces, it is the science of the coup-d'œil that makes everything; it must maneuver at large to know how to maneuver. This is so true that one of the greatest inconveniences of the current feebleness of our regiments is that they are not in the habit of grand movements, that they are exercised on too-small fronts, [and] that, when they must maneuver in line, the cavalry being ranged on war footing, the squadron chiefs and the regimental commanders will find themselves lost in proportions with which they are not familiar. It will require time, and unfortunately perhaps checks, to form their heads and coup d'œil. This is the same reason that militates so strongly for the cavalry to be maintained in peacetime on almost the same footing as it is in war. Otherwise it would be useless; otherwise we would carry in war only the burden of cavalry maintenance; war would arrive; we would raise new regiments [and] new companies, that is to say that we would place recruits on remounts; and all this *pospolite* would go as it could.[17] Moreover, it would [work] like the enemies'

---

17 [The Dictionary of the Académie Français defines "*pospolite*" as the assembly of the Sejm of the Polish-Lithuanian Commonwealth. The Sejm was a unique institution in contemporary Europe: a national assembly of nobles that elected the monarch of the Commonwealth and often decided other important national issues. The Commonwealth may be said to have been Europe's first modern large democracy, although it served as a cautionary tale for contemporaries, as it proved unable to resist the absorption of the state by neighboring Prussia, Austria, and Russia between 1772 and 1795. See Norman Davies, *God's*

cavalry, which, being neither more maneuvering nor better constituted, would fundamentally have no more merit and would have less of the French impetuosity than ours. Today, everything has changed: the discipline and science of maneuvering have made the cavalry an almost-new arm, a formidable arm, but therefore quite costly. The great powers alone may maintain cavalry. I demand grace for this digression; it is born of my subject, and I let myself go to it, because it is not foreign to it.

I return to Mesnil-Durand. In attaching a company of horse grenadiers to each of his *plésions*, he founds himself on the necessity and on the advantage of intermingling the arms; this was the doctrine of Folard, and he is faithful to it. But Folard was excusable in advancing this opinion more than fifty years ago; it is hardly possible for Mesnil-Durand to revive it today. In the times of Folard, cavalry was still in its infancy; today, it has made immense progress. Mesnil-Durand should have marched with his century. Independently of the example of the ancients, the master and the disciple both support themselves with the authority of some of the great modern captains like Alessandro Farnese, duca di Parma, Castro, e Piacenza; Henri de la Tour d'Auvergne, vicomte de Turenne; [and] Montecuccoli, but these great men were good in their times, and they would act differently in ours.[18] Their genius would seize knowledge acquired since then. What may have been appropriate in a time when cavalry was still partially armed with lances, covered with defensive armor, [and]

charging at the walk and making use of fire surely is not appropriate today. What role would the infantry platoons play now, intermingled with our squadrons and charging with them, as the ancient Gascons did, as Gustav Adolf [and] Henri IV., etc., practiced, as Mesnil-Durand proposes for his horse grenadiers?[19] And the cavalry platoons intermingled in their turn with the battalions or supporting them at a hundred paces of distance! And the orders of battle *en échiquier*, alternatingly intermingling infantry and cavalry brigades in such a manner that the infantry would be behind the cavalry and the cavalry behind the infantry, as Folard teaches![20] It is not a question of *intermingling* the arms today; it is of [their] *supporting* [each other]; these words are not synonyms, and their meanings are quite distinct; it is [a question of] forming each in its place, that is to say in the place that the terrain and the circumstance assigns them; it is, in any case, [a question of] not morseling them out, nor intermingling them, because by their nature, they may almost never make simultaneous efforts. One marches, and the other flies; one has its principal force in fire, and the other only has it by shock; one is essentially defensive, [and] the other may never be and only ever acts offensively.[21]

We pass to the second manner in which Mesnil-Durand proposes to employ cavalry: behind the infantry in such a manner as to support it and be able to debouch by the intervals of its columns. In this second version, Mesnil-Durand would not at all have cavalry on the infantry's wings, because it must be recalled that he posed in principle that an army in his system does not have any flanks and thus it has no need of supporting them. Let us leave this strange principle, which we will return to in its place, and respond only to this second manner of disposing of the cavalry.

Playground: A History of Poland Volume 1: *The Origins to 1795* (New York: Oxford University Press, 2005); and Wladyslaw Roczniak, "The Polish-Lithuanian Commonwealth," Oxford Bibliographies Online (2019), https://www.oxfordbibliographies.com/display/document/obo-9780195399301/obo-9780195399301-0119.xml.]

18 [Alessandro Farnese, duca di Parma, Castro, e Piacenza, was another great captain. He served the Spanish crown in a variety of martial roles, including being present at the Battle of Lepanto in 1571 when a Venetian-Habsburg fleet defeated an Ottoman fleet. He is best known as Governor of the Spanish Netherlands from 1578 to 1592, where he skillfully fought both the Dutch rebels commanded by Maurits of Nassau and the French under Henri III and Henri IV as part of the French Wars of Religion.

Turenne was arguably the greatest general of the seventeenth century and one of six men named Marshal-General of France. He was from an old French noble family and spent his life in military service. He turned against the royal government during the Fronde before returning to royal service and defeating the Frondeurs in several important battles, securing the throne for the young Louis XIV. He commanded armies in the War of Devolution and the Dutch War before being killed at the Battle of Salzbach in 1675, which will figure in Guibert's narrative. He was recognized as a master of maneuver warfare and a great captain. His reputation was such that even the radical Revolutionaries did not destroy his body as they did those of many royals and Old-Regime generals, and he was eventually interred in the Invalides overlooking Napoleon's tomb.]

19 [Henry IV was King of France from around 1590 until his assassination in 1610. He was a leading Protestant commander in the Wars of Religion that consumed France for most of the second half of the sixteenth century. His conversion to Catholicism and his martial prowess brought an end to the conflicts and stability to the kingdom. See David Buisseret, *Henry IV* (London: Allen & Unwin, 1984); Nicolas le Roux, *Les guerres de religion (1559–1629)* (Paris: Bellin, 2009); and Eric Nelson, "Henri IV, King of France," Oxford Bibliographies Online (2021), https://www.oxfordbibliographies.com/display/document/obo-9780195399301/obo-9780195399301-0087.xml.]

20 [See Folard, *Nouvelles découvertes sur la guerre*, 339–388.]

21 [Guibert continues his illustration of the importance of combined arms and at what level the arms were best combined. He castigates Mesnil-Durand and Folard for binding infantry to cavalry and vice-versa, giving both the deficits of both arms without gaining the benefits of either. Instead, he argues that the arms must be combined at higher levels in ways that complement each other, as subsequent passages will reveal.]

Cavalry charges have effect, and grand effect, only by their ensemble and by the unanimity of shock, and this ensemble and this unanimity may exist only by the adherence of the squadrons [to each other]. They procure the victory in making irruption[s] and gap[s] in the enemy order of battle and in separating the parts that compose it. It is because of this that, in the modern cavalry tactics, we have, with reason, established as a principle that charges will always be executed *en muraille*, that is to say without interval[s] between the squadrons.

This posed, what [advantage] will Mesnil-Durand pretend to draw from his cavalry placed behind his columns? Making it charge in passing by the intervals, but these intervals are only fifty-six paces [wide], and they must be even smaller in the parts of his order that Mesnil-Durand destines to attack. Often he must insert his second line into them, and then the intervals will be reduced to around twenty paces. What cavalry will debouch by such gaps! But I suppose even the entire intervals and those that Mesnil-Durand establishes in his primitive order; a squadron would be at pains to debouch by each interval, and what will then become of the debouche of these intervals, this line of squadrons morseled with distances between them almost equal to their frontage! Will it go thus, both full and empty, to attack the enemy? I leave to my readers to appreciate the success of such a charge. Will it halt to re-serry its intervals, or will it work to re-serry them on the march? I again leave to my readers to appreciate this movement.

"But," Mesnil-Durand will say, "my cavalry will only debouch when my columns will have pierced the enemy order of battle, and then it will only be a question of following the fugitives and of completing the victory." Here thus is cavalry condemned by Mesnil-Durand to only ever acting depending on the infantry and [making itself a] subsidiary to it. [It is] thus reduced, according to him, to going to make prisoners and to preventing the rallying of the fugitives. But we see if this small destination will only be possible to accomplish by the manner in which Mesnil-Durand disposes the cavalry.

I would that the columns of Mesnil-Durand have pierced the two lines of enemy infantry; they will find the cavalry reserves and the dragoons supporting them if the disposition is made in conformation with the true principles of modern tactics. Other cavalry corps drawn from the second line of the wings will rapidly carry themselves there. This second line will have had nothing to do, the first having been more than sufficient to act on the flanks and on the rear of the order of battle of Mesnil-Durand. Carrying itself from the interior parts of the two wings to the center of the infantry, where Mesnil-Durand ordinarily makes his attack, will not be a difficult or slow movement for a maneuvering cavalry. What will then become of the cavalry of Mesnil-Durand? The reserve alone well-united, well-serried, charging in the current method, will add to the stampede of squadrons; the corps coming from the wings will arrive at the same time by the flank. If there were a hundred squadrons, the disorder and the confusion will be even greater, because once the disorder begins, it always grows in proportion to numbers. The means of repassing by the intervals that will become the defiles! The enemy will push, will press, and will finish by knocking out all the cavalry in all these unfortunate columns and by beating all of them pell-mell and one after the other. We have seen at Vaussieux this test of cavalry passing by the intervals of the columns to charge the enemy, and there was no one in the army who did not tremble in seeing the danger of this movement.

We will terminate this examination of the second disposition of Mesnil-Durand with a single reflection: in the case in which one wishes the arms to support each other, one must never lose sight of the advantages and the inconveniences that result for each of them as well as the ultimate consequences of the disposition that one takes. Thus, one must never place the cavalry in the case of charging in advance of the infantry, because, if it is beaten, the infantry courts the risk of being swept away by it. In our current tactics, we do not miss this principle when we support a line of infantry with a line of cavalry because, if the infantry is beaten, and the cavalry advances to charge the enemy, the gap is fortunately always large enough to allow it all the liberty to act and to charge in its habitual order. If the infantry is beaten and one wishes to pursue the enemy with cavalry, then the infantry forms itself in column by battalions or by regiments, leaving to the cavalry intervals large enough for it to liberally debouch and to pass in the case of a check. We add to this that our infantry, having always for [a] principle to preserve intervals equal to its frontage when it forms itself in column, may form parts of the line at need, whether on its front or on its flank, to protect the retreat of the cavalry with its fire in its turn.

The third and last version of Mesnil-Durand on the manner of employing cavalry appears to us to be more fortunate than the two preceding. He pretended to respond to the objection that was made on the isolation and the nudity of its flanks by it. But at the same time that he feebly remedied it, here are other great inconveniences into which he has fallen.

In taking his cavalry three-hundred paces behind the flank of his line of infantry, Mesnil-Durand first pretends that it well covers the flank of this infantry, because one would not be able to attack it without readying one's own cavalry. He then has for his objective, he says, to hold it outside the range of fire and consequently more in reserve, more fresh, and more in a state of acting. It would have been simpler to return in good faith to conventional wisdom. But when one has made a system, there is a cost to be paid when one approaches what one has blamed and what one wished to destroy. One wishes to palliate this return, and one well prefers to fall into the extraordinary rather than to not propose changes.

War may have positions and circumstances in which it is advantageous to place oneself behind the point that one wishes to defend. Thus, for example, it perhaps better merits defending entrenchments, a river, [or] an advantageous height to be within range of falling on the enemy as soon as they will have penetrated rather than along the obstacle itself. Thus, in applying this principle to tactics, hooks on the wings [and] bodies between the lines and behind the flanks are perhaps good to protect them and to cover them. Caesar gave an example of it at Pharsalus, and several tacticians have, with reason, proposed them since as excellent resources to employ when one is inferior in number and superior in maneuvers. I said in the *General Essay on Tactics* that I believed above all [that] these [are] excellent means to employ on the points of the cavalry wings because the advantage in all cavalry fight[s] must necessarily rest with those that would gain the enemy flank last and that would have the last fresh troop to make move.[22] But employing this principle indifferently to everything, and making it, as Mesnil-Durand does, the base of his habitual order, is to be strangely mistaken. We examine what would result from it.

I would [that] Mesnil-Durand [be], despite the opinion that he established in his system, equal in cavalry to his enemy, as this would not leave him the resource of saying that he was attacked with unequal arms. Both thus have one-hundred squadrons; Mesnil-Durand will place twenty-five on a single line behind and on the flank of each of his infantry wings, and the fifty others behind his infantry to support it and to attack by the intervals of his columns at need. The enemy, conducting itself according to modern principles, will place forty squadrons on each of their wings and twenty in reserve behind the center of their infantry. These forty squadrons of the wings will be on two lines, the first of thirty squadrons without intervals and the second in two corps or reserves of five squadrons formed equally *en muraille* and placed one behind the center of the fifteen squadrons of the right and the other behind that of the fifteen squadrons of the left, all ten united behind the center of the wing, all ten behind the point of the wing to support it and assure the defeat of the enemy cavalry, or finally all ten behind the interior extremity of the wing if one wishes to hold them within range of falling on the flank of the enemy infantry after the defeat of their cavalry. As one sees, the circumstances and the objective determine this disposition, which is susceptible to many varieties and combinations.

I will direct the movement of the enemy right wing against the left wing of Mesnil-Durand in supposing the first enemy line ranged as I have said and the ten squadrons of their second line behind the left flank of their wing; the objective that I give to them on this occasion is to attack the cavalry of Mesnil-Durand [and] then to embrace his rear and his flanks. I will detail only the movements of a single wing, the other having what the position and circumstances will indicate to it on its side.

I suppose here the two respective wings opposite each other while Mesnil-Durand's infantry shakes itself out to march on mine. Immediately after I will begin moving, I will decide to charge the wing that is before me. His line is twenty-five squadrons; mine is thirty. I consequently outflank him by five squadrons that I of course will not unmask until the moment of my movement, holding them until then in columns behind the point of my wing. I have a second line, and he does not. All the probabilities are thus for me. His line reversed, I will follow him by the middle of mine, and I will then fall back with the fifteen squadrons that remain and the ten squadrons of my second line on his columns, on his cavalry that supports them, or even on both at the same time, my ten squadrons of the second line charging the flank of his infantry and my fifteen squadrons at the same time taking his cavalry in the flank which, morseled [and] separated by intervals, will be much at pains to make face. What will thus become of his columns? Will they arrest themselves to receive me and to make face on the flanks? Then they will no longer march on my infantry; they rest in range of my artillery. This order, mobile and offensive par excellence, will become stagnant and defensive. If they will continue to march, I will have a great game of charging them, because what composes this uncovered flank? One or two columns at most. Now suppose the cavalry of my other wing acts with an equal success because it has the same superiority; suppose it only occupies the cavalry that is opposite it, and it prevents them from leaving. We remember that, while I act thus offensively and victoriously on the wings while I put to flight or hold all the enemy cavalry in check, I have behind my infantry center a reserve of twenty squadrons, not morseled, not obliged to debouch by intervals barely equal to their frontage, like those that Mesnil-Durand has behind his, but [rather] contiguous and able to debouch on whatever front they will judge appropriate, because

---

22   [Abel, *Guibert's General Essay on Tactics*, 135–136.]

my lines will ploy themselves to let them go to their place, and then, deploying themselves, they will always re-find their own. I could push these hypotheses further; I could, in exhausting all the probable consequences, demonstrate how the false and poor use that Mesnil-Durand makes of cavalry may cause the dishonor and the ruin of an army in a moment. But hypotheses, whatever degree of probability and evidence that they have, are a genre [that is] vague and empty for good spirits, and when one has proffered them, it is better to abandon them to themselves.

What perhaps is not apparent to Mesnil-Durand, and what is the greatest vice, the primitive vice in every part of his system with regard to cavalry, is that it is absolutely contrary to the nature and the propriety of this arm, which is to be active and offensive. Thus attaching cavalry to infantry, intermingling it with it, binding it to its movements, [and] even ranging it behind it and in its support when it may only carry itself forward by the intervals that oblige it to tear itself and almost to defile, are to remove from the cavalry the liberty of terrain, of movement, and of action that are essentially necessary to it. Placing it three-hundred paces behind the wings in lieu of placing it at the height of the infantry is to also assign it a defensive destination contrary to its objective; it is to distance it from the enemy that it must charge; it is to augment "its career," that is to say its charging movement, by three-hundred paces; finally, it is to deprive it of the support of the infantry if it is beaten, because, in the current system, it is in advance of the order of battle that it engages the fight, since it goes in front of the enemy, and it is on the flank of the line that it returns to search for protection and rallying if it is beaten. It finds this protection in the fire of the flank brigades that are formed *en potence* on the flank of the order of battle [and] in the fire of the large artillery with which these brigades must be reinforced, and it would certainly not find the same on the flanks of Mesnil-Durand's order of battle, which is only composed of one or two battalions in column at most.

In thus placing his cavalry three-hundred paces behind the rest of his order of battle, Mesnil-Durand alleges that he draws it outside the range of enemy fire and consequently [leaves it] more fresh and more in a state of acting, but it is truly a question of forming it outside the range of enemy cavalry on the wings. It is it that must engage the fight; it is it that must swoop down on the enemy as soon as the general disposition of the army is formed. Let him thus reflect that it is truly the enemy cavalry that he has before him, and it is thus not musketry fire [that he has] to fear, [and] that, with regard to that [fire] of the cannon, if it is within range of it to the height of the infantry, it will not be in retreating a hundred *toises* that he will be sheltered from it,

but let him reflect above all that it [cavalry] is for attacking and not for resting *en panne*. A single circumstance may oblige the cavalry to form itself thus behind the rest of the order of battle: this would be when it would have infantry before it and when it would wish neither to attack it nor, of course, to submit to its fire. But, in this case, what cavalry has ever believed itself chained to the infantry alignment, and what need does one have to give to a precept to avoid that which may harm without purpose?

It must ceaselessly be repeated [that] the great default of cabinet tactics is to always go after ideal suppositions. One sees on paper, in the primitive orders of battle of modern tactics, that the infantry is at the center and the cavalry on the wings. From this, one believes to have found a sore spot, to have discovered the source of all lost battles; one heats oneself up, one blinds oneself, one writes, [and] one overturns [the system]. Eh! Messieurs, against what do you animate yourselves? You make war on an abuse that does not exist. You attack this order, [and] you find it feeble, dangerous, [and] absurd, but this order is nothing; it is only the primitive disposition, and, if I may express myself thus, the disposition of waiting and organization. Leave paper; it is, yet again, only the tableau of the army that fills the gazettes, that is affixed to the doors of the headquarters, [and] that is sent to the court the day that one enters into the campaign. Transport yourself to the terrain, follow real orders of battle, and you will see that, at the first movements, this primitive order extinguishes itself [and] that one encamps, one marches, [and] one fights relative to the terrain and to circumstances. You will never again see cavalry irrevocably fixed to the wings, wings of equal strength and always on two lines of the same proportion; you will see that all this changes, varies, combines, [and] modifies itself according to places and cases.

In one place, the cavalry will all be in the center, as Marshal Broglie placed it at Bergen, because the center of his position was an uncovered countryside, and his right and his left were posts into which he had thrown his infantry. It will all (if the terrain permits) be in the shelter of a height, as he then placed them on this great day, because it is both useless to expose troops who are outside the range of acting and to [allow] the enemy to count them so as to consequently regulate their disposition.

In another place, one will have them only on a single wing, because there is no position other than a part of the plain, and this plain finds itself on one of the wings, or one will considerably reinforce a wing, because it is by it that one wishes to act, and one will refuse the other wing in supporting it with posted infantry, with much artillery, or on some obstacle, whether natural or artificial, that hinders the enemy from attacking them.

On another occasion, the combat's being reduced by the nature of the terrain to an attack of several posts and the cavalry's not being able to act on a great front or being able to act only as a subsidiary to the infantry and only after the posts will be carried, one will form them all behind the infantry, or one will divide them into several corps destined to follow the operations of the several infantry corps charged with points of attack.

I will abridge these examples. This is enough to enlighten those who wish to be and too much for those who have decided to refuse the evidence. It will be objected to me that these changes, these modifications to the primitive order almost never take place and that I have made gratuitous suppositions here. I have proven that [this is not the case]. I have cited what Marshal Broglie did at Bergen, and I would have been able to cite what he did on ten other occasions. At Sandershausen, his cavalry was at the center, and, this cavalry having been pushed back, it was an infantry regiment *in deployed order* that covered its retreat and that arrested the enemy cavalry. This regiment did nothing but form itself *en potence* and fire a timely volley. I would be able to cite the King of Prussia [and] Prince Heinrich, and I would only have to recapitulate all the actions of war that they commanded. I would be able to cite the Austrian generals, now his emulators after having been his students. When I make the apology for modern tactics, it is [for] modern tactics well employed and not [as] abandoned to the routine of mediocre generals.

It only remains for me to speak of a great advantage that the adoption of the system of Mesnil-Durand would lose the two arms: it is the analogy that exists today between their tactics, [a] quite-useful analogy established in the Cavalry Maneuver Ordinance of 1776, [an] analogy from which one may draw the greatest fruit, [but an analogy] that may yet be perfected, that may dissipate the absolute ignorance [that] the officers of one arm were too often in on the resources and on the maneuvers of the other, [and] that finally, in forming true general officers, will render to this grade all the extent of its functions, since the name "general officer" supposes knowledge of all the arms; a general officer must know how to command indifferently, as much separated as united.[23]

I will terminate this chapter in inviting cavalry officers to relieve my errors or my omissions. It is a matter of their cause, and there are many more among them in a state to defend it than I.

---

23 [*Ordonnance du roi concernant la cavalerie* (1776), in *Recueil des nouvelles ordonnances du roi relatives à la constitution actuelle de l'état militaire*, 5 Vols. (Collignon: Metz, 1776–1777), I:162–181.]

CHAPTER 5

Examination of the System of Mesnil-Durand Relative to Artillery

Of all the tacticians who have spoken on artillery in their works, I am the one whom Mesnil-Durand must suspect the least of prejudice and partiality.

I elevated in my *General Essay on Tactics* against the *militaires* who attribute too great a preponderance to its effects. I reduced to its just value the assertion hazarded in some works written by artillery officers that "artillery [is] the soul of armies," [an] expression that we may in effect regard as a pardonable expression of esprit de corps and love of the art that [they] cultivate. I advanced that artillery was not, properly speaking, even an arm, and that it must be regarded only as an accessory, the name "arm" belonging only to infantry and cavalry when one wishes to speak with precision, because it is these corps that are essentially and necessarily the constituent parts of an army, and because an army does exist without them.[1]

Above all, I elevated myself with force against the abuse of the prodigious multiplication of artillery, [an] abuse that we draw from foreign armies, which the example of the King of Prussia has unfortunately consecrated and that may only be reformed by another man of genius supported by as many victories, [a] phenomenon that may perhaps be at pains to reproduce itself for several centuries.[2]

But this is far, and quite far, from saying as Mesnil-Durand [does] that artillery is not redoubtable [and] that it [has] an effect so uncertain in its execution that one may regard it as almost null, provided one determines oneself to march on it.

This is [also] far from taking no account of it in the reasons that must influence the determination of a system of tactics and to then throw oneself into a thousand calculations (I will not say in bad faith, but in prejudice and prestige) to justify one's opinion.

I will not at all engage myself here in reviewing all that Mesnil-Durand wrote [to try] to prove that all the objections that were made to his system relative to artillery are without foundation. This produced, during the first proofs made of the system at Metz three years ago, a quite-lively polemic between him and the late Philippe-Charles-Jean-Baptiste Tronson du Coudray. Nothing more assuredly better proves to what [degree] the spirit of system on one hand and the esprit de corps and profession on the other hand may mislead than this polemic.[3]

According to Mesnil-Durand, columns have less to fear from artillery fire than deployed columns. Half of the rounds must pass through the intervals. A ball may not kill more than three or four men in a file. Oblique and ricocheted rounds do not have a great effect. Finally, his columns are for artillery "what a hare is for a hunter" (these are his expressions).[4] They are always in movement; they go so quickly, so quickly! Quite quickly indeed, as he pretends that their speed must be three times that of battalions marching in line, and then [comes] his curtain wall of grenadiers and chasseurs that covers them, that prevents enemy cannoneers from perceiving them, that itself fires at these cannoneers and destroys them or thins them so much so that the last rounds that may have been the most redoubtable hardly take place: all bristling with calculations of ranges, of times, of distances; all denied by reason, by theory, and by practice.

---

1 [Abel, *Guibert's General Essay on Tactics*, 151–170. An anonymous essay entitled "Lettre d'un officier-général d'artillerie aux auteurs de ce journal au sujet d'un livre nouveau en deux volumes qui à pour titre *Défense du système de la guerre moderne ou réfutation complette du système de Mesnil-Durand* par l'auteur de l'*Essai général de tactique*," *Journal encyclopédique ou universel* 4 (1779): 300–306, argues that Guibert references *Essai sur l'usage de l'artillerie dans la guerre de campagne et dans celle des sièges* (Amsterdam: Arckstée et Merkus, 1771), probably written by Edmé-Jean-Antoine du Puget d'Orval, who served with Guibert in Corsica; see https://recherche-anom.culture.gouv.fr/ark:/61561/tu245pjimqx. Paul-Gédéon Joly de Maïzeroy, *Mémoire sur les opinions qui partagent les militaires* (Paris: Jombert, 1773), 122–126, provides an analysis of Puget's work in a similar vein to Guibert's, perhaps influenced by his.]

2 [As R.R. Palmer, "Frederick, Guibert, Bülow: From Dynastic to National War," *Makers of Modern Strategy from Machiavelli to the Nuclear Age*, ed. Peter Paret (Princeton: Princeton University Press, 1986), 91–122, notes, Guibert was both blinkered towards and incorrect about artillery, both in his own time and in future wars.]

3 [Philippe-Charles-Jean-Baptiste Tronson du Coudray was an artillery officer descended from a family of officers and public servants. He was a member of the household of Charles-Philippe, comte d'Artois, future King Charles X, and a client of Jean-Baptiste Vaquette de Gribeauval, the most important artillerist of the period. As Guibert intimates, Coudray engaged in a pamphlet war after the 1776 Metz exercises, including *L'ordre profonde et l'ordre mince considérés par rapport aux effets de l'artillerie: réponse de l'auteur de l'*Artillerie nouvelle *à Mesnil-Durand et Maïzeroy* (Paris: Rualt et Esprit, 1776). He also wrote on the science of mining and was elected a correspondent to the Académie des Sciences. He died an early death, as Guibert intimates, in Philadelphia as one of the first French officers to serve in the American War of Independence.]

4 [Mesnil-Durand, *Fragments de tactique*, 28.]

Le Coudray defended a good cause; he had only to hold to responding to Mesnil-Durand without exaggeration and without prejudice, as he had said in the commencement of his refutation, opposing him with simple and solid reasoning and supporting it with results on the ranges and on the execution of artillery, as we have always done under the eyes of the schools.[5] But he soon heated himself, he engaged in following Mesnil-Durand in his hypotheses [and] in his suppositions; he opposed batteries to columns, [and] he calculated lines of direction, paces, minutes, [and] the dead [and] the wounded. According to Mesnil-Durand, his columns would arrive healthy and safe; according to le Coudray, they were annihilated before arriving. [These are] jokes that I leave to my readers to appreciate the genre and the taste [that] brought this strange polemic to its apex. In one, Mesnil-Durand takes up the [math] underpinning le Coudray's calculations [and] proved that he had not drawn all he was able to from them and that, by following them with rigor, he killed a hundred more men than composed his column.

As for me, when one disputes, as it is always to the truth that must be reached [and] as nothing is more vague than the manner of reasoning by supposition and by hypothesis, I will bound myself here to the principles and the simple facts and evidence whose consequences I will not at all exaggerate so that, in the end, I do not at all fear that any educated *militaire*, and above all [any] practitioner, will be able to disavow them.

I know, as Mesnil-Durand does, that artillery, machines, agents, powder, projectiles, [and] milieu, all, in a word, contribute to rendering gun ranges uncertain, whether in their aim or in their range; that, when one aims a cannon at an isolated object that presents [a small] surface, it must fire perhaps ten, perhaps one-hundred rounds before touching this object, even at point-blank [range]; that, if one waits, the following blow, fired at the same angle, by the same cannoneers, with the same charge, [and] with the same quantity of powder, departs more or less sensibly from the same target; [and] that, consequently, the cannon, considered in its individual effect and pointed at an isolated target, is a little-redoubtable machine.

But this is not at all how artillery should be considered in fights. There, it acts at large and consequently with less uncertainty. There, it is no longer a question of isolated and individual points. It acts on lines or on the mass of troops; it acts to beat spaces [and] debouches. There, if one knows how to employ artillery, one forms large batteries; one takes prolongs and reverses; one makes use of the ricochet; one attaches oneself uniquely to carrying one's projectiles into the vertical plan of the enemy ordinance; finally, one accomplishes not the small objective of demonstrating a cannon or killing some men on a given point, but the great objective, the decisive objective, which must be to cover, to traverse with fire the terrain that the enemy occupies, and, above all, that [terrain] by which they would wish to advance themselves to attack. Thus placed, thus executed, artillery is certainly formidable.

I know that the outré partisans of artillery much exaggerate its range when they suppose that it acts in a decisive manner at six- or seven-hundred *toises*. But Mesnil-Durand does not exaggerate less in the opposite [way] when he does not believe it to be murderous at two- or three-hundred *toises*.

Between these two versions, both extremes, there is a true middle, and I give it in the following table. This middle is conformed to the constant results of all the proofs, even in admitting that the shortening of pieces in the new system has diminished their ranges, since these proofs were made with pieces of the new dimension.[6]

I do not at all exaggerate the effects of cannon on corps of troops ranged on a great depth. I thus do not think that a ball traverses a column from one extremity to the other, that is to say that it kills everyone that it encounters without slowing or stopping, but I do not believe either, as Mesnil-Durand does, that a ball kills or cripples three or four men at most. I have seen some hit as many as eight or nine men, and officers who I believe as much as

---

5 [Professional military education, as it would be termed today, was a relatively new and highly contentious subject in eighteenth-century France. Artillery schools first appeared in the late seventeenth century, most notably at Douai, and a school for the *génie* (engineers) was established at Mézières in the 1740s. More general education for officers was a subject of intense debate throughout the period of Guibert's life. The *Ecole Royale Militaire* was established to educate future officers in the early 1750s but dis-established in favor of a series of regional schools by Saint-Germain in the 1770s, likely with Guibert's approval and participation. Haroldo Guízar, *The Ecole Royale Militaire: Noble Education, Institutional Innovation, and Royal Charity, 1750–1788* (New York: Palgrave, 2020), provides an excellent overview. See also Rafe Blaufarb, *The French Army 1750–1820: Careers, Talent, Merit* (Manchester: Manchester University Press, 2002), 12–45; and Jay Smith, *The Culture of Merit: Nobility, Royal Service, and the Making of Absolute Monarchy in France, 1600–1789* (Ann Arbor: University of Michigan Press, 1996), 191–262.]

6 [Guibert refers to the Gribeauval System, which lightened and shortened the artillery of the previous Vallière System to make it more mobile and thus more useful in mobile warfare. Proponents of the siege-type weapons of the Vallière System were not convinced that lighter guns would be powerful enough, which is why the debate was not fully settled until the 1770s and 1780s. See Kevin Kiley, *Artillery of the Napoleonic Wars 1792–1815* (Mechanicsburg, PA: Stackpole Books, 2004), 25–121; and Bruce McConnachy, "The roots of Artillery Doctrine: Napoleonic Artillery Tactics Reconsidered," *The Journal of Military History* 65, no. 3 (2002): 614–640.]

TABLE 1   Estimative table on the distances over which one may commence counting on the effects of field artillery

Caliber of pieces	Distance of ball	Distances for pieces loaded with cartridge	
		Large balls	Small balls
	Toises	*Toises*	*Toises*
16	500–550	400–450	To 300
12	450–500	350–400	To 250
8	400–450	250–350	To 200
4	350–400	150–250	To 150

Note: One may certainly make use of cannon at more-considerable ranges, since a 16 pointed at fifteen degrees carries to around 1,200 *toises*, and a 12 of the new model carries to 800 *toises* at an angle of six degrees, but beyond the limits indicated by the second columns of this table, one may count on a decisive effect only by compensating for the irregularities of the greatest ranges with a great number of pieces.

I believe myself have seen more murderous blows. Above all, I believe in the terrible effect that cartridge has on a column, and I think that, if the artillery is numerous, well-placed, [and] well-served, and that the cannoneers do not abandon their pieces until the last extremity, the last discharges being the most decisive, it is quite likely that the column will not arrive on them, or at least it will arrive so thinned and so strongly disordered that the enemy troops that support it will have a good time repulsing them and thus charging them with advantage.

As to the rest, artillery must not be considered only relative to the real ill that it can do. It acts on morale; it unsettles imaginations by its sound, by its damage, [and] by the horror of the wounds [it causes]; this effect also wants to be calculated, since in war, to vanquish is as much a question of frightening as it is of killing. This is what Voltaire so fortunately expressed in his *History of Karl XII*, because [his] spirit is good for everything, and it makes one divine what one has not seen when it says that "it is not so much the number of dead that wins battles as it is the fear that one makes in the living."[7]

This effect will certainly be sensed more in a column than in a deployed battalion, because the rounds that carry into the column will do more ill; because, making more ill, they make more impression on spirits; [and] because, the column assembling a great quantity of men in a very small space, these impressions of terror and disorder are more communicative there and [thus] more dangerous. In a deployed battalion, on the contrary, the rounds that fall there are less murderous, and they consequently act less on the spirit of soldiers. Each individual sees only the files that neighbor him; those that arrive some paces more distant are ignored by him. Thus, if some impression of horror or tumult is elevated within [the battalion], as it [the impression] only takes place on a point, it communicates itself with more difficulty and may perhaps be contained more easily by discipline. It has been said elsewhere how, in this last regard, the organization of the deployed battalion, above all with the current disposition of officers and *bas-officiers*, part embedded in the ranks [and] part dispersed on the wings of the platoons, in serrying the files, in supervising, if I may express myself thus, the soldiers, is more advantageous and more sure than the organization of a column, whatever it may be, and particularly the column of Mesnil-Durand. But it does not suffice to examine the effects of artillery on the column in itself, or on a single column; what they would produce on the ensemble of the habitual disposition of Mesnil-Durand must be seen, that is to say on his line of columns substituted for a line of deployed battalions.

One recalls that his columns must only commonly have half the distance of a deployed battalion between them [and] that, above all, to attack the enemy and consequently in the parts of his order of battle destined to accomplish this goal, these intervals must further diminish. Suppose the enemy posted to receive them: this enemy will likely not have missed to place its artillery in advantageous points in advance, and principally on the wings of their position. They will above all search to place it in such a manner that it can cross its fire and take reverses on [their opponent]. The attacked ordinarily having chosen the position that they occupy, it is always apparent that they may procure themselves this advantage.

The columns of Mesnil-Durand, following their usage, take no account of positions; they do not waste time in

---

7   [Voltaire, *History of Charles XII, King of Sweden* (Edinburgh: Black, 1887), 55.]

maneuvering on flanks, in turning, [or] in working to extinguish the fire of the salients of the enemy position by a superior artillery or by more-skillful posting: small, good means in modern tactics but disdained in an order where one has need only of marching to vanquish. They thus advance audaciously. But, as in war, whatever Mesnil-Durand says, it does not suffice to always march on the enemy, here is what will arrive on them.

Far from fire and in the tranquil peacetime maneuvers at the Camp of Vaussieux, we saw how it was difficult for a line of columns to march *en bataille* in observing their intervals. Almost all movements were failed by this fault. At each instant, it was forced to stop itself to realign itself, reconnect itself, and regain its distances by flank maneuvers. Mesnil-Durand always speaks of commanding his columns at the run, but all the army will attest with me that never has a line of deployed battalions marched with this slowness and this maladdress. Thus in war, and in the attack that I suppose, the enemy artillery will beat the front and the flank. [The] mechanical movement, the almost irresistible tendency of a troop heated by its flanks, is to press on its intervals, as much to distance itself from the fire that beats it as in the false idea of finding support in approaching the troops that neighbor it. These intervals, already so difficult to observe, will thus close themselves more and more. The line of columns will diminish its frontage in proportion to [the degree to which] they close themselves, and consequently, these columns will be beaten and taken in the reverse by a quite-great quantity of artillery; from this [results] new closing of the intervals, and by this closing, new enemy batteries embrace the flanks in such a way that the infallible result of these effects will be, if they may [even] arrive on the enemy, arriving there composed only of a mass of columns, an unformed mass incapable of maneuvering in case of a first advantage and, in case of poor success, susceptible to being enveloped and destroyed.

This is not at all the place to speak of the movements of troops that the enemy may oppose to a similar attack disposition. I will treat them in examining the system of Mesnil-Durand relative to orders of battle and to combat action. I have only for my objective in this chapter to consider his system relative to the effects of artillery.

My readers may believe that I have gratuitously supposed a disposition for the artillery in the manner most favorable to my refutation above. But I call on all those who saw the maneuvers at the Camp of Vaussieux. This dangerous disposition was repeated every time that attacks were figured there. One day, we saw thirty-two battalions marching on two lines of columns to go to attack the enemy posted on an advantageous height and garnished with artillery on a front that did not have four-hundred *toises* of development and that was flanked by two villages.[8] The gap where the thirty-two battalions engaged themselves to march to this attack imperceptibly narrowed in mounting a glacis towards the position that the enemy occupied. They were beaten in front and on the reverse. They had no woods, hedges, or undulations of terrain that favored them. They did not at all have an opposing height from which they could, not extinguish, but only balance the fire of the enemy artillery; all [the artillery] that could have opposed them would have to have fired from the base of the height against troops that were covered up to the belly behind a species of dike that ran along the height. The majority of columns that had fifty-six paces of interval between them in taking their primitive disposition did not have twenty-five [paces] by [the] halfway [mark]. A part of those of the left was even obliged to double on several lines because of a narrowing of the terrain [that was] more evident in this part. Not a single cannon shot would have been uncertain against such a disposition. Reverse and oblique rounds would have traversed the columns in every sense, and the second line would have been the drain for all the rounds that would have crushed the first. With this, as there were no balls, as these thirty-two battalions represented the army, and it was said that the army must beat the corps that was before it, they always marched, and they reached the summit of the position.

See now by what means Mesnil-Durand pretends to not take account of artillery fire or to balance its effect. I have responded with a fact of experience to the pretention that he had of commanding his columns at the run. I will support this fact with reasons and raise here a strange error of Mesnil-Durand's.

Mesnil-Durand speaks on all occasions of marching rapidly, of doubling, [and] of tripling the pace, in a word, of running. If he wishes to make some movement with his columns, it is as at least at the maneuver pace that he shakes them. If it is in march order, and if [in it] would be doublings, re-doublings, [or] passages of defiles, it is again at the maneuver step that he joins the portions of the troops resting behind. If he must attack, it is at the maneuver step that he puts them in movement; it is then at the run when he is within a hundred or a hundred and fifty *toises* of the enemy. His grenadiers and chasseurs have no other speed, and they will again be at pains to arrive on what is required of them, but in war, it is not at all thus

---

8 See, on the map of the environs of the camp that is added to this work, the punctuated position between the villages of Rucqueville and Martragny. [See Appendix A, 177.]

that one handles infantry, because in war, the infantry is laden with equipment, and it is not like it is on garrison esplanades or in peacetime camps. In war, when the infantry is marching or moving, one does not know what the circumstances may require of them, or even the day or the next day, and one must consequently be frugal with one's forces. In war, the infantry thus marches at a pace [that is] moderate, equal, and that it may sustain for several hours. When one is in march order, one must not at all place the parts of the troops that doublings, re-doublings, [or] passages of defiles or obstacles have left behind at the maneuver step; one must relent the pace [in order to] not lose time in giving those that are lost the possibility of rejoining. But never, [or] at least [only] in extremely rare cases, must any troop double the free and natural step that it must take in forming in march order. If one maneuvers it, as all the maneuvers of an army are only ever marches, one must observe the same principle.[9] If one attacks with it, one must also march at an equal and moderate step, because it is only with this step that one preserves order. One may form oneself at the maneuver step at most one-hundred or one-hundred and fifty paces before one arrives on the enemy. The pace accelerates itself thus by degrees in such a manner that the run or elan is only reached at the last term of the movement. There is nothing on this to prescribe. All depends on the head, on the coup-d'œil, [and] on the example of the man who commands [it] and the moral impulsion that he knows how to give to those who follow him. I have raised elsewhere the inconvenience of always placing the unfortunate grenadiers and chasseurs at the run, but above all the grenadiers, [the] troop [that is] elite and of constancy, whose true employment is to make [a] corps with the battalion and to always serve in support of it.

I know that, if one must believe the partisans of antiquity, the Roman legionaries marched and even ran several *stades* laden like camels, but, whether that which comes from so far away is always aggrandized by tradition, the human species has degenerated, or education and habit have missed us in this regard, I know that we cannot require the same efforts of current infantry, and, while we wait to have the century and the race re-founded, we must conduct our soldiers according to their strengths.[10] What I know is that, the ancients being, by the nature of their arms, in the case of fighting [in] quite-close [quarters] and on quite-short and quite-narrow battlefields, it was also facile for them to go to the enemy and to maneuver at the run, [and], for opposite reasons drawn from the nature of our arms, this is impossible for us today.

We thus reject as illusory the means of rapidity by which Mesnil-Durand pretends to endure artillery fire for so little time and so little murderously, and see in his columns, in lieu of "mobile, light, [and] impalpable points" (as he represented them in his enthusiasm) masses, on the contrary, slower and heaver than our deployed battalions, more susceptible to disorder, and certainly more of a prize, in every sense, for artillery fire.

We pass to the second means of Mesnil-Durand against enemy fire, to the curtain that he throws in advance of his columns. I have already analyzed the composition of this strange curtain. Reduced to single companies of chasseurs, as it was forced to be at the Camp of Vaussieux, it is not even (if one wishes to take the pain of counting the front of the columns and their intervals) a contiguous line of fusiliers on a single rank; it is scattered and sparse tirailleurs, but, if one would even join the grenadiers to it, this curtain would only ever be a poor response that he tried to make to the powerful objections that were formed on the disadvantage of marching on the enemy without making fire, a supplement that he imagined since he re-founded his system of *plésions*, [as] he saw himself forced to abandon the pretention that columns were proper to fire action; [and] finally, a dangerous front line that only palliates the vice of his order and procures him no advantage. We examine it below relative to artillery.

Mesnil-Durand believes by his curtain to have shielded the march and the direction of his columns from the enemy artillery, or at least rendered it so confused that it will aim at them with uncertainty. The proofs of Vaussieux were not necessary to judge the insufficiency of these means. A sparse line of tirailleurs on one or two ranks at most covering the columns that march two-hundred paces behind it! This is a little like if someone pretended to hide their corps behind their hand; it is to not have reflected on the first notions taught by the perspective and habit of seeing troops.

The second part that Mesnil-Durand counts on drawing from his curtain is, in some regards, a little more real. It is to disquiet the enemy cannoneers with a little musketry fire, but this idea does not at all belong to Mesnil-Durand; it was known before him; it was written everywhere; I indicated it, or to better say, I recalled it (as one "indicates" only that which is new) in my *General Essay on Tactics* in the chapter on the attack in column. There, I threw scattered companies of chasseurs in advance of the march of the columns with instructions to profit from all the

---

9 [Guibert continues to develop an idea he first articulated in Abel, *Guibert's General Essay on Tactics*, particularly 172–197.]

10 [The Dictionary of the Académie Française defines a *stade*, or stadion, as "one-hundred twenty-five geometric paces," which would be around one-hundred fifty yards.]

advantages of the terrain to approach the enemy batteries and to attach themselves to inconveniencing the cannoneers.[11] To inconvenience them is in fact all that one may expect from such means, as to silence them, as Mesnil-Durand pretends [to do], is to exaggerate and to lose sight of what can be done in war; in effect, if the enemy is not deprived of the first military notions, when they will see these tirailleurs, they will throw other tirailleurs that respond to his and to oblige them to wait for the immediate support of their columns in advance of their position and on the flanks of their batteries, so as not to interfere with their execution. The enemy is supposed to be on the defensive and consequently posted, and thus it is apparent that the terrain or the precautions they will take give their side these small advantages more so than the attacker's side.

A third means against enemy artillery remains in the system of Mesnil-Durand: employing its own, as it must come to that, and despite all the clichés about valor, audacity, [and] the genius of the nation, when the enemy kills you at 500 *toises* and during the entire time that you travel the distance to them, the best part that one may take is to work to return it [the favor] to them.

This did not apparently enter into the first ideas of Mesnil-Durand, as, in his *Treatise on* Plésions, it was only ever a question of being contemptuous of and taking artillery. In none of his dispositions, in none of the diagrams that represent them does one at all see him make use of it. The universal complaint[s], the power of objections, or perhaps only his condescension to our prejudices has him approach our century a little in his later works.[12]

The French Order thus admits artillery; Mesnil-Durand intermingles it with his columns and wishes to protect their march by it; he goes further, as in his *Fragments*,[13] he appears to wish to bring the opinions on the artillery corps back to his system. He justifies himself in the contempt that had been attributed to him on it. He promises it that the French Order will value it more than Prussian tactics. He promises it that this order will furnish it "more ease, more liberty, [and] more terrain." Finally, he proposes it "a good peace, a durable alliance, the two parties conjointly reserving to each other to make the thin order and the enemies of France pay the costs of the trial."[14]

From this cordial return of Mesnil-Durand to artillery, I only have one point to examine. Does his system procure "more ease, liberty, terrain, and advantages" for the artillery? This question will be easily resolved.

Artillery only makes its greatest effect when it is posted. The fire that it makes in marching or in changing position at each instant is always little assured and little redoubtable. It is in this first that modern tactics is quite favorable to artillery, and artillery, for its part, seconds them well. In effect, as we will expose in greater length in treating the manner that must be used today to engage it in and to command it in fights in the chapter on battles,[15] one does not brusquely attack a post when it is advantageous and defended by a numerous artillery; one searches to embrace it, to turn it, to extend the fire of the parts that flank it, [and] to fatigue the troops that defend it by a murderous fire; this requires preliminaries during which the artillery acts posted and necessarily plays a great role. Then, when the moment of the attack is determined by the advantages that one has procured oneself, the artillery acts posted to support the troops that undertake it. Finally, battles and fights, seeing the discipline and the progress of the art, wish to be considered today not as irruptions into which one must always walk, attacking the enemy head lowered and without relenting, but as a succession of de-postings and of dispositions. If one chases the enemy from a position, one must, if the enemy is not absolutely routed, commence to establish oneself there by supporting one's flanks and then by working from there to combine a new attack disposition. Thus, from position to position, from parallel to parallel (if I may express myself thus), one advances on the battlefield to the enemy, and one drives them from it. Artillery, consequently, must second these movements and also pass from position to position, which necessarily makes it always act posted.

Following the system of Mesnil-Durand, one appears to need to fight in a completely different manner: it is always a question of marching forward, of attacking, of penetrating. Superior, one attacks right away, but inferior, there is no halt; one attacks again. Orders of battle are taken at four- or five-hundred *toises* from the enemy. Simple oblique, double oblique, perpendicular order: they are all equally taken with a rapidity that the eye is at pains to follow. From this, one marches, one beats, one disperses, one arrests oneself only when one no longer sees any more enemies. With a system of this genre, the artillery doubtlessly has little to do, and I see it, as soon as this army has thrown itself, reduced to letting it run to victory and to being a witness to its success.

Mesnil-Durand assures us that artillery, "thus employed and no longer acting for so long a time will destroy fewer

---

11 [Abel, *Guibert's General Essay on Tactics*, 88–96.]
12 [See especially Mesnil-Durand, "Mémoire sur l'artillerie," *Fragments de tactique* [Memoirs 7–9], 1–38.]
13 "Mémoire sur l'artillerie," 37–38.
14 [Ibid, 37–38.]

15 [See 116–150]

people and will no longer decide battles alone."¹⁶ Yes, without doubt [regarding] his [own], but [with regard to that of] the enemy, I guarantee that it will destroy double in return and that it will decide battles on its own.

What I do not hear is how Mesnil-Durand, at the end of this first assertion, promises to artillery "that his tactics will offer the means of always being superior in the part where it will decide the fight; that it will leave it more terrain and liberty for its emplacements and its movement; that it will give to it more ease for it to make use of its wagons [and] more facility for maneuvers by hand, which will shorten their durations and distances; [and] finally, that it will form it in a state of acting in advance of the line without really masking it and always being supported in such a manner as to never fear." It is true, as he adds in a note, that "perhaps this will demand a little explication," and that he does not give it; I console myself a little for my lack of penetration, and I take the part of waiting for someone to come to my aid.¹⁷

While waiting, here are some objections that present themselves to me. Artillery may act efficaciously only as long as it has sufficient terrain over which to extend itself. It does not take reverses, and we know how this advantage is decisive for it as long as it is on the flanks of the object that it beats. To be on the flank (or to see the flank, which amounts to the same), it must outflank, and to outflank, it must occupy a greater front. This principle is so evident that from it is derived all the superiority that the artillery of the besieger always takes over the besieged. The latter almost always has more artillery, and its artillery is covered. But that of the besieger acts with more liberty and on a greater development. All its effects stretch from the circumference to the center; it thus always finishes by embracing, flanking, prolonging, enfilading, and destroying that of the besieged. How will the system of Mesnil-Durand give this advantage to the artillery when it so prodigiously shortens the front of the orders of battle, when it places only fifty-six paces of interval between each column, [and] when it announces that, for its decisive attacks, it will reserry its columns yet more, or, what amounts to the same, that it will insert its second line into them? How will his artillery hold against that of the enemy, which will always outflank it, which will consequently beat it in the flank, *en rouage*, [and] at the ricochet, and prevent it from resting formed *en batterie*? Finally, where will this artillery place its carriage, indispensable for combat consumption, in such an order? In the intervals! I ask if this is [even] possible. In advance of the front! How would the columns then march? Yet again, I do not at all comprehend the means on which are founded the promises of Mesnil-Durand to the artillery, and he has great fault for not developing them. The masters of the art may announce the secrets that they hold in reserve, but Mesnil-Durand and I, who are [only] students [of artillery], do not have the same right. We are obliged to state everything, as one must neither believe us nor demure tranquilly on the faith of our promises.

What I saw at the Camp of Vaussieux, and what all the artillery officers who were there will attest with me, is that the maneuvers only had six pieces per division of eight battalions; that these pieces were only of 4 and 8 [and] hauled, as in peacetime maneuvers, by two or three horses only; that they had no sort of baggage [with them]; and that, even with these advantages, they did not know where to march, where to place themselves, or how to untangle themselves from the maneuvers of their division.

I leave the rest to the artillery officers themselves to discuss, in relation to the immediate and interior aspects of their art, the influence that the system of Mesnil-Durand would have on it if it were to be adopted and to furnish proofs of more-complete detail in this regard. There are so many enlightened people in this Corps, [people] who have made their métier truly an art, that it will doubtlessly present itself. I have treated the question only as a tactician, that is to say in the relation of the artillery to the troops and to the great parts of tactics; I will esteem myself fortunate if I am neither disavowed nor relieved of error by any of them in this work.

---

16 [See ibid., 36.]
17 [Ibid.]

BOOK 2

THIRD PART

Examination of the System of Mesnil-Durand Relative to Strategy, or the Tactics of Armies

∴

The subjects become more important and more vast in proportion to how much we advance. We are [now] at what concerns armies. When I treated this great part in my *General Essay on Tactics*, it was said that I had committed a crime; it was said that I placed my hand on the Ark of the Lord, that I wished to give lessons to the generals.[1] If someone asked of me again today by what right I treat it again, my response would be simple: by the same right that Mesnil-Durand had to treat it, with the difference that, if there would be audacity and vanity in discussing subjects so great, then this accusation must be imputed to those who make a system to upset received ideas rather than to those who write to defend them. But I am far from agreeing to these pretend accusations. The theory of an art is the resource of every man who thinks, and misfortune to the century and to the country where one has only had the right[s] to think for fifty years and to study the command of armies [only] when one would have [already done so]!

Among the advantages attributed by Mesnil-Durand to the deep order in general, adopted as [the] habitual order, and to his particular system, he insists above all on that of assembling more troops in the same space, and in one smaller at need, [and] in consequently re-serrying positions; on shortening orders of battle; on most-commonly finding advantageous camp [locations]; on passing without them without risk, if the country does not furnish them; on not at all having flanks; on being equally strong everywhere: in the end, on giving to the general, by the shortening of positions and orders of battle, the possibility of embracing the ensemble and the details of his defense or of his attack in a coup-d'œil, and of commanding operations himself in either circumstance.

I will analyze these pretend advantages and discuss them successively in the form of questions to this end.

---

1 [Guibert makes a rare Biblical reference to the Ark of the Covenant, the container in which the holy objects of early Judaism were stored. The specific reference is to a story in 2 Samuel 8, in which Uzzah, who had not been given permission to touch the Ark, prevented it from falling and was killed by God as a result.]

CHAPTER 1

If One Would Adopt the System of Mesnil-Durand, Would It Then Follow That One Would Be Able, as He Announces, to Re-Serry Positions, Camps, and Orders of Battle?

[We] must return here to the bases that were established in the chapter that treated the primitive and habitual order.[1]

It is in an army as [it is] in a troop, because an army is only a collection of many united troops. It is from the state of repose that an army passes to the state of action. Before acting, before fighting, or, to better say, in waiting for it to act or to fight, and [also] when it neither acts nor fights, an army must be established in a position.

This position must be such that this army may camp in it, subsist in it, [and] defend itself in it if it is surprised and attacked; cover or menace the points that interest it; and finally debouch [from it] with [the] liberty to march where it may be necessary for it to carry itself.

These conditions may be, according to circumstances, more or less interesting to reunite in a position; this depends on the degree of inferiority or superiority of the enemy [and] on the nature of the war that one has before one, on its greater or lesser proximity, etc., but it is always true that even a superior army, even [one] on the offensive, may not, up to a certain point, dispense itself from establishing itself in the positions that procure it these advantages, because, if it has an affair with a skillful and maneuvering enemy, they [the enemy] may find occasion to punish it [the army] for having neglected them [positions].

The choice of positions is thus one of the principal branches of the art of war today. Positions are tied to camps, since it is according to positions that camps are determined; to orders of march, since the objective of marches is always to carry the army from one position to another; to orders of battle, since, when one is on the defensive, it is according to the position that one occupies that the one that one must take must be determined, and, when one is on the offensive, it is according to the position that one wishes to attack that it must then be determined; [and] finally to subsistence, since it is positions that furnish it, cover it, or procure it.

The Ancients did not put any value on positions, and, as I have already explicated in the chapter that treats the primitive and habitual order, they were founded in reason in this.[2] The nature of their arms rendered them not only more proper to the offensive than to the defensive, but it also even rendered the defensive disadvantageous. Inferior or superior, they had to attack when they wished to fight, and consequently, they searched for plains as we search for posts.

I have demonstrated in the same chapter (and if this is useless to repeat in detail, this résumé is at least important to recall) that, for opposite reasons also drawn from the nature of our arms, the defensive today has become more advantageous; that, as such, the defensive order has necessarily and naturally become the most-frequent order; that the deployed order is more proper to the defensive than the deep order; and that it consequently follows that this [deployed order] must be the primitive and habitual order.

Now that these preliminaries are posed, to respond to the question posed by this chapter, we believe that three points must be examined: if the deployed order must necessarily take extended positions, if the deep order would dispense with taking them, [and] finally if it would be possible and advantageous to shorten them [positions]. These points are so analogous and interrelated that it is impossible for us to treat them separately; [thus], we are reduced to making them one subject of discussion.

It is strangely mistaken to believe that it would be the deployed order, adopted today as the primitive and habitual order, that determines armies to take extended positions. The extension of positions is drawn from other motives that would command the same of the deep order. Extended positions being necessary by these motives, the deployed order is the most proper and the most advantageous to occupy them and to garnish them. The deep order would be forced, if it did not wish to deploy itself to attend to the same objective, to augment the intervals of its primitive disposition; this would return to the same result as the pretend inconveniences of the extending of orders of battle, and [it] would certainly defend positions less well.

It is beyond doubt that, in general, shortened positions are not more advantageous to defend than extended positions; it is beyond doubt that, if a general could equally

---

1 [See 65–71.]

2 Ibid.

accomplish all the objectives that he must have in his view, relative to circumstances, it would not be personally more advantageous [for him] to choose a shortened position than an extended position, since, in the shortened position, he may embrace all, see all, [and] command all, in lieu of [the fact that], in the extended position, a part of his troops, of his terrain, and of his disposition being almost always outside of his view, he is obliged to rely on others than on himself, and thus he finds himself in the painful situation of being responsible for events and not always being able to command them.

But, as there are few of these fortunate positions that, in being re-serried, equally accomplish all the objectives that a good position must accomplish, [and] as there are almost always superior reasons that force it to extend itself, what follows from this? That the generals of the Ancients, not at all being subjected to making wars of positions and consequently always keeping their armies under their eyes and in hand, made a war that was much less difficult and much more advantageous for them; that modern generals have need of more art, more combinations, more activity, better organs to supplement the extension [of positions], more promptitude of judgment to repair faults and accidents, more sagacity to foresee them and to divine in some way what they do not see, [and] finally a head more vast and that contains, if I may dare to express myself thus, more terrain, more hypotheses, and more resources. To be a great general, [and] I intend by "great general" not a man who has partial success or even great success in which hazard played a part, but a long suite of victories, of good retreats, of wise campaigns, like those of the King of Prussia, for example, he must have genius, and genius of the highest degree.[3]

What will the result then be? It is that the art, [after] having experienced this revolution, fortunate or unfortunate as one will wish, but which exists in the end, it is [then] not at all [a question of] pretending to change it to render it more facile, easier, or more advantageous to the generals, but of studying it and reducing it to a theory so that the generals may employ it as it is and elevate themselves to it.

We return to our subject. Mesnil-Durand speaks of extended positions, of shortened positions, of the inconveniences of the one and the advantages of the other, etc., but all that he says on this subject is as vague as the air, because a position in itself is neither shortened nor extended; it only acquires this denomination in considering it relative to the strength of the army that must occupy it and to that of the enemy that may attack it. A position may not be disadvantageous despite being extended [or] advantageous despite being re-serried. The extended position may be covered in obstacles in such a manner that it reduces the attack to points and that an army that would be insufficiently in a position in the same development in a more-open terrain suffices for it. The re-serried position may, on the contrary, be disadvantageous; it only has to lack depth; it only has to be able to be embraced by its flanks. There are, as one sees, distinctions [and] modifications without number to establish, and, if one would wish to support each of them with an example, one would find as many positions disadvantageous by their re-serrying as by their extent.

But it is not only relative to the subject of fighting and to the number of troops that one has to occupy it compared to that which the enemy has to attack it that a position is good or bad. A position will be re-serried and unassailable in vain, [or] at least it will be a bad position, if the troops there are without commodities for their encamping and for their needs, if it does not cover the points from which an army draws its subsistence or the other points that is important for it to cover, [and] finally if it does not favor its ulterior operations at the same time as it is contrary to those of the enemy. In envisaging positions in all these aspects, it will be easy for me to prove that they almost always impose the necessity of extending oneself and that re-serried positions ordinarily procure many fewer of these advantages and are consequently more often defective than extended positions.

It is thus to these aspects that the extension of positions holds today and not, as Mesnil-Durand believes, to the deployed order. When a general chooses a position, it is they that he first has in view. He then combines the position that offers itself to him, and what it appears to accomplish for him, with the strength of his army. Whether he finds them proportional to each other will determine if he establishes himself there. If he finds his army too feeble to defend it, and if he perhaps fears to be attacked there, he renounces occupying it. If he finds himself more numerous than the extent of his position requires, then he applauds this as more of an advantage than his position, and this excess number does not at all embarrass him: he redoubles his lines, places troops in reserve, detaches them to an important point, or he even employs them in a useful expedition. To read Mesnil-Durand, [one] would believe that modern tactics teaches only taking positions at their measure and to find them good only when all the army has the necessary place to deploy itself in its [parade-ground] order!

We continue. The following chapters will develop more and more the great question that I treat.

---

3 [See Clausewitz, *On War*, 100–112, where he articulates a similar idea, that genius must be repeated in order to be present.]

CHAPTER 2

May Current Castrametation Change Form and Consequently Permit the Shortening of Positions?

When Folard attacked the principles of castrametation in use in his time for the excessive elongation that they gave to camps, he doubtlessly did so with good reason, but that Mesnil-Durand starts from these [same] principles [that are] outdated and fallen into disuse to propose a new system of encamping is not conceivable.

In all the classical works printed on castrametation, whether before Folard, in his time, and even today, the principle is posed to give to each battalion and each squadron the same extent [of territory along] the front of the camp that each battalion or squadron must have *en bataille*. In taking this principle as the base of his critique, Mesnil-Durand has a good game of amusing himself with the excessive elongation that would result for modern camps, as, supposing an army of one-hundred battalions and one-hundred squadrons, each battalion having only two-hundred files and each squadron seventy, the camp of this army on two lines would occupy 7,236 *toises*, which would be three great leagues. But where has Mesnil-Durand seen camps formed on this principle? Where has he seen an army of this strength take positions of this extent?

1. An army of this strength is not all assembled on a [single] point; it is often encamped on more than two lines, or at least it has several reserves that encamp on [a] third line. Independently of these reserves that are drawn from its order of battle, it has detached corps [and] advance guards. It must thus lose a great third of the army employed outside the line and diminish the pretend front that one has given above to one's camp by as much.
2. The principle of giving each battalion or squadron the front of their order of battle at the camp was relegated to old school arguments a long time ago. Since the war before last [the War of the Austrian Succession], we have no longer followed it, and we have much re-serried the front of camps. [During] the last war [the Seven Years War], Marshal Broglie established in his Regulations that we would always camp by platoons.[1] Finally, in the Provisional Ordinance on the campaign service, which he executed at the Vaussieux Camp, the form of camps when the army is in movement and operation activity, which will thus consequently be the most habitual form in the course of a campaign, is indicated as thirty-five *toises* per battalion, including its interval, and at thirty-five *toises* per squadron, which hardly makes two-thirds of the front that a battalion of two-hundred complete files would make and that which a squadron of seventy would occupy. We suppose with reason in this ordinance that the incomplete, the ill, the detached almost always reduce the effectives to a third below the [paper strength]. The form of [a] camp above is by half-company in the infantry and by company or by squadron in the cavalry.[2]

The same ordinance establishes, and I believe quite wisely, a second form of camp that is by quarter-company in the infantry and half-company or half-squadron in the cavalry, which is seventy *toises* per battalion and fifty per squadron. This formation is indicated for camps of convenience, for camps late in the season, and when one wishes to *barraquer* the troops.[3] It offers one more advantage: being able to hide from the enemy the knowledge of the troops that would be detached during the night, the battalions, regiments, and brigades that find themselves alongside the detached troops having only to split their camp in half to fill the interval that they would occupy in the line.

These are the principles of castrametation established today, simple principles that shortened the camps in a just proportion in leaving them the facility to extend themselves when it is necessary; principles consequently applicable to all circumstances. Thus, I demand the pardon of Mesnil-Durand; I find that it is quite advantageous that a system modify itself, bend itself, accommodate itself to the times, events, and to cases, because absolute and exclusive systems always extinguish themselves in practice; and that from nature, which acts in space, to man,

---

1 [See Victor-François, duc de Broglie, *Correspondance inédite avec le Prince Xavier de Saxe, comte de Lusace pour servir à l'histoire de la Guerre de Sept Ans*, 4 Vols. (Paris: Albin Michel, 1903), 1:9–24, which contains Broglie's 1759 orders to the army to form divisions, the first such in French history.]
2 [*Règlement provisoire sur le service de l'infanterie en campagne* (1778).]
3 [Ibid., 200. The word Guibert uses here, "*barraquer*," can mean either to bivouac or to send to winter quarters; the latter meaning is probably intended, given the context.]

who acts on a point, all appears to me to be full of exceptions, distinctions, and varieties.

Mesnil-Durand explicates with his ordinary clarity the system of castrametation that he would substitute for that which exists. First, however, he wishes to pardon the parallel form and agree that this form is quite convenient, because, each troop taking [up] arms at the head of its camp, the army finds itself formed in its habitual order of battle, and he seems to wish to content himself with this, provided that this parallel be that which he calls "shortened" so as to render castrametation analogous to his system. But soon after, he avows that

> this form of camp, tending directly and immediately to the parallel order of battle, is not the one that he would prefer, because it is not necessary to have too much tendency to the parallel order, which is not the best, and in which one would perhaps fight so rarely, and he would like better that the army encamp in such a form that, in the moment when it takes [up] arms, it would find itself disposed in double and assembled columns, because, in this state, it will pass in an instant to [whichever] order of battle that it will please the general to employ, and, in waiting, it will hold the enemy in an entire uncertainty on its disposition.[4]

One would believe that Mesnil-Durand would then explain the form of this camp, but [this] is another one of the secrets that it is very easy to hold in reserve. He thus says that "it is a small problem that he leaves to the reader for his amusement [and] that only, in waiting for his solution, he observes 1. that a camp of this species would be quite easy and quite beautiful; 2. that the different camps, always essentially the same and equally accomplishing the objective, would be susceptible to a great variety; 3. that, for the same reason, this new castrametation would accommodate itself to all sorts of terrain [and] would be neither more scrupulous nor more delicate than its dispositions and maneuvers, and that thus one would be able to easily and conveniently encamp in such a place where an army today would not decide to lodge itself; 4. that, just as there are for encamping, there are emplacements everywhere, [and] in advance of these emplacements, there are battlefields everywhere, good as soon as they are found and well reconnoitered, but sometimes quite singular; 5. finally, that this variety and this singularity of battlefields and camps would render them indecipherable for the enemy and that they would not at all be able to see, as

[they can] today, the number of troops by the extent of the camp, [and] by this number, by their emplacement, and by the terrain in advance [that is] always so open, the order of battle in which the army would present itself if it would be attacked."[5] Here, Mesnil-Durand is silent, and me, I avow that I remain in the shadows, and I leave his problem there.

It was said to me at the Camp of Vaussieux that it was in column that Mesnil-Durand would pretend to make the infantry encamp; this manner would have in effect some analogy with the announcement of his problem, but how to encamp in column? My imagination is lost. Will it be in double and assembled columns, that is to say *en jumelles*, such that a phrase of this problem seems to make itself heard, since he says that he would that the troops, in leaving their camp, find themselves formed in this disposition? This would seem impossible to me. Where would the tail of such a camp go? Would it be in column by battalion? This depth would be yet more terribly inconvenient. Where would the officers encamp? At what distances would the last companies find themselves from the front of the camp, which is the natural assembly point, since it is the line of defense and the part that faces the enemy! Again, I am lost, and I am obligated to leave here what my reason cannot admit.

I do not know if I abuse myself, but in waiting for Mesnil-Durand to reveal his secret to us, current castrametation appears to me [to be] all that is the most reasonable, the best extended, and the most analogous to healthy tactics.

We first see this in its details. It preserves each company in its habitual order. It places the soldiers between their weapon bundles on one side and their kitchens on the other. The former find themselves distributed on the line of the front in such a manner that, in case of alarm, to run there and find themselves in the habitual formation, which is at the same time the defensive formation, is the affair of a moment for all the soldiers who compose this battalion. The kitchens find themselves behind the companies' tents [and] consequently within range of them, under the eyes of the soldiers and in such a manner as to not at all be fearful of causing fire accidents. We follow all the rest of the distribution of the camp. The officers find themselves within range of their troops, each grade in its separate alignment, each officer with the terrain he precisely requires in such a manner that in no part of the camp is there either embarrassment or confusion. The camp finds itself well aired on all sides and pierced by avenues that are both convenient and hygienic. Some

---

4 *Fragments de tactique*, 186–187.

5 [Mesnil-Durand, *Fragments de tactique*, 186–187.]

serve the companies for them to assemble themselves and for all the interior details of discipline, [and] others for all the details of hygiene and for the flow of water. In advance of the camp is a sufficiently spacious *front de bandière*, which is the place for the battalion arms. By this *front de bandière* all the parts of the camp may communicate with each other, while the great intervals of the battalions serve at the same time as debouches for traversing the camp and for the communication of the lines.

We now pass to the results. All position[s] must first be defensive. The current form of our camps occupies and garnishes them along their entire front. The primitive and habitual order of battalions must be the deployed order, because they take it with the most facility, promptitude, etc. The form of our camps is relative to this order.

Mesnil-Durand says that the flank of our camps is the feeble part. Who denies it! But this is why positions are taken. This is why the choice of them is such an important part of war today. If the position is good, it thus has its flanks advantageously supported. Independently of this support, there is always an infantry brigade encamped on each flank, [an] excellent institution and [one] that we still have in our armies [thanks to] Marshal Broglie. But when one would encamp in columns by battalions in lieu of encamping by battalions in deployed order, would the camp have fewer flanks? To not have flanks, it would have to encamp in square order, or so much approaching square that the difference between the smallest side and the largest would hardly be sensible, or better yet, in the circular order. Mesnil-Durand had for [his] example the Romans in the former case and nominally the Orientals and the Turks in the latter. When he has searched in Chile for authorities in favor of the column, one may well accommodate oneself to the examples of castrametation that one would find in Turkey.

But speaking seriously, at least of one of these two dispositions, it is clear that, whatever may be the depth that one occupies, whether one camps on two, on three, or on several lines, if the enemy comes to take a position or to attack you on one of your flanks, you will still be obliged to take a new position to face them, because what makes the disadvantage of being taken in the flank is that the smallness of the front that one then presents gives to the enemy the possibility of embracing three of the faces of the position that one occupies.[6] Now, there would only be a single means of preventing this inconvenience, which, in truth, would be barbarous in view of modern tactics and weapons: camping in round or square order, as we have said.

Default[s] of terrain alone would almost always place [an] obstacle to encamping on a greater depth or in multiplying the lines. Already one finds quite few positions in which it would be possible to encamp on two lines with reserves and all the baggage that accompanies an army. Many positions lack depth, and this must occur often, because it is not in open country that one takes positions; it is on heights or in country[sides] embarrassed with obstacles. But here is what Mesnil-Durand ceaselessly loses sight of. He seems to always suppose that one makes war in plains, [but] it almost never [happens that way], first, because plains are more rare than unequal and covered country[sides], and second, because, of the two armies that operate against each other, one of the two is almost always on the defensive and necessarily abandons the plains to search for posts.

As for the rest, it is not in relation to castrametation alone that the question of the possibility of shortening positions must be examined. We go to find the other major reasons we oppose it.

---

6 [Guibert's description of the dilemma posed by a flanking maneuver is strikingly similar to the box concept developed in Antoine-Henri, baron Jomini, *The Art of War*, trans. G.H. Mendell (St. Paul: Greenhill, 1992), 77–84. Jomini argues that most situations begin with each army controlling two of the four sides of a box that surrounds them and that the victorious army will be the one that seizes a third side, usually by a flanking maneuver. Jomini published the majority of his work between 1805 and 1840, including what is erroneously titled *The Art of War* in many translations.]

CHAPTER 3

Relationship of Positions to Subsistence. May One, Relative to Subsistence, Adopt the System of Shortening Positions?

Mesnil-Durand doubtlessly has not reflected how subsistence, this so-important part of war, depends on positions, and how it would suffer from their shortening. It is by extended positions that one places behind oneself much country[side] and consequently many means [of subsistence], that one better covers one's communications and one's magazines, [and] finally that one puts oneself at ease for one's fodder and for one's needs of every species. This truth is so incontestable that, in late-season camps, and in all those where one foresees having to rest for a long time, one is forcibly obliged to elongate oneself, [and] that, if the position that one occupies is of such a nature that one may not extend without denaturing it or without enfeebling it, one takes the part of detaching corps that elongate themselves outside of the principal position and that make extensions in some way, save when they retire on it or approach it in case of the enemy's marching on them but that have for their objective to embrace more country[side], to aggrandize the rear of the army, and to procure it at the same time more ease and means for subsisting.

Subsistence depends so much on positions, and positions are sometimes so subordinated to subsistence that generals are forced to choose them relative to this sole consideration and sacrifice all the others. One thus sees them, to procure themselves subsistence and to cover the points that furnish it, sometimes obliged to take hazardous positions, whether because they are too extended, and by being extended, they are no longer in proportion to their army or they lose *points d'appui*; because their army is morseled into several corps, and one of these corps finds itself taken; or finally by other circumstances that their infinite variety dispenses us from detailing. This is the same [place] where the superior man hazards more than the mediocre man, because, at the same time that he would well know the inconveniences that he hazards, he would well foresee, combine, and [prepare] preservatives and resources.

Thus at the end of the 1761 campaign, Marshal Broglie saw himself forced to separate his army into seven or eight corps, all encamped several leagues from each other and embracing a great extent of the country[side] by this, to make it subsist more easily. Prince Ferdinand, who was retired and dispersed towards Hamelin, twelve or fifteen leagues from it, wished to profit from this circumstance by surprising him in this position. He assembled his troops and marched as quickly as possible towards Einbeck, where Broglie had his headquarters with only four infantry brigades and some cavalry. Broglie learned of this movement in the evening of 4 November. He immediately sent orders to all his detached corps to unite on him. At daybreak, he mounted his horse, chose a position in advance of Einbeck, and established the few troops that he had with him there. The head of the enemy army was already appearing. He sent a large detachment in advance of them. This detachment stopped it, contained it, [and] obliged it to form itself with the rest of the army and then to march with precautions. Time passed, the day advanced, [and] our troops arrived successively and garnished the reconnoitered position; finally, it was three hours before Ferdinand found himself within range of making dispositions for the fight. He counted on surprising, [but] in lieu of that, he saw before him a formidable position occupied by an army whose countenance did not at all appear uncertain and that he as such must have supposed to have been completely assembled. The day thus ended in a violent cannonade on both sides, and Prince Ferdinand, seeing his project lost, retook the Hamelin road that night.[1] Aside from the battle that did not take place and that I believe would have completed the analogy if it had been given, it was almost the same event as at Bergen: the same imminent danger, the same battlefield without troops for several hours, the same presence of spirit, the same coup-d'œil, the same justness of combinations, the same man, in the end, saved everything.[2]

And what was this position, so skillfully [and] so promptly untangled by Marshal Broglie in a country[side] so cut, so unequal, that, by force of presenting positions in every sense, he threw an ordinary talent into embarrassment, and almost always into error? I will enter into some details in this regard. This small digression will be neither foreign nor insignificant to my subject.

---

1 [Waddington, *La guerre de sept ans*, V:182–190. See also Szabo, *The Seven Years War in Europe*, 360–362. Guibert neglects to mention that the 1761 campaign cost Broglie his command.]
2 [See 57, 84–85.]

This was a position of a league and a half of development, although we had less than 40,000 combatants to occupy it; this was a position cut in half at its center by a valley in such a manner that the army was in effect divided into two corps. This species of valley or bottleneck debouched onto the Einbeck plain, which Broglie occupied with the greater part of his cavalry. But of what import was this extent of position, since his front was advantageous and the attack on it was necessarily reduced to the points that the army was sufficient to defend? Of what import was this separation of the army into two parts, since the enemy could certainly not have engaged itself in this bottleneck, behind which all our cavalry formed a respectable curtain wall while the two branches of the position seated on the heights formed salient parts or bastions? [With] less extension, taken conforming to the principles of the system of Mesnil-Durand, the position would have had no value; it would have been susceptible to being turned; it would have imposed on the enemy only on the first day. But we recall again that Mesnil-Durand did not content himself with wishing only to re-serry positions; he goes so far as to say that, with his system, one may go without them, and that "his order is an excellent post, that an army will [win] everywhere."[3] The good role indeed that we would have played at Einbeck if the order in columns was our only resource!

We continue to demonstrate the relationship between positions and subsistence. I have just shown an army obliged by the motive of subsistence to do more than elongate itself in its position: to morsel itself out, to divide itself, and to draw itself from this dangerous crisis only by the skill of its general. I will cite another army taking, relative to its subsistence, the position [that is] the most extraordinary, the furthest from common rules, the most dangerous in appearance, and, at its base, the most judicious, the wisest, and, I will even advance, the surest. Moreover, this example proves more than any other how positions relate to subsistence; it will perhaps prove to Mesnil-Durand that talent does not at all admit exclusive principles, that it is the enemy of unique methods, and that its true attribute is to have quite-varied resources and combinations for all terrains and for all cases.

This example is duc d'Orléans, the future regent, when he commanded the French army in Catalonia in 1708. He has always seemed so curious and so interesting to me that I have a true pleasure in placing him under the eyes of the public. This trait alone may not make it [to where] Orléans must be considered as a great man of war, but it confirms what history has said of this prince: he was born with genius and that he only missed opportunities, as it is only a man of genius who has grand and just thoughts beyond the route beaten by the vulgar.

Orléans made war in Catalonia, and he had before him the Army of the Archduke, commanded by Guido Wald Rüdiger, graf Starhemberg. Operations were finished, and it was only a question of knowing who, in procuring himself the most subsistence, would stay on campaign for longer and remain master of the country. This was, according to history, the situation in which the two armies found themselves. I will, to treat it in itself, copy what Feuquières said in his *Memoirs*. He would lose by not being extracted literally, and I will add on my end only the "plan" that I made fifteen years ago of this position to better represent to myself an example that struck me deeply. Those of my readers to whom this example appears as interesting as it does to me will perhaps be grateful to me for putting this plan under their eyes.

> Orléans was obliged to draw his bread from Balaguer, a small city in Catalonia, with the constraint of not being able to distance himself beyond the range of making convoys there in a day [because of] the lack of crews for *vivres*. It was also necessary that he procure himself enough subsistence for his cavalry to remain in this position for longer than the enemy would be able to remain with him. Starhemberg was camped on the Segre three leagues above the camp that Orléans had resolved to take to accomplish the two above objectives.
>
> It was thus a question of having the waters of the Segre for the army, the forage of the two sides of this small river for the cavalry, and, at the same time, of protecting the convoys from Balaguer and not distancing [himself] from this city.
>
> To give himself all these advantages, Orléans imagined to place the course of the Segre between his two lines and to face the two plains, on one side for the surety of his convoys and the other to procure himself more forage. To this end, he carried the right of his first line to a village that was on a height and accommodated to this village, where he put an infantry brigade, and the left of his second line facing this village, where there was a stone bridge. At the same time, he placed two bridges by battalions and as many by squadrons all along the stream so that the two lines would be able to communicate with each other by the rear of their camp.
>
> By this position, one sees that the army appeared to present to the enemy only the right flank of its first line and the left flank of its second.

---

3 [Mesnil-Durand, *Projet d'un ordre français*, 437.]

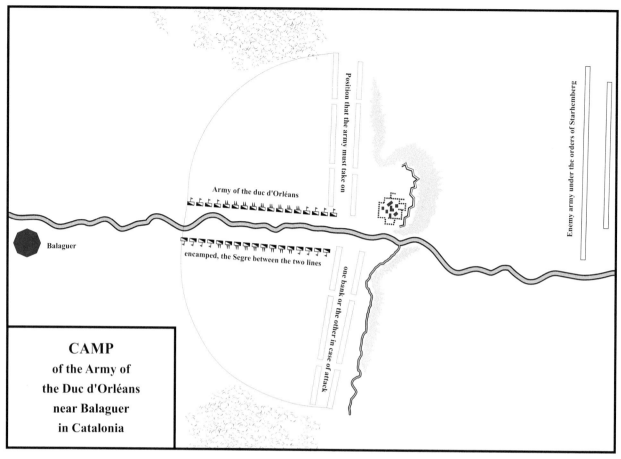

FIGURE 5 Diagram VI

If Orléans had been obliged to receive the enemy in this disposition, it would have been quite bad, but he remedied this inconvenience in procuring himself a battlefield on the two sides of the stream.

He made the village on his right the point of both his right and his left and found in this disposition of the country[side], and by the communications that it procured him, the means of making this village the right of the front of his army, in case the enemy came at him by a side of the small river, or the left of the same front, in case they came by the other side.

Thus, the two flanks of the right and the left of the first and the second line[s]' being equally covered, it is evident that this prince took one side or the other of his battlefield at need by a species of quarter-conversion on the extremities distant from this village that made it the pivot.[4]

While admiring the ingenious and audacious singularity of this camp, this quarter-conversion nevertheless disquieted Feuqiuères a little. Because he adds that "the country[side] had to be quite open for it to be susceptible to the advantage of carrying troops to this battlefield by a movement as grand as the quarter-conversion of the entire front of an army appears to need to be."[5] Today, this "great and difficult" movement would be regarded as quite facile and quite simple. This would be a change of position in the class of marches. But today, tactics has become maneuvering, and it was not then. This is why today a skillful general may, in making positions, extend himself, separate himself, [and] finally hazard more than one dared to do then.

An example like the one I have cited is doubtlessly rare, and it would require exactly the same conformity of circumstances to reproduce it, but other circumstances differently combined in the hands of a man of talent may produce other examples that would similarly be outside of the common rules. But the example that I have previously

---

4 [Feuquières, *Mémoires*, II:345–348. See also Alan Francis, *The First Peninsular War 1702–1713* (London: Benn, 1975), 275–276; and Lynn, *The Wars of Louis XIV*, 325–326.]

5 [Ibid.]

cited of Marshal Broglie renews itself often, and there is no campaign (above all when it commences at a good hour or is prolonged, because then subsistence becomes more difficult) that does not produce similar situations. But in the end, one takes extended positions to embrace more of the country[side] daily in war, and one embraces more country[side] only to procure oneself more means of subsisting. Almost all operations today unroll from this great base, and nourishing the armies that they command has become one of the most important and most difficult objectives for generals.

"But," Mesnil-Durand will say, "how then did the Ancients, who gave so little importance to positions, manage? Above all, how did the Romans, who encamped in a so-serried position, manage?" The Romans, yet again, had armies [that were] less numerous, and, above all, less overloaded with embarrassments and baggage than ours. The Romans had little cavalry. The Romans had methods of subsisting [that were] simpler and less consuming than ours. One has only to recall their distributions of raw grain, their hand mills, their extreme sobriety. Roman camps, always entrenched, were species of citadels where they had their magazines, their workshops, [and] their establishments of every genre. They rarely changed these camps. When they sortied from them, it was to fight. When they closed themselves in them, it was for surety. There are no examples in history of a Roman camp forced, or even attacked. Also, their genre of war may not be compared to ours in any aspect. I have already said, and I will repeat it as long as Mesnil-Durand will require, that the Roman methods would, in many regards, be better than ours. Their constitution, their education, [and] their customs were certainly more military. But when one does not wish to throw oneself into vague and chimerical systems, when one cannot regenerate either one's century or one's nation, when one wishes to think and to write to be useful, one must work with what exists and what can exist. It is not a question today of nourishing a Roman army; it is a question of nourishing a modern army, and, what is more, a French army, with all its inconveniences.[6]

Mesnil-Durand, to found the apology for his system, will fall back on the armies of the previous century, on those of Gustav Adolf, of Turenne, [and] of Condé, in the end on the times when the habitual order was deeper; I will respond to him that the positions of these armies, proportionate to the number retained, was more extend than ours.[7] I have followed, I have studied on the site[s], many of these positions: those of Franz Freiherr von Mercy around Freiburg,[8] those of Turenne and Montecuccoli in their famous campaign of 1675, [and] those of Marshal François de Blanchefort de Créqui, marquis de Marines, in his good defensive on the Saar and the Moselle.[9] These positions are all quite extended relative to the armies that occupied them, so extended that one would be at pains to conceive how armies [that were] so weak could have been able to garnish them if one would not recall that their battalions and their squadrons, which were, in truth, some eight and then six deep, and others four and then three, formed themselves *en bataille* in line, both full and empty, and consequently with intervals at least equal to their front, [and] that these armies often had only their reserves for their second line and that they thus extended their first line as much. The same reasons we have today forced them to take the positions of a great development. But, as I have already observed above, this elongation has fewer inconveniences today than [it did] then, and, in the

---

6 [Goldsworthy, *The Roman Army at War 100 BC-AD 200* (New York: Oxford University Press, 1996), 111–113, disproves Guibert by noting that that "there are many dramatic accounts by Roman historians of camps' being attacked and broken into," although he does continue by saying "it is hard to find an account of one being stormed without the Roman troops' having first been defeated in the open field." See also Southern, *The Roman Army*, 317–318.]

7 [Louis de Bourbon, prince de Condé, known as "the Great Condé" or simply as "the Condé," was a commander in the mid-seventeenth century. He won the signal victory of the French over the Spanish at Rocroi in 1643, which is often presented as the point of transition from Spanish to French hegemony in the early-modern period. Condé was Turenne's contemporary and rival during the Fronde, having been defeated by him and sent into exile for several years. He was rehabilitated and fought for Louis XIV until his death in 1686, including assuming command of Turenne's army after his death in 1675. Along with Turenne, he was and is seen as the greatest French commander of the period.]

8 [The Battle of Freiburg took place in August 1644 during the Thirty Years War. The Imperial army of Franz Freiherr von Mercy took Freiburg with around 16,000 men and pushed Turenne's army back, uniting it with Condé's to form a French force of around 20,000 under Condé. Over multiple days of fighting, Condé launched frontal attacks that pushed Mercy back from his prepared defensive positions but inflicted significant casualties on the French army. Although Mercy won the battle, he had to retreat, allowing the French to recover their position on the Rhine and take the fortress at Philippsburg. See Wilson, *The Thirty Years War*, 678–684.]

9 [The Moselle River is one of the major rivers of northern France, running from modern Koblenz through Metz and Nancy. The Saar is one of its tributaries, dividing from the main branch of the Moselle north of Luxembourg City and running near Forbach and Sarrebourg. Several key fortresses lay on the river system, including Metz, Nancy, Thionville, and Toul.

François de Blanchefort de Créqui, marquis de Marines, was a mid-seventeenth-century French commander who served in many of the wars of the period. Guibert likely references his campaigns in 1677 and 1678 at the end of the Dutch War that defended French acquisitions from an Imperial army and led to a favorable peace in the latter year. See Lynn, *The Wars of Louis XIV*, 150–155.]

hands of a skillful general, the perfection of modern tactics saves almost everything.

There remain many things to say on subsistence, but the objective of this chapter was only to envisage it in a single way: relative to the extension of positions. Permit me to invite my readers to read the chapter where I treat this important part in more detail in the *General Essay on Tactics*.[10]

---

10 [Abel, *Guibert's General Essay on Tactics*, 256–272.]

CHAPTER 4

Other Great Obstacles to the Re-serrying of Positions and Orders of Battle Drawn from the Nature of Operations and from the Circumstances to Which Armies Are Subjected

It does not suffice that a position be susceptible to the defense and that it favors the subsistence of the army that occupies it. There are other great objectives that it must accomplish. If one is on the defensive, it must hold the debouches or points by which the enemy may embrace [its] flanks or carry themselves on the objects that one covers. If one is on the offensive, it must hold the debouches by which [an enemy] may march on it, it must menace the points that interest it, [and] finally, it must extend itself to embrace them [the enemy] and to oblige them to extend themselves, and, by this, to enfeeble themselves.

These objectives almost always require that a position has a certain development. Of what import is it to the enemy, in the supposition that it has the offensive, that you occupy the position [that] is the most formidable in itself if they may leave you there and act on your flanks? Of what import is it to them, if they are on the defensive, that you take a sole debouche to arrive on them if they occupy all the others and if they may thus oppose you with almost all their forces on a [single] point?

Thus, there are few of these unique positions that occupy both many points and little space; one only defends a country[side] in extending oneself; all the art is in extending oneself without danger [and] in shortening this extension by skillfully seized points [and] by fortunately chosen salients that dispense with occupying the intermediary [ones]. All the art is sometimes in knowing to form oneself on the center of an extended defense line with the project and the well-calculated possibility of falling on the flanks of the enemy if they try to penetrate it. Similarly, one only attacks a country[side] [or] a position by extending oneself. All the art is also in extending oneself without making oneself a prize, in embracing without disuniting oneself, in tying one's operations or one's attacks together, in taking flanks without offering them, [and] finally in giving check without receiving it.[1] This is what one will certainly not do, either on the defensive or on the offensive, with the principles of Mesnil-Durand, which are to always shorten oneself [and] to always re-serry oneself on the center, but this is also what requires a general to have a vast [mind], profound thoughts, and rapid judgment.

This grand manner of making war [does not belong] solely to our times; the King of Prussia perfected it [and] facilitated by his tactics. But the foundation, the genius of this manner, if I may express myself thus, belonged to all the great generals of the last century. It belonged to Turenne, Condé, [and] François-Henri de Montemorency-Bouteville, duc de Piney-Luxembourg.[2] It was Créqui's, whom a single campaign places after them, because this campaign was sublime, and because, in all species of science, what must assign a man to the first rank is, it seems to me, to have elevated himself once to the highest degree of the art.[3]

I have been accused (because what is prejudice not capable of?) of having spoken lightly of the generals of the century of Louis XIV. With this calumny supported by clichés about my youth, my audacity, [and] my amour-propre, this was more than enough to indispose against me those who do not read, or those who read without understanding. The fact is that I dared to say that Villars was more fortunate than grand; that Louis-Joseph de Bourbon, duc de Vendôme; Nicolas Catinat; Berwick; and, in our days, Maurice de Saxe, were in the class of generals of the second order; [and] that, until the King of Prussia, no modern general was [a] tactician.[4] But relative to other

---

1 [Guibert uses a term from chess, in which a check requires the opponent to move their king out of check. The analogy, as the passage suggests, is to create an offensive opportunity without opening oneself up to a counter-offensive.]

2 [Luxembourg was, after Condé and Turenne, the best of Louis XIV's commanders. He was from an ancient military family, the Montmorencies, and his father was famously executed by Louis XIII for participating in an illegal duel. He served under Condé before being given command of an army in the 1672 invasion of the United Provinces; his army committed what would now be called war crimes there. His most famous action was to withdraw his small force of around 15,000 men from Utrecht to Charleroi in the face of an enemy army of 70,000, which won him his marshal's baton. He continued to serve, including his celebrated victory at Neerwinden in 1693, until his death in 1695.]

3 [This statement perhaps contradicts Guibert's earlier argument that genius must be repeated to be present; see 98.]

4 [See Abel, *Guibert's General Essay on Tactics*, 22–23.

  Louis-Joseph de Bourbon, duc de Vendôme; Nicolas Catinat; and James FitzJames, duc de Berwick, were generals in the later wars of Louis XIV. Vendôme came up under Créqui and Turenne before commanding his own armies in the War of the League of Augsburg and the War of the Spanish Succession, including help secure Felipe

great parts of war, who more than I prostrated themselves before the glory and the talents of Turenne and Luxembourg? I am not at all bounded by this sterile homage. I have followed, I have studied, [and] I have meditated my best on their immortal campaigns; I have drawn the theory that I expose from them; I have seen that the manner of the King of Prussia and that of these great men was the same at the base, [and] that the former had only perfected two things: knowing the troops as instruments and the maneuvers as means.

I have seen Turenne making a war of positions and movements for six weeks against Montecuccoli in the glorious campaign that terminated his life, a war absolutely similar to that which generals of the same order would make today with modern tactics. He commanded an army of 26,000 men, and Montecuccoli had 30,000. Montecuccoli, by this superiority, thus had the offensive; he searched to cross the Rhine and penetrate into Alsace. Strasbourg, then an Imperial Free City, openly preferred him, and it offered him a facile debouche. What did Turenne do? In lieu of following ordinary routine, which is to dispute the passage of the river that one wishes to defend, [a] routine that seems quite excusable when the river is a barrier as imposing as the Rhine, he passed it himself; he then placed himself between Strasbourg, which he left four leagues to his left, and his bridges that he raised at Altenheim and that he thus established four leagues to his right, detaching only a corps to cover them. Between the Rhine and Montecuccoli flowed the Schutter, [a] small river [that is] quite encased, quite deep, and almost always flowing along the heights that are on the Alsace side. Turenne made this small river his line of defense; he observed that this river always flows circularly in such a way that the arc was on Montecuccoli's side and that he occupied the chord. Thus, whether Montecuccoli wished to carry himself to Strasbourg, or he wished to march on his [Turenne's] bridges, he had to pass it [the line of defense]. It was on this fortunate nature of the country[side], but of which only a genius like his would have been able to grasp the advantages, that he founded his defense. He had the Rhine behind him, but of what import was the Rhine if, by means of the invincible obstacle that he had on his front, he was not in the case of fighting in this position? What if Montecuccoli tried to pass the Rhine above or below him? Then, he [Turenne] would have marched on him and attacked him during the passage, or else he would have taken his defensive in another sense, supporting his right or his left on the Rhine and his other wing on this same Schutter that he has before him. It is thus in this narrow theater, which was eight or ten leagues long by four or five wide at most, that these two great men deployed all the resources of the art for five weeks. Several times, Montecuccoli tried to surprise the passage of the Schutter. Turenne, having always the shortest route, only prolonged himself on his line of defense and presented himself before him [Montecuccoli], preventing him from executing his passage.[5] One time, the head of the corps of Guy Aldonce de Durfort, duc de Lorges, which, detached on Turenne's right, covered the bridges of Altenheim, was pushed [forward] by Montecuccoli, and he disposed himself to force the passage of the Schutter. Turenne rushed over, and Montecuccoli was obliged to retreat. Montecuccoli, tired of having this eternal barrier before him, abandoned [the position] and descended the Rhine. Turenne followed, going alongside him, always placing himself between the Rhine and him [Montecuccoli]. The Renchen, another small river, became his new line of defense. The two armies then passed fifteen days in this position. Finally, Turenne took the offensive in his turn; he found the occasion and the moment for it. Montecuccoli was fatigued by marches and countermarches; he had attempted everywhere without success, and the superiority of operations had thus passed to the side of his enemy. Turenne discovered a ford on the Renchen, which was two leagues from his right. He departed with his second line at the beginning of the night, passed the Renchen, and took a position on Montecuccoli's flank. Montecuccoli was only informed of this movement come day, and the entire camp of Turenne, which he still saw before him, threw him into uncertainty. He only left when he saw this camp slacken and the entire first line march by his right to pass the Renchen and carry itself to the support of Turenne. He marched himself, but Turenne's movements were combined with so much precision that his entire army was formed in its new position before Montecuccoli was in range of attacking. As such, Turenne made Montecuccoli retreat before him. Finally, the two armies found themselves near the village of Salzbach. There, Turenne was killed in advancing on a height

---

V's throne in Spain. He was particularly skilled at re-assembling armies that had been defeated under lesser commanders. Catinat was from a bourgeois family and won his rank through skill in military command. He was defeated by Eugene in Italy during the Spanish Succession and forced to resign his army command; he spent the rest of the war capably commanding armies under other marshals. He became a paragon of positive qualities, and the Académie Française's 1775 essay contest had him for its subject. Guibert competed for the prize, which was won by one of his literary rivals; see Abel, *Guibert*, 121. Berwick was the bastard son of the deposed James II of England, who lived in exile in France. Berwick served under Luxembourg before commanding armies on several fronts during the War of the Spanish Succession. He was killed at the Siege of Philippsburg in 1734 during the War of the Polish Succession.]

5 [Guibert describes a concept later defined as "interior lines" in Jomini, *The Art of War*, 72–178.]

to reconnoiter the enemy and to place a battery. There, he raises the most interesting military problem that exists: what did Turenne count on doing? Would he have wished to attack Montecuccoli, or would he have wished only to receive the fight? Did he say, a moment before his death, these famous words, recounted by several historians: "finally, I have it," astonishing words from the mouth of a man as prudent and as withdrawn as Turenne, and which, if they are true, must have only escaped him after an intimate conviction of the superiority of his position over that of Montecuccoli? In any case, and it had to be [so], his secret perished with him. The Council of War that assembled itself immediately after his death opined that it must retire and recross the Rhine. Today, all the officers who have reconnoitered this interesting position have not known how to explain these words, and, in case they were fabulous, how to at least judge what was coming to pass. It is to great generals alone, it is to geniuses of the first order, to divine the last words of Turenne and to take up the thread of his projects. It is permitted to the other men to exercise their imaginations, but they are forbidden to publish the result, under pain of a ridiculous pride.[6]

I have followed all the positions of Turenne and Montecuccoli in this memorable campaign, and I have seen them all much more extended than the principles prescribed by Mesnil-Durand. I have seen them all such that their armies were only able to garnish them [positions] only in ranging themselves in an order [that was] both full and empty, that is to say in having intervals between the battalions and squadrons equal to their frontages, which returns to the extension of our modern order without having its advantages and its solidity. At Salzbach notably, the two positions had more than a strong half-league of frontage, and they were armies of [only] 20,000 combatants.

I have followed a part of the encampments of Marshal Créqui in his beautiful campaign of 1677, and I have seen his positions almost always conformed to current principles. I have seen that he extended himself to oppose and to cover [and] that his army almost always occupied immense terrains in proportion to the front that they had in a plain or in chimerical hypotheses in the cabinet. I saw that the science of Marshal Créqui was, more or less, that which the Austrian armies had to employ in the last campaign against the King of Prussia, since, with a line of defense on an immense development [that] covered Bohemia, they reduced the King of Prussia to not daring to pierce it and to consuming the entire campaign in movements without combat.[7]

I have followed the campaigns of Marshal Luxembourg (this great man is the general of the last century who commanded the largest armies and who moved them best and most skillfully), and I saw that his offensive consisted, like that of the King of Prussia, of outflanking, of turning, and consequently, of extending himself. I have seen the Battle of Fleurus given on the principles of Leuthen.[8] I have seen Luxembourg always march, encamp, and fight on large fronts. The only difference[s] between those times and ours are that today, with modern tactics, the dispositions, the movements, [and] finally the means of execution, would be more facile, prompter, and better extended, [and] that today, for example, one would not be forced to arrive and to form one's disposition one day to attack the next day, as Luxembourg did at Neerwinden. Marching, arriving, menacing the enemy on a point, attacking them on another; taking one's order of battle relative to the moment, to the terrain, and to the circumstances; doing, in a word, what the King of Prussia did at Leuthen: here is what Luxembourg would have done in his time, if his genius had been joined to the enlightenment and to the knowledge of ours.

I applaud myself for having found in this chapter a place to consign my procession of respect and admiration for the greatest captains that France has had, for men whose glory I have been said to search to abase in ceaselessly opposing the King of Prussia to them. It would have been maladroitly praising this prince to slander the reputations that he himself consecrated in his works.[9] Of all the calumnies that have been brought against me, this is one of them that I have the most heart to respond to; it would attack my discernment and my patriotism at the same time. I do not pardon the enemies that it may make me, who have not taken the pain of judging me for my own work; moreover, it is quite natural to be indisposed against a man who attacks the objects of a cult so justly founded.

---

6 [See Lynn, *The Wars of Louis XIV*, 140–142. Guy Aldonce de Durfort, duc de Lorges, was a scion of the powerful and military Duras family, and Turenne's nephew. He served as an effective commander under Turenne, as Guibert indicates, before receiving his own commands and performing ably in the War of the League of Augsburg. He died in the early years of the War of the Spanish Succession.]

7 [Prussian armies invaded Bohemia on several occasions during the century, but Guibert likely references the campaigns of the War of the Bavarian Succession, in which Austrian forces successfully defended Bohemia (and Moravia) from a Prussian advance. See Showalter, *The Wars of Frederick the Great*, 343–350.]

8 [The Battle of Fleurus took place in July 1690 as part of the War of the League of Augsburg. Luxembourg, with around 35,000 men, found his opponent Georg Frederik van Waldeck-Eisenberg in a defensive position near Fleurus with around 38,000 men. Luxembourg conducted a double envelopment of Waldeck that won an "overwhelming victory" that was "truly Napoleonic," according to Lynn, *The Wars of Louis XIV*, 207–209.]

9 [Friedrich wrote extensively, and much of his work was published in his lifetime; Shrier, "Frederick the Great," provides an effective introduction.]

CHAPTER 5

System of Mesnil-Durand Considered in Relation to Marches and March Orders

In examining the elementary part of the system of Mesnil-Durand, I have demonstrated how his column adapted to marches is defective, useless, and subject to inconveniences. It remains to me to prove here that the ensemble of his system is even less favorable than its details to this important part of war.

Marches are necessarily tied to positions and to orders of battle. They hold to positions because they are in some way only the transport[ing] of the army from one position to another. They hold to orders of battle because it is they [marches] that prepare them [orders of battle] and command them. This has need of being more amply developed.

So that an army march (I intend here a maneuvering march, that is to say a march made within range of the enemy and with the possibility of being attacked while it is being executed) be conducted according to the principles of the art, in departing the camp or from the position that it occupies, it [the march] must transport the army on a front somewhat similar to that which it would occupy in the camp or in the position that it proposes to take.

Thus, if the march is a front march, that is to say that an army must occupy a parallel position or [one] somewhat parallel to that which it would occupy, the columns must have the distances necessary to form themselves *en bataille* between them, and the interval of the front of the march must be equal to the eventual front of the order of battle. The nature of the country[side and] the obstacles that it produces may often bring modifications to this principle. [In one place], the columns may be obliged to separate themselves; [in another], to re-serry themselves; elsewhere, to double themselves, etc. But the country[side] reopening, the obstacles being passed, the march must re-enter into the principle established above. In the end, this must be the primitive and habitual order of march and the objective that the officers charged with the reconnaissance and the opening of the march must have in view.

Thus, for the same reason, if the march is a flank march (that is to say that the army marches parallel to the enemy and that consequently the position or the camp that it goes to occupy must be on the prolong of the position or the camp that it would occupy), contrary to the preceding supposition, the columns must march as assembled as possible in such a manner that, by a right or a left, the army may form itself *en bataille*. It is thus the case of marching by line or by half of the line at most. The country[side] may yet stymie this disposition, but every time that it [the countryside] permits, it [the army] must return to it [the order], and the march must consequently be open.

Independently of this, the army must have one or several positions reconnoitered in advance between the position that one quits and that one goes to take that it may reach and occupy if the enemy carries themselves unexpectedly to attack it. Thus, all the times that the country[side] permits, the columns must be able to communicate freely. Above all, [this] is necessary in approaching their eventual positions, and, to this end, the officers charged with the opening of the march must have practiced transverse communications from the right to the left of the march.

I will not extend myself any further here on these principles, because I would only be able to repeat what I have developed in my *General Essay on Tactics*.[1] [I] must go to my objective, which is to examine the system of Mesnil-Durand relative to army marches.

Marches being intimately tied to positions, [and] positions necessarily dictate orders of battle and almost always having need of being extended in lieu of being shortened, as Mesnil-Durand pretends, how might his system tally with the true principles of army marches? What! the nature of the country[side], the great objects of war will force him to quit his natural order or at least to extend his position, and he will pretend to re-serry himself before forming himself in march order and thus marching re-serried! But, in the course of his march, he will be obliged to unexpectedly take a position to make face to the enemy. But, in arriving at the end of his march, the position that he will take will again necessarily impose on him the obligation of extending himself. It will thus be forced to enlarge itself anew. What useless system carries itself thus on false bases! It must thus float from variation to variation and from error to error.

The Camp of Vaussieux demonstrated these inconveniences to us. Each time that the army would march, it was forced to commence by re-serrying the battalions on the center of the regiments, the regiments on the center of

---

1 [See Abel, *Guibert's General Essay on Tactics*, 171–188.]

the brigades, and the brigades on the center of the divisions. Finally, before the twins were formed, we had lost a great hour to maneuvering, or perhaps to "trampling" in advance of the fasces. An army forming itself in march order by the means of current tactics would, in lieu of this, only form its columns by the right or by the left and debouch in advance or behind its front, all without preliminary maneuver, without embarrassment, [and] without difficulty, its columns having approximately their necessary distances or taking them gradually by the direction of the routes that would be open, marching at the first movement at the same pace that they had preserved during the entire march, that is to say at a free and natural step, not the maneuver step, not the running step, sorts of steps that, as I have already said, are good to employ only in forced circumstances or in short and partial movements, but never in army maneuvers or in general movements, or, above all, in war, where the soldier is overloaded and has need of managing his strength. In the end, it would have made a league in the time that that of Mesnil-Durand consumed in preparatory and useless maneuvers at the head of the camp.

But suppose the army of Mesnil-Durand, away from the camp guards (I do not at all speak here of the inconveniences of his system relative to great objects): the least obstacle slows his columns, [and] the least defile becomes a maneuver for it. Obliged to internal movements of doubling and re-doubling, as they do not at all have the distances in their organization necessary for these movements, I would see his entire columns forced to stop themselves until they would be finished from head to tail. In lieu of this, the army in march order according to current principles always goes [through] the same movement and at the same pace, nothing is an obstacle for it, [and] a defile does not require running or the stopping of any of its parts; never will one of its columns have need of halting because of its individual movements; it will be forced to be [halted] only by particular orders relative to the views of the general or to combine itself with its neighboring columns.

Arriving at the position or at the camp that one will take, this army enters it and forms itself there, again without any embarrassment. What if it is simply a camp that it would be a question of occupying? It always enters it at the same step, prolonging itself on the *front de bandière*, not at all maneuvering; the entry into the camp is only a moment of repose and the end of the march for it. What if it is a position [that is] important and before the enemy that it must occupy? As the premier points that it must reach and garnish are almost always those by which the wings must be supported, because it is always there that the enemy searches take first or to attack, the exterior columns direct themselves on the flanks of the position. What if one wishes to outflank the enemy? One deploys all one's columns outside. All these movements are simple and facile with columns formed by the wings.

In lieu of this, one recalls the columns of Mesnil-Durand that were seen at the Camp of Vaussieux embarrassed [even] in reentering into the camp, that is to say in the simplest and most facile movement, and thus obliged to maneuver. One will next observe that, in war, this will be even more embarrassing for them, as in war, it is often a question of maneuvering in a similar case; [an army] must enter into its camp by the shortest route. This route may not always be found before the front [of the camp]. It must sometimes pass by battalion intervals, in the middle of the embarrassments of a camp that marks itself and that establishes itself. Care must be taken with the forage and the grains that are found on the terrain of the camp. For this, the battalions often enter into the camp by the flank, elongating themselves before their *front de bandière*, and thus open only a route. Imagine the twins of Mesnil-Durand in similar circumstance [and] the time, the space, and the combinations that are required to decompose these machines. And if it is a battlefield that it acts to take, and thus it would be important to occupy the points of the wings promptly, because the enemy would attempt arrive there before the army, other embarrassments, other slowdowns, other counter-marches, other inversions [would be required]. The officer most accustomed to moving troops in this system would find themselves mired in it. We saw it at the Camp of Vaussieux; it was officers [who were hand-picked], adepts of the system, who commanded the maneuvers of each column, and we have never seen so much heaviness [and] confusion, and [so many] false movements. This is enough, as I would again fall into the inventory of the intrinsic defaults of the system of Mesnil-Durand, and I examine it here only in its general aspects.

I have not at all exhausted the great reasons that the science of marches furnishes against the system of Mesnil-Durand. Here is one drawn from the memoir of chevalier de Chastellux, which appears to me to be both new and important. If the position in which one encamps has for its objective to cover a place, a country[side], magazines, etc., and, if the movements of the enemy oblige it to take a new position, whether in advance or to the rear, in which it must always accomplish the same objective (this case is quite frequent in war), the march must continue to cover the same points. It is thus necessary that the development of the front of the march be parallel to the position that one leaves as much as possible, often even more eccentric, but more or less [so] according to the nature of the country[side] and always such that the enemy may not be able to extend past the flanks of the army and march on its rear and consequently on the points that it covers without meeting it and being forced to fight it.[2]

This principle [that is] so justly established by Chastellux appears to me to necessarily extend to flank marches when they are made in the same circumstance. Thus, when the two armies are in parallel movement, one with the goal of guarding its line of defense and covering the points that interest it, and the enemy with the objective of penetrating it, the march order of the former must always be, as much as it will be able [to be], relative in extent to the habitual extent of its battle front and to the elongation of the enemy in such a way that the latter may not be able to extend past the flanks of the defensive army and penetrate its line of defense without finding it [the former] before them and without being reduced to fighting.

If defensive marches almost always have need of a development proportionate to positions, offensive marches must occupy greater spaces still; their objective always being to embrace, to attack, to turn, this may only be done in directing them on a great number of points at the same time.

Thus, when Marshal Broglie wished to de-post Ferdinand from the Camp of Saxenhausen near Korbach, his movement had five great leagues of development. This was to menace Ferdinand on his front while the corps of Lusace disquieted his left flank, the corps of Muy more decisively turned his right flank, and several other large detachments made him abandon this important position.[3]

As we saw at the Camp of Vaussieux in the only maneuver of the great genre that was done, the passage of the Seulles that was supposedly defended by the enemy was executed not on four columns shortened and re-serried according to the principles of Mesnil-Durand, but on four columns that embraced the points of Creuilli, Saint-Gabriel, Mares, and Vienne from their right to their left, which was more than a league and a quarter.[4] The army was only of thirty-two battalions, and, if the enemy really had been forced to defend the passage of the Seulles, it is apparent that the columns of the left that passed Vienne that were destined to turn their right flank could have then taken their turn further and passed one or two leagues above so as to steal a march on the enemy, which, by their position, uncovered the point of Vienne too much, and consequently the effort that would be made against it.

Mesnil-Durand will thus pose in vain the principle that [an army] must re-serry itself on the center, attack by the center, [and] hold less space so as to assemble more forces on a point; practice will always oppose his theory. Marches in war, being always made to conduct to positions or to combat dispositions, will be obliged to be as extended as they are. Broglie himself furnished the demonstration [of this] in all his great operations in the last war. He renewed them at the Camp of Vaussieux, and he will renew them all the times that he will act in war or in [the] maneuvers that resemble it.

---

2   [Guibert likely refers to one of the many unpublished memoirs that the Ministry of War received and kept in the Dépôt de la Guerre, the main Ministry archive, at the Invalides. These are now housed at the Château de Vincennes in the Service Historique de la Défense.]

3   [François-Xavier-Louis Auguste Albert Bennon de Saxe, comte de Lusace, was the son of Augustus III, Elector of Saxony and King of the Polish-Lithuanian Commonwealth. When Friedrich invaded Saxony to begin the Seven Years War, Xavier became a commander in the French army in charge of the Saxon corps. He returned to Saxony to serve as regent for his nephew Friedrich-Augustus III between 1763 and 1768. He purchased an estate in France and lived there until the Revolution, resuming his service in the French army under the title "comte de Lusace." His correspondence with Broglie, *Correspondence inédite*, is a foundational document for understanding Broglie, Xavier, and the Seven Years War.]

4   See the map of the camp environs. [See Appendix A, 177.]

CHAPTER 6

Examination of the System of Mesnil-Durand Relative to Grand Maneuvers and to Army Movements

I will not at all attach myself to following Mesnil-Durand in the different maneuvers or army evolutions that he proposes in his works. This task is beyond my strength, and I would fatigue my readers without furnishing them new enlightenment on the base of the system of Mesnil-Durand, all these maneuvers being either useless or impractical in war and all departing from a false base. It is this that [the reader] will judge by the summary account that I will render of those that were made at the Camp of Vaussieux.

The army, after having passed an hour in forming itself, in re-serrying itself on the center, etc., as I said in the preceding chapter, finally shook itself out to maneuver: the first improbability, as an army does not have need of preliminary dispositions to maneuver, or, to say it better, an army does not maneuver. All its movements may only ever be simple marches. It is this that I will prove in the course of this chapter.

The army always executed general maneuvers by voice, the lieutenant general commanding the four infantry divisions' placing himself at the center and his commands being repeated by each division's lieutenant general, whose are repeated by their *maréchaux-de-camp*, etc. The second improbability: I will prove, in opposing the below to this manner, the sole method that I believe may be admitted when one wishes the maneuvers in peacetime camps to resemble those made in war.

The army has ordinarily changed its entire front on the same terrain as its position. These changes of front or of position, which have been habitual maneuvers, are in effect the great means that Mesnil-Durand proposes in his works, "for varying the disposition in arriving on the enemy, reinforcing parts of the line [and] refusing others, avoiding terrain [that is] too difficult or too defended, attaching oneself to convenient points, passing from the parallel order to the perpendicular, etc.," he says. They all executed themselves by voice for the evolutions and for the evolutions [that were] affected, calculated, [and] arranged in advance, all with a slowness [and] with a fumbling of the directions, the distances, [and] the alignments, of which it is difficult to make an idea. The third improbability. We demonstrate the same below.

We sometimes marched one or two leagues, always in the middle of maneuvering, often in line of columns and consequently much more lengthily and with much more difficulty than we would have in a deployed line, if we had decided to attempt it, which is evidently against the principles of modern tactics. When we marched thus in line of columns, we ceaselessly halted them to realign them [and] to connect the small masses that, in the immensity of the plain, appeared only as points and continually lost [their] alignment, direction, and intervals. As such, the army halted. We supposed an obstacle. We deployed half the line behind this obstacle. We made much fire, then we made [a] passage of lines, the second replacing the first, and the fire continued. Only two times did we form a species of [the] "perpendicular order on the center." It is thus at least that we believe we may call it by the analogy that we have found with some diagrams in *Fragments of Tactics*. It is in this maneuver that we employed the cavalry in the usage proposed by Mesnil-Durand, remembering to sustain the infantry and to charge by the intervals of the columns. All other times, whether [because] their small number did not permit them to [act] decisively, or [because], as a consequence of the system of Mesnil-Durand, the infantry must be in effect always the acting and principal arm, the cavalry always rested passive and almost always as an aside in the maneuvers of the army's corps, and it followed them without taking part in them.

These were the maneuvers that we constantly repeated at the Camp of Vaussieux. I will not do any further analysis of them. They are not a tenth part of those proposed by Mesnil-Durand in his *Fragments of Tactics*. I will only fight everything by a single argument: an army must never make movements by maneuvers, and all the movements of an army belong to the class of marches and may only be executed by them. This principle, of which I have begun the exposition in the first part of this work in speaking of changes of front and of position, has need of being more amply developed.

A battalion, a regiment, a brigade, [or] two brigades at most may be in the case of changing front to make face to an uncovered flank or to an inopportune movement of the enemy, and this change of front or position may be executed by a maneuver. But all the times that it must be a grand corps [or] an army, for a stronger reason, it is no longer a question of maneuvers, and all the changes of front or position must be executed by marches.

It may be said to me, "what difference do I pretend to make here between a movement executed by a maneuver and a movement executed by a march?" A great, an essential [one]: a maneuver is an instantaneous movement that may be commanded by voice, that acts in a small space, [and] that executes itself with a sort of mechanical precision and that consequently holds all the individuals that take part in it in a state of attention [that is] always a little forced and consequently painful. A march, on the contrary, is a long-winded movement by which one covers greatest spaces [and] that cannot be commanded by voice [but] that directs itself only by a known route or towards a given point: a movement, in the end, that has need of more ease and liberty [than a maneuver], because it must last for longer.

Thus all the movements of a battalion, of a regiment, of a brigade may execute themselves by maneuvers when they make themselves in a space circumscribed by time and terrain. All the movements of a great corps and of an army, being instead relative only to great spaces and terrain, must necessarily execute themselves by marches.

A battalion, a regiment, [or] a small corps may change front or position in making the parts that compose it pass the new line of direction by a given point, and this movement, always quite short and quite rapid, must execute itself by a maneuver. But an army ordinarily does not at all change front on the place that it occupies and makes the same passing of the direction of its new line of front by a battalion of its order of battle. When an army changes front, it is to take a new position, and it is quite rare, if not to say impossible, that this position may be found in maneuvering thus on itself and on its old battlefield. All changes "of front" or "of position," which appear to me almost absolutely [to be] synonymous for an army, being consequently a grand movement, may execute themselves only by march columns and [thus] evidently belong to the class of marches.

It results from this that an army is never in the case of executing maneuvers properly speaking, or, to speak more exactly, that all its maneuvers reduce themselves to marches and are only marches. What if it would be within range of the enemy [or] in the presence of the enemy? These marches will be made with more precaution, that is to say that these columns will march more serried and more ready to form *en bataille* [and] that they will observe their intervals with more precision, etc., but its movement will not make it less of a simple march.

It results from this that, when our ordinance indicates the maneuvers of changes of front or of positions, these maneuvers have their utility for one or two battalions, regiments, or brigades at most, but they must not at all be adapted to great corps, and, for a stronger reason, to armies, as this is where the analogy may no longer exist and where these maneuvers become true child's play that war may never furnish the application of.[1]

Mesnil-Durand thus deceives if he believes that an army led according to the true principles of modern tactics will change front or position by the maneuvers indicated in the ordinance. These maneuvers, one more time, are applicable only to small portions of the line or the order of battle like a battalion, a regiment, [or] one or two brigades at most. An army will only ever move itself by simple march columns. If it changes front, it will be to take a new position, and this transport from one position to the other will only ever be a march.

Mesnil-Durand deceives when he makes an army maneuver other than by marches, when he forms it in maneuver disposition during its sortie from the camp, when he holds it full maneuver for hours and entire leagues, when he also makes it march for hours and entire leagues in line of columns, [and] when he pretends to execute all his movements by voice, as one would on an esplanade, and with small means of alignment and direction by pennants, which are good only for partial maneuvers and not for movements that make themselves with a great quantity of troops and in great spaces.

Does Mesnil-Durand wish to have an idea of the manner by which an army must maneuver according to the true principles of modern tactics? Here, in a few words, are what this manner would be:

All the maneuvers of the army will execute themselves by marches and only ever be marches. March orders will take themselves with the greatest celerity and the greatest simplicity, each division forming its column, if it is a front march; or each its line or its half-line, if it is a flank march. It forms itself *en bataille* at the head of the camp, forming itself in march column by the right or by the left according to the situation of the route that it must follow, [then] finally marches; all this is done without preparatory dispositions, without pomp, without maneuvers, [and] without general voice commands in such a way that the entire army is already outside its camp and in open march while that of Mesnil-Durand still makes its preliminary movements to re-serry itself on the center.

The army, once in open march, will always continue by an equal and uniform movement without defiles' [or] obstacles' obliging any of its parts to maneuver [or], above

---

1 [As Guibert indicates, the largest coherent echelon that contemporary commanders used was the brigade, and he uses "great corps" for what would later be called divisions and corps. See Abel, "An Aspect of the Military Experience in the Age of Reason."]

all, stopping itself. Arriving at the position, what camp will one wish to occupy? I have said above how and with what facility one would enter it. No terrain, no circumstance will embarrass, slow, [or] retard the troops for a moment. Until the moment when they prolong themselves on the new line to form themselves *en bataille* or serry themselves to deploy, there is not at all any maneuver for them, and they only continue the march. What if one must take an order of battle that would not be analogous to the order of march and would [instead] be relative to the terrain and the dispositions of the enemy? Then these changes, these new combinations make themselves by advancing or retarding columns, by directing them on some point, by reinforcing one by the others, [and] in employing, above all for this last objective, first the advanced guard and then the parts of the columns destined to form the second line or the reserves. All of this interior mechanism is developed in the *General Essay on Tactics*, and I will be permitted to return to it.[2]

With regard to changes of front or of position, I have demonstrated that they must only ever execute themselves by simple marches. If the changes of front depart from the march order, then they execute themselves by a simple change of direction in the march of the columns; if they depart from a taken position or from a formed order of battle, it is then only a simple march executed with more or less precaution according to the proximity of the enemy.

All the art of movements or grand maneuvers of an army resides in the head of the general. It is in knowing how to move his march columns that he arrives at everything. But for this, he must keep them in hand, and what I call "keeping them in hand" is not placing himself in the midst of them or immediately at their head, [or] maneuvering them by voice or by means of the detailing of a general officer, but in marching with his advanced guard at a half-league or a league from his army to reconnoiter a part of the terrain and the enemy, and also to observe the ensemble in its proper march order, and to command, advance, or retard his columns according to circumstances and relative to the measures that they dictate to him.

[For example], the army being in front march order to go to occupy a position that would be parallel to the position or to the movement of the enemy, [suppose that] the general will learn in the midst of the march that this enemy marched by his right flank and that they go to present themselves on his left flank. All his army will thus be forced to change front to make face to them. It is to him to untangle, to choose, to create, so to speak (this choice must be rapid) a position on his flank, and to send orders to the general officers commanding his columns to direct themselves on a particular point to occupy the new position, if he wishes to hold himself to the defensive, or to form an offensive disposition, if he finds it more advantageous to attack the enemy.

It is then to the general officers to know, rapidly and without fumbling, how to execute these orders, direct their columns on the new points that are indicated to them, judge the distances and the intervals, [and] choose the best manner of making the troops enter into the new position or disposition relative to whether the columns that they command arrive by the right, by the left, [or] by the center in advance of or behind the front line, etc. The current ordinance furnishes them with means for this [that are] simple, facile, [and] susceptible to bending themselves to all terrains and to all circumstances. This is the perfection of the ordinance in this regard: by means of the excellent methods that it includes, one may, when one knows how to take advantage of it and not weigh them down, form a troop, a column, [or] an army *en bataille* by the shortest way and with a mathematical precision on the given points.

I will not extend myself any further on this subject. I would that we renew the demonstration that Rochambeau made at the Camp of Vaussieux for all the *militaires* who were not there, [a] demonstration that was so decisive in favor of the maneuvers of the ordinance and in which Rochambeau had all the army's officers for [his] judges and admirers.[3]

---

2 [Abel, *Guibert's General Essay on Tactics*, 171–188.]

3 [Many of the camp's records are contained in SHAT 1M 1819, including accounts of the camp's exercises contained in 20, "Lettre de Wimpffen."]

CHAPTER 7

[The] System of Mesnil-Durand Considered in Relation to Orders of Battle and to Battles

We have arrived here at the most important part of tactics, to that which is [both] the complement and the goal in some way, because armies exercise themselves, instruct themselves, [and] toughen themselves only to form themselves in a state of winning battles, and it is battles that decide, and almost always led to the success of, all the other operations.

I know the inconvenience[s] that there are for an officer in treating this great material. I know all the clichés that are elevated without fail against those who [work on it]. They are accused of dogmatizing on what they cannot know. It is inferred that, since they reason on battles, they have the stupidity to believe themselves capable of giving them and commanding them. And then come the declamations against the incompetence of age and grade, against the insubordination of spirits, [and] the so-often ill-applied example of the Rhetorician of Ephesus, giving lessons on the art of war, etc.[1] I wish for once, since I have the occasion, to respond to all that was said or that will be said in the future, whether against me or against particular officers whose zeal and application will engage [them] in the same career.

First of all, I declare, for this that concerns me (and I do not doubt that, in similar cases, they do not all have the same modesty) that, because I write on war, because I have not ceased to study, to deepen, and to research the extent of the theory of my art, I do not believe myself more capable than another to command in war and to have success in it. Study and knowledge may inspire a prejudice favorable for the one who has these advantages. One may hope for him, but this is his only right, and it is a suitably flattering recompense. Talent, talent: here is what theory does not give, but practice does not give it either, because, as Friedrich wrote to Friedrich Heinrich Karl Freiherr de la Motte Fouqué, "practice without reflection is only ever an insufficient routine. A mule that made ten campaigns with Eugene is not a better tactician. In effect, marching when one marches, stopping when one stops, encamping when one encamps, eating when one eats, beating when one beats: this is war is for the majority of officers who do it."[2] Talent, I repeat: this is what one is born with; this is the privileged gift, the gift of nature, the gift before which obstacles, jealousies, [and] enmities must all abase themselves and extinguish themselves when it exists to a certain degree. An officer who will have written like Caesar, like Friedrich, like Montecuccoli will know how to teach the science of these great men in a perfect manner; other great men will develop themselves by reading their works; if he lacks talent and he finds himself placed in grand occasions, all his theory will support him in vain; it will not give him faculties, organs, judgment, courage, or character. A man will elevate himself, perhaps resting until then in the crowd and in insecurity, a man who will not make a name for himself by his words or by his writings, a man who will meditate in silence, [and] finally a man who will perhaps ignore his talent, who will have felt it only in exercising it, and who will have studied quite little. This man will seize opinions, circumstances, [and] fortune, and he will say to the great theoretician what the practicing architect said to the architectural orator before the Athenians: "what my rival said to you, I will execute."[3]

After this profession of faith that must, I hope, shield me from all the pretentions that have been gratuitously supposed of me, I will respond to the reproaches of incompetence of age and of grade, of insubordination of spirit, that have ceaselessly been made to young people and to particular officers, first by opposing generalities to generalities:

---

1 [After the Second Punic War, Hannibal Barca became a mercenary commander in Greece, which took him to Ephesus. In a story recorded in Marcus Tullius Cicero, *De oratore*, 3 Vols. (Cambridge: Harvard University Press, 1979), II:254, Hannibal attended a lecture on warfare by Phormio, the "Rhetorician of Ephesus," that he denigrated as insanity. Guibert makes the same reference in Abel, *Guibert's Essay on Tactics*, 238.]

2 [See Friedrich II, *Recueil de lettres de S.M. le Roi de Prusse pour servir à l'histoire de la guerre dernière* (Leipzig, 1772), 72.
   Friedrich Heinrich Karl Freiherr de la Motte Fouqué was a childhood friend of Friedrich who commanded forces in the Seven Years War. Their correspondence was a valuable contemporary source for the Prussian perspective of the Seven Years War.]

3 [Several authors identify this passage as an oracular prediction about Napoleon. See, for example, Jacques Bainville, "L'uniforme d'artilleur," *Napoléon* (Digicat: 2022); Louis Garros, *Napoléon, cet inconnu* (Paris: Beaudart, 1950), 103; Frederic Natusch Maude, *The Leipzig Campaign, 1813* (New York: MacMillan, 1908), XIII; E. Mayer, "Le général Jean Colin, *Revue de Paris* 4 (1918): 827–849; and Théodore Pavlovitch, *L'idéal démocratique et la discipline militaire* (Paris: Chapelot, 1911), 77.]

If it is a question of commanding and of acting, youth, or at least maturity, is the age of strength and talent; the greatest generals were young and demonstrated at the beginning of their careers almost all that they would after; without recalling the ancients who would give me the most complete victory in the case [like] the examples of Alexander, Caesar, Publius Cornelius Scipio Africanus, Hannibal, etc., the best modern generals commanded armies at an age where one would be at pains to be a general officer today: Turenne, Condé, [and] Luxembourg all commanded armies before thirty years of age; [and] even today, Saxe and Broglie commanded them at forty.[4]

Perhaps even great generals may only be formed in advancing men who announce talents quite rapidly and during their youth because they must contract at a good time the habit of command, of turning details into results, and of thinking and acting at large.

But, as unfortunately today the enormous multiplication of superior grades, the engorgement that results from it, the prejudices on the *ordre de tableau*, an infinity of other vices of our constitution, and, more than this, [and] the length of peacetime that makes no talent spring forth with éclat, render the advancement towards the eminent grades in war, and towards command, more difficult and slower than ever, there is only one remaining means that may develop emulation and prepare some talents for the nation: young people and particular officers [must] apply themselves, study, and work to supplement the practice that they lack with a wiser theory.

In applying themselves and in studying thus, there must necessarily be some among them who would be tempted to communicate their ideas, their research, [and] their observations to the public, because all men have a goal in working, and there is not at all a man who would work if he were condemned to [simply] burying the fruit of his hard work.

The just deference due to age and to grade doubtlessly imposes on young people and particular officers the need to take counsel of experience; of never forming their opinion, in person or directly, in the presence of those men that age, grade, and, for a stronger reason, personal reputation, have placed above them; [and] in a word, to doubt, to hesitate, [and] to examine for a long time before opposing themselves to them.

But when a deep study finally makes them take this opinion, and they believe the development useful to the good of the service and to the progress of the art, they are permitted to submit it to the judgment of the public; the public is, in the long run, the true, the great, the irrecusable arbitrator, and, in pleading in its tribunal, one may expect truth and justice sooner or later.[5]

In these sorts of military controversies, all personal precedence must cease; opinions appear nude; they have neither age, nor rank, nor grade, and their respective rights are the reasons that support them.

Of these generalities, if it is now permitted for me to pass to that which may more directly serve as apology for the liberty that I take in treating the great objects of this chapter, I will represent to my readers that this youth, which was made a so-great crime when I published my *General Essay on Tactics*, unfortunately escapes me every day, and that at thirty-five years old, one is almost no longer guilty of it. I will dare to add that this youth is not perhaps completely denuded of experience; that, elevated in the camps, it had seven campaigns behind it; [and] that I had seen some battles and that I had studied almost all those that were given in Europe over the last century on the sites where they took place. Finally, I will repeat what I have already said, that my rights are at least the same as those of Mesnil-Durand, and that, moreover, I always march with a system that is not mine for [my] base and [with] the greatest generals for [my] guide.

We come to the subjects that I have to treat. I will first speak of orders of battle in themselves and then of the manner of taking them and forming them. From there, I will speak of battles, that is to say of the action of combat and of the manner of conducting it. I will place, relative to these diverse regards, the two systems in opposition to

---

4 [Publius Cornelius Scipio Africanus was one of the great generals of the Roman Republic. Descended from the patrician Cornelii, he entered military service and was instrumental in rescuing Rome from near-defeat at the hands of Hannibal in the Second Punic War. See Goldsworthy, *The Punic Wars*, 197–330.

Army command in eighteenth-century France generally went to senior commanders, which is why they were older than the great captains Guibert recites, and his contemporaries Saxe and Broglie only received commands after a succession of other generals had failed.]

5 [Historiography on the public, public opinion, and the public sphere is immense, particularly after the mid-twentieth century and around the theories of Robert Darnton and Jürgen Habermas. T.C.W. Blanning, *The Culture of Power and the Power of Culture: Old Regime Europe 1660–1789* (New York: Oxford University Press, 2006), especially 103–184, provides an effective introduction. See also Roger Chartier, *The Cultural Origins of the French Revolution*, trans. Lydia Cochrane (Durham: Duke University Press, 1991); *The Darnton Debate: Books and Revolution in the Eighteenth Century*, ed. Haydn Mason (Oxford: Voltaire Foundation, 1998); Arlette Farge, *Subversive Words: Public Opinion in Eighteenth-Century France*, trans. Rosemary Morris (University Park, PA: Penn State University Press, 1995); Jürgen Habermas, *The Structural Transformation of the Public Sphere: An Inquiry into a Category of Bourgeois Society*, trans. Thomas Burger (Cambridge: MIT Press, 1991; and Roche, *France in the Enlightenment*, 485–640.]

each other. Nevertheless, I will warn that I will not burden myself with that [system] of Mesnil-Durand; this would be to attach myself to his debris, and I have a more interesting goal to attain: achieving the development of the modern system.

1   Orders of Battle, According to the System of Mesnil-Durand

Mesnil-Durand, always faithful to his manner, which is to divide and subdivide to infinity, establishes in his *Fragments of Tactics* (this is his most-recent work, and that to which I will consequently attach myself here) "that all the orders of battle may be ranged under four classes, and these four branches comprise all of grand tactics. These four orders are," he adds, "the parallel, the oblique, the perpendicular, and the separated."[6]

1.1   *Parallel Order*

"The parallel order," says Mesnil-Durand, "is an order that spreads its forces equally over all its front and that engages itself in all parts."[7] Mesnil-Durand adds that this is a quite-bad order; we fall into accord with him, but this will absolutely not be for the same reasons. For example, one of the [reasons] on which he extends himself the most is that "the parallel order, having all its front extended and contiguous, and going to the enemy all of a piece, may only march with much pain and slowness without deranging the line and opening it in several locations, even when the terrain is quite accommodating; for example," he adds, "if one takes a line of any fifty battalions and one measures this march to the *toise* and with a watch."[8]

I have demonstrated in the course of this work how Mesnil-Durand has little-just notions on modern tactics in this regard. Who has ever thought in these tactics of marching in order of battle "all of a piece!" Eh! what an order of battle again! Mesnil-Durand supposes it of fifty battalions in line.

Mesnil-Durand then distinguishes three sorts of parallel orders: the "elongated parallel," the "simple parallel," and the "double parallel," and he defines them and then explains them in the following manner:

The elongated parallel is the habitual order of our time, and it is good only for fire and in the case when it is not possible to close [with the enemy].

The simple parallel is no less extended than the elongated order but does not leave two battalions opposed to each enemy battalion because it only has one line in lieu of two. It is true that this sole line is truly two that act against the first, independently and distinctly, although together.

The double parallel is only different from the simple in that it has double forces on an equal front and its battalions on two lines of assembled columns. It is with it that, in closed terrain, one may fight with great advantage an inferior, equal, or superior army, [and] that, in an elongated order like this, one would fight equal forces.[9]

I bound myself to citing. What to respond to this chaos of distinctions and definitions? What to respond to Mesnil-Durand when he believes that, in modern tactics, one would be reduced to fighting with equal forces against an inferior enemy? Is it that one would not act on their flanks? Of two choices—one where the enemy would not be posted, [and one where] they would be—if they would be in a plain, one would outflank them, one would envelop them, [and] one would carry only the troops on one's front necessary to attack them or to contain them; if they would be posted, one would turn their position just the same. Perhaps one would be obliged to take oneself a little further, but in the end, one would de-post them without attacking them on any point with equal forces. I see in history superior armies making stupidity of fighting inferior armies on equal front and getting themselves beaten by them. But these are the Persians at Thermopylae, the Burgundians at Morat, [and] the French at Azincourt, and modern tactics does not teach to take them for models.

We again take up the abridged account that I render of Mesnil-Durand's orders of battle; it is always he that I will faithfully extract.

1.2   *Oblique Order*

The oblique order is that which reinforces a part of the army's front to engage the combat uniquely with this part and to assure it the victory by the superiority that one has arranged, and, to this end, refusing all the others, holding each of them more or less remotely according to whether it is more or

---

6   *Fragments de tactique*, chapter on orders of battle.
    [See Mesnil-Durand, *Fragments de tactique*, 124–187. Mesnil-Durand's orders are drawn from Vegetius, *Epitome of Military Science*, 104–107, which he acknowledges throughout the memoir.]
7   [Ibid., 130.]
8   [Ibid., 131.]

9   See "Memoir on orders of battle," *Fragments de tactique*. [See Ibid., 133–136.]

less distant from the attacking party in such a manner that the ensemble of the refused parts is oblique and not parallel to the enemy line.

"The oblique order may attack by the right, by the left, by both, or by the center," says Mesnil-Durand, but he prefers to always attack by the center, and he makes it a general principle; his reasons in this regard are that, by means of modern dispositions, the flanks are often unattackable; that battles engaged by the wings are never decisive enough; that, when the oblique has no other objective than to outflank and to turn, this so-vaunted order becomes [a] quite-little thing; [and] that, in lieu of this, in attacking by the center, one pierces the enemy order of battle, one separates it, and the destruction of their army is the infallible [result]. It is thus in effect that he made his *plésionettes* play so great a role in his first works in making them make the maneuver that he named "dividing by manches." His columns must today accomplish the same usage.[10] One recalls what I have said in this regard in the first part of this work.[11]

"The oblique order formed on the center," concludes Mesnil-Durand, "is thus the only true, essential, universal [order], the only [order] that, always being in season whether one outflanks or one does not outflank, gives means to attack the enemy."[12]

Mesnil-Durand adds to this definition of the oblique order a mass of principles that I will dispense with extracting and fighting. The principle of attacking by the center appears to me to be the only one that merits the pain.

I agree with Mesnil-Durand that it would certainly be advantageous to pierce the enemy order of battle, to separate their army into two, and, thus taking their disposition in the reverse on both sides, to destroy this army to the last. This is perhaps what an attack by the center could operate if it were feasible, as proposed by Mesnil-Durand, that there would be nothing to counteract the success that he promises himself, and above all that the enemy would do nothing to oppose it. But similar suppositions may not make themselves in our days. There are no longer barbarians in Europe, and, in still supposing a quite-inferior army to another skilled in maneuvers and in leadership, of which the Seven Years War offered examples, simple good sense, the sole evidence, [or] the enlightenment of a single general or superior officer suffices to indicate the remedies to an attack on the center and the means of turning it against the enemy.

The attack on the center has evident disadvantages. 1. The enemy may more facilely and more promptly reunite their forces against it, since they are all more within range [of doing so].[13] 2. They [the enemy] may, in reuniting themselves, embrace and envelop the army that attacks. 3. In attacking on the center, one is necessarily and naturally outflanked. Mesnil-Durand says truthfully that "it is a thing on which the decision is made."[14] He then adds, and one must recall that it is a principle ceaselessly announced in his works, that to be outflanked is only an inconvenience for the extended order, that his [order] is above this pusillanimous fear, [and] that it does not at have flanks or weak parts. We will examine this last assertion in the course of this chapter. We return to our enumeration of the disadvantages of the attack on the center.

4. Attacking on the center and winning a complete battle in this manner, it is certainly more disastrous for the enemy. But, for the same reason, in giving it, one compromises oneself more, [and] one courts the greatest risks. If a first success has you penetrating into the enemy order of battle and then the lateral parts of this order of battle, the second line, the reserves know how to properly maneuver and have a return to fortune; if the enemy, more skillful yet, knows how to retreat adroitly before you until they have prepared their maneuvers on your flanks, as we have just now proven that Mesnil-Durand has flanks, it is you in your turn who courts the risk of a complete rout. The more you will engage in the enemy battlefield, the more return and retreat will become difficult.

These are, in short, the inconveniences of attacks on the enemy center. We will demonstrate, in developing the modern system relative to orders of battle, that attacks on the wings, which are one of the fundamental principles of our tactics, unite all the opposing advantages, and others [that are] more important still. We go to the pretention that Mesnil-Durand has that his habitual order has nothing to fear on its flanks and, to speak his language, that it does not even have flanks.

Without doubt, a battalion of a frontage of sixteen men on twenty-four of depth, also known as a *plésion* or a column, does not at all have flanks, and it is [approximately] equally strong on all its faces when it is standing still and when it makes face on four different fronts. But it is a singular consequence to conclude from this that a line of columns, which is the habitual order of Mesnil-Durand, also does not at all have flanks.

---

10   [Mesnil-Durand, *Fragments de tactique*, 138.]
11   [See 18–20.]
12   [See Mesnil-Durand, *Fragments de tactique*, 92–93.]
13   [See Jomini, *The Art of War*, 72–178.]
14   [This does not appear to be a direct quote of Mesnil-Durand, but it does accurately reflect his thought on the issue.]

For an army to have an order of battle without flanks, it would have to, as I have already said in relation to castrametation, range itself on a square, or almost-square, order, in such a manner that the difference between the smallest and largest sides would be difficult to sense. It is this proportion between the front and the depth of the battalion in column that makes its individual strength. But this proportion, and consequently this strength, no longer exists from the moment that there is a line of columns. Mesnil-Durand may well shrink his intervals [and] insert column on column in them; the side of this disposition, if his army is of fifty battalions, will still be shorter than the frontage in relation to one of fifty, and it will not be less necessary, if the enemy presents themselves on his flank, that he make a conversion movement or change of front of the totality or of a part of his line to make face to this flank.

It is thus a strange error of Mesnil-Durand's to believe that his habitual order does not at all have flanks and consequently does not at all fear being outflanked. This outflanking is not only as destructive to him as it is to the extended order, but it is also even more so to him, because, as he occupies a smaller space, the enemy may embrace and envelop him with more facility. It may act on three sides of his order at the same time. Finally, if he arrives at being put into disorder, this disorder is almost without recourse, since the re-serrying of the troops and of space must necessarily augment it, and the effects of enemy artillery are yet more destructive and redoubtable. Finally, if the enemy knows to press and push without relenting, it may be that, in an entire army in such a disposition, no one escapes to go to carry news of the disaster. I will return to this in treating the conduct of the action of combat in the course of this chapter. Meanwhile, we pursue the exposition of the other orders of battle of Mesnil-Durand.

1.3 *Perpendicular Order*

This is the order invented by Mesnil-Durand, whose glory he does not wish to share with Folard, that he believes to be quite superior to the oblique order, and, in the end, according to him, [is] the best of all the orders and that on which the choice must fall the most often. But we place Mesnil-Durand himself under the eyes of our readers.

> The perpendicular order has for its objective, like the oblique [order], to attack a part of the enemy front with a great superiority, refusing the fight with all the others. It differs in that, in the oblique order, supposed to start from the parallel, the refused part front marches only retarding successively by echelons in such a manner that, in its ensemble, it effectively becomes oblique, [while] in lieu of this, the perpendicular [order] marches by the flank to form itself in column, prolonging the flank of the attacking part and consequently becoming really perpendicular to its front and to that of the enemy.[15]

Definitions ordinarily have for their goal to clarify; those of Mesnil-Durand sometimes accomplish the opposite goal, but I will dispense with furnishing commentary on them; we see if they will be found in the following.

> This order may form itself as the preceding, by the right, by the left, by both at the same time, or by the center, and these two different cases will represent one square, two [squares], or a double [square].
>
> In all these cases, rarely will the square employ the entire army, and more often some parts will remain outside and behind, parallel to the front that will further protect and assure the perpendicular line, [which is] already assured by its disposition, which would entirely protect it from the enemy, and by its proper strength, which it would be able to put into action at need without a maneuver other than a single [one] to the right or to the left by man.
>
> The perpendicular has all the properties of the oblique; [it] even refuses the part that it does not wish to engage more entirely, and (if one may count on this advantage for something) [it] holds [the refused portion] within closer range of reinforcing the attacked part; it is yet simpler and more clear [and] consequently would appear generally preferable. It is true that the perpendicular line, more shielded than oblique echelons and yet less susceptible to diversions, for the same reason [is] less within range of arriving, as soon as the attack has succeeded, on the front of the non-attacked parts to achieve and complete the victory. Only if the attack is obliged to advance itself quite far to reverse a third line, this perpendicular line, which always follows, finds itself quite well placed to immediately carry itself frontally on the uncovered flanks that remain in line and promptly sweep the battlefield. It is to the general to combine these different properties and choose between the two orders according to the circumstances. But I am persuaded that the choice will fall most often on this one.[16]

---

15 "Memoir on orders of battle," *Fragments de tactique*, 172 and following.

16 [Mesnil-Durand, *Fragments de tactique*, 172–173.]

Mesnil-Durand then extends himself, as much in the text as in the notes, to assure himself of the propriety of the invention of this order. He says that Folard did not at all doubt it; that the sixth order of Vegetius "which is, if one wishes, somewhat perpendicular,"[17] has nothing in common with his; [and] that Maïzeroy has maladroitly given us, in his *Cours de tactique, théorique, et pratique,* a fight of the Maccabees in the perpendicular order.[18] Finally, he proves that this order is his and that no ancient or modern historian, nor Holy Scripture, can abduct the discovery from him. We assuredly leave him this glory and bound ourselves to doubting that this order never procures any for the generals who would be tempted to make use of it, etc.

Here are the reasons on which I found my doubts. First, the perpendicular order of Mesnil-Durand will be even more outflanked than any other of his orders, and it will be in a quite dangerous manner. In effect, which is the order of battle of Mesnil-Durand thus elongated on a perpendicular: as he gives it in Diagram V of his *Fragments of Tactics,* or as we have seen a representation of it, in truth quite unformed, at the Camp of Vaussieux? It is an order whose point or head is six battalions' frontage, while the two branches or flanks of this order are two lines of columns elongated on the two perpendiculars. In the end, this is, to reduce this order to a known figure, a parallelogram whose small side makes front to the enemy.

We suppose this parallelogram, [in] making face to the right or the left, represents an army on two lines that, in lieu of a brigade of four battalions on its flank, as is the usage in modern tactics, will have one of six placed. What! it is with this same order turned towards the enemy front that Mesnil-Durand seriously proposes to attack, to penetrate, and to destroy the army that will be opposed to him! How does he not sense that this disposition, which he persuades himself to be so decisive and so formidable, is only in fact composed of three flanks; that he puts himself in contact with the enemy in the most unfavorable manner by it; [and] that the most skillful and the most fortunate maneuver that the enemy would be able to make to attack him in the flank themselves would never furnish them so complete an advantage [as this disposition]? In effect, what could be more advantageous and better foresee the most complete victory than to find oneself already formed on the flank of an enemy army with all one's forces developed and ready to act? One believes to already have, and in effect has, a so-great advantage when one turns the enemy flank, when one outflanks them and embraces them with some troops. Here is quite another thing. The flank of Mesnil-Durand (as it will be well objected to me that this is not his flank and that it is the front of his attack, I call "flank" the side [that is] the shortest and consequently the weakest in an order of battle) I say is opposite the enemy center, since it is the center that it pretends to attack, and consequently the two larger sides of his order are outflanked on both sides by half the enemy army.

Mesnil-Durand will say that his order will always march, attack, [and] pierce. But if it marches, the larger sides of his perpendicular order will thus certainly become flanks in every sense of the expression, as columns may not both march and make face on the flanks. What if it will be stopped? Then it will be on the defensive. It will be the butt of the dispositions of every species that the enemy may form against it [and] to the superiority of their artillery that, acting on a quite-great development, taking reverses on it, and beating the masses accumulated in a small space, may only shake it and commence its defeat.

I will not extend myself further on the perpendicular order. I pray only that my readers recall that it is this order with which he must "approach the enemy; charge them with the *arme blanche*, even when they will repair to inaccessible obstacles on ninety-nine percent of their front; and be sure, although inferior, of beating them in so-advantageous a post, etc."[19]

1.4 *Separated Order*

This [order] is not absolutely the creation of Mesnil-Durand; it is one of those spoken by Vegetius.[20] One sees it in Charles le Beau, *Histoire du Bas-Empire en commençant à Constantin le Grand,* employed by Narses, Justinian's general.[21] In truth, these were not the good years of the military science. If the mania for erudition would wish to seize me, if I would wish to furnish the twin of the example of a perpendicular order of battle found in Maccabees,

---

17 [Mesnil-Durand, *Fragments de tactique*, 172–175; and Vegetius, *Epitome of Military Science*, 104–107.]

18 [Mesnil-Durand, *Fragments de tactique*, 174n(a), and Maïzeroy, *Cours de tactique, théorique, et pratique*, II:94–97. The story Maïzeroy references is found in 1 Maccabees 16, in which a Jewish army commanded by Judas and John Maccabaeus defeat an Antiochian army under Cendebaeus, governor of the Levant, at the Battle of Modein.]

19 See the first part of this work, 24–25.

20 [Vegetius, *Epitome of Military Science*, 104–107.]

21 [See Charles le Beau, *Histoire du Bas-Empire en commençant à Constantin le Grand,* 27 Vols. (1757–1811), XII.

Narses was a Byzantine general who served under Emperor Justinian I in the sixth century. His military prowess enabled the Byzantines to re-conquer much of Rome's lost territory, pushing the Eastern Roman Empire to its greatest extent. See also John Haldon, *Warfare, State, and Society in the Byzantine World 565–1204* (New York: Routledge, 1999).]

I would find in that of Gideon the origin of the separated order, as, when Gideon attacked the camp of the Midianites, he divided his three-hundred men into three troops and attacked on three sides at the same time.[22] But leaving aside Vegetius and Narses, the Maccabees and Gideon, it is the system of Mesnil-Durand in which it is a question.

Mesnil-Durand says [that]

> The separated order is that in which each division makes separate corps and fights independently of the others, which become separated and even distant from each other. The three preceding orders are in successive lines, the first right, the second broken into echelons, and the third broken into square. This one is not at all a line; it is a regiment of three or four *plésions*, [which is] an approximate parallel to what a brigade in the accustomed order would do. As to the rest, it has for its objective, like the oblique and perpendicular [orders], to attack only some parts of the enemy front, refusing combat to the others, and assuring itself the victory by the extreme superiority granted to the parts that alone decide it.[23]

I will not give myself the pain of either analyzing or refuting this order. It returns to the preceding order, since, according to Mesnil-Durand, the divisions must each form their perpendicular attack, and it is more dangerous yet, since the same inconveniences are more multiplied here. In addition, there is always a grand objection to make against these separated attacks: they are always either too close or too distant from each other. In the former case, they do not accomplish the great goal, which is to throw the enemy into uncertainty and to much divide their forces. In the latter case, they almost always lose for want of concert between them; their distancing [and] the nature of the country[side] are often such that they may not see, hear, or rescue each other, and, in case of ill success, they may be cut or dangerously compromised.[24]

Mesnil-Durand would that his separated order attack by divisions and consequently on three or four points at least. But the more he multiplies the points of attack, the more the above inconveniences are augmented [and] the less these separated corps have constancy and their attacks have decisive effects. It must be added to this that rarely does a position, at least if it would not be quite ill-chosen, offer three or four points [that are] feeble and consequently susceptible to attack. "But," Mesnil-Durand will say, "how will modern tactics work, whose principle is to embrace and to act on great fronts?" In modern tactics, an offensive disposition embraces much terrain [and] menaces several parts, but it is rare that it makes a true attack on more than a single one. The attack may embrace several points, as long as these points are dependent on each other, but they all only form a general disposition to which the points are tied and that places the greater part of a general's forces in hand and under his eyes, particularly those with which he acts. Thus were all the great battles of the King of Prussia and of the great modern generals given. It is on this that we will have occasion to return in treating orders of battle according to the current system.

2 Orders of Battle According to the Modern System

I will be somewhat forced to repeat here what I have said in the *General Essay on Tactics*, as having to speak on the same subjects and not at all having changed opinion since, I do not have a new version.[25]

"Order of battle" in current tactics may and must be understood and defined in two manners. It first signifies the primitive and fundamental order in which an army disposes itself to encamp and to fight, [an] abstraction made of all local or accidental circumstances. It then signifies all dispositions whatsoever derived from this primitive order with any modifications or changes relative these circumstances. I will clarify this double definition.

Considered as [the] primitive and fundamental disposition, the order of battle of an army is the tableau that one forms at the commencement of the campaign to regulate the emplacement and the disposition of the different corps that compose an army. It is after this that the troops are disposed on two lines, the infantry at the center and the cavalry on the wings; this first arrangement is founded in reason when it is only the preparatory disposition and, if I may express myself thus, the disposition of waiting and of organization, but it becomes abuse and error when it degenerates into routine, when one takes it indifferently in all circumstances and in all terrains, [and], above all, when one makes it the combat disposition.

I say that this arrangement is founded in reason when it is only the disposition of encamping and of organization; in effect, when one assembles an army, it is good to establish a primitive and habitual order in it, an order that would be the base from which one may depart for operating and

---

22   [Judges 6–8. Guibert likely derives this reference from Maïzeroy, *Cours de tactique, théorique, et praticque*, 1:22.]
23   [Mesnil-Durand, *Fragments de tactique*, 181.]
24   [Guibert speaks of the opposite of interior lines, what Jomini, *The Art of War*, 72–178, refers to as "exterior lines."]

25   [See Abel, *Guibert's General Essay on Tactics*, 189–197.]

to which one may return when the circumstances that [caused one to be] departed from it no longer exist. I say that this arrangement becomes abuse and error when one does not depart from it according to circumstances [and] when one blindly makes one's combat disposition from it. In effect, it is easy to sense that incidents, circumstances, and vices without number must oblige to make changes to the primitive order; it is easy to sense, for example, that, although following this order, the army must be formed on two lines, the infantry being at the center [and] the cavalry on the wings, and all the corps that compose each line being contiguous with each other, circumstances in war may require that the cavalry be placed in the center and the infantry on the wings, fighting on one line, forming oneself on two or three lines, [or] even separating the army into several corps to make each act on [a] different point; however, all these derogations from the primitive order do not at all hinder the totality of the disposition from being an order of battle, because it has for its goal to fight.

Considered as [a] disposition dictated by the terrain and by the circumstances, the order of battle of an army is and may thus almost always only ever be the primitive and fundamental order, as rarely does one find oneself in plains where the army may be formed on straight and contiguous lines. Rarely does the nature of the country[side] permit it to compose the entire center of infantry and the wings of cavalry. Often, one weakens and places outside of being made a prize a part of one's disposition to reinforce another with which one wishes to fight. These circumstances produce modifications and variations to infinity; ceaselessly does one depart from the order of method and take dispositions that have little relation to them. The more a general is skillful, the more his army is maneuvering, the more he departs from elementary routine so as to carry unforeseen and decisive blows to his enemy. Finally, between the disposition of method and the disposition of circumstances, which may both be named "order of battle," [is] an essential difference: the former takes place only in peacetime camps, on paper, and in the dreams of tacticians, [while] the latter is that which takes place in war, in which one gives battles, and, above all, that which wins them.

There may only be two manners of giving battle to the enemy: the first, in engaging, or in forming oneself within range of engaging, the combat on all the parts of one's front at the same time; the second in attacking only on one or several points. After this, I believe [it possible] to be able to reduce the seven orders of which Vegetius speaks, and, for a stronger reason, the four of Mesnil-Durand, with their variants, to two orders alone: "the parallel" and "the oblique." I will, in separately treating each of these two orders, define them, assign them their principles [and] their goal, and demonstrate how all dispositions hold to these two orders and are only derived from and modifications of them.

2.1   *Parallel Order*

A battle disposition whose front develops parallelly to that of the enemy so as to be able to enter into the action with all the parts that compose it at the same time must be called this. When I say "parallelly," one must not read this word as geometric precision, as there are few country[sides] that may permit two armies to extend themselves on fronts exactly parallel to each other. The name "parallel order" thus belongs to any disposition that places all the corps of the two armies opposite each other, in proportion [to each other], and in range of fighting.

This is certainly how armies must have been disposed in the first ages of the military science. They were not as numerous as today; they formed themselves on a less-extended ordinance; they were armed in such a manner as to have need of approaching each other to damage each other. They did not at all know all the finesse of tactics; in proportion to their being less enlightened, they had perhaps more courage. Each wished to fight; each wished to take part in the danger and in the glory. As such, these battles, so much more terrible and so much more bloody than our current fights, which are only games after theirs, make us almost regard them as fabulous. One still sees two savage nations today violently animated against each other and not knowing the usage of our firearms: their brave [people] assemble, march one against the other, join, and their disposition will extend itself so that they can all fight and each [can] find his man. Thus do all the nations in America that the Europeans have not armed fight each other; also their wars sometimes finish themselves by the entire destruction of the vanquished people. Thus all the first races of men that inhabited Europe fought until hazard, ambition, and reason gave birth to some illumination among them.[26]

One sees that, the parallel order being the natural and the most simple, it must be the oldest disposition known, as it is not the words that make things, and, since the savages perhaps did not know either the word "order," or certainly the term "parallel," it is this unformed and instinctive disposition that they took to all approach the enemy at the same time and to fight them; it is it that has perfected itself

---

26   [This passage, and several that follow, mirror arguments made in Abel, *Guibert's General Essay on Tactics*, 19–20 and 192–193.]

little by little, and the words born with the ideas became and named [it the] "parallel order."

In proportion to [the degree to which] men enlightened themselves, armies superior in number had to search to draw the advantage of their superiority, and, to this end, to envelop the enemy and to embrace their flanks. From this [results] the disposition in the form of a crescent that still subsists today in Turkish and Asiatic armies. Thus, skillful generals, finding themselves at the head of inferior armies, had to search for the means to compensate for this inferiority by the perfection of tactics; they had to sense that, in presenting themselves parallelly to an enemy superior in number, they would have exposed themselves to being enveloped and beaten, [and] that there was some other sort of disposition, some science of movements by means of which they would have been able to carry the elite of their forces to one of the points of the order of battle, engaging the combat only on this point, and placing all the other parts of their position outside of being a prize; from this [resulted] the oblique order and all the other derogations of the parallel order. Finally, between generals who were a little enlightened on both sides, the parallel order ceased to take place in battles, because, superior or inferior in number, they calculated with reason that there were other, more advantageous dispositions.

This proves what the origin of the different orders of battle must have been in antiquity [and] is what we have seen reborn in the same progression. The military science fell with the Roman Empire and annihilated itself. Centuries of shadows succeeded it. Ignorance extended itself over everything; it extended itself particularly on the manner of making war, as it must be observed in passing that then, much more than today, it was the most ignorant of the nations that devoted themselves to arms; the inhabitants of cities were not at all warlike, and the small number of men who delivered themselves to studying studied for the altar, for the Scholastics, or for some of the arts that escaped the general barbarity.[27]

They thus then returned to fighting each other as in the first times; it was multitude against multitude, hazard against ignorance; armies approached each other and engaged each other along all their front. Thus did Clovis give battle against Atilla, Charles Martel against the Saracens, [and] Charlemagne against the Saxons.[28] The proof that they give for this is that an incredible number of combatants perished. The chronicles of these wars say often that few of the victorious saved themselves from the carnage of combats. These armies took the parallel order without knowing it; it took place for a long time after; it took place as long as tactics rested in infancy; it was found at Marignano, at Agnadello, [and] at Pavia, where, above all, the armies had the time to form themselves *en bataille* the day before and the possibility of closing on each other along all their front[s].[29]

---

27 [Ibid., especially 19–20. Guibert argues the "Dark Ages" myth that posits a collapse of culture and learning between the end of the Western Roman Empire and the rise of the western European states. While academics have largely set aside the term, it remains in full use in popular histories and imaginations. See Janet Nelson, "The Dark Ages," *History Workshop Journal* 63, no. 1 (2007): 191–201.

The Scholastics were medieval philosophers influenced by Aristotle and his works, as transmitted through Greek, Jewish, and Muslim sources. See Peter Adamson, *Medieval Philosophy* (New York: Oxford University Press, 2019), 3–360. Guibert intends the reference to be to a small group of erudite people isolated from and not representative of society.]

28 [Guibert identifies four prominent leaders and commanders of the early medieval period.

Clovis I was the leader of the Salian Franks who conquered much of modern France in the mid-sixth century. He made the critical decisions to accept Christianity and to adapt to extant Gallo-Roman culture rather than impose Frankish culture on Gaul, resulting in a hybridization of the two. He created the Merovingian Frankish state that Guibert and his contemporaries refer to as the "first race" of French kings. Atilla was the early fifth-century Emperor of the Hunnic Empire that terrorized the late Roman Empire before his defeat at the Battle of the Catalaunian Plains in 451 and death in 453. Guibert is incorrect in having Clovis fight Atilla, as Clovis would not be born for at least a decade after Atilla's death.

Charles Martel was Mayor of the Palace in eighth-century Frankia. He ruled in the name of Merovingian kings, but his Carolingian family served as de facto rulers of Frankia. He defended the Frankish state and expanded it through conquest. He is most famous for his victory in the 732 Battle of Tours, in which he led a Frankish coalition that defeated the Umayyad ("Saracen") army of Abd al-Rahman ibn Abd Allah Al-Ghafiqi, largely ending the threat of Muslim conquest of Gaul. His son Pepin was the first Carolingian King of the Franks, inaugurating the "second race" of kings.

Charlemagne, Pepin's son, was the greatest of the Carolingian Frankish kings. He spread Frankish rule across western Europe, from the Spanish March to modern Poland, the Balkans, and Italy. As Guibert notes, he conducted several campaigns against the Saxons, forcing Christianity on them. He is usually regarded as the first Holy Roman Emperor and the "Father of Europe," along with both France and Germany. The polities that eventually became France, Germany, and Italy evolved from his empire.

See Patrick Geary, *Before France and Germany: The Creation and Transformation of the Merovingian World* (New York: Oxford University Press, 1988); Edward James, *The Franks* (New York: Blackwell, 1988); and Janet Nelson, *King and Emperor: A New Life of Charlemagne* (Berkeley: University of California Press, 2019.]

29 [Guibert cites three battles from the Habsburg-Valois Wars that roiled Europe between the 1494 and 1590. The wars originated with a French claim to the Kingdom of Naples that several kings attempted to press; they quickly expanded into a pan-European

When the military science commenced to be reborn, [its philosophes] made the same reasoning that the Ancients did, and they consequently departed from the parallel order. They searched to maneuver, to turn their enemy by their flanks; there were almost no battles engaged on the totality of the front; there were many fewer still when armies became more numerous and ranged themselves on a thinner ordinance. This meant, in effect, that there was not some obstacle that prevented them from joining each other on so-extended fronts! They then adopted a new genre of war founded on the nature of the terrain and on the choice of positions. Inferior armies began, whether by entrenchments or by natural obstacles of the country[side], to shelter themselves from all attacks or to reduce the possibility of the attack to some points. All combats became affairs of posts; there were no longer general battles, [and] consequently, [no] more parallel order. Since the end of the last century, one may not cite an action where the armies engaged the combat on all their fronts.

What must most contribute to rejecting the parallel order now, other than the immense frontage of the armies and the difficulty of equally joining [the enemy] on all the points of their front[s], is the necessity that is in all states of not compromising their strength, the armies that make all their strength and their destiny, in a general action. Today, no nation is warlike in its customs or by its constitution; today, peoples have for their defense only a certain number of troops; outside of these troops, all the rest of the citizens are only a lazy multitude without any idea of war or discipline, ready, consequently, to subject themselves to the yoke of the vanquisher; the respective politics of governments wishes that the generals leave nothing to chance. We have seen how the result of parallel orders put into execution on the day of battle was to render the action general; how it became more terrible, more decisive, [and] more bloody; [and] how it might have brought about the total destruction of the vanquished. [Imagine] the distress of one of our modern nations if one would have said to them, as was said to the Romans after the day of Cannae, "the enemy arrives; the army that covered the capital engaged in a general battle, and this army is no more."[30]

The parallel order, taken in the sense that I gave it at the commencement of this chapter, is thus never executed in battles today, but this name may remain for the primitive and habitual disposition of an army's organization and encamping, since all the parts of its disposition find themselves of equal strength and ready (the obstacles of the terrain left aside) to enter into action with the enemy if it wishes to attack with all its front at the same time.

From [the fact that] the parallel order, employed as the attack disposition, is no longer in use today, does it follow that it is never advantageous for an army to make use of it? Doubtlessly no; a superior army, whether by number or by the species of troops, will do well to employ it if the enemy is so ill-advised as to furnish it the occasion, that is to say that they present themselves to it in a plain or in a position approachable along all its front, as the battle that a similar army would win in this disposition would entirely ruin the opposing army. But other than to surprise one's enemy on the march in an absolutely open country[side], and [one] that affords them no recourse of any position, one never has occasion to thus engage battles with all of one's front, as the enemy on the defensive always occupies a position [that is] advantageous by nature or by art, and then the attack necessarily reduces itself to points, the parallel order no longer being able to take place.

Nevertheless, we found the fortunate and rare occasion of surprising an inferior enemy on the march and of being able to attack on all their front in an absolutely open plain without obstacle once in the Seven Years War. This example offers a too-great lesson in several respects for me to allow it to pass in silence.

In 1758, the French and Allied armies, each being on the move, approached and encountered each other on the march without suspecting [that they would]; they both formed *en bataille*. But chance had placed all the advantages on the side of the French army. The position that it found quite naturally on the right flank of its march, towards which the enemy presented themselves, was a chain of heights [that was] advantageous [and] almost dominant, in the form of a semi-circle a plan of around a league and a half of depth that extended itself from the heights of Frauwiller up to the small Erst River. Other than

---

conflict that was staged between the Valois and Habsburg families and took place largely in Italy. The Battle of Agnadello took place in May 1509 as King Louis XII led an army of French and Italian states against the Venetians; he won the battle and pushed the Venetians out of Lombardy. The Battles of Marignano and Pavia were commanded by King François I. At Marignano in 1515, François and allied Venetians defeated the Swiss, breaking their vaunted pike-and-shot formation and ending willing Swiss participation in wars. At Pavia in 1525, François suffered a devastating defeat at the hands of a Habsburg army that virtually annihilated the French army in Italy and resulted in his capture. As Guibert intimates, the dense formations of the period required significant planning and exertion to maneuver into position for battle. See Michael Mallett and Christine Shaw, *The Italian Wars 1494–1559: War, State, and Society in Early Modern Europe* (New York: Routledge, 2019), 89–92, 126–131, and 150–153.]

30 [This paragraph, and parts of the preceding, are repeated nearly verbatim from Abel, *Guibert's General Essay on Tactics*, 193.]

this superiority of position, we had that of numbers, and we came to take the offensive. Ferdinand, on the contrary, found himself in the most destructive position, [with] this small river behind him, since he was achieving its passage when he discovered our columns: one of his bridges broke [with] the greater part of his artillery on board; [there was] no *point d'appui* for his wings [and] no obstacle on his front; he could not have chosen another position, the country[side] offering him none and his army having only the time to form itself *en bataille* in haste. It was nine in the morning at the moment when the two armies thus encountered each other. A part of the day was employed in forming *en bataille*, in consulting, [and] in reconnoitering. For reasons that do not belong to me to judge, the attack was postponed until the next day, and Ferdinand re-crossed the Erst without any loss during the night.[31]

In a similar circumstance, if one would be determined to give battle, it would doubtlessly be a case of making use of the parallel order; it would be a case of descending from the heights that we occupied to attack, at once and along our entire front, this army that floated in a plain without obstacles and that did not at all have a retreat. But such a confluence of position and circumstances is so rare that this example changes nothing of the general principle that today rejects the parallel order. It only proves, in making an exception, that a general principle is not at all exclusive and that healthy tactics admit nothing of this genre [exclusivity].

But a great lesson that must be drawn from this example is relative to the theory of marches, [a] theory that has always unfortunately been in its infancy in our armies, [and a] theory on which I have first dared to hazard some new ideas to make it march alongside the progress of modern tactics.

Our army marched leaving the Erst on its right flank, and, in its march, it constantly followed the same direction. Prince Ferdinand was on the other bank of this river. It was thus clear, by his position and by ours, that the march that we were going to make was of the class of flank marches and that it must consequently be open. Conforming to the principles established in our theory, the army should have thus marched on two columns, each line forming its own, or at most on four [columns], each of them being composed of half a line; these columns (the nature of the country[side] permitted [this] easily, as it was without obstacles) should have been open [and] quite close to each other, in such a manner that the army would only have had to make a right to form itself *en bataille*, and the interior march columns would have had only the least terrain possible to cover to approach the eventual position that the army would have been able to have been in the case of taking. Marching thus, we would have been *en bataille* in a moment, and, some hours gained, because we lost fewer, would perhaps have made [us] take the part of the attacker. In lieu of this, the march opened itself and followed the accustomed routine, which was to not at all distinguish the species of march that we had to make and to believe that there was always gain [to be had] from multiplying the columns when the nature of the country[side] permitted it, [a] principle evidently good when it must be a front march but evidently false when it must be a flank march. The march was thus on six columns, and the interior column of the march, that is to say the column of the left, was a league and a half from that of the right. When it [the army] had to form itself *en bataille* on the right flank, it upset the entire march order, arrested the columns, decomposed others, [and] made those of the left arrive by a long circuit; we add to this that the troops were less maneuvering then [and that] that the general officers, the superior officers, no one knew the simplest and promptest means of reaching what the terrain and circumstances required. Four or five hours were thus lost in forming everyone in order and before the left was absolutely formed. This was not anyone's fault; it was the vice of the times and the result of the imperfection of tactics.[32]

2.2 *Oblique Order*

The oblique order is the order of battle [that is] the most used, the wisest, [and] the most susceptible to combinations, the order that conforms equally to inferior and superior armies, to the latter for making a great use of the superiority of their forces [and] to the former for supplementing their inferiority. It is the most-famous order of the ancients, but none of their tacticians made known its interior mechanism to us. The King of Prussia is the first modern who executed it by principles and who adapted it as current tactics.[33]

For an order of battle to be reputed "oblique," it is not necessary that the front of this order exactly draw an oblique line in relation to the enemy front, as rarely do the terrain and the circumstances permit such a regularity to be able to take place. I thus call "oblique" any disposition in which one carries a part and the elite of one's forces on the enemy and draws the rest out of range of them, any disposition, in a word, in which one attacks with superiority

---

31 [See Szabo, *The Seven Years War in Europe*, 180–182.]
32 [Ibid.]
33 [See Claus Telp, *The Evolution of Operational Art, 1740–1813: From Frederick the Great to Napoleon* (New York: Frank Cass, 2005), 5–34.]

one or several points of the enemy order of battle while one gives the change to the other parts and [thus] forms oneself outside of being able to be attacked by them.

After this definition, almost all battles that have been given for a century were in the oblique order, as they were all reduced to points of attack. But this order was taken by chance and without great combinations. These advantages have not been at all deepened; their finesses are not known; the manner of taking it rapidly on a point indicated by the circumstances of the moment, and that would not at all have been foreseen in the march order, is ignored.

To perfectly develop the theory of the modern oblique order, is necessary to enter into some details here.

I will first distinguish two different species of the oblique order. One is the oblique order *in principle*, the oblique properly said, that is to say an order in which the army is disposed exactly *obliquely* to the front of the enemy; the other is the oblique order *of circumstance*, that is to say an order in which the army, despite not at all being disposed obliquely to the enemy, nevertheless finds itself, whether by the nature of the terrain or by the skill of its movements, in the case of attacking on one or several points, and of being outside of being a prize on others.[34] I will speak on each of these two species successively and make known their differences. The oblique order, properly said, may execute itself in two manners: "by lines" or "by echelons. "By lines" means the disposition forms an oblique front at a half-quarter conversion, all the battalions and squadrons being contiguous and on the same alignment, in this form:

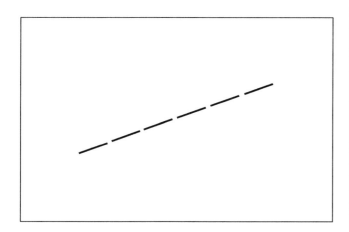

"By echelons" means that each battalion and squadron allows itself to be passed on the side on which one wishes to attack by the battalion or squadron that is next to it by a certain number of paces more or less considerable according to the number of troops that compose each column and the degree of obliquity that one wishes to give to the order of battle; all the parts that must attack thus form a species of hammer in advance and are ranged in the ordinary disposition, in the following form:

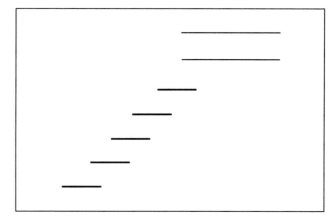

This disposition by echelons will be better still if, in lieu of being formed by battalion and by squadron, it is [formed] by brigade or by division, these corps being disposed in such a manner as to be able to hold hands at need and to occupy the positions that may be the most formed outside of being a prize and make illusion to the enemy. Thus, for example, AB is the hammer, the part of the order of battle destined to attack the enemy placed at I, and CDEF are four army columns that are formed *en bataille* by echelons [and] occupying different points in which they accomplish the goals indicated above.[35]

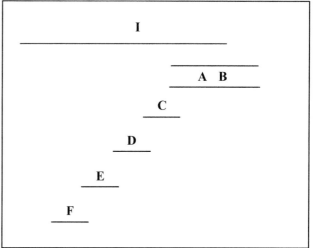

---

34 [Guibert's italics.]

35 [The smaller diagrams in this chapter are taken nearly wholesale from Abel, *Guibert's General Essay on Tactics*, 194–195.]

Of these two manners of taking the oblique order "by lines" or "by echelons," the first is elementary and purely of method. It is good to execute it in a camp of instruction so as to commence making known to the general officers what the oblique order is and what its goal is. The second, which is only a sequel to the first, is simpler, more facile in its deployment, more applicable to all terrains, [and] more susceptible to maneuvers and to action when the order is formed. It is this one that must serve in war, above all when one forms, by brigades or by great corps, the echelons destined to refuse themselves to the enemy or to make illusion to them.

The oblique order may form itself on the right, on the left, or on the center, that is to say that one may attack the enemy on one of these three points and refuse to them the rest of the order of battle by means of this order. But, as I proved in refuting the favored principle of Mesnil-Durand, which is to form attacks on the center, it is always by the wings that it is the surest and the most advantageous to attack, and this principle, absolutely opposed to that of Mesnil-Durand, is one of the bases of modern tactics.

I will add to the reasons that I have already given in this regard to combat the principle of Mesnil-Durand [and] to support the modern principle

1. that attacks on the wings accomplish a great objective, which is that of turning and menacing the enemy rear. Mesnil-Durand regards the truth of this advantage as [worthy] of little consideration, but his doctrine on this point does not have many proselytes.
2. that attacks on the wings always find less strength united against them and that the enemy has fewer resources to oppose them, because it is certainly farther from all the parts of an order of battle at one of its extremities than at its center.
3. that it is more facile to the enemy to untangle and to judge an attack disposition that one forms on their center than it is one that would be formed on their wings, as what passes on the center is perceived on two parts, and, the enemy outflanking this disposition on both sides at the same time, not a single movement must escape them. On the contrary, the attack disposition formed on their wings makes itself towards the extremity of their order of battle, and it may thus be perceived only by a single side at most, but more often still, it makes itself outside the enemy order of battle, and, by this, almost outside of their view, since every attack on the wings ordinarily embraces the flank and searches to turn it.
4. that, in attacking the wings, above all in the oblique disposition of modern tactics, the entire army may successively carry itself at need to the support of the part that attacks in order to sustain it, to refresh it, or to reinforce it, and in thus supporting the part engaged in action, it draws all that it wishes to refuse outside of the range of the enemy. It is this that the attack on the center cannot do, as first, the parts of the enemy order of battle that outflank it may, with facility, embrace it and take the two parts in the flank. In addition, in proportion to [how much] the corner or the head of the attack engages itself in the enemy battlefield, or even to penetrate it, it is obliged to make itself supported and sustained more and more by the lateral branches of the disposition; these branches, in advancing themselves, necessarily approach the two parts of the enemy order of battle that overlap them and outflank them and very much form themselves as a prize.
5. that, if an attack on the wings does not succeed, it compromises nothing of the army that formed it, up to a certain point; the corps that were engaged in action only then fall back on the corps that refused themselves to the enemy, and these latter make the rear-guard. In addition, the beaten army then retiring to the rear and outside of the position occupied by the enemy, it finds itself immediately outside their range and outside the range of being pursued, because, for the victorious army to be in a manner redoubtable for it [the pursuit], it would be necessary for the army to commence by making a change of front that returns it within range of it [the beaten army], [a] movement during which the latter would gain time in order to advance to place itself in cover. On the contrary, I have demonstrated how an army that would be beaten in attacking by the center would find itself exposed by its defeat to a total ruin.

Despite this general principle of attacking on the wings, favorable exceptions may nevertheless present themselves. But, one more time, exceptions do not constitute a general principle when it [the principle] is that which must be habitually followed; they [general principles] are only what is not exclusive, and we avow that no principle of modern tactics has this pretention.

I will give some examples of these exceptions here, and consequently the case[s] in which it would be advantageous to attack by the center. [One is when] the enemy has the ill-address to compromise their center in occupying a post [that is] too detached from the rest of their position in such a way that one may, in attacking, cut its communication and separate them from the order of battle that supports it. This was the village of Lauffeld, since our cavalry, after several successive attacks in which this village was taken and re-taken several times, was able pass between this village and the Allied army to charge it in the flank and dissipate the infantry that was refreshing the troops charged with the defense of the village and winning it as soon as we had taken it.[36]

[Another is when] the enemy composes the center of their order of battle in such a manner that the arms would not be employed relative to the nature of the terrain, to circumstances, and to the rules of war. [For example], at Blenheim, the center found itself composed entirely of cavalry, because the two united armies of Tallard and Marcin were encamped as if they were separated, and the common center of the two orders of battle consequently found itself formed of one wing of cavalry from each of the two armies.[37]

[A third is when] the enemy has exposed their center in a nude and open position, or one that that has been too ungarnished with troops to reinforce its wings. I would then be able to cite other exceptional cases and support them with examples, as poor generals have many manners of forming themselves as a prize, and faults of ignorance are yet more varied than combinations of talent.

But when one has an affair with a skillful enemy, such examples may hardly renew themselves, as, once the wings of a position [are] well supported, if the position does not have an extent disproportionate to the army's strength, [an] inconvenience one avoids falling into, there are many means of forming one's center outside of being a prize. One entrenches; one reinforces it with artillery, and art soon makes it a formidable point; one pulls it back in the form of a reentrant in leaving one's two wings, which one has placed in a good defensive position, as bastions in advance of one. Finally, as to the repartition of troops, the center is always necessarily the strongest part of an order of battle, because one always makes it, seen at its greatest and its equal proximity to all the other parts, the emplacement of reserves and the point of distribution from which all the reinforcements and supports come.

We return to that which concerns the oblique order.

The oblique disposition's degree of obliquity, whether this disposition makes itself by lines or by echelons, must be combined on the enemy's strength, on its science, on its hardiness, and, most particularly still, on the nature of the terrain and on the points [that are] advantageous for the defensive that this terrain may furnish to the parts of the order of battle that one wishes to refuse. Thus, the more that an enemy army is superior, the more this enemy is skillful and maneuvering, and the more that one must pay attention to distancing the feeble and defensive parts of the order of battle from it, the more that the direction of obliquity on which the army is ranged must form an open angle with the enemy wing that one attacks. It is hardly possible to give some positive principle too the rest, as the nature of the country[side] may be such that, on certain points, one may, without inconvenience, approach the enemy with the parts of one's disposition that must rest on the defensive, because, by the means that this position will offer these points, one will have between the enemy and one obstacles that will prevent their making an offensive movement on these feeble points. But this case enters into the second species of the oblique order.

This second species of oblique order, which I have named the order of "circumstance" in my definition, as I have named the first the order of "method," is that in which the army, despite not at all being disposed obliquely to the enemy front, nevertheless forms itself, whether by the nature of the terrain or by the skillfulness of its movements, in a situation to attack on one or on several points, and to be itself outside of being made a prize in the parts of its disposition that it wishes to refuse. This order is the one that one is most habitually in the case of taking in war, because it is rare that battles give themselves in absolutely flat and uncovered plains and in which dispositions consequently may be made without relation to the terrain and in the regular obliquity established in principles. One is perhaps almost always subjected to departing from this regularity to profit from advantageous positions offered by the nature of the country[side], whether to favor the illusion that one wishes to make to the enemy or to form the defensive parts of the order of battle more in surety.

Thus I name the disposition of the Battle of Leuthen an oblique disposition, although the Prussian army was not ranged obliquely to the Austrian front. But it attacked their left wing with the elite of its forces, took it in the rear, and destroyed it, while it profited from a chain of heights that was opposite their right and their center to make illusion to them, to hold them in check, and to place the rest of its army, enfeebled by the reinforcements that he carried to its right, in an excellent defensive [position] there.

Thus I name the disposition of the army of Prince Ferdinand at Krefeld an oblique disposition, because he turned and attacked our left with the elite of his forces while the rest of his army, separated into several corps, contained the center and the right of our army by demonstrating on several points at the greatest range of our cannon.

---

36 [The Battle of Lauffeld was fought in July 1747 between the 125,000 French commanded by Maurice de Saxe and the Pragmatic Army of 100,000 commanded by Prince William Augustus, Duke of Cumberland. Maurice was attempting to open a siege of Maastricht, which Cumberland maneuvered to protect. The battle was hard-fought, including in the destroyed village of Lauffeld, which served as the anchor for the Allied line that Fontenoy had for the French in that battle. Maurice prevailed, but he could not open the siege that year, although he did the following year. See Browning, *The War of the Austrian Succession*, 313–317.]

37 [See Lynn, *The Wars of Louis XIV*, 290–294.]

Thus could I say that almost all the armies that have engaged in battles over the last century engaged them in the oblique order because they reduced their attack to points, and I would say, [even] if it were not true, that, in the majority of these battles (I except those that were given by the King of Prussia), this order was taken by quite imperfect means and without having a reasoned and theoretical knowledge of its mechanism and its goal.

The oblique order of the second species' being that which is adapted most easily to terrains and circumstances, generals must thus particularly make their study of it. And where might this study be made with success? It is in instruction camps; it is in war, which offers the widest-varied and truest lessons; [and] it is, if I may express myself thus, by dint of handling troops and circumstances. Theory may pose principles where there were none, but it is then to the genius to make application of them.

Formation of Orders of Battle According to the System of Mesnil-Durand

It is not at all easy to render account of the principles and the means by which Mesnil-Durand pretends to arrive at the formation of his orders of battle. The Camp of Vaussieux did not at all furnish us with positive illumination on this, because, as we have already seen, not a single order of battle was executed there relative to terrain and to circumstances. Everything was limited to maneuvers in line of columns, to some changes of front, and, a single time, to an unformed representation of a disposition that appears to us to have some analogy with the perpendicular order exposed in Diagram V of *Fragments of Tactics*. It is thus in these *Fragments*, which are the most recent work of Mesnil-Durand, that we are reduced to searching for some details that may give to our readers an idea of the manner in which Mesnil-Durand forms his orders of battle. In reading these details, our readers will be grateful to us for not having multiple citations, and, above all, for not being elongated in commentaries and in refutations. It was the case, or never, of remembering that "the secret of boring [people] is that of saying everything."[38]

We first see a small résumé of Mesnil-Durand on parallel orders:

> The simple and double parallels are, according to circumstances, quite capable of extension and contraction. The simple may, without inconvenience and without much enfeebling, give some more *toises* to its intervals, and, by this means, outflank an enemy of equal strength elongated on two lines; it may give them less to oppose not two battalions to one, but six to two. It may, without being doubled along its entire extent, be reinforced in some parts by reserves, etc.

The formation of the parallel order is the ordinary development of the habitual march order, [a] development [that is] always the same for each of the three species but more or less long according to whether it will be more or less total. Thus, the double parallel will be more formed than the simple, which will itself be more formed than the elongated parallel, and the development of the first two is nothing more than that of the last stopped at some point.

The formation of the simple, as it is presented in Diagram II, is, counting from the moment when the commencement of the double columns *approaches* and separates by an avenue of twenty-six *toises*, a maneuver of four to five minutes, supposing that there are twelve battalions in the march of each column:[39]

	Proof	
Extension:	5×34	$= 170$
Shortening:	$\dfrac{5 \times 12.5}{3}$	$= 21$
Total:		$\underline{191 \text{ toises}}$

The formation of the double, in the same case, is ten minutes more:

	Proof	
Extension:	2×34	$= 68$
Shortening	$\dfrac{2 \times 12.5}{3}$	$= 8$
Total:		$\underline{76 \text{ toises}}$

The parallel, elongated on two lines, having to extend itself no more than the simple on one, would be no longer in forming than the thirty-two *toises* that must be counted for the particular development of a battalion.[40]

But these partial and truncated extracts may always appear to be suspect, imposing on our readers the obligation to read an entire example of a formation of the oblique order

---

38 [Guibert quotes from Voltaire to Friedrich, 6 August 1738, *Oeuvres completes*, Volume 1 (Paris, 1830), 201–204.]

39 [Guibert's italics.]

40 [Mesnil-Durand, *Fragments de tactique*, 136–137. The proofs are reproduced from notes (a) and (b).]

by the center. I have already said that all the examples of formations of the order of battle that Mesnil-Durand gives in his works are by the center, his favorite principle being to preferably engage attacks on this point.

Mesnil-Durand says

> there is an army of forty-eight battalions, seventy-two squadrons, and seventy-two guns in the [artillery] park. I set aside any additional light troops that there may be, and even the reserve, as pieces foreign to the base of the maneuver and disposition, as well as accessory usage that the general will wish to make use of them.
>
> This army, which marches on its habitual order on four columns, arrives on the alignment where it wishes to deploy itself *in double assembled columns*, as they always are at the moment of development.[41] This army of 32,256 infantrymen [and] 6,912 cavalrymen holds 1,556 *toises* of frontage for the infantry, 420 for each wing, totaling 2,408, because it wishes to equal the front of its enemy, elongated in modern style, having formed for this only one line in which each battalion that is again in French column draws, as much for it as for its interval, thirty-six *toises*; it only has four battalions in the second line, two in the center [and] one on each flank. The grenadiers and chasseurs on six ranks are aligned on the heads [of the columns] in the intervals, [as are] the regimental guns, if there are any, in such a manner that everything presents an almost-contiguous line. Twenty-four squadrons are placed, as one sees, behind the battalion intervals; the rest [of the cavalry] is divided between the two wings, each of the twenty-four squadrons on two lines having between them intervals equal to half of their fronts. These wings are two-hundred and forty *toises* behind the infantry line. The twenty-four squadrons of the right wing are the eighteen of the first column and the six last of the second. It is the same on the left: the four artillery divisions, at the moment of the development, carry themselves on the front, passing by the avenues of the double columns and immediately forming themselves *en batterie*.
>
> We have previously seen that the development of this parallel order is five minutes at the most moderated redoubled step, and even four for all the army's battalions except four. We have also seen that the formation of the cavalry is not any longer.

I suppose that the army, which first formed itself thus, wishes to make an oblique attack on the center on a frontage of six battalions, comprising one-hundred eighty-eight *toises* and consequently arriving on that of three enemy battalions.

For this, the four battalions of the center, with the two that they have in the second line, will only march forward without thinking to maneuver, occupying themselves only with closing on the enemy by the shortest route. They will only begin the redoubled pace after having covered thirty-six *toises* at the ordinary pace;[42] at the same time that these six battalions will shake themselves out, the five that are to their right (9, 4, 2, 1, 3)[43] will march by the left, always at the redoubled pace. After having thus covered thirty-six *toises*, (9) will reform on front to march the second line after (10); (4), having arrived at the same time in the position that (9) occupied, will reform itself also on front and will march aligned on the front of the attack whose right it will hold; (2) will then arrive at the same point [and] form itself in the second line following (4); finally, (1, 3) will reform themselves on front, when they will find themselves in the third line behind (9, 2), on which one may remark that these last (1, 3) have covered thirty-six *toises* more than the others; [given] from where they will arrive if they do not force speed for a time, this third line will be a little more remote than is demonstrated in the figure, but this is a quite-insignificant thing, as it must be remarked that, in this movement, each battalion preserving in advance of the one that precedes it only the thirty-six *toises* that it [had] in line more advanced towards the left, it finds only these thirty-six *toises* from the first line to the second, including one of the two lines' thicknesses, and that there would be no inconvenience if these lines were a little less close.

---

41 [Guibert's italics; Mesnil-Durand's original italics are only on "assembled."]

42 [Mesnil-Durand's note:] "They may neglect this small attention without any inconvenience. Because, as we have already observed, our maneuvers are not *scrupulous*. What would arrive if, in outflanking the enemy, the four battalions of the center of the front would find themselves advanced these thirty-six *toises*? The battalions of the right and the left (4, 3) only at the points where the figure presents them (2, 1)?* The disposition would not be less good; I would not be astounded even if it were found to be better, and, if I would re-commence the diagram, I would form thus, to suppress this bagatelle of thirty-six toises and to render to the battalions that have the head of the attack the time of the order's change exactly null."

43 These figures are the numerals that Mesnil-Durand attached to his battalions and squadrons to facilitate the intelligence of his maneuvers.

At the same time that the five battalions of the right will thus maneuver by the left, the five of the left (5, 3, 1, 2, 4) will maneuver the same by the right, and this will only form, in the order as we see it, the division of sixteen battalions that must make the attack. But I will speak no more of the maneuver of the left, entirely parallel to that of the right.

We only well remark, before going further, that to form this attack division as we see it, and to carry it to this point three-hundred and thirty-six *toises* in advance of the parallel position, it only took the time that it had taken its first battalions to cover three-hundred seventy-two without any maneuver, so that the change of order is really a minute longer for this entire division, or perhaps this length is exactly null, as we have seen in [note 42].

While the head of the attack will form itself and advance thus, the eight battalions that are to its right and that must form the first echelon will march together by the left. When they will have covered the thirty-six *toises*, the first four (5, 6, 7, 8) will reform themselves on front and will march, the three will follow (12, 11, 10) by the left one-hundred eight *toises* more then will reform themselves on front and will march in the second line behind the preceding, [and] finally, the last (9) will march thirty-six *toises* more before reforming itself and marching in the third line behind (10). The formation of this echelon is thus a total of one-hundred forty-four *toises*, as the last battalion that marches thirty-six toises more by the left then has less to cover in advancing, and, these one-hundred forty-four *toises* being made by the first line at the ordinary pace, the echelon will finish forming itself, as one sees, at the moment when it will be one-hundred eight *toises* in advance of the parallel position and one-hundred eight *toises* behind the front of the attack in such a way that this echelon will cover thirty-six *toises* more at the ordinary pace, if one wishes that it would, according to the figure, one-hundred forty-four *toises* behind the attack. As to the rest, to better mark the maneuver, one may first draw the front of the echelon to the height of that of the attack, save then forming them at the ordinary step, or even arresting them quite quickly, as much as they can, to lose the one-hundred forty-four *toises*.

The second echelon will be formed by the eight battalions of the right of the army in the state where they would find themselves in the parallel position. The figure represents it at one-hundred ninety-two *toises* from the first because it supposes that this has stopped, as we have seen, at one-hundred forty-four and the maneuver has commenced at three-hundred thirty-six from the enemy, although it may be done much closer.

The third echelon is formed by the wing in its position two-hundred forty *toises* behind the infantry [and] five-hundred seventy-six from the enemy. But it is quite easy to advance these last echelons as far as one will judge appropriate; the affair of the maneuver in itself is to refuse them completely naturally, at least as much as they have need of being.

As for the twenty-four squadrons that would be behind the infantry in the parallel order, the four columns of the center, each of four demi-squadrons, will follow the attack as indicated corresponding to the figure, and, for this, will only march in advance, resting a little on the center. They were placed behind and to the right of the intervals of the front in such a manner as to be equally able to leave in advance to dissipate beaten enemies or by the side to charge in the flank that would wish to march against the front of the first echelon. The four squadrons (5, 6, 7, 8) I always say are of the right, resting a little on their left, will go to place themselves, as one sees, to the left of the first echelon to protect the flank of the attacking division. Finally, the four others (9, 10, 11, 12) that were behind the infantry's right will place themselves on a line to the left of the second echelon. One sees how these cavalry movements do nothing and will not keep us waiting; one also sees that, to better mark the maneuver, one may, before it commences, carry these two parts of cavalry on the front of the infantry by means of which all the battalions that have marched by the flank will be covered either by this cavalry or by other battalions marching in advance.

At the same time, or even before the maneuver commences, the two artillery divisions of the center, reinforced by the artillery reserves, if there are any, will carry themselves brusquely forward to the distance and to the place [that are] the easiest for protecting the attack, and, above all, to thunder against all the batteries that will present themselves. As to the divisions of the right and the left, half will rest in advance of the third echelon, [and] the other half will carry itself, as one sees, on the flank of the first.

It would injure the reader for me to arrest myself too much in showing them how this disposition and maneuvers are advantageous. No more is necessary than for me to prove how the enemy may not be able to hold for a moment against this attack, neither three battalions to which it is addressed resisting sixteen supported by eight squadrons nor, if one wishes to count only the first line, although the second supports so closely and in such a way that they may really act together, that these three battalions may not hold against six reinforced yet more by the grenadiers and chasseurs of six others. It is not less obvious that, the enemy line's thus being pierced with the greatest facility and the battalions' immediately being dissipated by cavalry with the same facility, this attack would pierce a second, and, if it existed, a sixth; that the breech would open itself rapidly, and the pierced line would itself crumble, the collateral parts only being able to wait to be charged from the front by the [follow-on] echelons at the same time that they would be [charged] in the flank by the victorious division and by the cavalry that follows it; that, as long as this division thus wins the battle, the enemy will not be able to engage the combat in other parts; that they will not be able to charge the flank of this division, nor that of any [follow-on] echelon, nor even the fronts of these echelons, without themselves being charged in the flank; that there is not even the time to arrive on these echelons; [and] that no accident or contrariety may arrest the effect of the maneuver nor hinder all the pieces that follow their vocation and accomplish their goal, the echelons always following the attack movement without any slowing or change of direction [and] without slowing the attacking division by a step, nor does it have need of thinking of them until all the enemy lines are reversed and its army is beyond the battlefield.

It is no less evident that, when the maneuver would be as distant as we will suppose and, at the pace of forty *toises*, much too slow, the enemy would not be able to see it and to judge it in time to carry themselves there to remedy it. In effect, only eight or nine minutes would pass from the first step of this maneuver to the moment where it would pierce, of which they would lose a good part before they would see it clearly, as the first echelons would first appear to march as well as the attacking part; the second [echelons], if they do not at all march or promptly cease to march, may yet only give [them] quite-vague suspicions, above all [in] being quite ill-seen by some troops thrown in advance for a moment and seeing the maneuvers that signify nothing, [as] the maneuvering parts are marked; finally, the wings, supposing them tranquil in their posts of the last echelons, say nothing; otherwise, they do not press to fire but may arrive at the gallop at any moment. Of these eight or nine minutes, the enemy will thus lose at least four or five. And then what will they make of the other four or five?

It will be much worse if the maneuver makes itself, not at three-hundred thirty-six *toises*, but at two-hundred, [or] if, in lieu of the forty *toises* per minute, one covers sixty; then, from the first step of the maneuver to the first bayonet blow, it will not be a question of nine minutes, but of three or four. The enemy will have one or two minutes to see, judge, and parry this. In a word, the change of order and the charge will be the lightning and the thunder.

If at present we add to this formation that of the parallel order itself, and we suppose that the army came to form this at three-hundred *toises* from the enemy to deceive them by the display of this false disposition, then immediately after forming the oblique and attacking, *from the first step of the development to the first bayonet blow*, there will be (at the pace of forty *toises*) thirteen and a half minutes, of which [there will be] five for the parallel deployment, one for the change of order (that we need not count) and seven and a half to arrive.[44]

We believe ourselves dispensed from engaging ourselves here in a deep analysis. How to refute in form what refutes itself in simple reading? Who could believe, If I did not expose the entire text here, that such maneuvers were seriously proposed? That, first at three-hundred and then at two-hundred *toises* from the enemy, one will hazard similar movements, one will form these echelons to the *toise*, to the minute, sometimes at the ordinary step, sometimes at the redoubled step, one marching in advance, [and] the others halting; others marching by their flank; [and] finally others forming front! And this strange use of cavalry! And the columns of the center each composed of four demi-squadrons that must follow the attack, and, for this, only "march forward, resting a little on the center," then "placing themselves behind and to the right of the intervals of the front in such a manner as to be able to equally go in advance to dissipate beaten enemies or alongside to charge in the flank that which would wish to march against the flank of the first echelon!" And the four other squadrons, which, "resting a little on their left, will go to place themselves to the left of the first echelon to protect the flank of the attacking division!" And finally, these four others "placed on one line to the left of the second

---

44 "Memoir on Orders of Battle," *Fragments de tactique*, 170 and following.

[Mesnil-Durand, *Fragments de tactique*, 150–157.]

echelon! The good role that the cavalry thus morseled and exposed to all the fire of an attack would play, because it must accompany the movements of the echelons! And the two artillery divisions "that carry themselves brusquely in advance to protect the attack and to thunder on all the batteries that will present themselves!" This would be artillery in good surety when it would be thus dispersed in advance of the echelons! Above all, it would be quite advantageously posted, the enemy artillery not being able to fail to beat it in the flank, because the disposition of Mesnil-Durand is flanked on both sides! And the infantry "that must cover sixty *toises* a minute!" And "the change of order and the charge," which, by means of this prodigious speed, "must be as the lightning and the thunder!" And the attack "that must penetrate their lines with the same facility as a single one!" And "the breach" of the enemy order of battle "that must open itself in a moment!" And "the pierced line that must crumble itself!" And finally, this single division of the army of Mesnil-Durand that must "win the battle all by itself, without the enemy's being able to engage the combat in other parts, without their being able to charge the flank of this division, nor that of any [follow-on] echelon, nor even the fronts of these echelons; in a word, without any accident or contrariety being able to arrest the effect of the maneuver nor hinder all the pieces from following their vocation!" etc.

What to say to the other examples of [the] formation of orders of battle given by Mesnil-Durand? They are all maneuvers of the same genre and begin from the same principles. None of them offers [any] relation to the terrain. They are always figures and points that move themselves at [his] pleasure and without obstacle on blank paper. We will show modern tactics in opposition [to them], reckoning a little more with means and circumstances, and giving by this hypotheses [that are] true and that war may realize.

4 Formation of Orders of Battle Following Modern Tactics

It is on the formation of orders of battle that modern tactics has made, or, to speak more justly, is in the process of making, the most important and the most complete revolution. Before it, armies were neither divided nor constituted in a fashion to be able to be maneuvering. The different corps that composed them could move themselves individually only by movements [that were] slow [and] heavy and of which they did not even have the habit. General officers did not at all have the habit of handling troops. From this ignorance and from this general ill-address, as much on the part of the agents as on the part of the conductors, resulted that it took several hours to form an army *en bataille*, [and] that, once this army [was] *en bataille*, one dared not make the least change in its disposition for fear of confounding everything, of losing everything. In the end, [this] resulted in one always combining the order of march on the disposition that one wished to take.

Thus, for example, one formed oneself in march order with the objective of attacking the enemy on some point, [and] one consequently reinforced some columns; arriving in the presence of the enemy, the order of battle was dictated by the order of march and consequently taken. Then what followed? Often, this order of battle found itself vicious, either because one had false knowledge of the terrain or the enemy position or because the enemy had made changes in their disposition. How to remedy this? The means of rapidly changing one's primitive disposition with so-imperfect tactics! When a general would sense the genius capable of undertaking it, how to dare to attempt it with troops and general officers incapable of any grand maneuver? It was such a lengthy operation, forming an army *en bataille*! What would then arrive? [With] the army employing an infinite amount of time in passing from march order to battle order, the enemy was able at leisure to judge the strength of its columns, the point against which they were directing themselves, [and] the objective that they had in view, and [then] make [their] dispositions consequently. If examples to support what I advance here are needed, I would be able to cite them *en masse*, and the Seven Years War would furnish me many.

In modern tactics, one arrives at the formation of orders of battle in a totally different manner. For example, what if one wishes to go to attack the enemy? As one is not able to know precisely the position that they occupy, as, even when one would know it, one may not be sure that, although instructed in the movement that one makes on them, there will not be some changes in their position or disposition by which they intend to defend it, one forms the army in march order in the habitual order, the columns being all equal and each formed of a division. Thus disposed, the army advances, the general being in advance of it, at the head of the advanced guard. One arrives within range of the enemy, and then the general determines his order of battle relative to the nature of the terrain, to the position that the enemy occupies, and to the disposition that they have taken. To this end, he reinforces or enfeebles columns as he judges appropriate, advancing one and halting another or leaving it in the rear, directing one [column] on a point and another [column] on another [point]; then, when his general disposition is done, [he] gives the signal for the formation of the order of battle. Instantly, all his troops, who are accustomed to the execution of grand maneuvers, who have simple and rapid methods for accomplishing them, take the particular disposition that was ordained for them, whether in forming themselves *en bataille*, or in holding in columns on agreed points, ready to deploy themselves, to debouch, or to make illusion to the enemy and to menace them if this is their goal; the parts destined to attack engage the action at the same time in such a way that they [the columns] commence before the enemy has had the time to untangle where they wish to strike them or, if they do untangle it, to change their disposition to parry them.

But this is not at all the entire usage that a skillful general may make of modern tactics. Recall that, marching at the head of his advanced guard, he has behind him all his columns that he holds, so to speak, in hand and ready to take the dispositions that he will indicate to them. Arriving within the enemy's view and not finding them to be in a disadvantageous posture, he maneuvers against them, [and] he searches to give them the change; he employs all the resources of terrain and tactics to give them illusion on his project. He feints offensive movements on one wing to form his attack on another point then and at the same time. In one place, he makes a grand display of strength, whether in presenting columns at open distances or in multiplying the heads of columns to conceal their depth; in another place, he hides his forces in holding his troops in serried columns. He knows so well, in a word, that, if the enemy is not as skillful as he is, they take the change [he dictates], abandon or occupy a post that forms them as a prize, or even enfeeble themselves on a point, whether in leaving too few troops there, in leaving too few of the arm proper to defending it there, or in leaving the least-good troops in his army there; as I have already observed, there are many ways to be beaten in war. Then, this fault is seized, and the skillful and maneuvering general immediately carries efforts on this feeble part. However, if the enemy does not form themselves as a prize either by their position or by their disposition, then this general finds himself having nothing engaged, nothing compromised. He retires, takes a position, and gives birth to a more-favorable occasion.

This is the true science of the formation of orders of battle. This is of what the King of Prussia gave us the precepts and examples. Until then, it must be agreed, the practice of this science was concentrated in his head and in his army. We have no idea, or to speak more justly, no habit, which amounts to the same thing, of this great genre of war, of this manner of reconnoitering the enemy with all one's forces, of presenting the combat to them, [and] of inducing faults in them and profiting from them with rapidity. We do not at all know how to take momentary orders of battle combined on the terrain and on circumstances. In the end, we are ignorant of the art of moving and maneuvering armies. But we are not the only ones who are ignorant of it. The Austrians, who have made an entire war against the King of Prussia, who had proof that this art gave him superiority, are similarly ignorant of it, and, until they have given and won what I call a maneuvering battle, I am justified in saying that this art is still a mystery for them.[45]

"But," it may be said to me, "the Austrians, who sometimes beat, surprised, [and] contained the King of Prussia during the Seven Years War, who still come at the commencement of the Bavarian Succession to render all his efforts useless for two months, do [they really] not know the art of maneuvering armies?" No, they do not know it, as one practices what one knows, and they have never practiced it. They have never even made it an objective of study in their peacetime camps, or, when they have wished to study it, they have employed poor methods and false principles. The immense science of war is composed of an infinity of parts. The Austrians know how to take positions, entrench, and fight. At Kolin, they were able to frustrate all the resources of the art employed by Friedrich on this great day by the goodness and the valor of their troops. They were able to surprise him at Hochkirch, cut off and envelop General Friedrich August von Finck at Maxen, take unattackable positions in the last campaign [the War of Bavarian Succession], and skillfully hold themselves in a wisely chosen line of defense.[46] But the art of moving armies, of giving battles, of winning by the ascendancy of maneuvers, is another branch of war, and it is unknown to them at present.

We doubtlessly also know about the great parts of war. We know how to win battles of posts, have partial success,

---

45 [Guibert probably references the War of the Bavarian Succession, but the analysis applies to any of the various wars pitting Prussia against Austria during the period.]

46 [The Battle of Hochkirch took place in late 1758. An army of 80,000 under Daun encamped close to Friedrich's of around 30,000 in Saxony. Friedrich contemptuously dismissed the Austrians, believing them to be unwilling to attack, but Daun did, inflicting around 10,000 casualties on Friedrich, as well as a serious blow to his prestige. The Battle of Maxen took place late in the following year. Friedrich and Daun once again faced each other in Saxony, and Friedrich dispatched a force of around 15,000 under General Friedrich August von Finck to Maxen outside Dresden in only loose contact with the main Prussian army. Once again, Daun pounced on Friedrich's hubris and induced Finck's surrender after a short battle; the loss was the most significant numerically for Prussia in the war outside of the Battle of Kunersdorf. See Szabo, *The Seven Years War in Europe*, 195–199, and 252–254.]

[and] make war by corps and by detachments, but we lack the art of grand maneuvers and general movements even more than the Austrians. The Austrians, habituated to making war against the King of Prussia, have learned, if not how to maneuver at large themselves, at least how to balance the superiority of this prince in this regard via a vigorous defense, and [one that is] well extended in many regards. Experience has taught them to hold themselves on guard against this superiority and to not compromise themselves against the King of Prussia in open country, on the march, or in maneuvering. We lack this experience, and, if we were in a state of suddenly finding ourselves in the presence of a maneuvering army commanded by a skillful chief, it would be able to arrive on us as it arrived on the Austrians: to be astounded for some time by a genre of war that would appear new to us and to acquire the same experience only by misfortunes.

This manner of never making war *en masse*, that is to say of not at all maneuvering with all one's army at the same time, of not at all daring to give great battles, [and] finally of morseling oneself, of ceaselessly compromising oneself in separated corps [and] in detail movements, is so habitual for us that I may dispense myself of returning to it. It is totally opposed to the principles of modern grand tactics; it must only take place when the army that one commands is maladroit in grand movements, when one may count on neither the general officers nor on the troops that compose it, [or] when one has need of toughening it by degrees and of supporting it with some small successes in lieu of general and decisive operations. In the end, [this] is only a degradation of the art and a true diminutive of great war. This is too important and holds too directly to the objective of this chapter for it not to be developed in more detail.

There are doubtlessly operations, positions, [and] circumstances that impose the necessity of forming detached corps and advanced guards, but, as much as it is possible, these corps must not be permanent and indefinitely composed of the same troops and the same general officers. Above all, they must not be attached to the *état-major*, and they [must] never constitute a reserve or a separated corps. These small corps have great pretentions: they become useless to the general and to the army; they animate themselves with a particular spirit that is almost never that of the army; they combine exclusively for themselves, occupying themselves with preserving the most integrity and the most independence that they can and become indifferent to success[es] and to checks that are not their own. This principle [is] prudently adopted everywhere, but [it] is above all [necessary] in a French army, but we pass [from it] to more general motifs and draw grand reasons from war.

[What if] one is superior to the enemy? [Then], one must rarely morsel oneself, as one descends to their level by this morseling; one exposes the corps that one detaches to being beaten and to losing in detail the advantage that one had in remaining together. [What if] one is inferior to the enemy? [Then], for a stronger reason, one must make war without morseling oneself, because, in dividing oneself thus, one reduces oneself to being on the defensive, in inquietude, and exposed to checks and to coups de main everywhere. [What if] one is on a decided offensive and in a grand operation within the enemy's range? [Then], for a stronger reason, one must hold oneself together; one must even recall one's detached corps and light troops. In effect, if one wishes to attack, why uncover oneself, announce oneself, [or] form oneself as a prize on some point? It would be desirable that, when the enemy would see the first troop arrive, the entire army would support it, and that there would be no time to parry the blow that it would bring. If one is on the defensive, if one fears being attacked, is there a better disposition than that of being united and ready to make resistance where the enemy will wish to make [their] effort?

If this excellent principle of morseling an army as little as possible were to be contested, if an authority were needed to support it, I would cite that of the King of Prussia. All the times that he is in offensive march order within enemy range, his advanced guard always holds to his columns, and it is never more than a half-league distant from them. This advanced guard is composed of hussars, of dragoons, [and] of grenadier battalions with some cannon. He is there in person [along] with the general officers commanding his columns. It is from here that he reconnoiters the enemy and determines the order of battle that he wishes to take, holding all his columns in movement behind him, then indicating to each column commander the points to which he must carry himself and the objectives that he must accomplish; [he] masks with his advanced guard, if he can, what passes behind him; then, at the moment of the formation of the order of battle, [he] carries this advanced guard as reinforcement to the point of attack and engages the combat with it while his columns develop themselves in his support; all this interior mechanism meanwhile operates itself with so much accord and speed that the astounded enemy untangles the disposition that he will take [only] with difficulty.

For the same reason that the King of Prussia, in his marches of offensive maneuvers, has his advanced guard almost immediately at the head of his columns, his rear guard holds to his army in the same way in his retreat marches within range of the enemy; he has also never had an affair with the rear guard. The means by which little-maneuvering armies engage themselves in attacking an elite rear guard sustained by an army skillful in arresting themselves, in forming a disposition, or in taking an offensive movement forward at need! Light troops and advanced guards will certainly not compromise themselves there; they only have coups to gain there.

After the general views concerning the formation of orders of battle exposed above, we pass to the details that relate to them.

The parallel order being only an order of battle of method and of principle, as I have demonstrated, I have no need of extending myself here on the details of its formation; they are so simple that they have no need of explication. I refer in this regard to the *General Essay on Tactics*. One will see there, in the maneuvers of the camp of instruction, three marches followed by the formation of a parallel order taken alternatively by deployments on the right, on the left, and on the center. It would only be necessary to adapt to these maneuvers the current methods of the ordinance which, relative to some details, merit more than those that I proposed. The *General Essay on Tactics* was written ten years ago, and details have been deepened and perfected since.[47]

But one more time, the parallel order, and, above all, the regular and contiguous parallel order, may never be of any use in war; it is only good to form it in a camp of instruction for only the first few days and uniquely to well-affirm the troops and the general officers in the details of the primitive organization of the army like the formation of march columns, the march in itself and then the movements preparatory for deployment, the observation of distances between columns, deployment, etc.

Permit me to return again to the *General Essay on Tactics* for all the details of the formation of the oblique order. One will see, in the maneuvers of the camp of instruction, different orders of march following the diverse formations of the oblique order that I exposed above in the article that treats this order. It is by these diverse formations, whose first [few] are purely elementary, that the troops will arrive at more-composed formations, that is to say to those that will be made relative to terrain and to circumstances.[48] Before speaking of the latter, I have to treat two important points on which modern tactics is too distant from the principles of Mesnil-Durand to not arrest myself.

Mesnil-Durand would that we always deploy by the center [and] that we always arrive by the center of our terrain, and he wishes it so much that he is far outside of being able to do otherwise [because of] his central formation adopted as [the] unique and exclusive method. On the contrary, modern tactics rejects the central formation and prefers [deployment] by the wings on all occasions. Here is one of the great reasons on which he founds his preference and on which I have not been able to extend myself in the discussion of the details of the system of Mesnil-Durand, because it holds to grand tactics, and I wished to put each thing in its place.

The oblique order almost always forming itself on one of the enemy wings and its objective then being to outflank it and take it in the reverse, as soon as the general has determined which [wing] he wishes to attack, the columns must direct their heads and march obliquely towards this flank in such a manner that, by means of the deployment, the wing that must engage the combat outflanks the enemy and may take it in the flank.

To procure themselves the advantage of outflanking the enemy more facilely, when the oblique order must execute itself by the right, all the army's columns, or at least the troops that are destined to form the attack, must deploy themselves on the right, and they deploy themselves on the left if the oblique order must execute itself on the left. By these means, one gains the terrain on the flank and outside the order of march where the column of the wing deploys itself. From this principle, it does not follow that one may never be able to deploy columns on the center in a similar circumstance. This species of deployment, being shorter by half, must on the contrary always be employed when, by the direction of its march, the army has already accomplished the objective of outflanking the enemy.

Mesnil-Durand may in truth respond that his tactics have no need of outflanking and that he proves this assuredly in preferring to always attack by the center. But it is no more than a question of knowing if his tactics have reason, and it is on this that our readers will pronounce.

We pass to the second subject. Mesnil-Durand counts the effect of artillery for nothing, pretend[ing] to form his orders of battle at three-hundred *toises* from the enemy, [and] often closer. It cannot be denied that it would be quite advantageous to form a disposition quite close to the enemy to be able to arrive on them rapidly and in one effort. But how to propose to form a disposition, that is to say to maneuver, and, above all, to maneuver with columns, under the most murderous fire of enemy artillery? At three-hundred *toises*, one is beaten at point-blank by the smallest calibers and by park calibers with cartridge. We believe to have thus begun from a most-just and most-reflected knowledge of the effects of artillery in establishing as principles what follows.

One of the first objectives of all attack dispositions being to astound the enemy and to not leave them the

---

47 [Abel, *Guibert's General Essay on Tactics*, 207–235.]
48 [Ibid.]

time to reconnoiter it, this disposition must form at a distance from the enemy well-enough combined so that the fire of enemy artillery may not trouble the formation of this disposition and throw it into disorder, and at the same time, the troops [must] not have too long a space to cover under enemy fire to arrive on them. This is to the coup d'œil, to the experience, to the talent of the general officer who commands the part of the order of battle destined to attack to determine this distance. Theory may not assign any precise rule on this. All depends on the circumstances and on the terrain. The disposition may sometimes form itself quite close if the enemy has little artillery, if this artillery is little redoubtable or dominated by a quite-superior artillery, or finally, if one may debouch on it from cover. It must form itself quite far if their artillery is numerous and redoubtable and if the terrain to cover to arrive on them is flat and open, because despite what Mesnil-Durand may say, we believe that one may not untangle, one may not deploy, one may not maneuver columns in any way under the fire of a numerous artillery; we also believe that battalions in line must suffer less from this fire in traversing a long and open space than troops in column.

The species of troops that one commands must again enter much into consideration relative to this objective. Are they brave, warlike, maneuvering? One may hazard [more] to form one's disposition, to deploy, to maneuver quite close to the enemy than when they are without discipline and without vigor. What if it is cavalry that one must form for the attack? One must form them *en bataille* further away, because for one, cannon do more damage to a column of cavalry than one of infantry, and for another, cavalry may cover the terrain that separates them from the goal of their attack more rapidly. What if it is infantry? One may, for the contrary reasons, deploy quite close to them.

In the end, the only general maxims that may be given in this regard (and general maxims rest, for good reason, subordinated to all the varieties of terrain and of circumstance) are to deploy oneself or to form one's disposition at distances where enemy fire would not be deadly enough to throw disorder into the troops' maneuvers [and] at the same time to not deploy oneself at too-distant distances, because then one loses the advantages of reforming oneself in march columns, which is easier and more facile than reforming oneself in line; of hiding for the longest time the quantity of troops that one is able to carry against them; and of being able to bring one's troops, in one effort, from the point where the attack disposition was formed to the point of the attack.

It remains to me to speak of the most important subject in this chapter: the application of orders of battle to terrain and to circumstances. It is by this that I wish to make known not only how modern tactics are superior to those of Mesnil-Durand, which is not a great triumph for them, but also how they are at once simple and sublime, how they bend themselves to all possible varieties of places and cases, and finally how they may furnish resources to [both] good generals and to interior armies. It is this last advantage that eminently distinguishes them in my eyes and makes them a science of genius in my ideas.

I am forced here to resort again to the *General Essay on Tactics* for an extract of what I have said in this regard. I may return my readers to it, as I have done above, for some maneuvers of principle and of method. But I cannot pass up examples of [the] application of orders of battle to terrain and to circumstances here. They form the complement of this work and the most victorious argument in favor of modern tactics.[49]

In seeing me thus sometimes returning to the *General Essay on Tactics* in the course of this work [and] sometimes extracting passages adapted to the current work, the enmity that always searches to devour will perhaps accuse me of a crime. It will say that I always cite myself, that I thus have the pretention to being an authority, etc. I have already foreseen some part of this ridiculous accusation, but the apology must be repeated, and it is still often insufficient, until it becomes evidence to this class of men who, by prejudice or malignity, alternatively feign ignorance of what they know and knowing of what they are ignorant, accuse against their conscience and search to envelop a work with the vague reproaches of presumption and pride that they make to its author. I thus declare that I only cite my *General Essay on Tactics* as one recalls old means of defense and that I only extract from it when having the same things to say, [as] I cannot dispense myself from repeating myself. I find myself in the double case here.

My goal in the maneuvers below would be to furnish examples of the application of orders of battle to terrain and to circumstances. And here is how I have worked to accomplish it.

I am obliged to recall, to make these maneuvers intelligible, that I would suppose them to need to be executed in a camp of instruction by an army of eighty battalions and eighty squadrons. The eighty battalions would be divided into three divisions, each of twenty-four battalions, with twelve in the first [line] and twelve in the second line, and in two flank brigades, each of four battalions. Each cavalry wing would form its division and would be composed of forty squadrons, with twenty in the first line and twenty in the second. I return to the *General Essay on Tactics* for

---

49 [Abel, *Guibert's General Essay on Tactics*, 227–235.]

the greatest details of the organization of this army in all other aspects, and on the motifs and principles on which it is established.[50]

In beginning with this order of battle as the primitive and habitual disposition, the army is supposed [to be] formed on five columns, each composed of a division in all the orders of march, and it is as such that the following maneuvers must be considered.

5 Application of Orders of Battle to Terrain and to Circumstances

Of all the maneuvers that I have described, there is perhaps not one that would be in the case of being executed in war by combinations exactly like those detailed, as terrain and circumstances absolutely change the given [combinations], and, in war, the nature of terrain and circumstances rarely being able to be foreseen, movements are not at all premeditated, and it is ordinarily the moment that determines them.

However, whatever infinities, whatever varieties of combinations that one may be able to form, because it is nevertheless by the same mechanism that one executes them, I had to first teach what this mechanism was in isolation and with no relation to terrain and to circumstances; I consequently had to always indicate to the army, in the orders of march, the species of order of battle by which it must conduct itself. Now, the primitive objective and the principles of the orders of battle being known, the general officers and the troops having formed [their] coup d'œil and [their] intelligence by simple and premeditated maneuvers, the sphere of instruction will extend itself and become more interesting. Suppose that the preceding maneuvers made themselves in terrains [that were] absolutely nude and uniform [and] that they consequently did not oblige any local consideration. Now, the examples will have more truth, and one will always maneuver relative to terrain, and to terrain varied like the country[side] will offer.

The army will thus form itself in march order as in war to carry itself on some point, and it will only be from the advanced guard and relative to the nature of the country[side] that the general will determine the order of battle that it will have to take. As, I must repeat, it is the advantage of this organization of the army and of the disposition of its orders of march that the army may rapidly and according to circumstances take any order of battle whatsoever and reinforce or refuse any part of this order.

The general marches at the head of his advanced guard, [and] behind him, all the columns that he commands advance, retard, arrest, and deploy according to his projects. What would Turenne, Condé, [or] Luxembourg have not done if they had known the simplicity and the possibilities of this mechanism!

Thus, for example, the army debouching in plain A (Diagram VII) to go to attack the enemy occupying position BC, the general, arrived at the head of the advanced guard at L, will see that the enemy left is susceptible to being attacked and outflanked, and he will immediately give the signals for the army to dispose itself to take the oblique order by the right. He will instruct the general officers commanding the divisions of the points on which they must direct the columns, the points of alignment of the wings, the manner in which the columns must deploy themselves, and the general objective of the disposition.

He will have to determine this disposition via making a coup-d'œil of the advantages that the terrain offers to the offensive and defensive parts of his order of battle.

He will consequently direct the first and the second column on point F, because he will wish to profit from the plain to form his right and to attack the feeble left and discover the enemy.

He will arrest the third column on the heights [at] G so as to give a defensive position there to the part of his order of battle that he wishes to refuse, and, covered by these heights, he will carry his brigades of the second line of this column to his right so that they will form there the second line of the second column, which will deploy itself all in the first line.

Covered by these same heights, the twenty squadrons of the tail of the left column will carry themselves to reinforce the right to form the second line of the first column, which will deploy itself all in the first line.

If he would have need of a grand reinforcement of infantry on this right, he would draw it from the brigades of the second line of the fourth column, or he would form it within range of [being able to do so] in having them approach the heights of his center and thus leaving fewer infantry to the left.

He will leave some light troops on the *rideau* H and will file his entire advanced guard behind this *rideau* to reinforce his right.[51]

He will profit from the woods that are in advance of the columns of his left to menace the enemy right wing and

---

50 [Ibid.]

51 ["*Rideau*" typically means a screen or curtain, often of men or fortifications, but in this instance, Guibert uses it to refer to a natural terrain feature that provides concealment of a body of troops behind a small patch of higher ground, as the diagram shows.]

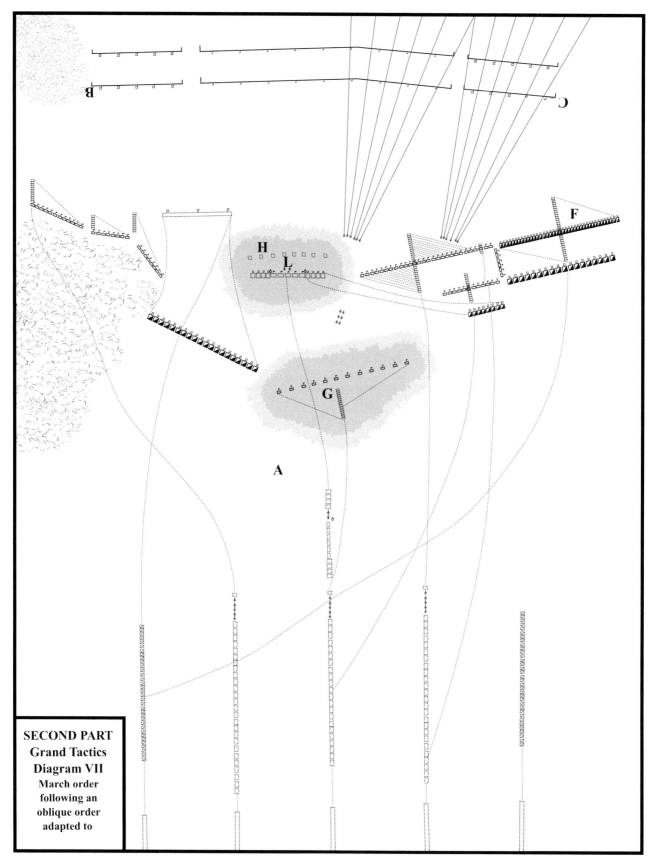

FIGURE 6 Diagram VII

to engage their attention there. To this end, he will order the fourth and fifth maneuver columns along [this] chain of woods to present more column heads there at open distances; to make, in a word, the greatest ostentation of strength and offensive possible; to then re-fold, forming *en bataille* along the chain of woods; and to concur with the general objective of the disposition. The twenty-eight battalions that compose the fourth column will entirely form the army's left, and the twenty squadrons that rest in the fifth will rapidly come to form themselves in the gap that is between the woods and the heights of the center.

He will not subject himself, as one may see in the diagram, to any irregularity in the alignment and in the obliquity of the disposition; his center will find itself far behind the degree of obliquity that we have established in the order of principles, because it will have wished to profit from the heights to hold itself further outside the enemy's range; his left will be placed strongly forward, because it is covered by the woods where the enemy will certainly not wish to attack and where it makes a bastion in some manner on the curtain wall of his order of battle.[52]

The total objective of his disposition will nevertheless have all the advantages of the oblique order because it refuses and holds the center and the left of his army outside the range of the enemy, and he only attacks with his considerably reinforced right.

The preceding example makes known how the oblique order must be applied to terrain. What I have given above will show how, having determined after the first disposition that one would form the oblique order on one point and the army's having consequently commenced its movement, if the enemy came to change their disposition, one would be able to rapidly change the plan of attack and form the oblique order on another point.

The army forms itself in march order in the accustomed order to go to attack the enemy posted at AB (Diagram VIII). Arriving within range of reconnoitering the enemy, the general sees that the center of their position is impregnable, that the right presents difficulties, and that the left is, by the nature of the terrain, the least strong and most accessible part. He consequently determines to attack by his right and makes his army commence the necessary movements to form the oblique order on this wing.

However, arriving more within range of the enemy and continuing to observe more and more their positions and the movements that his approach makes them make in their disposition, he sees, I suppose, that the enemy, counting on the goodness of their right and fearing the feebleness of their left, carry there [to the left] the greater part of their troops. He sees that, by means of this change of disposition, the left, which had appeared and was in effect the most feeble side in the primitive aspect, becomes, by the number and species of the troops that carry there, the point least susceptible to attack, while the right, more difficult by the terrain, rests almost abandoned of its local forces and is defended only by a small number of troops; immediately he changes [his] project and resolves himself to form his oblique order on his left. A signal indicates this change to his columns, which then take by their left the echelon of obliquity that they had commenced to form by the right; if there are some parts of troops that would already be in movement to carry themselves to reinforce this right, they arrest themselves and re-march on the left in such a manner as to re-join the columns from which they were detached.

At the same time and as soon as the general has determined his new disposition, he sends trusted officers to the columns to show them the new disposition that he wishes to take, the direction that they must follow, and the points where they must form themselves. As for him, he carries his person to the left of the army so as to follow the execution of the interesting part of the movement.[53]

According to his first disposition, he would have to form the oblique order on the right, reinforcing this cavalry wing with twenty squadrons drawn from his left and forming them at C to attack the enemy left; his first infantry column, reinforced by the brigades of the second line of the second and third columns and the troops of his advanced guard, would have to support this wing and engage the attack in concert with it, while the rest of his third, fourth, and fifth columns would have to deploy themselves to the rear by echelons and, as a result of the advantages of the country[side], hold themselves outside of enemy range.

The movements that the enemy made engaged him to change this first disposition and to take the oblique order by the left. Consequently, here is the new profit that he draws from the terrain and the orders that he sends to the columns.

The enemy right, with the exception of a small part of the plain where they left around twenty squadrons, is on heights of difficult access and fortified yet more by redoubts and batteries, that is to say that this wing is better-posted than the left, which is in a razed and uncovered

---

52 [The exercise Guibert has designed here is strikingly similar to the French deployment at the 1745 Battle of Fontenoy in which Maurice de Saxe anchored his left wing on a forest and refused his left behind a series of fortified artillery positions. See Browning, *The War of the Austrian Succession*, 206–214.]

53 [Guibert provides an unwitting illustration of the difficulty of tactical maneuvers, much less operational, at the time, given that orders had to be carried by "trusted officers" by hand.]

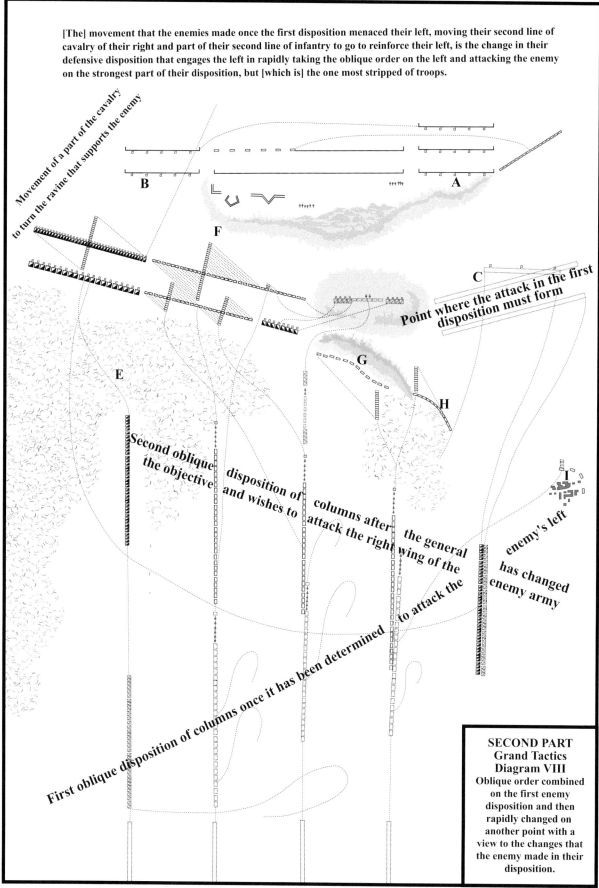

FIGURE 7 Diagram VIII

plain, but the enemy counts too much on the advantages of terrain, de-garnishing it of troops and leaving there [on the right] only those on which they would count the least so as to considerably reinforce their left, for which the nature of the country[side], the facility of debouches, and the view of the first attack disposition gave rise to fear. This is the fault that the general of our army seizes, and, to this end, he sends orders to his cavalry column of the left, which is rejoined on the way by the twenty squadrons that had already commenced to carry themselves towards the left, to direct itself on point D, marching at serried distances and working to hide its strength as much as possible.

The objective of this cavalry is, at the signal of the deployment, to form itself *en bataille* opposite the squadrons of the enemy right; to profit from its superiority to outflank them; even to turn them, if it can, by carrying some squadrons outside the ravine that supports them; and finally, to attack them vigorously while the infantry that is to its right attacks the right of the enemy infantry at the same time.

The first infantry column of the left, composed of twenty-eight battalions counting the flank brigades, traverses the grand woods E [and] advances itself at serried distances towards point F; arriving on this point, [it] deploys itself all on a line, is sustained in second by the six brigades of the second and third infantry columns of the left, and [is] further reinforced by the grenadiers and dragoons of the advanced guard that come to place themselves to its right. This disposition made, it immediately marches on the enemy, profiting from the premier advantage of the cavalry to turn the great *rideau* F, against which the redoubts of the right are supported, and finishes, by all appearances, by carrying a position in which the inferior enemy, whether by number[s] or by the species of troops, has only little resistance to oppose to it.

The second infantry column of the left carries itself on the heights G, which, disposed as in the diagram, extends itself in distancing itself from the enemy, and it forms itself there on a single line, having its left covered by the dragoons of the advanced guard. The three brigades of the second line of this column are carried in the second line behind the left, as was said previously.

The third infantry column forms itself in the same way on the chain of woods H; these woods, yet further to the rear than the heights G, hide its strength and furnish it a favorable position. The three brigades of the second line of this column have made the same movement as that of the second column.

These two columns only take their position to the rear at the moment of the general deployment; until then, they must present themselves in advance of the heights and of the woods, mounting several column heads at open distances and appearing to menace the enemy center and right.

Finally, it is the fifth column that is particularly charged with giving them the change, and it consequently advances itself audaciously to traverse the great plain as if it would have to in effect commence the attack so that, in the first disposition, it divides itself into several columns at quite-open distances; then, at the signal of the general deployment, it retires itself at the great trot and goes to form itself *en bataille* under the protection of the infantry of the right and of hamlet I, where the flank brigade has thrown itself.

The facility with which one executes it, the illusion that its execution must produce in the enemy, and the appearance of infallible success that must result for the attacked army must be seen in the plan of the general effect of this disposition. In effect, what may the enemy be able to do? They would be at pains to untangle the target of the new disposition when their right would already have been attacked by infinitely superior forces. What if they searched to maneuver by their left and by their center to carry themselves on the feeble and distant parts of the oblique order? They have a great distance between them, [and] odds are that they would be recalled by the disasters on their right before they achieved so great a movement. In addition, this oblique will only have to retreat before them, always supporting itself in its retreat towards the left of the army so as to not separate itself from it. What if they carried reinforcements to their attacked wing? It is apparent that they will arrive only to be witness to the defeat of this wing. Finally, even when these reinforcements would appear to reestablish the fight there, even when the battle would [seem to] be lost for the army that attacks, it only has one of its wings engaged; this wing retires covered by the other parts of the disposition. It may arrive that an attack made in this order by a vigorous and well-commanded army fail, but it is rare, [and] it is almost impossible that it [would] turn into a rout.

It remains to me to cite the Battle of Leuthen to support this example; this is more or less how it was conducted. The King of Prussia maneuvered for two hours before the Austrians. He first menaced their right, which was the most feeble by the nature of the terrain. They reinforced it with a great number and the elite of their troops. They accounted their left [to be] well-seated on the heights and supported at their base by land that was believed to be marshy, and they left only the Bavarians and some Imperial troops there. The King of Prussia seized on this fault: his disposition, uncertain and suspended for a long time, rapidly determined on his right. A light curtain of heights hid the nature and the movement of his columns. The left wing of Charles-Alexandre-Emanuel, prince de Lorraine, was taken in the flank and knocked over after a half-hour of combat. The Austrians arrived, but it was too late: two lines were already formed on their flank; all that presented itself [to them] was reversed, and the victory of the King of Prussia, who hardly had 35,000 men against 60,000, was one of the most complete and most decisive of the war.

This is a quite-great and quite-little-known advantage in our armies: holding in columns until the order of battle that one wishes to take would be determined. By it, one perfectly draws one's army into one's hand; one may handle it more easily and with more speed, make interior movements that escape the enemy, make illusion to them, menace them first on one point and then on another, induce error in them, and yet never form oneself as a prize. By it, one may, with all one's forces, march to the enemy, feel them, maneuver before them, work to engage them in a false movement or in a false disposition, and, if they fall into the trap, profit from it with rapidity. At worst, if one does not succeed, one retires, and it is a reconnaissance that runs the risk of neither danger nor shame.

I will give a third example: a flank march order following a front order of battle determined by the unforeseen appearance of the enemy army at the head of the march and combined on the nature of the country[side].

With the army in march order like AB (Diagram IX), the light troops that clear the head of the march would advertise to the general that the enemy appears at CD and advances frontally towards the army to attack it on its march. The general carries himself immediately to the head of the columns, making his advanced guard follow, and, when he has reconnoitered the enemy, he immediately makes his disposition to oppose them. In advance of him and on his right is a stream, to the left of which extends a chain of wooded heights; it is on this stream that he will anchor his right, then extend himself along these heights. The center of his position will hold the plain D, and it will consequently carry the greater part of his cavalry. His left, composed of infantry, will occupy the woods F and anchor on village G, to which he will carry an infantry brigade. The rest of his cavalry will be *en bataille* behind this village and in the different gaps that are along the woods of the left so as to support the infantry that defends it. His position determined, he will indicate to the general officers commanding his divisions the points to which they must carry the troops and the general plan of his disposition. The two lines of his right wing of cavalry that are at the head of the march carry themselves rapidly to plain D and form the center of the army on a single line there, anchoring their right on the heights and their left on the woods. The second line of infantry that forms the second column directs itself towards the right part of the position that it must occupy. The six brigades of the head of the column, counting the flank brigade, must form the first line of this right, and the four brigades of the tail the second. To this end, this column divides itself into two or three columns so as to arrive more promptly on the points on which it must form itself. The first infantry line, which composes the center of the first column, must occupy the left of the position in the new order of battle; consequently, it similarly divides itself into several columns to achieve its movement and directs itself on the points on which it must form itself. The flank brigade, which is at the tail, carries itself directly to the village on the left. The five brigades of the head of the column form the first line of the right, and the four brigades of the tail the second. With regard to the first line of the left wing of cavalry, which forms the tail of the first column, it directs itself in advance of the left to form itself *en bataille* behind the gaps in the woods that were occupied by the infantry of this wing, and the second line of cavalry that is at the tail of the second column, continuing its movement forward, goes to form itself in the second line behind the center. The advanced guard has carried itself in advance of the center into some advantageous position from which it covers the army's movements and from which it is in range of carrying itself to reinforce the most feeble part of the order of battle according to the disposition that the general will wish to make to the enemy. This order of battle entirely inverts the primitive order of the army, but it rapidly faces an unforeseen circumstance. The troops arrive on the points that they go to occupy by the shortest route, and, in war, method must not enchain; it must not degenerate into routine.[54]

By this example, one senses that, if the terrain of the position chosen by the general would require other combinations in the emplacement of the troops, they would execute them with the same facility. One also senses that, if, in lieu of simply occupying a defensive position, the general would find it advantageous to immediately pass to a counter-offensive movement on the enemy, he would equally be able to. Once an army is well organized, once it has acquired the habit of grand maneuvers, if the man who commands it has genius, there is no machine that would be more manageable, simpler, and susceptible to more varieties in its combinations.

---

54 [The final sentence of this paragraph is repeated from Abel, *Guibert's General Essay on Tactics*, 234.]

[THE] SYSTEM OF MESNIL-DURAND CONSIDERED IN RELATION TO ORDERS OF BATTLE AND TO BATTLES

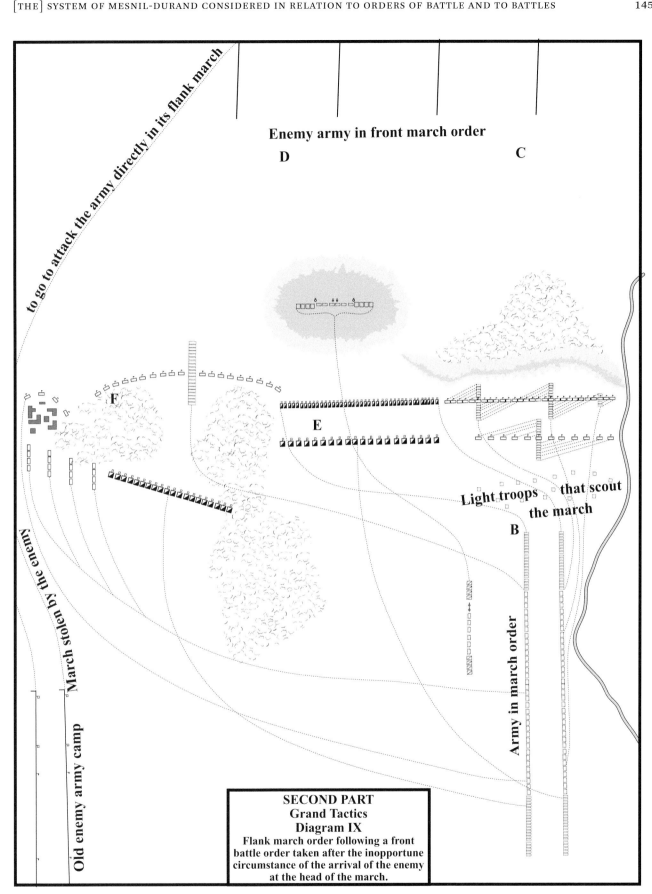

FIGURE 8   Diagram IX

6 On Combat Action and the Manner of Conducting It

In the course of this work, we have already given samples of the manner in which Mesnil-Durand pretends to engage and conduct the combat action in his system. We have seen that "fighting and vanquishing are always synonymous" for him. He does not take into account the positions, the dispositions, or the maneuvers that may be opposed to it. He does not at all march; "he runs, he flies;" if he is attacked, "he penetrates, he reverses, he dissipates." Of little import to him to be inferior! This inferiority "will only be an occasion to acquire more glory" for him. Obstacles do not at all arrest him; "provided that the enemy be approachable in one percent of their front," this suffices for him; "it is there that he charges to pierce them." I advance nothing here that I have not proven by verbatim citations from his works. We saw that he regards artillery as quite little redoubtable, as he proposes to form his disposition at four-hundred *toises* at most from the enemy, and sometimes at two-hundred. Not only does he believe the maneuvers for turning, for outflanking, for enveloping the enemy [to be] useless, but he also does not fear forming himself as a prize to the enemy in this regard, and it is as such that he always prefers attacks by the center. Finally, he takes, he changes, [and] he varies his orders of battle [and] his dispositions with such a rapidity that the eye is at pains to follow them. When he forms the oblique attack by the center, of which we have rendered account above, he says that "the four battalions of the center with the two that they have in the second line will only march in advance without considering the maneuver of the rest, nor [will they] occupy themselves with anything other than joining the enemy by the shortest route."

Six battalions thus divided to go to attack an army completely alone, while the rest of the maneuver forms [the rest of the troops] to support them! I leave what the result might be to the imagination. What Mesnil-Durand says of cavalry I have spoken about in the chapter that concerns it, [describing] the manner in which he would count on employing it in his orders of battle. Permit me to add here the manner in which he pretends to make it fight. This citation is again extracted from his *Fragments of Tactics*, and it is his last [word] on the disposition of cavalry in combats:[55]

> Behind the column intervals, one sees my cavalry in column by demi-squadrons. In the first position, it is quite held back so as not to fire uselessly. At the moment of the shock, it is close enough to find itself within range of charging that which would dare to throw itself into the intervals as well as to sortie, in whole or in part, to dissipate the enemy broken by the infantry charge. In addition, this cavalry, first held back, arrives at the gallop at the moment when the infantry columns appear to debouch through the line of fire that continues its *tapage* and when, ready to strike the enemy, these columns sound a great cry; all this composes a quite imposing tableau, and [one] that will have its effect on both parties.
>
> One also sees that the first enemy line, thus charged by doubled forces, may not hold for a moment; that it will be immediately destroyed by the cavalry that vomits from the intervals; that a similar charge thus supported must make the same blow to knock over the second line, and the fourth, if necessary; that, when these [lines] would wish to hold, at least astounded by the defeat of the first, stunned by the tempest that so brusquely broke on them, embarrassed and deranged by their fugitives, they would be reversed more facilely still. It is understood that our battalions will get carried away, which will be quite easy to obtain from them, etc.

I will not push this extract any further, and I will not add any reflection to it.

Modern tactics, we admit, proceeds with more slowness and method. It has need of preparing and combining its dispositions. It makes a case of the artillery; thus, on one hand, it has for [a] principle to form itself outside of range of or sheltered from the lively and deadly fire of that of the enemy [artillery] so as to have the time and the liberty to create more ensemble and accord in all the parts of its dispositions, [and], on the other hand, it searches to give itself the space, the development, and the advantages of the situation so as to be able to act with more success, whether by extending the fire of the enemy artillery or at least by balancing it and [thus] sustaining the troops that attack.

I return to what I have said in this regard in the chapter that relates to it.[56]

Modern tactics regards embracing, turning, [and] flanking the enemy as an important objective and vice-versa as a quite great disadvantage to be by them. Thus, other than its marches, in its positions, [and] in its orders of battle, it constantly has this objective in view, [and] it even preserves it in the action of combat. All the art of a good attack disposition thus consists, in modern tactics,

---

55 "Memoir on orders of battle," *Fragments de tactique*, 134.

56 [See 76–85.]

of procuring oneself this advantage, as all the art of a good defense disposition consists of avoiding the enemy's taking it.

When one attacks, it is thus not uniquely a question, as Mesnil-Durand seems to believe, of assembling many forces in a small space and of taking a disposition that permits them to be contained in this space. It is a question of employing all one's forces in the most advantageous and the most decisive manner. Or, it is surely to turn, to flank, and to embrace the enemy, which procures the greatest advantage and the most decisive advantage in an attack. It is a question of having the least possible [number of] useless forces. This is what necessarily arrives when one has for [a] principle to concentrate oneself, to re-serry oneself, [and] to assemble many troops in a small space. Add to this that this re-serrying necessarily produces crowding at the first check, and crowding [necessarily produces] chaos. If there would be need of recent examples, we saw proof in the attack on Saint Lucia of the destructive effect of several columns re-serried on a small front and beaten in the flank in this situation by a violent fire.[57]

Every time that one has an affair with a posted enemy, which is almost always the manner in which war is made today, there is no attack that is well-understood and followed by a fortunate success other than that which embraces and that flanks the attacked, and consequently, that which develops itself on a front greater than theirs. Wishing to attack with other principles is to give to the attacked the advantage that one must take for oneself; it is to expose oneself to losing the premier faculty that the attacker must have: acting with liberty and always by their flanks.

I believe [that I can] rest having sufficiently established in the second part of this work, in the chapter on columns, that modern tactics is not at all exclusive, [and] that it admits, that it even recommends, the usage of columns for attacks of posts, etc.[58] I will thus not return to it here. It is evident that it is [relative] to circumstances and to the talent of the man who commands to determine the details of his disposition. There are only fundamental principles from which he may not depart, and one of these principles is certainly that which we have demonstrated relative to the general objective of all attack dispositions.

But this principle is not applicable uniquely to the first attack disposition; it must continue to be observed during the entire course of the action. It is that, in turning, in flanking, in embracing the enemy more and more, one successively de-posts them from all the points that they occupy and all those in which they attempt to make themselves firm. To win a battle today, it is not only a matter of making a head-bowed irruption into the enemy order of battle; in piercing it at one point or in carrying a post, the troops must always preserve as much order, ensemble, and space [as possible in order] to be able to pass immediately to a new disposition. It must, when the enemy is chased from a post and they are not in absolute rout, commence by establishing itself there and by well-supporting its flanks so as to not be chased in its turn. As such, it must combine a new forward movement in always continuing to turn and to flank the enemy. Finally, to make use of a definition that I already employed in the chapter on artillery, a battle may be regarded as a continuous succession of de-postings and dispositions by means of which the attacker, ceaselessly passing from one parallel to the other and always embracing the enemy more and more, pushes them outside their battlefield and makes them abandon it.

To engage and command a battle according to these principles is not a matter of "running, of flying, of penetrating." It is not a matter, as Mesnil-Durand pretends, "of expediting the affair and of beating, of dissipating, of destroying the enemy army in less time than is needed to read half of one of these chapters." It requires method, circumspection, even length sometimes, and always ensemble and discipline. Often, one does not know the details of the enemy position well, and one may only know them when one approaches it. One is thus often obliged to wait to reconnoiter and to form one's disposition in consequence, or to make changes in that which one has formed. Finally, I would that, knowing the first enemy position, having beaten them on a point and having carried one of their posts, one would not know the position that they have taken to the rear; they suddenly offer you a new nature of country[side]; one must stop oneself and reconnoiter again; a new disposition must be made; arms must sometimes be transported there and their primitive disposition changed.

But an infinity of other circumstances that war gives birth to (and the officers who have made it with reflection know the importance and the variety [of them]) necessarily throws delay and slowness into the movements of an

---

57 [The Battle of Saint Lucia took place in late 1778 after French entry into the American War of Independence. A British naval force landed marines on the French colony, allowing them to establish a defensive position. A French fleet under Jean-Baptiste-Charles-Henri Hector, comte d'Estaing, fought a series of naval engagements with the British fleet before landing 7,000 troops to attack the British position. Estaing divided his force into three columns, as Guibert notes, and launched a series of unsuccessful attacks on the British defense before withdrawing. See Georges Lacour-Gayet, *La marine militaire de la France sous le règne de Louis XIV* (Paris: Champion, 1905), 183–187.]

58 [See 71–75.]

attack. Often, one is obliged to combine the disposition of a collateral part that must often attack in concert with distant corps that, without being destined to strike decisive blows, must nevertheless work with them. Often, one has pierced and beaten on the point that one attacks, but the collateral attacks find more resistance or are repulsed. One of them succeeds, and the other does not: here is a case that requires a combination. Both lose at the same time; an absolutely different combination is required.

It is relative to all these considerations that one cannot conceive of the different attack projects presented by Mesnil-Durand in his *Fragments of Tactics*. They must all execute themselves in six or seven minutes. This rapidity is necessary to suppose when one proposes an ordinance of depth for the habitual ordinance, which does not permit resting under artillery fire without exposing it to an infallible destruction. But how to admit such a supposition? It is evidently contrary to all the possibilities and to all the rules of war. It is because one may not run, always go before one, or "expedite battles in a moment," [and] it is because the necessary measures, and then the delays, the obstacles, the unforeseen accidents, often force [one] to hold oneself in inaction within enemy range and under their artillery fire that modern tactics cannot admit the order in columns for [its] primitive and habitual order. It admits it for cases, for moments, and it is sagely appreciated for this, calculated and taken in its [proper] place.

I will bound myself here to my discussion on the manner of engaging and commanding the combat action. I have wished only to prove how, in this regard, the principles of the two systems are in opposition and how those of modern tactics are superior. Moreover, this is part of execution. The varieties of circumstances and means are thus infinite, and it is respecting the genius, it is knowing all the extent of its resources, to pretend neither to dictate to it the application of principles to circumstances nor even to always subjugate it to principles.

It only remains to me to terminate this chapter by considering orders of battle in relation to the defensive. It is there that one achieves seeing how modern tactics are anti-exclusive and how the writers that have critiqued them are far from having known them.

7 Application of Orders of Battle to the Defensive

Until now, I have only considered orders of battle relative to the subject of the offensive. I have demonstrated the advantages that may result from the combination of marches and deployments, whether to deceive the enemy as to the strength of the columns and on the point of attack or to rapidly take a disposition. I have shown how these advantages must be immense when the attacked army, following accustomed routine, would make its disposition in advance and would stretch its lines on the position that it would have to defend, as then the enemy general commanding according to the principles of modern tactics would arrive at the head of his army, would reconnoiter this disposition, would count the number and the species of troops that defend each point, and would determine his order of battle in consequence.

Tactics would be a quite-imperfect science if it did not offer to the army that is on the defensive the means of balancing these advantages. It offers them, [including] the art of mines [and] of the attack and defense of places. Equally susceptible to being employed by both parties, they will more decisively serve the one that possesses and applies them better.

Suppose a general [who is] skillful and [a] tactician in the necessity of receiving a battle: he will only reveal his defense disposition after he will have reconnoitered the points where the enemy may wish to make [their] effort. He will hold his army in columns on the battlefield that he will need to occupy so as to determine the repartition of his troops only on those of the enemy troops. Finally, he will oppose finesse to finesse and maneuver to maneuver, that is to say that he will be continually in movement before the enemy [and] that he will search to throw them into irresolution, to induce error in them, to give them illusion on the number and on the disposition of his troops, [and] to present to them a point ungarnished in appearance so as to engage them in directing their attack on this point, that is to say that he will not always bound himself to a simple defensive disposition, and that, if the enemy forms themselves as a prize on some point, he will know how to make an offensive counter-movement on them.

It is not a question here of the defensive positions [that are] so advantageous that the land necessarily reduces the attack on them to a point, because then, as there can be no uncertainty on the part where it is necessary to carry one's greatest forces, there is no inconvenience in determining one's order of battle in advance. But it is not the same in positions that are susceptible to being attacked on several points, because there it is only a matter of determining one's disposition on that of the enemy so that there is not one of these points that is ungarnished at the same time that the others will be uselessly occupied by a too-great number of troops [and] so that the enemy is not able to engage the strong part [of their force] against a weak part; one must occupy the points of attack by the heads of the troops and hold the rest of one's army in columns behind and between them so as to carry one's forces where the enemy will carry their efforts, and sometimes where they will form themselves as a prize and render themselves susceptible to being attacked. For a stronger reason, in positions in [a] plain, one must only determine one's order of battle on that of the enemy, because, in these positions, it is the number of troops, it is a more- or less-strong wing, [or] it is some arm rendered superior in a part of the order of battle that decides the success of the action.

What will the enemy general do then? He will see the heads of the troops in the principal points of the position that he wishes to attack, and, in lieu of an army *en bataille* and disposed to allow itself to be counted and beaten, [he will see] this army divided into columns whose depth nor purpose he will be able to judge. What if he will maneuver? This army will also maneuver. What if he will search to give it the change? It will hold itself *en garde* against him; it will search to make illusion to him in its turn. What if he will decide to attack a point and reunite his forces to carry it? The forces of this army will reunite themselves to defend it. Between two similar armies, it will be in the end to that which will carry genius and celerity in its maneuvers.

This application of tactics to the defensive is yet more unknown and yet not less important than their application to offensive battles. I have demonstrated how, for want of this latter, attacking armies have lost battles. Blenheim and Ramillies furnish, in the opposite sense, examples of attacked armies that were beaten by having maladroitly spread the openings of their dispositions and invited the enemy to advantageously combine an offensive disposition on them by this.[59] One must thus occupy oneself essentially with defensive dispositions in camps of instruction. One must familiarize the troops and the general officers with them there. It is above all when one will divide the army into two corps that one may give quite credible lessons in this regard.[60]

When I say that the troops must be familiarized with this manner of taking defensive dispositions, [what I mean is] that it would much surprise them if one would go to employ it in war without reasoned examples in peacetime having made known its advantages. We are generally of the opinion that an army that must be attacked cannot be too quickly disposed *en bataille*. Consequently, we are in the routine of forming our lines on the position that we chose before the enemy makes their disposition. How would a general not upset opinions and customs if, the enemy debouching to attack his army, he would carry it in several columns on the reconnoitered battlefield; if, in lieu of then forming himself *en bataille*, he would then wait for the enemy to do so; [and] finally, if he would skillfully combine [to the point that] it would suffice for him to have achieved his disposition at the moment when the enemy would arrive on him? It is only the well-considered habit of this new manner that, in light of current prejudice, could reassure the troops against this countenance, and, without this, they would regard it as the effect of uncertainty on the general and as a dangerous situation.

As a consequence of this principle, it may arrive that the general only forms *en bataille* the parts of his army that are susceptible to being attacked and entering immediately into action and that he holds the others in columns until the moment when the enemy disposition or movements put them in the case of being made use of. It may arrive that a general officer commanding a part of the order of battle even holds, in whole or in part, his troops in columns on the position that they must occupy, as it is not necessary to be developed in line to occupy a position; it suffices to hold its principal points with column heads and to be able to form oneself *en bataille* there before the enemy would be within range of attacking it; finally, as I said in the chapter on the column considered as the attack disposition, columns may be employed with success in offensive dispositions, whether to act separately on the posts that they must carry, to support deployed battalions, to attack in concert with them, [or] to attack [while] being sustained by them; I will say here that columns may even be usefully employed in defensive dispositions, whether to defend the obstacle that forms the position by holding themselves behind it and charging the enemy if it attempts to pass them, in supporting the deployed battalions that may garnish the position and defending it with their musketry, or in supporting the attacked post and debouching by the flanks or by the center of this post to repulse the enemy that would take it. These are the interior details of the disposition whose choice and employment are dictated by the circumstances and [are] in the hands of the man who commands them. Modern tactics, and our maneuver ordinance particularly, bend themselves to all these modifications, and to refuse this evidence is not having understood [their] spirit [or] known [their] means.

---

59 [The Battle of Ramillies took place during the War of the Spanish Succession. Matching armies of 60,000 under Marlborough and Marshal François de Neufville, duc de Villeroy, met in May 1706 in the Low Countries. Villeroy placed his army in an extended defensive position across a three-mile frontage, leaving gaps in it that Marlborough exploited, as Guibert indicates. The resulting defeat cost over 13,000 French casualties to only around 4,000 Allied and was a disaster for France. See Lynn, *The Wars of Louis XIV*, 302–306.]

60 [Guibert means to divide the camp's force into two corps that oppose each other in exercises, as was done at Vaussieux.]

Let Mesnil-Durand not yet infer from this that we search to reverse ourselves, to palliate the vices of modern tactics, and to adopt his system with the tacit bad faith of appearing not to adopt it. It may be seen, in the *General Essay on Tactics*, Book II Chapter XIV, that this manner of employing columns in defensive positions is not new and that I am not indebted to his system for it. But for achieving to prove to him that neither modern tactics nor I have borrowed anything from him in this regard, I must demonstrate that, although we employ columns here, there is nevertheless no analogy between our manner [of doing so] and his, [due to] the difference of means and of principles.

Why would we propose above to hold part of our dispositions, whether offensive or defensive, in columns on many occasions? Why would we particularly propose this means in all the preliminaries of dispositions and in the parts of these dispositions that are not immediately destined to enter into action? It is to hide the disposition that one will take for as long as possible from the enemy and to work to always regulate it on theirs; it is to hinder the counting of the number of troops that one carries on them if one attacks them and that one opposes to them if it is by them that one is attacked. It is evident that one better-accomplishes this double objective with columns than with lines of deployed battalions. Movements in columns always have something confusing to the eye that masks their direction and their strength, [compared to those in] a line, [where] nothing escapes the enemy; finally, it is to carry the troops on menaced points more easily and more conveniently or to support troops that are in action, as it is incontestable that, for rapidly traversing great spaces, columns are more easily handled than lines.

But we first observe that this principle of maneuvering for as long as one can in columns and of forming oneself *en bataille* only for entering into action is subordinated in modern tactics to many circumstances that do not permit it to be an exclusive principle, nor even [a] habitual [one]; that it is particularly subordinated to the nature of the terrain and to the quantity, the proximity, and the effect of enemy artillery; [and] that thus, for example, it is not under a lively and murderous fire of this artillery that it may be a question of maneuvering in columns, of resting *en panne* in columns, [or] of marching for a long time in columns; then, it is necessary to go to the deployed order. In the system of Mesnil-Durand, on the contrary, columns are the primitive, habitual, and exclusive order. One must never march or maneuver in another order, whatever the nature of the terrain or the violence of the enemy fire may be; one quits it only to range oneself behind an obstacle that must be defended by musketry, and it is expressly forbidden to take a step in the deployed order in this system.

Beyond this, we observe that we intend by "columns," on the occasions in which we have spoken of them above, to always [mean] columns of maneuver or march (these are synonymous in modern grand tactics), that is to say columns of a certain strength and consequently susceptible to making illusion to the enemy as to their depth and their strength. In the system of Mesnil-Durand, on the contrary, his primitive and habitual order, the order from which he departs to take his dispositions [and] to take his orders of battle, consists of a line of columns of a single battalion each. This order is at least as difficult to move as a line of deployed battalions, and it is not susceptible to making any illusion to the enemy. The enemy will count battalions in column more easily than battalions *en bataille*. In this case, the order of Mesnil-Durand joins the inconveniences of the deployed order to all of its own.

With regard to columns employed in defensive dispositions and actions, they return to what I have said in my second part on the column considered as attack order, since in this case, they defend by attacking, and they may have no other property. I have proven in this same part that Mesnil-Durand was not founded in claiming them [as his own]. They do not belong to his system, and they were made use of before him. I have cited above all the excellent use that Marshal Broglie made of them at Bergen.

I will terminate this chapter here. I desire that its importance saves its length. I have worked both to forget nothing and to not at all weigh myself down.

FOURTH PART

Résumé

∴

CHAPTER 1

The System of Mesnil-Durand Is Not Admissible in Any Respect. It Is a Matter of Holding to the One That Exists and Only Consolidating Our Constitution and Perfecting Ourselves in Modern Tactics

In what respect does it remain to me to examine the system of Mesnil-Durand? I have followed all its details. I have considered it relative to elementary and grand tactics, and above all, I believe I have demonstrated that it is not admissible in any respect. Will I now engage myself in following Mesnil-Durand into the diverse operations in which he conducts his *plésions*? He first speaks of ambuscades, and he employs a chapter in proving that *plésions* are more proper for them than battalions. Here are his literal proofs; they are always of a nature for me to dispense with refuting them:[1]

> The *plésions* run to the enemy, which has them in their arms at the same time as before their eyes. This lightness means that one does not have time to cut their retreat; they pass through everything [and] accommodate themselves to all sorts of issues, not at all losing the time to defile and to re-form themselves with each step. When they are cut, they are not lost. They have the gift of piercing all that they encounter, above all cavalry, which is that which one encounters the most [often] in similar cases. [...] If the country[side] is a little too uncovered, it is not easy for battalions to find a place to make an ambuscade. *Plésions*, more collected, hide themselves everywhere. A small hedge, a small round or square depression of no importance suffices to mask them. [...] Nature perhaps does not [produce] a league of plain so exact that it does not have some small niches where one or even several *plésions* might be able to hide themselves without being perceived.

And then comes the citation and the detail of an example of an ambuscade dressed by Hannibal in the Gerunium plain by means of a great number of caverns and holes in rocks that he found there.[2] Mesnil-Durand continues:

> With my order, one would not fail to repeat this favorite maneuver of Hannibal enough, which, until the present, has been quite rare. For the same reason that I have reported, these niches would serve much less well if they were small and separated as those of Gerunium, where the largest held two-hundred men. One would not think of drawing from them all these small troops, some more close, some more distant, each turned to their own side, and forming battalions from them. My *plésions* would be accommodated quite well there, etc.

He then goes to attacks of the rear-guard.[3] [A] new chapter and new proofs of the same genre:

> The lightness and the security of the flanks render the *plésion* perfect for this operation. One cannot go too fast to engage in combat people who wish to avoid it. But to go quickly is not all. The army that follows does not absolutely go the same way. One thus finds oneself often more feeble than the enemy. As such, it is a quite-dangerous commission for the battalions that feebleness of flanks forms in so-great peril when they have an affair with a superior enemy. [...] If they [the units] are *plésions*, they will attack the last enemy corps brusquely, will reverse them, and will never fear engaging them. They know that the danger will not last and that, as long as they support each other for some time, aid will come to them; they will push their point and will attack others. It will arrive from this more than once that the enemy, pressed in such a lively way and hoping for nothing but the worst, since the army approaches during this time, will lose countenance [and] will take flight, as sailors say, in such a way that, without some combat,

---

1 *Projet d'un ordre français en tactique*, page 326 and following.
  [Mesnil-Durand, *Projet d'un ordre français en tactique*, 326–329.]
2 [Ibid. The incident to which Mesnil-Durand refers took place during the Second Punic War in 217 BCE. Hannibal, having defeated two Roman armies, made his way into central Italy. Quintus Fabius Maximus, namesake of the Fabian Strategy, shadowed his movements and contested them whenever possible. His subordinate Marcus Minucius Rufus, desiring to attack Hannibal directly, won a skirmish and co-command with Fabius. Minucius was then ambushed and defeated by Hannibal, who made use of rough terrain as Mesnil-Durand says. See Polybius, *Histories*, 3, https://www.perseus.tufts.edu/hopper/text?doc=Perseus%3Atext%3A1999.01.0234%3Abook%3D3.]
3 330.
  [See Mesnil-Durand, *Projet d'un ordre français en tactique*, 329–330.]

without having employed a tenth of one's forces, one will have the pleasure of seeing the entire enemy army in rout,

etc.

I would be able to much extend this analysis, as "army surprises, river passages, descents, mountain wars, attacks and defenses of entrenchments, sieges:" Mesnil-Durand treats each of these operations chapter by chapter with the objective of proving that his system is the best and the most advantageous on every occasion.[4] But this would abuse the arms that Mesnil-Durand has furnished us. If the obligation of refuting his system imposed on us the necessity of not leaving behind any of the means that may have been able to destroy it, this objective being accomplished, moderation and honesty make it a duty to not at all accumulate citations that are not necessary for us to combat it.

May this work, which yet again I do not give as mine but as the concurrence of assembled modern enlightenment; as the result of what I have learned in studying, in meditating, [and] in consulting; [and] as commentary on the theory and practice of the greatest man of war who has existed, one day shed light on the question that it has elevated, and, rallying opinions on the path of the truth, make us finally work usefully to form an army!

It is doubtlessly time; it is time, after seventeen years of peace, to consolidate our constitution; I say "to consolidate" because, by strength of variations, attempts, and errors, it has become almost impossible to perfect it. So many changes [that are] well- or poorly understood, but all ephemeral, all contrary, infirm, [and] destroying of one another, have thrown discredit on future innovations. The machine is so fatigued that even a man of genius would only be able to tremble to touch it. His genius would not suffice to guarantee him success. He must be, if I may make use of an expression that I hazarded in my youth, a "King-Minister" or a "Minister-King."[5]

If this is the situation of our military constitution; if, in this situation, it must perhaps be to use it as it is with destroyed bodies to which one dares apply no other remedy than palliatives, it is at least a part that may be perfected, and without risk, because it is to instruction and discipline that it is relative. But to perfect it, we must hold to the current system; we must maintain our maneuver ordinances, which are seated on the best principles and contain the best means. Finally, considerable camps must be formed every year. The one that was assembled this year [Vaussieux] must, more than ever, make their necessity obvious.

The following chapter being in some way beyond the work of the refutation of the system of Mesnil-Durand, and it consummating, to speak properly, this refutation, I cannot, it seems to me, consign to a more convenient place the protestation that I form of not responding to any work published against it. I found this revolution on two reasons: the first is that I have exhausted all that I have had to say and that it is insipid to write books to repeat oneself. The second is that all polemics, in prolonging themselves, fatigue the public more than they enlighten it and that, above all, in a profession that requires more actions than words, they always end up throwing a sort of ridicule on the authors who write them.

---

4 [Ibid., 340–384.]

5 "Preliminary Discourse," *General Essay on Tactics*.
 [As Guibert suggest and as the introduction notes, he draws much of the analysis in these concluding chapters from the Preliminary Discourse of Abel, *Guibert's General Essay on Tactics*, 4–31.]

CHAPTER 2

[The] Current System of War Examined in Relation to Politics and to the Administration. It Would Be Impossible and Even Disadvantageous to Change It

This System, Beyond That It Is More Perfect and Wiser Than Any That Has Existed, Is Less Ruinous for the People [and] More Proper to Maintaining the Peace and Hindering Conquests, Devastations, and the Great Revolutions That War Once Brought

This chapter no longer has immediate relation to the system of Mesnil-Durand, but it essentially and directly holds to the general objective of my work, since this objective is to defend the system of modern war in all its senses. I have made the apology for it in all aspects that relate to tactics. It remains to me to do so here in relation to politics, to the administration, and, I dare to add, to general human interest, [which are] more general and not less important.

What is almost unanimously reproached about the system of modern war is the necessity that it imposes of constantly maintaining large standing armies; the immensity of their baggage; the cost of these armies; the incredible expenses of our current wars, expenses that will often be purchased with what it costs to sustain them [from] the funds of the country where they were disputed; [and] the consumption of men that they bring [that is] more disastrous yet.

The philosophes, or to speak more justly, the people who make "philosopher" their profession, attribute quite-destructive effects to this system, because armies, they say, are both the instruments of oppression and the schools of slavery. It is by terror that they impose [the situation in which] no people dares to throw off its chains and look its tyrants in the face. However, considering armies only from this point of view forgets that, if there are unjust wars, there are [also] necessary ones, [and] that, if the troops are sometimes the accomplices of despotism, they are more often the safeguard of nations; they [philosophers] confound the scourge and the profession, passing the horror of one to hatred of the other, naming men of war "stipendiaries" [and] "satellites" and nevertheless sitting in the shade of soft idleness that the men of war procured them, whether in preserving the peace, because they keep watch over them, or in removing war from their homes, because they will fight and die far away for them.[1]

In these imputations made of the system of modern war, there are some truths mixed with many errors and injustices. I will undertake analysis and refutation of them. I will prove that, of all the systems of war that exist, the modern system is the wisest and the most perfect if one considers it from the side of art, and also the most advantageous to governments and to nations, [and] the least destructive, the least calamitous, [and] the most preserving of peace and empires, if one calculates its effects and its results. It is doubtlessly sweet for me to defend a science that I cultivate and a profession that honors me, but, this pleasure aside, the solution to this problem may usefully change the course of opinions. I must avow that I will sometimes be found in contradiction here with the Preliminary Discourse of the *General Essay on Tactics*. When I wrote that work, I was ten years younger. The vapors of modern philosophy aroused my mind and obfuscated my judgment. At the age when one does not reflect maturely, at the age when one draws, if I may express myself thus, all the spirit of one's soul, it is so easy to allow oneself to have illusions by which one believes to improve oneself and to aggrandize oneself![2]

First and before everything, we pose as an incontestable base that philosophy elevates itself in vain against war [and] that it will not destroy the custom of it. To destroy it would require annihilating passions; it would require creating angels of people. Even then, we see that pride and ambition finished by putting them at odds with their creator.[3] If war is an infallible result of the passions of the

---

1 [Guibert draws from Vegetius, *Epitome of Military Science*, particularly 2–8, in his condemnation of the "idleness" and "enervation" of the civilian populace, especially in urban areas. Here and in subsequent passages, he also reacts to contemporary anti-war sentiment, which was a thread of public discussion during the period; Christy Pichichero, *The Military Enlightenment: War and Culture in the French Empire from Louis XIV to Napoleon* (Ithaca: Cornell University Press, 2017), 110–150, provides an introduction to the topic.]
2 [See XXI.]
3 [This passage is one of Guibert's rare recourses to religion in his writings.]

human species, it thus requires an art to make it and men who consecrate themselves to it.

This base posed, declaiming against war in verse and in prose [or] carrying philosophical anathemas against it is to beat the air with vain sounds, as surely princes [who are] ambitious, unjust, or powerful will not be content [without it]. But what may and what must necessarily result from this [declamation] is to extinguish the military spirit little by little, to render the government less occupied with this important branch of the administration, and to one day deliver the nation, soft and unarmed (or, what amounts to the same, ill-armed and to not knowing how to make use of its arms) to the yoke of the warlike nations that have perhaps less enlightenment but more judgement and prudence.

I will speak of another error that is stranger yet: the one that makes men of much spirit but [who are] led astray by their hearts [believe] that there will be no more war one day [and] that peoples and sovereigns will give themselves to the evidence of reason and enlightenment, as if men, whether individually or collectively, would ever be able to cease to be animated by vengeance, by ambition, by love of glory, [or] by interest, all natural or artificial passions that have their source in the human heart or in the prejudices with which humans are imbued.[4]

The King of Prussia [and] Tsarina Ekaterina are certainly quite-enlightened sovereigns.[5] But I doubt that they would ever allow their neighbors to do anything that would wound their interests or their glory. We see the King of Prussia engage himself, at sixty-eight years old, in a war that perhaps his health would not allow him to either sustain the burden of or permit him to see the end of. But the interest of his power, the role of Protector of the Empire that was important to him to enlarge the heritage of his house, [and] finally, the phantom of posterity that besieges great men and that would have demanded an accounting of his treasures, of his forces, of his talents, of all his past glory if he had allowed the invasion of Bavaria to be consummated: this is what animated him.[6]

There is doubtlessly much philosophy and many philosophes in England. But these philosophes are above all [either] traders themselves or indirectly attached to the prosperity of trade; because of this, the interest of commerce for them is the premier and the most pressing of all.[7] It is this interest that makes them tear themselves from their brother Americans; this will always make them make war with us every time that we attempt to elevate our Marine; this makes a people so free and so proud of their liberty [be] so oppressive and such a friend of tyranny in Asia. It is this interest that renders the English so hard and so aloof in the vexations that led to the expulsion of our ambassadors from the Indies, that makes them tear up the canvasses that we order from the weaver's workshops, that makes them forbid our vessels to fire cannon into the Ganges, even on Saint Louis Day. It is this interest that made them destroy Pondichéry, because Pondichéry was the rival of Madras, and where there is rivalry, there can no longer be pity nor justice. The English sense that their conduct in this part of the world is inequitable and vexatious, but it is of import to them to humiliate us in the eyes of the natives of the country and to make themselves the preponderant nation there, as fear adds to prestige, and prestige is a real weight in the balance of nations.[8]

---

4 [Guibert speaks of writers like Charles-Irénée Castel de Saint-Pierre, whose *Projet pour rendre la paix perpétuelle en Europe*, 3 Vols. (Utrecht: Schouten, 1713–1717), was enormously influential on contemporary thought. See Stella Ghervas, *Conquering Peace from the Enlightenment to the European Union* (Cambridge: Harvard University Press, 2021), 29–81; and Pichichero, *The Military Enlightenment*, 162–165; see also *A Cultural History of Peace in the Age of Enlightenment*, ed. David Armitage and Stella Ghervas (New York: Bloomsbury, 2023).]

5 [Ekaterina II, commonly referred to as Catherine the Great, was Tsarina of Russia from 1762 to 1796. She spent a great deal of money modernizing Russia according to the culture of Western Europe, including importing experts like Denis Diderot. She saw herself and was seen by contemporaries as an enlightened monarch, as Guibert says. See Robert Massie, *Catherine the Great: Portrait of a Woman* (New York: Random House, 2011).]

6 [The War of the Bavarian Succession.]

7 [Guibert touches on two important contemporary debates here: national character, and the role of the nobility in French society. The former assigned traits to people based on their geography, history, and physiology, as it was understood at the time; see Abel, *Guibert's General Essay on Tactics*, 42–45. The second was a mid-century debate over the continued role of nobility within French society, particularly as militaries became more rational, professional, and disciplined. French nobles were banned from engaging in trade or commerce, although many did clandestinely, because their traditional duty was to fight for the crown and to subsist on their feudal dues, as argued in Philippe-Auguste de Sainte-Foy, chevalier d'Arcq, *La noblesse militaire ou le patriote français* (Paris, 1756). Gabriel-François Coyer, *La noblesse commerçante* (Paris: Duchesne, 1756), turned this tradition on its head by arguing that the nobility should engage in commerce as it did in other places, notably England. The debate continued through the end of the Old Regime, with many in the military favoring Arcq's view. See D'Auria, *The Shaping of French National Identity*, 162–167; and Smith, *The Culture of Merit*, 230–241. See also David Bien, et al., *Caste, Class, and Profession in Old Regime France: The French Army and the Ségur Reform of 1781* (St. Andrews: Centre for French History and Culture, 2010).]

8 [Throughout the eighteenth century, the English gradually expanded their control over parts of coastal India via the East India Company. This involved pushing out other European colonizers like the Dutch and especially the French, who were established at Pondichéry and other trading posts. The English were never strong enough to simply muscle out their competitors and dominate the indigenous Indian people, which required them to work with various polities

The English are assuredly philosophes, but their works, their theaters, their clubs do not resound with declamations against war and against the citizens who devote themselves to it. They honor their military Marine, which they regard as their bastion and as their true defense. They do not at all regret the enormous sums that they employ in it, and they only complain about it when these expenses have not resulted in formidable armaments. In the end, [they are] more considered than we are; when they wage war, they do not do it halfway, and they employ all the means of their power in it.[9]

The sole one of our modern writers who has envisaged war in its true viewpoint, and who has written as much as a man of state as as a philosophe, is the author of the *History of the Settlements and Trade of the Europeans in the East and West Indies*.[10] He detests war in itself; he dedicates the kings and ministers who make it unjustly to public execration with the warmest eloquence. But at the same time, he senses that war is an inevitable scourge, and even one that one must know how to go to; thus, he does not neglect any military detail in his immortal work; he extends himself on it with a care that makes known how much importance he attaches to it. Everywhere he invites the government to fortify, to aggrandize, [and] to improve its possessions, and, in inviting it, he enlightens it [the government] on the means of being successful in it [war]. We add that, in this work, which must be regarded as one of the monuments of the century, in this work in which we only admire the great extent of the research or the manner in which it was written, all the military details are made with a sharpness, a clarity that *militaires* admire even over those places of which he speaks and that prove on the part of the author a quite-just discernment of the material that has been furnished to him and of the sources from which he drew it.

But we enter into the material. To completely analyze a subject of discussion as complicated and as vast, it is necessary to return to its premier elements.

When war breaks out between two nations, doubtlessly it would be simpler, more expedient, and less bloody if they would wish to confide their destinies to a small number of combatants and to subscribe to receiving the law of the vanquishing party. Thus was sometimes the custom in antiquity. Thus did the Romans and the Alba Longans in the famous combat of the Horatii.[11] Thus we saw kings regard the obligation of combat for their nation as the first need of the throne, settling or proposing to settle the differences of their peoples between them. Some examples of these sorts of duels have not been able to be established in custom, and it must be agreed that nothing would be more absurd and more senseless. What! a people would be dependent on his strength, his interests, his glory, in a particular combat! A false step, a weapon of less-good temper, a man of more adroitness, more strength, or more bravery would decide if all of a nation must govern or obey! And if the sovereigns would have to fight personally, if, in the event that their combat would be attached to the destinies of their subjects, there would thus be no more genius or virtue, and it would be gladiators who would rule![12]

---

on the subcontinent, as Guibert indicates. There was also a debate in England about the propriety of Indian colonialism, which culminated in the trial of Warren Hastings at the end of the century; see Mithi Mukherjee, "The Colonial and the Imperial: India and Britain in the Impeachment Trial of Warren Hastings," *India in the Shadows of Empire: A Legal and Political History (1774–1950)* (New York: Oxford University Press, 2012). As with most topics in English history, English colonialism in India is relatively well covered in historiography; L.H. Roper, "English Overseas Empire," and Pramod Nayar, "English Colonial Discourse and India," *Oxford Bibliographies Online* (2023 and 2021), https://www.oxfordbibliographies.com/display/document/obo-9780195399301/obo-9780195399301-0468.xml and https://www.oxfordbibliographies.com/display/document/obo-9780190221911/obo-9780190221911-0114.xml provide an effective introduction. As is also true in Anglophone historiography, the French colonial efforts in India are much less well documented; see Nathan Marvin and Blake Smith, "France and its Empire in the Indian Ocean," *Oxford Bibliographies Online* (2019), https://www.oxfordbibliographies.com/display/document/obo-9780199730414/obo-9780199730414-0318.xml.]

9 [Guibert is somewhat stilted in his argumentation here. The English very much cared about the costs of war during the period, particularly as they escalated dramatically from the Seven Years War, although they had much more sophisticated debt instruments to manage them. On the other hand, he is absolutely correct that England did tend to wage more "total" wars during the eighteenth century, acknowledging the problematic nature of that term. See John Brewer, *The Sinews of Power: War, Money, and the English State* (Cambridge: Harvard University Press, 1990); and Lawrence Stone, *An Imperial State at War: Britain from 1689 to 1815* (New York: Routledge, 1994).]

10 [Guillaume-Thomas-François Raynal, *A Philosophical and Political History of the Settlements and Trade of the Europeans in the East and West Indies*, 10 Vols. (London: Strahan and Cadell, 1783).]

11 [One of Rome's many founding myths involved a ritual combat fought between three brothers each from the towns of Rome and Alba Longa; the Roman brothers were from the Horatii family. The Horatii victory led to Alba Longa's submission to Rome. The story originates in Titus Livius, *The History of the Roman People*, 1:23–26. Livy himself expresses some skepticism about the finality of the event, and it is generally accepted to have been mythical, as is much of Rome's pre-Republican history. See Kathryn Lomas, *The Rise of Rome from the Iron Age to the Punic Wars* (Cambridge: Harvard University Press, 2018), 3–98; and H.H. Scullard, *A History of the Roman World from 753 to 146 BC* (London: Methuen, 1961), 42–77.]

12 [Guibert provides a pointed critique of what is now referred to as judicial combat, which had fallen out of practice centuries

It passed through the head of some dreamers of the public good that wars could be able to be decided by small armies, that sovereigns could be able to agree between them to obtain armies only proportionate to the extent of their states and to their means. But this chimera faints at the first examination. If there would ever be a congress of sovereigns assembled to work for the goodness of the human species, it would be easier to realize the project of perpetual peace than to form such a convention [in the first place], because who would establish the proportion [of power with it]? What would the arithmetic scale of each power's armament be? Russia would pretend that its extent is the measure of its strength, [while] France would say that it is population, England commerce, [and] The United Provinces riches, [and] the King of Prussia would say that it is the talent and the genius of the sovereign.

Let us leave these chimeras and speak of the two most-used manners, the most habitual of all the nations, whether ancient or modern, that have been used to settle their debates. One is making war themselves, that is to say in arming themselves at the moment when war is declared, in choosing from among themselves the youngest, the most vigorous, the most ardent, the most noble, and going to fight with this more-or-less-informed assemblage under the name "communes," "men at arms," "arrière-ban," "*pospolite*," [and] finally "militia." The other manner is constantly maintaining standing armies at great expense, armies that peacetime prepares, disciplines, [and] forms for war, [armies] on which nations repose themselves from the care of their defense [and] behind which, in the end, if one excepts the countries that are the theaters of operations, they sow, reap, [and] enjoy all the pleasure of life, taking part in war only by curiosity or by personal affectation, and the events that it produces are already no more than the dreams of history when they reach them.

This first manner is entirely lost in Europe. The Turks alone preserve it; they pay dearly for it, and their last war with the Russians ruled decisively on the debate between the multitude and discipline. It still remains in the *pospolite* of the Poles; 9,000 or 10,000 Russians fighting in modern style have dissipated these helpless hordes everywhere.[13] In the end, in all of Europe, there are only nations today [whose people] more or less are not warriors and that pay regular troops, perpetual armies, armies always in view of each other, to fight in their place.[14]

It is now a question of examining which of these two manners is more advantageous to governments and less onerous to nations and to humanity.

The question is so evidently relevant to governments that I will not have need of arresting myself on it for a long time. Without armies, and without great armies, great states would not have surety, prestige, or [their own] politics. They would put themselves at the mercy of the first sovereign, who, [although] inferior in real power, in means, [and] in population, would wish to make an existence by arms with ambition and talent. Thus the King of Prussia, making of his court a [military] camp, turned all his strengths towards the military, and [who], also having the skill to enlarge them by calling many foreigners to his service, would have finished by cutting down the Habsburgs if they had not formed an army capable of balancing his in their own turn. But (without speaking of [examples] external [to the discussion] by descending from the great to the small to extend the question to states that may not at all maintain an army) without any military strengths, governments would have no authority, support, or coactive force. The form of government and the extent of the country only modify this principle, but troops are needed everywhere. From France to the Republic of Venice, in whatever proportion and in whatever form, soldiers must be maintained.

Here the philosophes will elevate themselves, [and] they will make resound the words "despotism" and "liberty," [which are] so ill-conceived and so vague. We examine on what their clamors are founded and reduce their wishes and their declamations to truth and, above all, to possibility.

Troops may sometimes doubtlessly serve as instruments of despotism, but did despotism not exist before there were regular troops? Does it not exist in the East, where it has only eunuchs and torturers for its agents?[15]

---

prior in most of western Europe. See Hunt Janin, *Medieval Justice: Cases and Laws in France, England, and Germany, 500–1500* (Jefferson, NC: McFarland, 2009).]

13 [Guibert speaks of the 1768–1774 Russo-Turkish War in which Russia inflicted significant defeats on the Ottoman Empire and gained important territory, particularly on the Black Sea, and contemporaneous Russian interventions into the Polish-Lithuanian Commonwealth. See Aksan, *Ottoman Wars*, 129–179, Herbert Kaplan, *The First Partition of Poland* (New York: Columbia University Press, 1962); and Stone, *A Military History of Russia*, 76–89. As Guibert indicates, that war may be seen as a referendum on the military reforms enacted in Russia during the century, although that point may also be exaggerated; see Eugene Miakinkov, *War and Enlightenment in Russia: Military Culture in the Age of Catherine II* (Buffalo: University of Toronto Press, 2020).]

14 [Guibert echoes the criticisms of Vegetius, *Epitome of Military Science*, 2–8, of societies that refuse to dedicate themselves to war.]

15 [Guibert engages in Orientalism by referencing eunuchs and torturers, both of which were found in the Byzantine and Ottoman Empires.]

Was Louis XI not more despotic without an army than Louis XIV, creator of grand armies?[16] Was it troops that executed the Saint Bartholomew's Day Massacre?[17] All the sovereigns of Europe have troops; in what barbarism, in what execution, in what blow of tyranny are they employed? It is when princes are feeble and armed with a half-power that they are perhaps more dangerous. It is then that defiance accompanies them and that resistance embitters them; it is then that they turn to spies and torturers. It is then that a Louis XI makes a citadel of his palace and the citadel the dungeon and charnel of his prisoners. It is then that a Henri III assassinates the Guises, whom he dreads.[18] It is then that the order is given to arrest Marshal Concino Concini, marquis d'Ancre, dead or alive, which is only another palliated assassination.[19] It is then that a Armand-Jean du Plessis, duc de Richelieu, always alarmed by the shadowy pusillanimity of his master, uses his name to extend his personal power and to lead pretend conspirators to the scaffold.[20] When authority is supported by armies, there are no more attempts or occasions of troubles. The ministers no longer have the pretext to kill their enemies. They can no longer accuse them of crime whose possibility no longer exists. The philosophes say that this tranquility is a destructive calm, that it is the calm of the tomb, but it is a matter of knowing if, for the interest of humanity, for the interest of this sacred portion, because it is the suffering and numerous portion, for the people in a word, if the convulsions of civil wars are not a hundred times more redoubtable? What does this unfortunate people gain from these shocks, from these pretend ameliorations of governments? Where do they have laws made for them? Where do they remedy the monstrous inequality of their fortunes? I interrogate impartial philosophy, true philosophy here, and I summon it to respond to me.

The custom of perpetual armies was destructive to humanity in the time of barbarity and ignorance; today, enlightenment, the evidence of reason, the softening of morals, in the end everything, down to the softness and enfeebling of characters, removes all the danger from this institution. Armies are the firmest support of legitimate authority, of authority contained in its just boundaries, and they are a tacit brake on tyranny at the same time. A Charles IX commanding his troops to massacre his subjects, a Nero wishing to burn his capital would find in his troops only instruments of his own deposing.[21]

---

16 [Louis XI was King of France between 1461 and 1483. His reign saw the formal end of the Hundred Years War with the 1475 Treaty of Picquigny and the annexation to the crown of large parts of Burgundy after the death of Charles the Bold in 1477. He also improved the efficiency of the royal government, increasing tax revenues by around four-hundred percent, for example. See Emmanuel Le Roy Ladurie, *The Royal French State 1460–1610*, trans. Juliet Vale (Oxford: Blackwell, 1987). As Joël Blanchard, "Louis XI, King of France," *Oxford Bibliographies Online* (2022), https://www.oxfordbibliographies.com/display/document/obo-9780195399301/obo-9780195399301-0491.xml, notes, "few kings have been tagged with such worn stereotypes, notably the simple and sinister image of the 'universal spider' that has clung to him over the centuries," as Guibert's criticism here and later indicate. Louis XI is a ripe topic for a scholarly Anglophone biography.]

17 [The 1572 Saint Bartholomew's Day Massacre was perhaps the seminal event of the French Wars of Religion. Sectarian violence had roiled the kingdom for the decade prior, splitting the kingdom into three groups headed by the Huguenots under Admiral Gaspard Coligny and Henri of Navarre, the ultramontanes under the Guise family, and the more moderate royals under King Charles IX and his mother, Catherine de' Medici. Despite a peace treaty, Charles decided to allow the radicals to enact a massacre of Huguenots in Paris, which took place from 24 August, Saint Bartholomew's feast day, until 26 August. Provincial massacres followed throughout the kingdom, resulting in the deaths of tens of thousands of Huguenots. While the massacres were largely perpetrated by paramilitary groups and the Paris militia, units of the *Maison militaire du roi* also participated, contre Guibert's statement. See Mack Holt, *The French Wars of Religion, 1562–1629* (New York: Cambridge University Press, 2005), 76–98.]

18 [Henri III was King of France between 1574 and 1589, the penultimate period of the Wars of Religion. He attempted to steer a middle course between the Huguenots of Henri of Navarre and the radical Catholic League led by Henri, duc de Guise. The religious question was also intimately related to the succession, as Henri had no direct heirs, leaving the throne to Henri of Navarre, who was a Huguenot, which allowed Guise to press his own claim. Open warfare broke out in 1585 between the three factions, marking the eighth such conflict in the Wars of Religion. Guise seized Paris in mid-1788, leading Henri to order the assassination of Guise and his brother, Louis Cardinal Guise, in December of the same year. Henri was himself assassinated the following year, one of only three Capetian kings to die by violence. See Holt, *The French Wars of Religion*, 123–136.]

19 [Concino Concini, marquis d'Ancre, was favorite of dowager Queen and regent Marie de' Medici after the assassination of Henri IV in 1610. He secured royal power for the young Louis XIII, and great wealth for himself, by wielding the army against various rebellious factions, including the Condé and Guise families. Louis turned against Concini and ordered his assassination in 1617, which was carried out in brutal fashion first by royal agents and then by a mob, as Guibert indicates. See Emmanuel Le Roy Ladurie, *The Ancien Régime: A History of France, 1610–1789*, trans. Mark Greenglass (New York: Blackwell, 1996), 10–25.]

20 [As with Louis XI, a black legend grew around Richelieu, especially among those opposed to his efforts to restrain traditional noble autonomy and build a more centralized state, as Guibert intimates.]

21 [Nero Claudius Caesar Augustus Germanicus was Emperor of Rome from 54 until his suicide in 68. He was the last of the Julio-Claudian emperors, and his death contributed to the civil war known as the Year of the Four Emperors. Beginning with contemporary chroniclers, historians have almost universally viewed his emperorship as negative. The specific event and myth Guibert references is the Great Fire of Rome, which took place in 64 and gutted the city. Nero attempted to blame Christians for the

Without doubt, liberty is lost; without doubt, it is almost impossible to recover everywhere sovereigns have formidable armies. But would liberty (I intend by "liberty" the right to govern oneself, as this is what it must be reduced to in policed nations) be suitable for almost all the great nations of Europe? The majority of them are neither situated nor constituted to form republics. To taste this form of government, there must be a certain temper of character and of spirit; there must be morals, poverty, [and] simplicity; there must be no knowledge of all the poison and softening of luxury, of letters, and of arts. There would have to be a party of individuals in each nation that had not contracted the habit and the necessity of living in the graces and the abuses of all species that abound in the monarchic regime. Finally, there is a nation that has reached the point where, if it were made a present of its liberty, it would not at all know how to make use of it, would fall into anarchy, and would soon raise great cries for the government against which it declaims today.[22]

One will cite England. One will say that England is both rich and corrupt and thus strong and free. But it is to its fortunate situation, it is to the seas that surround it and that defend it, that England owes having maintained its form of government until now. It is this situation that permits it to pass over land armies, or at least to have an inconsiderable one. Its fleets take the place of ramparts and battalions. And this is the advantage of sea power, when it was founded like that of England on a great maritime commerce, when they even feed and sustain themselves via this commerce. It is even more to their advantage in that, defending England against outside enemies, they [fleets] do not place a dangerous power in the hands of the sovereign, as with a fleet, one is not master of a country. But suppose England in the midst of the continent like Germany; suppose only that it was not separated from France by the sea; then it would be obliged to have land armies. Then, under the first warrior and victorious king, the royal prerogative would extend itself, the counterweights to his authority would be enfeebled; in the end, all the equilibrium of this good constitution would be sapped by its foundations.[23]

Let us thus leave philosophy to feed on chimeras that can never realize themselves and speak of our own situation. We inhabit a great continent, [and] we have frontiers of an immense development [and] bellicose neighbors with powerful armies. Monarchic government is that which best conforms to such a position. It is it (although history furnishes some opposing examples) that is most capable of expedition, of secret, and of vigor; it is it that may best operate the reunion and the concourse of the means of so great a mass. As a consequence of this situation, we must have armies proportionate to our power and to that of the nations that border us. Poland had a sad experience of the abuses of republican anarchy; by a system destructive to liberty, it wished to have neither armies nor places of war; it feared placing itself into the hands of its sovereign, and it became the slave of and the prey to the powerful monarchies and formidable armies that surrounded it.[24]

Let us now examine first if it would be possible, then if it would be advantageous, for modern nations to make war themselves in lieu of making it by *suppôts*, that is to say by regular troops.[25]

The discipline and the progress of the art in every genre today have placed a so-prodigious difference between the armies that would passingly assemble to fight, like those that may have composed our militias or our arrières-bans, and armies constituted and maintained for a long time for this purpose that there remains no term of equality between the former and the latter [and] no reasonable possibility to hazard [a fight] with the one against the other, even with a great superiority of numbers, and finally that the nation that, surrounded by nations armed according to the modern system, wishing to return to the old system, and, if I may express myself thus, beating itself to gain its money, would be, relative to its neighbors, in the same proportion of disadvantage and feebleness as a

---

event, leading to their persecution and his continued vilification in later Christian sources. In particular, the axiom "Nero fiddled while Rome burned" arose from the event, portraying a callous emperor who may have even burnt the city for his own ends. Subsequent historiography has reconsidered both the event and the man, but the negative connotation largely remains. See H.H. Scullard, *From the Gracchio to Nero: A History of Rome from 133 BC to AD 68* (New York: Routledge, 1982), 288–321.]

22 [Guibert unwittingly provides an effective single-sentence description of the French Revolution, which began with the end of the Bourbon monarchy and ended with a military dictatorship-cum-monarchy.]

23 [Guibert anticipates the arguments of Alfred Mahan, *The Influence of Sea Power upon History 1660–1783* (Boston: Little, Brown, and Co., 1898), especially 29–81.]

24 [Guibert speaks of the ongoing dismemberment of the Polish-Lithuanian Commonwealth, which was in the process of being partitioned between Russia, Prussia, and Austria before its final demise in 1795.]

25 [The word Guibert uses here, "*suppôt*," is defined in the Fourth Edition of the Dictionary of the Académie Française as "someone who is a supporter and a partisan of one who is evil [or] who serves the ill designs of another." The older definition is of someone who works within a specific body, particularly a university like the Sorbonne. Guibert's use of it to denote regular troops here is one of the more intriguing passages in the book.]

disarmed man or one who does not know how to handle his arms against a man [who is] armed and exercised in the manner of handling his own.

The philosophes have not failed to triumph these last years in seeing the Americans resisting the English army with success; this example flatters their opinions. "Despite the armies," they would say, "there still remains an asylum for liberty on the earth! Despite the armies, discontented and oppressed nations will still raise themselves against their tyrants! Love of liberty will still, in raising a nation above itself, take the place of all the details of art and discipline so vaunted by men of war!"

This American resistance, this success, which will perhaps be ephemeral, has not changed my opinion. First, I believe that the difference that I have spoken of above, although apparently contradicted by the results, existed between the English army and that of George Washington, and even between that of John Burgoyne that laid down its arms and that of Horatio Gates that made it capitulate.[26] I believe that, if one would be able to consult the foreign officers who have seen this war, if one would be able to open the mouth of one of them who has made such a good name for himself there, that an expedition [that was] so personal, so chivalrous, [and] so generous, supported by so much conduct, prudence, valor, and modesty, has just placed in the tableau of his fellow young people on a plan so distinct and so separated, I believe, I said, that they would unanimously agree that the misfortunes of the English come only from their own faults; that their generals lost the plan, took false measures, [and] maladroitly divided their forces; [and] that, above all, they made the great fault of not sensing the superiority of their means well enough and of forgetting that regular troops that include militias even lose their principle advantage, which consists of the opinion that they must have of their superiority and that they give by this to these latter a little countenance and strength.[27] Finally, I believe that they would all unite to avow that they have often bemoaned this prodigious difference and that, in supposing that love of liberty exists unanimously among the Americans, this sentiment that sometimes makes heroes of individuals, is, for the multitude, a less-sure vehicle than discipline.[28]

But, even if the American War of Independence would not have the effect that I believe must be that of every war made between well-led regular troops and an armed nation, this example would prove nothing more against my opinion, as this war resembles that made in Europe in nothing. The English are two-thousand leagues from their country. Food; the embarrassment of transports; the slowness and the uncertainty of convoys; the nature of the land that, by its great rivers, its lakes, [and] its forests, presents much greater obstacles than our continent; the difficulty of advancing in land where one draws all one's subsistence from the coast and from one's fleets: all this may balance the superiority that discipline and the species of their troops gives the English over the Americans.

We return to the difference that the discipline and progress of the art bring today between armies and the collections of nations. This difference was already immense in the time of Louis XIV, and we were in the midst of having it proven in a terrible manner, because, if in 1710, in lieu of the fortunate event of Denain, the only, the last army that remained to Louis XIV would have experienced a misfortune like that of Blenheim, we would have seen that it [France] would have become the first kingdom in Europe to have no more armies. Some frontier places excepted,

---

26 [George Washington was the commander of the Continental Army during the War of American Independence and first president of the United States. The combat Guibert describes is the Battles of Saratoga, fought in late 1777 between the English army of John Burgoyne and the American armies of Horatio Gates and Benedict Arnold. Burgoyne, with around 7,000 men and First Nations support, moved south from Canada into New York late in the spring to open a second front in the region. Various American forces fell back south from Burgoyne's advance through August, when Gates assumed command of a mixed force of around 6,000 regulars and at least 6,000 militia. The two armies fought engagements in September and October near Saratoga, after which Burgoyne surrendered to Gates. Saratoga was a major turning point in the war, as it proved that the American Patriots could win a traditional battle against English regulars, which helped convince France to join the war the following year. See John Ferling, *Almost a Miracle: The American Victory in the War of Independence* (New York: Oxford University Press, 2007, 211–241.]

27 [Guibert's argument here anticipates generations of debate about the nature of the American Patriot forces and how they won the War of Independence. Contemporary propaganda emphasized the democratic nature of the Patriot forces, recalling the citizen armies of Republican Rome, creating a myth of a citizen-militia that defeated the regular English soldiers by fighting using irregular tactics, including those used by the First Nations. More recent scholarship draws on the leadership of the Continental Army, particularly Washington, to illustrate his emphasis on the need to train regular, professional, disciplined soldiers to meet the English on equal footing. This debate continues to the present, with popular memory and historians generally favoring the former view and academic historians the latter. Guy Chet, *Conquering the American Wilderness: The Triumph of European Warfare in the Colonial Northeast* (Amherst: University of Massachusetts Press, 2003); and John Grenier, *The First Way of War: American War Making on the Frontier, 1607–1814* (New York: Cambridge University Press, 2005), present an effective introduction to the voluminous debate.]

28 [Guibert perhaps evinces some bitterness at not being sent to America himself; see Abel, *Jacques-Antoine-Hippolyte, comte de Guibert*, 118–139.]

this kingdom would have been entirely [without]; twenty million inhabitants would have hardly heard the sound of the cannon, and then Prince Eugene would have arrived at the capital without obstacles. Struck with reason by these long calamities but still preserving dignity under their weight, the master of this vast empire would only have dared to hope for an honorable death in the case of defeat. "If you are beaten," he would have said to Marshal Villars on leaving, "I will convoke my nobility, and I will go to die at their head."

But it is in the epoch of the King of Prussia, which must justly be regarded as a new age in military science, that the difference between the system of modern war between armies and nations has become yet more obvious. This prince gave birth to a new order of things; he created a new discipline, a new [system of] tactics, a new genre of war. His army, always complete, always provided with all the necessary equipment, always menacing, has become like the formidable barrier of the legions that watched all along the frontiers in the good years of Rome. Rival of [Friedrich's] neighborhood and of glory, the Emperor has embraced the same system and marches in the same footsteps.[29] Finally, it is no longer a matter today, as was done under Louis XIV and as continued to be done for a long time after him, of levying great augmentations in war to then make great reforms in peacetime. The progress of the art, the necessity of its instruction, [and] the importance of discipline oblige making peacetime the school of war and maintaining armies on such a footing that they are able to enter into a campaign at the first signal.[30] From this, regular troops acquire more and more superiority over the collections of nations, [and] nations are less than ever in the case of doing without them and of being able to measure themselves with them.

Things being at this point, what great nation would dare to depart from the accepted system! But I will demonstrate that surety, apart from necessity, [and] the interest of modern nations is still in maintaining regular troops to make war rather than in making war themselves.

When nations are half-barbarous, when they have no enlightenment, commerce, riches, [or] luxury, the idleness of the nobles, the vigor of the young men, the ardor of the ambitious, the general ferocity of spirits, finally, the lure of the only species of glory that they would know carries many men to arms. Among the basic arts, there are almost only two occupations: laborer and fighter. Such were the Romans in the first ages of the Republic; the consuls planted their flags on the Campus Martius, and the young rushed headlong to arrange themselves on it.[31] Such was still the majority of the peoples of Europe two centuries ago. The troubles of religion, the anarchy of feudal government, [and] the maintenance of an almost-continual state of war. Each seigneur, each town, each parish had its banner. As they had neither discipline nor science, each was able to arm itself and fight at need. One recalls the facility with which they made emigrating armies under the name of "crusades." It is so easy to detach from their soil and lead to death men who do not know what to do with their lives! In our modern nations, enlightenment and riches have completely reversed everything in this regard. They have created a mass of new professions, opened opportunities in every sense, enervated bodies, softened courage, and made known the value of life. One would call citizens to the defense of their country today in vain, excepting the nobility, whose remnant of prejudice would lead it to go to [war]; all the other classes will be occupied; all have their bonds, their profession, their interests, their needs; there would remain only the last class of people entirely at the disposal of the government, [people] who would be directed there rather than led. The more that nations are rich, enlightened, [and] fortunate, the less that they may fight themselves [and] the more that it is both necessary and advantageous to commit and to maintain a small portion of them to avow themselves to their defense and to be their representatives.[32]

In any government, everyone must have their part in the cost; the public defense is doubtlessly a most-sacred need, and the tribute of one's blood is, above all, that which, in the primitive institution, no one has the right to refuse. This is the debt, this is the cost that the men of war maintained by the nation lift from the magistrate, the lawyer, the savant, the artist, the father of a family, [and]

---

29 [Guibert probably means Emperor Josef II, who reigned alongside his mother from 1765 to 1780 and then solely until 1790. He contested the War of the Bavarian Succession and engaged in several other martial projects, including a potential swap of the Austrian Netherlands for Bavaria, that did not come to fruition.]

30 ["L'origine des grandes manœuvres—les camps d'instruction aux XVIIe et XVIIIe siècles," *Revue militaire* and *Revue d'histoire* (1899–1900, 1901–1903), provides an in-depth study of the peacetime activities of the French army of the period, including its training camps.]

31 [Traditionally, the people of the Roman Republic assembled on the Campus Martius, the Field of Mars, on the banks of the Tiber in times of war to draw lots for membership in the legionary army. See Paul Jacobs and Diane Atnally Conlin, *Campus Martius: The Field of Mars in the Life of Ancient Rome* (New York: Cambridge University Press, 2015). See also Abel, *Guibert's General Essay on Tactics*, 47.]

32 [As with previous similar passages, Guibert repeats nearly verbatim the social arguments of Vegetius, *Epitome of Military Science*, 2–8.]

finally, from the useless citizen who weighs on the earth that nourishes them and who does nothing for it.

I leave it to be judged now if it is just to declaim against men of war, to search to debase the troops by the name "stipendiaries," and to appear to always regret the expense that they occasion. And what makes the men of war more stipendiaries than the magistrate who receives *gages* [or] the man of letters or the artist who receives a pension![33] If, in the general mass of salaries, one compares theirs [soldiers'] to that of the other professions, they make less than anyone. If one then compares the[ir] service, the other professions give their time, [while] they [soldiers] give their blood and their lives.

The excessive number of troops will be objected to me in saying that it is unwisely increased in several states, and much more than their populations would permit. The great number of arms that this removes from agriculture and the other professions; the more-than-real harm that this quantity of men of war, almost all single, all in the vigor of age, inflicts on the population; the cost of maintaining such armies in peacetime, a cost [that is] all the more onerous [and] all the more felt in that it no longer appears to be justified by need, will be objected to me. The system of war, becoming more expensive than before on all sides and in every way, will be objected to me; wars almost equally exhaust the vanquisher and the vanquished, making one bemoan one of his victories and not compensating them for it and making the other weep for their shame and ruin at the same time. These arguments contain more specious than solid objections. I will prove this by the following analysis and demonstrate that none of them concludes powerfully against the system of modern war.

We first return to that which concerns the prodigious quantity of troops; the objection raised in this regard may only regard three or four great powers, as the inferior powers, even counting the small German princes that traffic their troops as a commodity of their country, certainly have troops on a footing quite inferior to their population.[34] We thus go to these formidable powers, to these armed colossi against which a misunderstanding philosophy raises so many exclamations.

With the title "formidable military power," I must certainly not speak of France as the premier, as, seeing the current footing of its military, it is only the fourth in this class, but, as it is the premier by its real means; as it must be by its situation [and] by its politics; as the other powers have only usurped its place, which it will retake when its government will have the will and the vigor to seize it again; [and] finally as it is that which interests me, I will commence with it.

We will not begin here with the present footing of the kingdom's troops, this footing being certainly inferior to what it must be and to what our means permit us. We will suppose that it has a healthy politics, both exterior and interior, that must determine it. This double politics has positive bases, [ones] that we do not fear that administrators [who are] the most deprived of energy and ambition could contest.

France may wish to neither conquer nor extend itself. It may, preferring repose to war and making peace its premier goal, renounce the role of predominant power that its superiority in every genre assigns it. But it must at least hold its place and its rank among the great powers; it must at least not only be able to preserve its territorial possessions but also its prestige, its dignity, [and] its influence in the affairs of Europe, another genre of possession that all good governments must value. To maintain itself in this situation, it must at least be armed like the principal powers of continental Europe; I say "at least" because it at least has coasts and borders to guard [and] colonies to defend. Thus, for example, the peacetime footing of the armies of the Emperor and the King of Prussia, which are the two greatest military powers in Europe, is ordinarily 160,000 men in peacetime, counting only field troops [and not garrison troops]. Following this proportion, not counting its militias, the [footing] of France's troops must be 180,000, of whom 30,000 [must be] cavalry, all mounted. This excess of superiority must have for its objective to face the exterior garrisons and the great extent of our frontiers and our coasts in such a manner that the number of available troops, that is to say [those] ready to enter into

---

33 ["*Gage*" has several meanings in French, ranging from a simple payment or salary to complex and arcane payments related to ancient feudal obligations. In this instance, Guibert refers to the remuneration for holding public office, which was not necessarily a simple payment, which would have been referred to as a pension. *Gages* could be payments, the right to collect feudal dues or other forms of payment from a specific fief or other area of land, or even more complicated systems involving circular debt. Roland Mousnier, *The Institutions of France under the Absolute Monarchy 1598–1789*, 2 Vols., trans. Arthur Goldhammer and Brian Pearce (Chicago: The University of Chicago Press, 1979), provides the best overview of the concept and the French magistracy in general.]

34 [Guibert refers to states like Hesse-Kassel, which trained small professional armies for use as mercenaries. Such troops were ubiquitous in contemporary conflicts and often composed a significant portion of armies in a given campaign. See for example Friederike Baer, *Hessians: German Soldiers in the American Revolutionary War* (New York: Oxford University Press, 2022).]

[a] campaign, would be equal to that which each of these powers could place there.

This number, taken as the habitual base of our military constitution, is certainly far from being in proportion to our population and what it may furnish to the military state without enfeebling it if, as Jean-Baptiste Moheau's work entitled *Researches and Considerations on the Population of France*, printed in 1774, appears to prove invincibly: he demonstrates that it has twenty-four million inhabitants; deducting women, the elderly, infants, and all people below age sixteen and above age fifty, he determines the number of men in a state of carrying arms at 5,518,540; it follows from this calculation that the land military, constantly maintained on an effective peacetime footing of 180,000 men, would only make the [ratio] of men in a state of carrying arms [to total population] be 1:30.66; this proportion would be less onerous yet in supposing that, of these 180,000 men, there would be around 20,000 foreigners, thus placing [the ratio] at 1:33.66.[35]

But it must be truthfully be observed 1. that, of these 5,518,540 men, a just reduction to establish is to only count the men under forty-five years of age, because, although many men continue their military service beyond this age, one must neither enroll as a soldier nor class with the title of militia any man above forty, from which I believe to be able to reasonably establish the average of forty-five. 2. That the men that some infirmity or grave defect render useless for service must be deducted from these 5,518,520 men, [as must] those that a too-short height rejects, a custom perhaps quite misunderstood in a nation in which nature, and perhaps yet more, an infinity of vices that the laws may be able to remedy, have generally made of a lesser height and that seems to us to be much less reasonable than that of the Russians. This nation being no more elevated than our own, it has the good spirit to not at all consider height for [someone to enter into] the state of [being a] soldier and to content itself with the degree of strength capable of sustaining a great fatigue [in its soldiers]. 3. That those who are part of the order[s] of the clergy, the nobility, the magistracy, and then the professions of finance, commerce, [and] the arts must be deducted from these 5,518,540, considering, however, to not exaggerate this reduction; that the nobility furnishes its contingent to the military state, since it comprises the officers; and that it is truly necessary only to deduct the men between the ages of sixteen and forty-five from the other states or professions, since it is only this class of which we speak here. 4. That the men sworn to the service of the Marine, whether Military or Merchant, must also be deducted, in observing that this profession employs men below sixteen years and above forty-five [and] emigrants, deserters, or errant people in Europe, [an] unfortunately considerable number, and almost all coming from the class of those sixteen to forty-five years old, because this is the age of passions; [this is] a sort of national malady that is both the result of our lightness, of the sentiment of confidence that the French person has in their spirit and in the resources of their industry, and, what is saddest, of the excessive misery of the lowest class of the nation, [a] malady that a good government would be able to cure, or at least a contagion that it would be able to diminish.

I lack the knowledge and the research to be able to state positively enough what the residual net population [would be] that could furnish the maintenance of the land military in France [with] all these deductions made. This would be a work worthy of a citizen ministry animated with great views. This work has difficulties, but difficulties that obstinate love of the public good and truth would manage to vanquish, [but] once it was done, we would no longer float haphazardly and without principles; we would know the just measure of our strength, on one hand, so as to not exaggerate them and to not make efforts beyond them, and on the other, to not remain below our means; we would form a general plan for the partition of the militias based on this knowledge, [a] necessary supplement to armies, [a] supplement that, during peacetime, is neither an inconvenience nor a surcharge for the people and that, during war, is only a momentary effort and an indispensable reserve for guarding the kingdom, [managing] the slowness or the difficulty of levies and great reverses. Who would be able to believe that the current partition of the militia is not founded on any calculation of population; that it is routine, custom, [and] the protocol of bureaus that fix it; and that, as proof of this, these insufficient bases have not varied since their establishment?[36]

But without being able to furnish calculations as positive and as precise as I would desire in this regard, I believe to have said enough to demonstrate that the footing of our military is certainly quite inferior to that which our population permits us and that philosophical declamations on this subject are thus absolutely false. We go to the other great military powers.

---

35   [Jean-Baptiste Moheau, *Recherches et considérations sur la population de la France* (Paris: Moutard, 1778), Guibert appears to have mistaken the publication date, as the cited work is the first edition; the 1774 date occurs in both manuscripts of the *Defense of the System of Modern War*.]

36   [The French militia was technically liable only for defense of the region in which it was raised, but it often ended up being the manpower pool for the army during the Old Regime. See Gebelin, *Histoire des milices provinciales*; and Lynn, *Giant of the Grand Siècle*, 371–379.]

The Holy Roman Emperor, the King of Prussia, [and] even Russia are certainly more formidably armed than we are, if one compares the habitual footing of their militaries to ours, and yet the population of their states is quite inferior to ours, as the Emperor has only around thirteen or fourteen million inhabitants in his united possessions and the King of Prussia seven or eight million, including their acquisitions in Poland for both. Russia has no more than sixteen or seventeen million inhabitants, and this population is spread over an immense surface that, in dispersing it and scattering it, doubtlessly enfeebles it. But these powers have neither commerce nor colonies; they do not have our luxury, our arts, our religion, or our malady of emigration; above all, they do not have a mass of citizens that philosophy, letters, riches, and, it must be added above all, the maladroit indifference of the government on this important subject, have rendered cosmopolites and useless to their country like we do. The King of Prussia, with a feebler population [and] seeming to have carried his military onto a footing that has no proportion to it, has the art of sharing with his neighbors, and even with France, the burden of this enormous apparatus of war. The great majority of his troops is not composed of [people of] his nation; [it is composed of] natives of the Empire, of deserters of all nations, of French, all then amalgamated by discipline and surrounded by a wall of bronze from which they no longer depart until he wishes them to go into the arena to make them fight.

Let us not thus go to these false speculations of a philosophy that can appreciate in the cabinet neither the localities of countries and governments nor the interests and the passions of sovereigns; do not believe that these great foreign powers would ever come to disarming and letting their military constitutions fall. These constitutions have become the base of their politics and their grandeur; they are analogous to the situation of their states, [and] to the spirit, the morals, [and] the character of their subjects. Nations more fortunately situated enjoy commerce, the arts, [and] riches; it may only remain to the peoples [from] nations isolated in the [the center of the] continent to be agricultural and warlike. There, luxury [and] the refining of spirits do not at all sap [or] relax military discipline and the taste for arms, as they do with us. There, there is only one state, one profession, one outlet for fortune and for glory; there, every man born is a soldier, and the entire nation is the nursery of the army. Finally, there, military power is the first objective, all expenses relate to it, and, to suffer the maintenance of armies, the courts have almost adopted the simplicity of [military] camps.

Does it follow from this that the system of these nations must be adopted to only become *militaires* like them? Doubtlessly no; we must play to all our advantages; we must profit from [our] abundant population that permits us to [engage in] commerce, the arts, agriculture, and war at the same time. We must reach the destination that nature seems to have assigned us to be a universal people, but we must have an army that sustains this grand destiny and that makes our neighbors respect us. The difference between them and us is that, to have an army, they are obliged to combine, to unite, [and] to exhaust all their means, [and] that, having an army, they have nothing beyond it. Here, the army may exist without harming the other parts of the administration; it must only be the safeguard behind which all the other professions, equally encouraged by the means that are relative to them, equally dear to the government, will be flourishing and fortunate.

But if the numerous armies introduced by the system of modern war do not contribute to the prosperity of the state as much as they do to its strength, it is the fault of governments and not of the system, as there would be numerous means of rendering the troops less onerous to nations. One could, as the Russians have done, not require a height so tall for the soldier and thus not remove the most beautiful species of man from the population. One could, as the King of Prussia and the Emperor practice, favor the marriage of soldiers, aid in the subsistence of their children, [and] raise the males in the profession of their fathers. This encouragement for marriages, this education for the children to whom they give birth, and a mass of other advantages yet would be the result and the fruit of the method of sedentary garrisons and quarters substituted for the errant and ruinous life in which we lead our regiments. In lieu of occupying the troops only in exercises [that are] puerile and almost foreign to war; in lieu of hoarding them in places of war, as if the enemy were at the gates of the kingdom and consequently on the frontiers, where food is always more dear and has the most outlets [and] where the inhabitants have the most resources and industry, one could disperse them in the interior provinces that lack vivification and variety and have more commodities than consumers. One could divide uncultivated land between them, employ them in public works, in the opening of several grand canals that we yet lack, [and] in the construction of roads and in the repair of those that exist.[37] There would be no regiment

---

37 [Guibert argues for the use of soldiers in public-works projects, which was the custom in Rome but also a contemporary practice. See Jean Meyer, "States, Roads, Armies, and the Organization of Space," *War and Competition between States*, ed. Philippe Contamine (New York: Oxford University Press, 2000), 99–128; and Southern, *The Roman Army*, 368–420.]

that would not charge itself with the maintenance of those of its canton, at much less expense than they cost. One could charge the troops with the guarding and the internal policing of the kingdom, functions fulfilled so poorly and in such a costly way by the Maréchaussée.[38] It is only in France that this Maréchaussée establishment exists. In all of Germany, the troops render aid to justice [and] to the civil authority, patrolling the roads [and] keeping watch over the public surety. And what better duty must the troops be able to accomplish in peacetime! Each regiment would be charged with and responsible for its arrondissement. When it would depart for war, its depot, under the name of "company," "battalion," or "garrison squadron," would be the depot of women, children, old soldiers who would prefer this retreat to the Invalides, [and] half-broken soldiers and too-weak young men who, not being able to sustain the fatigues of war, would be proper to sedentary service; this depot, I say, would accomplish the care of those who would be confined to it in the absence of the regiment.[39]

A military state of two-hundred thousand men thus constituted, thus employed in peacetime, would be less a cost to the population, to finances, to the kingdom, than one-hundred forty thousand men or so, as we have today, accumulated and consigned to garrisons, lost to idleness and debauchery, distasteful to their state, and so soft of body and heart that, when they quit the métier of soldier, they are capable only of urban and sedentary work.[40] Eh! does one believe that discipline and instruction are lost? They would gain both there. I intend here by "discipline" not the enchaining in fastidious minutiae and miserable details of uniformity that are so maladroitly confounded with it but true discipline, that which would harden the body, which would subordinate the grades, which would make both order and contentment reign, which would have need of neither casernes nor ramparts, and which would maintain itself entirely and equally well in villages and in tents. I intend by "instruction" that which is not bounded by exercises of detail and of the esplanade [but] that which would teach tactics like those I have presented in this work and would form all the grades in them and would be applicable to war. To this end, it would suffice to the troops encamp by regiments or by brigades every year for two months at the center of their quarters and then to assemble them for fifteen days in army corps at the center of a certain number of arrondissements.[41] I have seen Austrian troops thus encamp by brigades at the center of their "numerals;" this is the name that we give to their arrondissements. After these two-and-a-half months, the troops would re-enter their quarters; they would pass from military exercises, not into a state of inaction, but [rather] into another genre of exercises [that is] not less important: working the body outdoors, which must form the base of military education. What advantages, what immense gains would result from this genre of constitution and employment of troops for the state! In peacetime, economy; in war, victories; at all times, veneration and recognition for the military state by the other orders of citizens, because they would see them being equally useful at all times.

All these thoughts, which do not belong to me, which were thrown before the public a long time ago but which prejudice and abuse will perhaps always push back on, come despite me to present themselves in a mass under my pen. Which minister, or perhaps which sovereign, will reassemble them one day? It will be the one who will sense that the nation must have a formidable army but at the same time that this army must not be charged to it, and the one who will wish to immortalize themselves by the monument of this great problem resolved and put into execution.[42]

We go to the objection made to the system of modern war relative to the expenses that it requires. I cannot deny that this system has not increased them greatly. It has increased them first in peacetime, because, after the progress that has been made in discipline, in tactics, [and] in all the branches of the art, after the necessity of having troops [that are] maneuvering and always ready to enter

---

38 [The Maréchaussée was a mounted force intended to keep the peace and prevent brigandage in the French countryside, particularly on highways. See Iain Cameron, "The Police of Eighteenth-Century France," *European Studies Review* 7 (1977): 47–75.]

39 [The Invalides was founded in the mid-seventeenth century as a hospice for injured and invalid soldiers, which it still remains. Its location on the Champ de Mars and its gold-accented dome make it one of the most prominent landmarks in Paris, along with its housing of Napoleon's tomb. In Guibert's period, the Invalides maintained control over several units of older soldiers who worked on garrison duty around the kingdom. Command of the Invalides was both a mark of distinction and a sinecure, one Guibert's father held, as noted.]

40 [Guibert uses the term "*citadin*," which I have translated "urban" but may also be translated as "townie" or even "proletarian." It carries a negative connotation, as the passage indicates.]

41 [The term "army corps (*corps d'armée*)" does not reflect the later, formal Napoleonic organization; it simply denotes the literal meaning, of a body of troops that are part of an army. See Abel, *Guibert's General Essay on Tactics*, 36.]

42 [Guibert anticipates the role played by Lazare Carnot, the "Organizer of Victory," in creating the bureaucracy that ran the French army during the French Revolution, elements of which remain to the present. See Howard Brown, *War, Revolution, and the Bureaucratic State: Politics and Army Administration in France 1791–1799* (New York: Oxford University Press, 2004).]

into [a] campaign, peacetime does not admit almost any more reforms, and it becomes a prolongation itself of the state of war. It has increased them [expenses] much more in war by the immense baggage that great armies require; by its prodigious accumulation of artillery; by the cost of purchasing, maintaining, [and] replacing that which follows them; [and] finally by the genre of war that it has established. Campaigns have become longer, [and] the usage of winter quarters is almost hardly known anymore; because of this, consumption has doubled, replacements are continual, [and] every [army] may now only repair itself in haste and at enormous cost. In the end, this is the result of the system of modern war: money has become more than ever the nerve and the means [of it]; small sovereigns may only have standing troops in order to sell them, because they do not have enough riches to put them into action; great sovereigns consume the greater part of their revenues in suffering to maintain their troops on peacetime footing; and, in war, they are all reduced to loans and, at the end of some campaigns, whether vanquisher or vanquished, to being almost equally ruined and forced to desire peace.[43]

The result of this must be advantageous to rich powers; above all, it should have to be [advantageous] to France, which has immense riches joined to an immense population. Its revenues alone are stronger than those of the House of Austria, the King of Prussia, and Russia. But, by a fatality that Providence doubtlessly wishes to make the counterweight of its superiority, it is at pains to maintain a military as numerous as that of Russia at four times the expense, and one much less formidable than that of Prussia and the House of Austria at double the expense. Thus France is at pains today to maintain one-hundred forty thousand troops with one-hundred six millions that it applies directly or indirectly, in truth, and that passes through all sorts of networks, whether great or small, for the expenses of its land military, while Russia maintains one-hundred fifty thousand with twenty-seven or twenty-eight millions, Prussia around one-hundred eighty thousand with fifty-six millions, and Austria around as many for sixty-two or sixty-three [millions]. At least this was the state of things before the commencement of the war lit between these two powers.[44]

Placing these constitutions in opposition to ours would be an interesting tableau; we would discover there the sources of a difference so prodigiously to our disadvantage, but, other than that this is not my objective, it would move me away from the general truths that never bring inconvenience to engage me in a census and a discussion of particular abuses. I must remind myself that it is only in a war that there are coups to accomplish, because behind abuse are entrenched all the people who enjoy it or who live by it.

The expenses of these nations to maintain their armies in war more or less follow the same proportions as in peacetime. Thus Russia is the power that places its armies in action and that maintains them at the least expense. This economy draws from the health of the constitution of the Russian troops, from their sobriety, [and] from their methods of subsistence, which are infinitely less expensive than those of all the other nations of Europe. Russian regiments are like Roman legions: they carry all the workshops necessary for their needs. They are distributed flour, and often even unrefined grain; they have hand mills in each company; they make their bread themselves; often, they do without it, and biscuits or flour soaked and cooked in water suffices for their nourishment. Finally, money being quite rare in Russia, all the commodities, all the premier materials are found at a good price, and consequently, everything is much cheaper for the government.[45]

The King of Prussia is the next sovereign who makes war with fewer expenses. This economy is not at all drawn from the same causes as that of Russia, as the constitution of his troops is not as good in this regard, and it hardly differs from that of other German troops. Commodities and materials of premier need are not priced any better there than in the rest of Germany, but, as he is the sole sovereign in Europe who has a treasury, he pays for everything in cash. He does not at all know the usurious advances of the entrepreneurs, and, when he treats with them, it is again via cash in hand. His economy rests above all on the skill with which he makes it draw from the means and the resources of the country[side], whether friend or enemy; no general has commented and practiced the maxim of

---

43 [Guibert describes what is now referred to as the fiscal-military state in early-modern Europe. The European Fiscal-Military System 1530–1870, https://fiscalmilitary.history.ox.ac.uk/, provides an excellent introduction to the topic.]

44 [Guibert presumably uses the *livre* as his currency of reference in this paragraph. Calculating the value of historical currencies is extremely difficult, if even possible, so no effort will be made to do so.]

45 [As he does with Rome, Guibert euphemizes a military establishment of which he has little personal experience. Service in the Russian army could be brutal, and the Russians were no better at fielding and maintaining armies than any contemporary state. See Christopher Duffy, *Russia's Military Way to the West: Origins and Nature of Russian Military Power, 1700–1800* (New York: Routledge, 1985); and Miakinkov, *War and Enlightenment in Russia.*]

Marcus Porcius Cato as well as he has: "it must be that war nourishes war."⁴⁶

The House of Austria holds the third rank for economy in war expenses to the present. Perhaps the Emperor, commanding its armies himself and flattening many of the obstacles that always give flight to simple generals by his presence [like being] forced to account with a Council of War and a court, the military administration of the Austrians in times of war will perfect itself now as it has already perfected itself relative to peacetime expenses. But to the present, the science of drawing advantage from the country[side] is always not as well known to them as it is to the Prussian armies. They always have a great obstacle to any species of economic amelioration that, as we have observed, the King of Prussia does not have. Far from having funds in reserve and always leaving the check open, the court of Vienna still has debts from the last war to discharge: it was trying to begin its campaign, and it had already negotiated loans. As a result, there is only a step to enterprises and to all the abuses that follow them.⁴⁷

As for France, in supposing in the next war that we would change neither methods nor measures, the augmentation of expenses that the war would throw us into is almost impossible to calculate; ordinarily, they [expenses] double, [and], in the case of misfortune, they no longer have boundaries. The campaign of 1757 cost us two-hundred million [livres], and that of 1759 hardly less. This enormous difference between our expenses and those of the foreign powers doubtlessly emerges in part from all the commodities', all the furnishings', [and] all the premier materials' for the troops' usage, whatever species they are, costing more in France than elsewhere. But it also emerges from the most-decisive points; from the scarcity of money that the administration immediately finds itself in, and from this, our binding ourselves hand and foot in the hands of entrepreneurs at need; from our lack of skill in drawing on the means of the country[side] where we make war, [a] lack of skill such that the most abundant countries cannot suffice to nourish our armies; from our habit of not knowing how to do anything without enormous baggage and [paying a great deal of] money; [and] finally, from so many abuses, whether of routine, of ignorance, or of embezzlement, that I neither can nor dare to arrest myself on them. To indicate them *en masse* is to fall into declamation; detailing them and supporting them with proofs is a dangerous role, and what must arrest more than the danger is that, in charging oneself with this role, one is only devoting oneself without success. One must only attack abuses when one is armed with power, and, if one does not at all have the club at the same time, one must not advise oneself to make use of the torch.⁴⁸

Furthermore, what arrives in France is the fate of England for all its war expenses, and perhaps, in this regard, the vices of its administration and its abuses of every genre are even more wasteful, as if there are rich nations like opulent individuals who are condemned to no longer buying anything at the current weight and price and who even find the sources of their ruin in their riches, as if fate would wish to establish a sort of equilibrium between rich nations and poor nations by increasing the means of the latter by economy and enfeebling those of the former by waste!

But I touch here on one of the most important points of this chapter, on a proposition whose announcement will appear to be a paradox, so much does it shock current beliefs. I pretend that numerous armies and the necessary expenses that they require are not a burden without compensation for peoples and that the system of modern war, envisaged in this regard and compared to the old system, is quite advantageous to nations and to humanity.

Once, when only small armies existed, when war was made without much baggage and at little cost, when armies did not constantly stand on a war footing, and when armies only formed themselves passingly in times of war, and sometimes even only for the moment of expeditions, wars were much less frequent, and Europe was perpetually their theater. Each small sovereign, each seigneur, even with little power, had the right and the means to make war; it sufficed for them to convoke their vassals. For a stronger reason, war was even more facile for great sovereigns. At the slightest grievance, they ran to arms.

When the military art commenced to be reborn, when a-little-better-regulated troops took the place of this species of feudal militia, as these troops were still of a small number, as they levied and armed themselves at little cost, this did not at all yet reduce the furor and the frequency of wars. Plenty of small armies lived in Europe. Simple generals, having no right other than their swords, attached themselves to adventurers and made war on their account or sold themselves to sovereigns. Thus did Bertrand du

---

46 [See Abel, *Guibert's General Essay on Tactics*, 47. The Cato sentence is frequently quoted in works on logistics, both contemporary and modern.]

47 [See Christopher Duffy, *The Austrian Army in the Seven Years War*, 2 Vols. (Chicago: Emperor's Press, 2000–2008).]

48 [See Kennett, *The French Army in the Seven Years War*, 88–129.]

Guesclin;[49] Charles, duc de Bourbon;[50] Bernhard von Saschen-Weimar, etc.[51] From this [came] the stipendiaries with all sorts of names [like] *reiters, landsknechten,* [and] archers that Germany and Italy furnished for our armies.[52] The petit princes, who today pacifically sell their troops to [fund] the luxury of their small courts, the petit princes reduced today to placing themselves under the protection of great powers to not be despoiled by them, were all turbulent and ambitious then. They made war at the heads of their troops and for themselves. Even bishops involved themselves in it. I do not need to cite anyone beyond the famous Christoph Bernhard Freiherr von Galen, Prince-Bishop of Münster.[53] I must not neglect to recall that, independently of all these troops, there were great monarchies like France, for example, where the Princes of the Blood and the great seigneurs much maintained knights and men at arms. Our princes had guards, troops, [and] places of war, and many employed militaries at will.[54]

Thus, in counting all who were in arms then, there were perhaps many more men in Europe sworn to this profession than today, but neither great work nor great effects resulted, because they lacked the money and the methods to unite them, because the system of war did not exist in those times, and finally, because they did not have, as today, great masses of powers that annihilated all the others and, more despotic in their interiors at the same time, united all the scattered forces that composed the feudal old regime in their hands. What today forms the armies of five or six sovereigns in Europe had once been paid by five- or six-hundred masters. Serving for the sake of serving: it seems to me that those who are destined for it have gained from the change, because great tyrants, if these sovereigns were tempted to become them, have better composition than petty [sovereigns], and servitude ennobles a little [according to] the grandeur of the master.

Thus in these centuries, certainly more unfortunate than our own, wars were much more frequent and longer, and they were made on many more points at once. This will be easy for me to prove. Today, war being only made with regular troops, with numerous armies [that are] disciplined over time and constantly maintained on a standing footing, five or six great powers alone in Europe have the right and the means to make it [war]; I say "the right" because the secondary powers no longer make them; they are reduced to attaching themselves to powers of the first

---

49 [Bertrand du Guesclin was Constable of France and one of the most important commanders of the Hundred Years War. He descended from an old Breton family and was a renowned jouster and fighter, involving himself in the Breton succession before joining the French army. He rose through the French ranks to become Constable of France, the highest military rank, and helped rescue the French position after the disastrous defeats of Crécy and Poitiers by refusing to engage English armies directly and instead conducting a Fabian strategy. While he did serve a country that was not his own in France, Guibert's naming him a soldier of fortune is somewhat incorrect, as he did not fight primarily for his own advancement and was buried in the French royal crypt at Saint-Denis.]

50 [Charles, duc de Bourbon, was a scion of the Montpensier branch of the Bourbon family in the late fifteenth century, making him a Prince of the Blood. He inherited extensive lands across France from various family members, including Auvergne, Forez, and La Marche, along with the Bourbonnais, making him one of the most powerful men in the kingdom. Like many men his age, he went to war in the Italian Wars, including fighting at Agnadello and Marignano. François I made him Constable of France along with other court dignities, but the two men eventually became rivals. Bourbon left French service and allied with Charles V, hoping to carve out a kingdom for himself in southern France. He commanded the Imperial army that conquered Rome in 1527, and his soldiers murdered him before sacking the city, one of the landmark events of the period. Guibert wrote a play about Bourbon entitled the *Connétable de Bourbon* that was staged by Queen Marie Antoinette in 1775; see Abel, *Jacques-Antoine-Hippolyte, comte de Guibert,* 94–96.]

51 [Bernhard von Sachsen-Weimar was born around 1600 and became one of the most skilled commanders of the Protestant forces in the Thirty Years War. Within the chaotic construct of that conflict, he served a variety of states, including Denmark, Sweden, and eventually, France, all while seeking his own aggrandizement. He secured France's foothold in the war after the death of Gustav Adolf before himself dying in 1639. As with Guesclin, naming Sachsen-Weimar a soldier of fortune is somewhat inapt, as his military service was always first to the Protestant cause in the war.]

52 [Guibert refers to various types of troops, many of which were hired as mercenaries by the French to fight in early-modern wars. While the terms are no longer accepted to denote a specific kind of soldier, *reiters* were generally German cavalry units, *landsknechten* were elite German infantry units, and archers were light forces. See David Parrott, *Richelieu's Army: War, Government, and Society in France, 1624–1642* (New York: Cambridge University Press, 2008). Confusingly, "archer" also denoted a semi-ceremonial state officer in France charged with protecting officials and executing laws akin to a bailiff in England; see Mousnier, *The Institutions of France under the Old Regime.*]

53 [Christoph Bernhard Freiherr von Galen was Prince-Bishop of Münster for much of the seventeenth century. He fought in the Thirty Years War before studying for the Church. He engaged in several wars throughout his reign, including against his own capital city, and fought on both sides of Louis XIV's wars against the Habsburgs.]

54 [Guibert speaks of the period before around 1650, which was much as he describes. Major landowners and Princes of the Blood maintained or could raise military forces, often with foreign aid, and deploy them in their own interests, usually against each other or against the crown. The last significant instance of this was the Fronde of the Princes around 1650; by the end of that century, most internal fortresses had been demolished and lords' armies disestablished. No significant armed revolt against the crown by the nobility took place between 1653 and 1789.]

order and adjudicating their differences by them. It is already much [progress] that five or six people alone have the disposition of this scourge, and there are already many probabilities more in favor of peace, because the fewer the heads there are, the fewer rivalries, interests, and passions there are.

This is not all. When war is easy to make, when it requires only primitive advances, when it requires only to undertake assembling some men, arming them, and running to the enemy, then one is exercised for insignificant reasons; one obeys at a first movement, one declares war, and one goes like a particularist with sword in hand to repay an offense. This was how nations and sovereigns used to use it [war].

Today, war has become so difficult to undertake, it requires so much expense [and] so many advances, [that it is] such a ruinous wager; it offers, as we have developed above in considering the modern system relative to the art itself, perspectives of success [that are] so uncertain, odds [that are] so long, and a ruin [that is] almost equal for the vanquisher and the vanquished at the peace, that sovereigns balance for a long time before they determine on it. They dissimulate on small grievances [and] palliate the others; they negotiate, and, when the negotiations are made, the animosity chills, other interests surface, and the peace is prolonged. In the end, as a general system of politics today ties all the great nations to each other, whether by ties of union or ties of enmity, those who make peace always fearing, when a rupture arises between one of them, to be dragged into the quarrel, they hasten themselves to offer their mediation. This is the spectacle that Europe has offered us for seventeen years [since the Treaty of Paris 1763]. Three or four times, the appearances of war extinguished themselves in smoke. They had just sparked themselves between Prussia and Austria [when] the Allies reciprocally interposed their good offices, and these two formidable powers, after measuring themselves and sensing the equilibrium between their forces, were enjoined to reconcile.[55]

For the same reason that wars were once more frequent, they were longer, and they are shorter today for the same reason that they are rarer today. These results, [despite] appearing so opposed to each other, are the result of the difference in means that were then employed and those that are employed today. Then, one acted with few forces at the same time and consequently with little effort; as a result, one had to repeat these efforts often and prolong them for a long time. Today, one acts with immense forces and consequently with immense efforts. They [armies] must thus soon exhaust themselves and [then] have the need to repose for a long time. The Seven Years War, which was and which will truly be the most memorable of our century, put five-hundred thousand combatants under arms, and it lasted six years. The Thirty Years War, the most celebrated war of the previous century, placed no more than one-hundred thousand combatants in all the respective armies, but it lasted for thirty years.[56] I will not at all hazard to pronounce which of the two cost more human blood and tears, but several reasons appear to incontestably prove to me that the system of modern war is less murderous and less devastating than the old [one].

First, it is doubtless that the usage of firearms has rendered fights infinitely less sanguinary. The causes of this difference are too obvious, and history furnishes too many proofs of it, for me to have need of arresting myself on it. It is also doubtless that, seeing the art with which battles are engaged today, they may no longer be general and consequently also [neither] murderous [nor] decisive. I have explained, in the chapter on orders of battle, how modern science has substituted the oblique order for the parallel order.[57] It is the skill of the generals and the health of the dispositions that decide the fate of battles today more than the quantity of bloodshed. In the end, it is a game of calculation and combination that has succeeded a game of hazard and ruin.

But it is not in this sole regard that the system of modern war is more favorable to humanity. Today, wars have become less cruel. Blood is not shed outside of combat, prisoners are respected, towns are no longer destroyed, [and] the countryside is no longer ravaged. Philosophy, enlightenment, [and] the universal softening of morals have doubtlessly contributed to this revolution, but it is also the result of the system of modern war.

When war was made with the foundation of nations, when it was the nobility and their vassals passingly assembled that sustained it, the aftermath of a victory, the invasion of a country, [and] the fall of a town had to necessarily bring ravage and devastation. Any country defended by its inhabitants almost inevitably had to experience this genre of calamity. They hoped to intimidate them and make

---

55 [The War of the Bavarian Succession.]

56 [Guibert repeats an error from Abel, *Guibert's General Essay on Tactics*, 141–143, in arguing that the militaries of the Thirty Years War were smaller than those of his own period. In fact, they were roughly similar, with factions fielding total military strengths well above 150,000 at times, especially around 1630. It was not until late in the war, and especially the wars of the later century, that they declined to the kinds of establishments Guibert references. See David Parrott, *The Business of War: Military Enterprise and Military Revolution in Early Modern Europe* (New York: Cambridge University Press, 2012), 139–195.]

57 [See 116–150.]

them lay down their arms by this. The vanquisher thus regarded pillage as retaliation for the defense. By ravaging, by destroying, they believed to enfeeble their enemies, and they did enfeeble them in effect. In the end, it was difficult to not involuntarily go to treat with rigor the inhabitant who once bore arms. This rigor is almost natural right, because, in defending and in shedding blood of the vanquisher, the inhabitant with all that belongs to them appears to have become the objective and the prize of the conquest. Thus, in the famous Thirty Years War, Magdeburg, defended by its inhabitants, was nothing more than a heap of cadavers and ruins.[58] Germany was a theater of desolation in almost all its extent and in every way. We have recently seen in America that war becomes more disastrous and more cruel when the inhabitants take part in it. The English, who demonstrate themselves to be so humane and so generous in all their other wars, have committed horrors there.[59] Philosophy may reproach them for this, but all the reasons that I have just given may also justify them.

The system of modern war having made two absolutely separated classes of armies and nations in Europe, the inhabitants of the countries where war is made are only spectators. As such, a sort of tacitly unanimous convention serves to safeguard them and render them sacred even to vanquishers. We have seen towns carried sword in hand not being subjected to pillage in our days; this is [because] the inhabitants would have had no part in the defense, and it would have been barbarism for [the attacking army] to avenge itself on them for a resistance that they had not made. An army seizes a country: this country would be at pains to perceive that it had changed masters. The conquering army is no more dependent on it than that which defended it [was]. Often, what it pays in contributions is less onerous than what it paid in taxes to its sovereign, because military contributions are paid by more direct and simpler means than taxes [that have] the surcharge of financial collection, and all the abuses that it brings, joined to their weight. In the end, even if numerous armies and their immense baggage do exhaust the country where they sojourn, they are also obligated to observe more order and discipline to manage its resources; they spend more money in it than they draw from it and make by this the effect of torrents that fertilize by ravaging and that leave new germs of fecundity after them. Flanders has often made proof of this, and Hesse, which I saw ten years after the Seven Years War, offered the same tableau to me.[60]

It remains to me to consider here the system of modern war relative to the art in itself.[61] If one first envisages this art alongside the immensity and the difficulty [of war], it is superior to what it was in all the centuries of antiquity. The Ancients knew neither the science of artillery nor that of mines, sciences founded on abstract and profound speculations. What was the theory of their arms and their ballistics compared to that of Bernard Forest de Bélidor [or] Benjamin Robbins?[62] What was the *fouillage* of the Bessi and the Dacians compared to our art of mines,[63] comparted to the art so luminously perfected by Jean-Melchior Goullet de Rugy?[64] Will we place the science of fortifica-

---

58 [Guibert refers to the infamous 1630 Siege of Magdeburg in which a Catholic army stormed the city, then sacked and burned it, probably killing over 20,000, most civilians. The event was the culmination of a series of sacks and massacres of garrisons by both sides. According to Wilson, *The Thirty Years War*, 468–470, "the disaster became a defining event in the war and did much to shape its subsequent interpretation as a benchmark for brutality."]

59 [See Holger Hoock, "Mangled Bodies: Atrocity in the American Revolutionary War," *Past & Present* 230 (2016): 123–159.]

60 [See Guibert, *Journal d'un voyage en allemagne*, 1:112–124. As Julia Osman, "Guibert vs. Guibert: Competing Notions in the *Essai général de tactique* and *Défense du système de guerre moderne*," *Journal of Military History* 83 (2019): 43–65, notes, this and the prior paragraph are replete with exaggerations that Guibert makes to prove his point. It is highly unlikely that the inhabitants of any country would prefer occupation of their homes and lands by soldiers to paying taxes, no matter how onerous, and the era of sacking cities was not past, as the aforementioned sack of Bergen-op-Zoom by French soldiers in 1747 illustrates.]

61 [Guibert repeats much of this and subsequent paragraphs, including verbatim passages, from Abel, *Guibert's General Essay on Tactics*, 27.]

62 [Bernard Forest de Bélidor was a mathematician and physicist in the French army in the mid-eighteenth century. His major discovery related to the physics of gunpowder, particularly how to make its use more efficient, which made him an enemy of Vallière and those who supported his system. Bélidor wrote several technical treatises on artillery, fortification, and hydraulic architecture and was elected a elected member of the Académie des sciences in 1756 before his death in 1761.

Benjamin Robins was an English mathematician and physicist in the mid-eighteenth century. He engaged in scholarly debates with Johann Bernoulli before setting aside his Quaker upbringing and turning to military engineering and ballistics. Along with Bélidor, he worked to define the physics and mathematics of artillery ballistics, drawing on the works of Galileo Galilei and Nicolo Tartaglia, the latter of whom relied on the works of Archimedes. See also Abel, *Guibert's General Essay on Tactics*, 151–152.]

63 ["Fouillage" is a non-standard French word derived from "fouiller," which means "to dig" or "to mine." The Bessi and Dacians were inhabitants of the regions around the Black Sea during the Classical period; see Cosmin Onofrei, "Thracians in Roman Dacia. Military and Civilian Elements," https://arheologie-istoriaartei-cluj.ro/Articole/eph-XVIII-05.pdf.]

64 This skillful officer, who directed our Ecole de Mineurs established at Verdun, made a revolution in this science. It was once

tion of the ancients, that of their attack and defense of places, alongside that of Vauban?[65] The latter is founded on the reflected convergence of almost all the branches of mathematics; that of the ancients, if one excepts the fables of Archimedes, was only an uninformed art.[66] The Ancients did not have prodigious trains of artillery equipment [and] food, [which are] so difficult to move and to nourish. They did not have armies as numerous.[67] They knew little of the chicaneries of the *petite guerre*; they almost did not embarrass themselves with the choice of positions.[68] One does not see any topographical details in the narrative of the ancient historians. Armies had quite-small fronts, the species of weapons occasioned neither smoke nor tumult, [and] battles were necessarily easier to give and to command.[69] I compare the wars of the Greeks, and the majority of ancient wars, to those of our colonies on the other continent. I have seen five-thousand or six-thousand men fight each other there, the battlefields so close that the eye of the general may embrace all, direct all, [and] repair all. A good major of today could conduct the maneuvers of Leuctra and Mantinea like Epaminondas.

Would it then follow from this that the art is at the point of perfection? Doubtlessly no. There are, if we may be permitted to hazard this expression, some parts where its progress has even retreated and where, in extending itself, it complicates itself at the expense of its perfection. Thus the artillery and the light troops are too multiplied, [and] the frontiers of states are maladroitly bristling with places. This was necessary to serve as depots [and] rallying points [and] to guard the principal debouches. In lieu of this, second and third lines were constructed; there are [also] many too-small [ones] that have no objective. Places are then uselessly surcharged with too many fortification pieces; the majority of engineers' plans are too regular, too methodical, [and] too little-combined with tactics. The science of positions is harmful, in some armies [like] in those that are not at all maneuvering, [and] the science of movements and topographic details have acquired too much importance as a result. Armies, becoming immense, whether by the augmentation of combatants or by the baggage and embarrassments that they trail in their wake, are difficult to move. The details of their subsistence form a science of which armies in the good times of antiquity, [which were] less numerous, more sober, and better constituted, did not at all have an idea. Finally, the different arms, the different branches of the art each having become a great part, they elevate pretentions, whether exclusive or preponderant, that produce false consequences and harm the general perfection of the art at each step; as a result, each arm believes itself the premier and the most important; the infantry believes itself to be everything in armies, the cavalry says in its turn that it alone decides battles, the artillery imagines that in it resides all the great means of strength and of destruction, the engineers see all the sublimity of war in their angles and in their works, [and] the *état-major* of the army sees [the same] in its reconnaissance of terrain or in local combinations; as a result, the light troops become so numerous today and believe themselves the sole active and warlike corps, pretentions [that are] all false, or at least exaggerated, [but] all proofs of the ignorance and the rarity of great views, pretentions that

---

more favorable to be the attacker than to be the attacked. It is held today to be more advantageous to be besieged than to be the besieger. He created a system of subterranean fortification by means of which the fall of places prepared according to this system must be infinitely more lengthy and more difficult. The principles of this new science are still a mystery in Europe.

[Jean-Melchior Goullet de Rugy was an engineer and, as Guibert says, director of the School of Miners at Verdun. He invented an air exchanger for mines that eased the difficulties of working in them. Like Bélidor, he was a supporter of the Gribeauval System, working on artillery ordinances with the artillerist during the 1760s and running the Verdun school until the advent of the Revolution. He was recognized as an outstanding officer in his technical field and honored as such until his death in 1813. See Emile-August Bégin, "Jean-Melchior Goullet de Rugy," *Biographie de la Moselle*, 4 Vols. (Metz: 1832), IV:170–179.]

65 [Sébastien le Prestre, seigneur de Vauban, was one of the most important military figures in late seventeenth- and early eighteenth-century France. He was one of the premier military engineers of his day, designing fortresses that guarded the kingdom and systems for attacking fortresses that rendered most sieges perfunctory. He was also intensely interested in political economy, and he helped design the system of taxation that funded the wars of Louis XIV and Louis XV. He is one of two commanders, the other being Turenne, buried overlooking Napoleon's tomb.]

66 [Archimedes was a Syracusan polymath who laid the foundations for much of the fields of mathematics, physics, and engineering. He famously worked to prevent the Roman seizure of his home city during the Second Punic War, including deploying a crane that would disrupt Roman ships. In the many centuries since, fantastical inventions like a solar death ray have been ascribed to Archimedes, as Guibert intimates.]

67 [Guibert repeats a mistake from Abel, *General Essay on Tactics*, 151–152. While Roman armies were probably relatively small during the early years of the Republic, they were regularly of size similar to eighteenth-century armies by the late Republican and Imperial periods.]

68 [While the sources Guibert consulted likely did make the argument he presents here, subsequent research has shown the importance of the *petite guerre* and light forces to Greek and Roman armies; see Frank Russell, "Finding the Enemy: Military Intelligence," *The Oxford Handbook of Warfare in the Classical World*, 474–492, for example.]

69 [Guibert makes one correct observation: ancient battles did not have to contend with the smoke and fog generated by muskets and artillery.]

recall the apology that each member claims preeminence and believes itself the principle and the seat of life.

These are the abuses and errors that complicate the modern science and that await men of genius to classify all, reduce all, [and] contain all in just proportions, for, in a word, enlightened people of each branch of the military art to make beam of rays that constitutes the science and to consolidate it.[70] But in the meantime, it is a mélange of enlightenment and abuses, of knowledge and errors that, in overwhelming men of a mediocre spirit and in requiring more talent, renders and must render great generals so rare today. The man whose spirit must embrace all the parts of the military arts of the Ancients [and] who would well-command twenty-thousand Greeks or Romans, the man who would thus be a Xanthippus [or] a Camillus, would not suffice today for half the knowledge that comprises the modern science; he [would be] absorbed by the details, blinded by the immensity, [and] stunned by the multitude.[71] A hundred-thousand men whose movements he would have to regulate, the care of providing for their subsistence, all the obstacles produced by our poor constitutions, a hundred-thousand enemies that are opposed to him, a campaign plan of many branches,[72] the combinations without number that result from the multiplicity of objects, [and] so many thoughts, cares, and attentions to reunite them, form a burden beyond his strength. It [the army of a hundred-thousand men] remains fatigued and stunned under him; it is only good on some days and in some parts; finally, he is only a general of the second or the third order.

But there is a point on which the art of war has undergone a great revolution and by which it must become dear to healthy philosophy and to humanity. Formerly, the art of war was almost entirely directed towards the offensive. It had for its principal goal to attack and to invade. I have demonstrated in the course of this work that the Ancients' arms were more favorable to the attack than to the defense, that their unique and exclusive order was offensive as a result, [and] finally, that they knew how fight only by attacking. I have demonstrated that, as a consequence, the science of positions and all that is today called "defensive war" were almost unknown to them, that giving combat was always their objective, and that these combats, by the nature of their arms and by the species of their tactics, were more murderous and more decisive than ours. Thus three battles reversed the Empire of Darius, [an] empire almost as large as Europe.[73] The Battle of Cannæ would have destroyed the Roman Republic if Hannibal had not committed the fault of arresting himself at Capua, and that of Zama decided the fate of Carthage.[74]

Until the invention of firearms, as long as they had not been perfected, as long as tactics rested in its infancy, that is to say until the middle of the sixteenth century, war was made more or less on the same principles, [and] the science of positions and the defensive were quite little-known. Battles continued to be the great and the almost-unique operation and led to invasions and conquests.[75]

In this epoch, which was that of Parma, of Maurits of Nassau, [and] of Gustav Adolf, the art changed face: we began to place importance and price on positions, on entrenchments, [and] on places of war. It is to the wars in Flanders that we must give this revolution, because the Dutch, always struggling against the Spanish with an unequal number, were obliged to reinforce themselves by art and by discipline. It is to them that must be given the system of modern fortification, the usage of entrenchments adapted to campaign warfare, and the first elements of the genre of war by means of which, with inferior forces [and] aided by the obstacles of the country[side] and the resources of the art, one defends, one retards, one hinders invasions against superior armies.[76]

---

70 [As he does in Abel, *Guibert's General Essay on Tactics*, 29, Guibert uses a term, "beam of rays," from the physics of light that suggests the union of similar ideas into an epitome.]

71 [Marcus Furius Camillus was a semi-legendary figure that Plutarch, *Camillus*, credits with saving Rome following the Gallic sack of the fourth century BCE and establishing many of the institutions of the Roman Republic. See Scullard, *History of the Roman World*, 92–114.]

72 ["A campaign plan of many branches" appears to be an unambiguous reference to Pierre-Joseph Bourcet, *Principes de la guerre de montagne* (Paris: 1888), a work often credited with being one of the founding documents of operational-level warfare. The unpublished book circulated in the late eighteenth century, although clear evidence of its contemporary use and influence has been scanty. See Quimby, *The Background of Napoleonic Warfare*, 175–185.]

73 [Guibert speaks of the Battles of Granicus River, Issus, and Gaugamela that virtually destroyed the Achaemenid Persian armies.]

74 [Guibert is somewhat reductionist in the argument here. Hannibal had intended Cannæ to bring Rome to the negotiating table, but the city fought on, and he could not mount a proper siege of it. His turn to Capua was an effort to either draw the Romans out for another battle or force them to surrender by dismantling the Italian ally system that supported Rome.]

75 [Guibert continues to be reductionist, although he is not to be faulted for falling into the "Dark Ages" trope, as proper scholarship on the medieval period in general, and medieval military history specifically, hardly existed at the time.]

76 [Maurits of Nassau was the commander of Dutch forces in the early stages of the Dutch Revolt against the Spanish Empire in the late sixteenth and early seventeenth centuries. He avoided battle with the superior Spanish forces and instead focused on sieges, diplomatic efforts, and building a small, disciplined army and navy.

The century of Louis XIV and ours have received and perfected these documents. The defense has become one of the wisest and the most difficult parts of war. It is by it that Turenne and Créqui, and to a lesser degree Catinat and Berwick, immortalized themselves. It is the defense, founded on rivers, on places, on positions, that, in the misfortunes of the Spanish Succession War, preserved France from being invaded.[77]

In the end, today the system of modern war is more than ever turned to the defense. This may be an abuse, this may be a vice of the art, as the [cases] for and against may be equally supported by it, but it is a result [that is] certainly advantageous to the tranquility of nations and the surety of empires.

The predominance of the defense in the system of modern war draws from the species of our current arms, which are more favorable to the defense than to the attack; from the superiority that positions give to the troops that defend them over those that attack them; from the habitual custom that armies have today of posting themselves; from the favorable support that places of war lend them; from the immense train of equipment and artillery that our armies trail in their wakes; from the embarrassments that result from them for great movements and for subsistence; [and] finally, from the difficulty of acting offensively with all these embarrassments and despite all these obstacles, as, contrary to opinion consecrated by prejudice, (if one excepts the defense of the great genre like that Turenne made in his 1675 campaign, [a] defense that was both active and offensive) the part of war that we believe to be the most difficult to make today, seeing all these embarrassments and obstacles on one hand and the progress of the defense on the other, is certainly the offense. What confirms us in this opinion is that all mediocre generals more or less understand the defense [while] only those of the first order understand how to handle the offense. But this discussion would demand a great development, and it is foreign to my subject.

It follows from the major change that was made in the art of modern war that this art has essentially and primitively become protecter and preserver; it follows that, the defense's being more and more perfected and the offense's being more difficult, wars are necessarily less decisive; that they arrest themselves at the frontiers of states; and that they rarely penetrate into the interior; it consequently follows that the scourge traverses less space, that it concentrates on points, and that it makes fewer ravages. An army, formidable, skillfully commanded and making war with all the enlightenment of the modern system, is like the useful barriers that one establishes on the frontiers to keep contagion out.[78]

Now, the more the respective armies of great nations, the more instruction and discipline in these armies, the more the talents of their generals equally balance each other, [and] the more they mutually impose themselves on each other and the less they consequently undertake wars, as forces in equilibrium necessitate repose, when they do undertake them [wars], the less they will be decisive and consequently destructive to nations, [and], in the end, the less the possibility of conquests, subjects of temptation for ambitious princes, and revolutions of empires there are.

What are the results that I pretend to draw from this long discussion? They are reduced to these:

War is doubtlessly a scourge, but it is an inevitable scourge.

To render it rarer, to make itself more distant from it, France must be powerfully armed to remove the desire to attack from its neighbors, or at least to make it harmful to their interests.

In this paragraph, Guibert neatly summarizes what would later become known as "The Military Revolution," particularly in Michael Roberts, "The Military Revolution, 1560–1660 (Belfast, 1956). The Military Revolution argument is that a succession of Roman-inspired reformers, chiefly Maurits and Gustav Adolf, introduced discipline and professionalism to state armies, which then expanded to produce the militaries and fiscal-military states of early-modern Europe. As Guibert illustrates, Roberts based his thesis on scholarship from the eighteenth century. The Military Revolution was largely accepted in the mid-twentieth century, although it received significant amendment via works like Geoffrey Parker, *The Military Revolution: Military Innovation and the Rise of the West, 1500–1800* (New York: Cambridge University Press, 2016). Subsequent research, beginning with *The Military Revolution Debate: Readings on the Military Transformation of Early Modern Europe*, ed. Clifford Rogers (New York: Routledge, 1995), has decisively debunked the theory. In particular, critics have pointed out its reductionist nature, the undue weight given in it to Protestant states and commanders in northern Europe like Maurits and Gustav Adolf while ignoring military institutions like the Spanish, and the more general issues with its emphasis on Huntingtonian concepts like "the West" and monocausal revolutionary approaches. As such, it is generally out of favor in modern historiography.]

77 [Guibert continues to argue a strategy opposed to the offensive favored by Folard; see Chagniot, *Le chevalier de Folard*.]

78 [By the eighteenth century, governments had discovered that strict quarantines usually stopped the spread of plague. The last great plague outbreak in Western Europe took place in 1720, particularly in the port town of Marseille. The government reacted swiftly, using the military to quarantine the city. While many died within it, the plague did not spread far beyond it. See Cindy Ermus, *The Great Plague Scare of 1720: Disaster and Diplomacy in the Eighteenth-Century Atlantic World* (New York: Cambridge University Press, 2023), especially 13–64.]

The necessity of maintaining an army's being established, this army must correspond to the grandeur of the kingdom, to its population, to its political system, and to all the circumstances that surround it. It must certainly work to maintain this army with the greatest economy possible; it is doubtlessly a great misfortune that this expense is already two or three times greater than the other powers, but, if this is the constitution of the country, [and] we cannot, we dare not, or we do not wish to remedy the abuses that occasion this prodigious difference, we must close our eyes to the expense and make this army at whatever the price be. Because, whatever it may cost, it must be able to defend its possessions and reap what is sown there; it must preserve some prestige and shelter itself from invasion. What is most costly and most onerous is to have a half-army, because with it, one is never at the level of politics, rank, or role that one must play, and any expense that is insufficient is to be truly regretted.

Having an army, we must have one that is at least equal to, and, if it be possible, superior to, those of the other powers in discipline and in instruction. Because what is expensive, both at present and in the future, is a mediocre army, given that its expense in peacetime is not less than that of a good one and that one does not pay down the interest of war's cost via victories.

To have an excellent army, [a nation] must above all have a military spirit, [and], if this spirit is feeble in a nation, it must recover it and preserve it in its army; this must be one of the most-important cares of the government, the sacred fire that it must maintain, as this fire, once extinguished, was the end of Rome and its destinies.[79]

Any nation can wish, hope, [or] breathe only in peace, because all the other professions only flourish by it, but the army must have the thirst for war; this ardor may only be birthed by two means, both in the hand of the government: one is the sentiment of its strength that the government may inspire in it by forming it on a formidable standing, [and] the other is the extreme sobriety of graces in peacetime and the possibility of the abundance of graces in war.[80] These are is the utilitarian politics of the King of Prussia. His army burns with desire for war, first because it senses, it sees, it judges itself to be in a state of making it, and then because, during peacetime, there are neither advancements nor graces in this army. Uniform, pay, [and] busy work: this is all that one may expect during it [peacetime]. Also, at the lightest sound of war, all in this army wake themselves, rejoicing or hoping. Ambition or interest animates all the classes, advancement for some [and] money for others. No one in this army does not experience or promise themselves an amelioration of their fate via war. Even the foreign soldier, the unfortunate who moaned in the captivity of the garrison and under the yoke of discipline during the entire peace, yearns for war, [from which] they hope for more movement and liberty. I saw this tableau some years ago, in a moment when the troubles of Poland seemed to announce the next war. This entire army trembled with impatience and joy; it gave me the idea of a pack of hounds ready to launch themselves [on the hunt]; it seemed to wait for its master to deliver it a nation to devour.[81]

This must be the spirit of an army for that army to be redoubtable, as the métier of arms is not a métier of reason and philosophy; it is a métier against nature and in which movements must ceaselessly be smothered. It is a métier in which morals must not be too soft, because, if they are, they run the risk of enfeebling the military qualities; it is a métier that must be liked to be done well, and, with [two who have] equal faculties [for it], the one who likes it better always does it best; finally, it is a métier in which all the prestige of glory and honor that elevates and ennobles must be carefully preserved, because, if people who make it go to it by reasoning and sensing like philosophes, what they would certainly have to do best would be to abandon it or to make it with softness.

Thus, searching to decry both the art and the profession of war is a philosophy [that is] quite dangerous, quite misunderstanding, [and] quite deprived of enlightenment despite the arrogant pretention that it has spread. For a stronger reason, we would need to decry maritime commerce, because the storms, maladies, [and] accidents inseparable from navigation carry away many men every year; the possession of the Caribbean Islands, because they are the tomb of the vast majority of Europeans who pass them; [and] the exploitation of all mines regardless of their species, because they are never not unhealthy and destructive to the workers who work in them. In effect, we may, strictly speaking, dispense with corresponding with

---

79 [Guibert speaks of the eternal flame in the Temple of Vesta in Rome tended by the Vestal Virgins. It was extinguished in AD 391 by Theodosius I, which represented a symbolic if not literal end of the Roman Empire.]

80 ["Graces" refers to benefits bestowed by the crown on individuals in the form of titles, peerages, pensions, honors, etc. As David Bien, "The Army in the French Enlightenment: Reform, Reaction, and Revolution," *Pas & Present* 85 (1979): 68–98; and David Bien and Nina Godneff, "Les offices, les corps, et le crédit d'état: l'utilisation des privilèges sous l'Ancien Régime," *Annales. Histoire, Sciences Sociales* no. 2 (1974): 23–48, argue, Louis XV used them to bind the nobility to the throne and enable it to serve at the head of his armies.]

81 [See Guibert, *Journal d'un voyage en allemagne*, I:158–246 and II:119–234.]

the nations that nature has placed the immensity of the seas between them and us. We may dispense with sugar, coffee, [and] indigo; we may not have need of cobalt, arsenic, or fossil salt, etc., but it is of premier necessity to guard one's country and to be sure that another people, tempted by both its fecundity and our feebleness, will not come to drive us from it.

Finally, what results from this long discourse is that, for summary and general result, the system of modern war, despite the philosophical anathemas and maledictions, merits the recognition of people and the greatest attention on the part of governments.

I will be content if this discussion sways to my opinion not the mass of the coryphées of the philosophy du jour who neither deepen anything nor ever see beyond the surface of great subjects, having never wisely studied history and marched in the great theater of affairs and of passions, declaiming by echo, speaking on what they cannot know, and believing to aggrandize themselves by calling themselves citizens of the world and ceasing to be one of their countries, but [rather] the men made to be true philosophers, because they have an elevated soul and a vast spirit, the men who I could name if I would not fear wounding their modesty and if I would not best honor them by leaving them to the public to designate rather than designating them myself; they would have discovered and appreciated the importance and the advantages of the system of modern war better than I if it had been their profession to reflect and to mediate on what relates to it; it is to them that I will present the memorable words of a man whose name I have always heard them pronounce with veneration, of a man who, in a century of shadows, had foreseen or divined almost everything, the immortal [Francis] Bacon: "As soon as a naturally belligerent people will neglect arms and fall into softness, war will swoop down on them on all sides. An empire that degenerates thinks only of richness; it is bait for its neighbors, who, taking it in a time of feebleness, soon make it their conquest and their prey."[82]

I will be content if I reconcile to the profession of arms a gender that has become, after the philosophes, the second authority of societies of this country, a gender that used to be protector and friend of this profession. Modern declamations against war have misled its sensibility and have detoured it from its true destination: being the goal and the prize of glory. May the reader of this chapter, if this book falls into their hands, uncover their eyes, make themselves see that humanity has won in the revolution that is made in the art of war [and] that this art, today destined for defense and protection rather than attack and invasion, merits to be honored and encouraged more than ever. Today, it is no longer a question of great lance-blows or personal feats of arms, [as] the art of war has taken a vaster form; it is a question of a luminous and profound science, of a science that must embrace and fill the lives of those who cultivate it; it is not a question of acts of courage and passing movements of ambition and zeal; it is a question of a métier that must be liked and studied without relaxing, that must go to learn in garrisons, on voyages, in the places that were the theater of great wars, far from Paris, in a word, because Paris is the tomb of talents, because character is attenuated there, courage is enervated there, morals are corrupted there, [and] application is relaxed there, and, in the end, one only takes ideas of fortune in lieu of ideas of glory from it. This is what women must inspire in us. The work and the sacrifices are greater than they used to be, but also the greatest pleasures must follow the greatest privations, and the greatest glory [must follow] the greatest efforts.[83]

I will be content if, by this work, I give to *militaires* a greater respect for their art and a greater idea of the knowledge that it requires; if, above all, I throw a sort of emulation mixed with fear into the consciences of people whose birth calls them to command armies and who neglect to render themselves capable of doing so. In the end, I will have accomplished my goal if I excite the government to have an army; it is it that has the premier interest; it is to it to redress our prejudices in this regard or to put itself above them; it is for this that it has authority in its hands, and, when it will employ it thus, all the good spirits, all the true citizens will bless its use.

---

82 [Francis Bacon was one of the premier philosophers of the early modern period. He lived and worked in the late sixteenth and early seventeenth centuries, contributing enormously to the philosophies of empiricism, government, law, and science. The quote is likely from *Analyse de la philosophie du chancelier François Bacon*, 2 Vols. (Leiden: Libraires Associés, 1756), 1:408–409.]

83 [Guibert here presents a remarkable appeal to women as arbiters of polite society, one that is likely unique in military theory of the time. See Dena Goodman, *The Republic of Letters: A Cultural History of the French Enlightenment* (Ithaca: Cornell University Press, 1994).]

Appendix A: Diagram v: Vaussieux and Its Environs

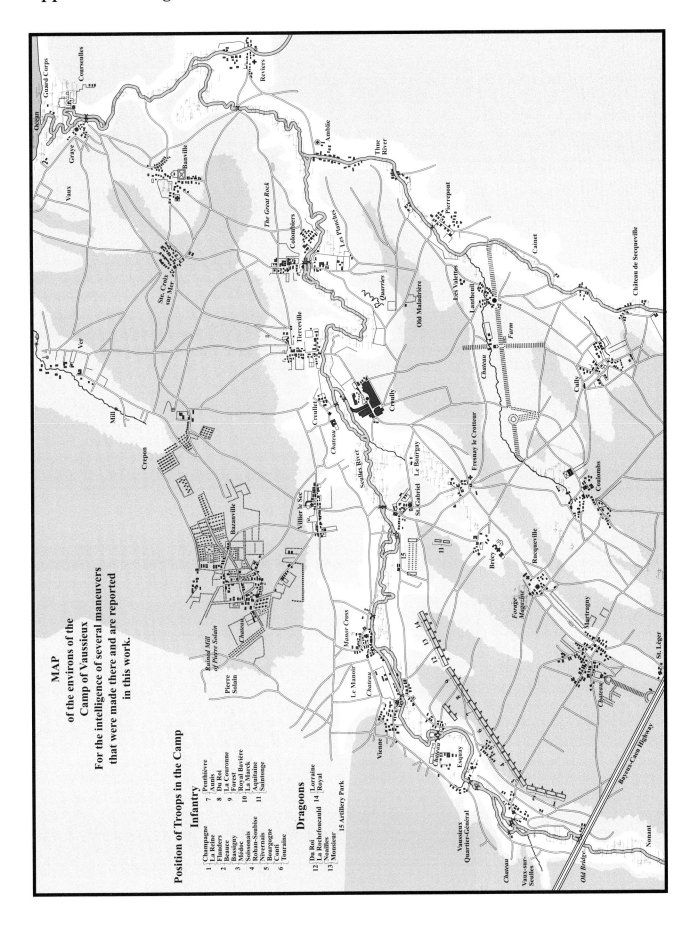

Appendix B: The French Army in the Eighteenth Century

Organization[1]

The eighteenth-century French army had three arms, to use contemporary terminology: infantry, cavalry, and light forces. These may be grouped into two categories: line and light forces, or the forces that arrayed themselves in linear formations and those that dispersed across the battlefield or theater, respectively. Infantry and cavalry proper fell into the former category.

The *Defense of the System of Modern War* largely concerns itself with infantry, although the other arms and branches are represented to some degree in the text, unlike many contemporary works. As such, the organization of the infantry is most important. The cavalry, light forces, and artillery usually operated with systems analogous to that of the infantry, if only for simplicity's sake. Generally, especially when comparing cavalry and light forces to infantry, the most significant changes in organization were the titles of certain officers. The more technical branches, particularly the artillery and *génie*, adapted these mores to suit their services.

Infantry

The infantry was the core of the army and composed the majority of its forces. Infantry was broken into two categories: fusiliers, or *fantassins*, and grenadiers. The former were the general-purpose infantry and were the bulk of any army. The latter were veteran soldiers expected to lead attacks and hold positions in defense; despite their name, they had long set aside their titular bombs and were usually armed like the fusiliers.

After 1700, infantry equipment was largely standardized. The average infantryman carried a smoothbore flintlock musket that was around four feet long, which extended to around six feet with its socket bayonet attached. It fired a solid lead ball of around .60 caliber. The contemporary musket, or fusil, to give it its proper name, was an inaccurate and inefficient weapon. Its effective range was no more than two-hundred yards, and soldiers fired between one and perhaps five rounds per minute, depending on their skill and training. The fusil was inaccurate and slow because of technical limitations. The concept of machining equipment to precise specifications was relatively new, particularly in mass production, and thus imperfect. The need to load the fusil from the barrel also required large barrels to accommodate a variety of balls, often roughly cast by the soldier himself. Because of this, barrel width could vary significantly, as could the caliber of the balls used. In addition, even one firing with black powder fouled the barrel, and repeated firings required frequent cleaning. As a result, the windage, or gap between the projectile and the barrel, could be significant, allowing exploding gas to escape around the ball and all but preventing aiming.

Infantry training consisted of the manual of arms and drill. Subalterns (non-commissioned and junior officers) had to instruct their charges first in the use of the musket, which had been honed over centuries into a science. They then had to teach the soldiers how to cooperate with each other by marching in formation, performing evolutions, and firing. While the army taught volley firing, almost every period writer acknowledged that volleys were relatively rare in combat, usually occurring only once or twice at the beginning of the fight and then degenerating into fire-at-will, known as *feu à volonté* or the *billebaude*. Following this, officers instructed men in ever-larger formations, up to the entire battalion. This training was collectively known as the "school of the battalion" and occupied most of the time and energy of non-commissioned and junior officers.

Cavalry

"Cavalry" to the French meant heavy shock forces. For most of the eighteenth century, the cuirassier was the standard unit of cavalry. Cuirassiers were armored with a cuirass, a metal breast- and back-plate, and a helmet. They were armed with a cavalry saber that was either curved for slashing or straight for stabbing. Some cavalry forces were also armed with pistols or carbines, but technical limitations rendered them largely useless on the battlefield; the effective range of a contemporary pistol was probably less than ten feet. Cavalry units were still familiar with the caracole, the orderly rotation of men forward in order to fire volleys, but it largely remained a relic of the seventeenth century.

Cavalrymen trained together with their horses, a process that took far longer than the training of infantry. They would first train as an individual rider, then in increasingly large formations like the infantry. A significant portion of training was dedicated to keeping horses and men in formation, especially once they determined on a charge.

---

1 This appendix is reproduced from Abel, *Guibert's General Essay on Tactics*, 273–285.

Discussions of contemporary cavalry tactics are replete with admonitions against allowing men to give their horses their heads and exhausting them before they contacted the enemy line.

Dragoons were another form of cavalry, albeit one that occupied an uneasy space that straddled the definitions of cavalry and light. Rather than being mounted infantry, as in later American historical practice, dragoons were cavalry units that were also trained in infantry tactics. They did not wear the full accoutrements of the cavalryman, with most eschewing spurs and even the cuirass and helmet. They were expected to perform a variety of roles within the purview of all three arms, including shock attacks alongside traditional cavalry, scouting, harassing, and fighting as infantry on occasion.

As the century progressed, the role of the cavalry diminished. Fire was the major reason for this, as even the best-planned charge could be stymied by coordinated defensive fire from enemy infantry, artillery, and light forces. However, cavalry was still seen as the *masse de décision*, expected to open an enemy line for an infantry assault, finish a wavering opponent, contest with enemy cavalry, and pursue a defeated foe.

Light Forces

Light forces were the third arm of the French army, and the newest. "Light" was a catch-all term that included all units that were not easily categorized into one of the other arms. Their use was inspired by fighting on the Habsburg-Ottoman frontier during the late seventeenth century, where battlefields often transcended the formulaic infantry and cavalry blocks of Western Europe. There was no standardization of light forces during the period. They could be mounted or dismounted. They were armed with a wide variety of weaponry, from standard fusils to rifled muskets capable of far greater accuracy. They went by a variety of names, including chasseurs, hussars, *jägers*, *Grenzer*, *carabiniers*, and many others; within the French army, they were generally referred to as "chasseurs." Confusingly, line units could be trained in skirmishing, the *tiraillerie*, and were usually called chasseurs themselves. By the later part of the century, most French regiments had at least one "chasseur company," although that term rarely denoted any specificity of role or equipment beyond designating the unit as elite.

The role of light forces was to supplement the line forces, particularly on campaign. They performed the majority of the scouting, intelligence collecting, and harassing in advance of the army's march columns. In the battle, light forces were expected engage in the *tiraillerie*, the skirmish with opposing forces, particularly if they were heavy in light forces themselves.

Artillery and the Génie (*Engineers*)

Artillery occupied a liminal space in the French army. It was not considered an arm equal to the infantry, cavalry, and light forces for two reasons. First was the role that artillery played in siege warfare, both traditionally and throughout the century. Second, and related, were technical limitations that the artillery faced, particularly early in the century.

French artillery originated in the fourteenth century as a weapon for attacking enemy fortifications. As siegecraft evolved through the age of Sébastien le Prestre, seigneur de Vauban, artillery remained a key component of the siege. Cannon needed to be large and heavy in order to fire the projectiles necessary to damage fortress walls, which could be dozens of feet thick. Additionally, artillery pieces were usually cast around a mold, which left a seam through the barrel and made it vulnerable to exploding if not properly cared for. Guns also suffered from the same issues of windage and fouling as did infantry weapons. As a result, artillery pieces were large, heavy, and virtually immobile. There was no formal organizational distinction between siege and field artillery. Gun crews were trained to move their gun, site it, and fire it at a relatively slow pace, whether at an enemy position or army.

The use of artillery evolved the most of any of the branches of the French army over the eighteenth century. The example of the German states and the implementation of the Gribeauval System both contributed to this transition. Early in the eighteenth century, Austria was believed to have the best artillery service in Europe. Austrian artillerists generally made use of artillery for sieges, but they also trained gun crews and officers to use cannon as field artillery as well. Friedrich II was rudely inaugurated into the use of field artillery by his Austrian opponents in the War of the Austrian Succession; by the Seven Years War, the Prussian army possessed nimble field artillery that helped it win several battles. While field artillery was not a new concept, the German states innovated and adapted various means of making guns lighter and more maneuverable that became the standard of field artillery across the continent, including France. Jean-Baptiste-Vaquette de Gribeauval, the foremost artillerist in France, had served in Germany during the mid-century wars and returned with a system based on light, maneuverable field guns that would support the combat arms. This system was implemented in the 1770s, and it transformed the French artillery away from a primarily siege-based force to one that would eventually become an arm proper, albeit not until after 1789. Until then, because of its limitations and inability to fight without support from one of the arms, artillery was not considered a true arm.

The *génie* was often considered alongside, or even amalgamated with, the artillery. This occurred in large part because of the natural synergy between the two services in sieges as well as the technical nature of both. In the 1750s, the two corps were combined into a single body, the Royal Corps of Artillery and *Génie*. Engineers travelled with the army as distinct units and performed the engineering duties typical to armies of any period like building bridges, clearing roads, constructing camps and defensive works, and engaging in siege operations.

Officers of both branches were considered to be technical specialists, and most attended specialized educational institutions. They rarely left the branch, and as a result, few rose to high command or even prominence; Vauban, who was Louis XIV's siege master and most prominent general after 1690, was one exception. Because of this, army commanders rarely appreciated the abilities of and constraints on the two services, particularly as the artillery evolved to be more mobile and thus more useful on the battlefield. This contributed to both the absence of the services from high command and to the lack of true integration of all arms and branches until after 1789.

Unit Organization

Throughout the century, organization remained largely at the whim of the regimental commander, its colonel-proprietor. Even after the reforms of the 1770s that ostensibly eliminated venality, regiments continued to be conducted in accord with tradition rather than War Department regulation. As a result, it is all but impossible to provide specific details of organization across the French army of the eighteenth century; only generalities are possible.

The regiment was the chief administrative unit in the three arms and could have from as few as five-hundred men to over 2,000. Infantry regiments and some light regiment analogs consisted of between one and four battalions of between three-hundred and 1,000 men each. The infantry battalion was also largely an administrative unit. Battalions were broken into companies of between forty and two-hundred men; these companies were the chief tactical unit. Generally, each battalion maintained a company of grenadiers, and some preferred to keep a chasseur company as well. Companies were generally broken into squads, but formal subdivisions either did not exist or were not implemented for most of the century. Regimental, battalion, and company commanders created a variety of subdivisions, including demi-battalions, demi-companies, platoons, squads, divisions, *manches*, and many others.

Efforts to standardize regimental organization were made in the 1760s and again in the 1770s. The former decade set a battalion at eight fusilier companies and one grenadier company each. The latter reduced the fusilier companies to four and added a chasseur company to the battalion, along with setting most infantry regiments at two battalions each. However, both because of fierce opposition and disagreements over the propriety of reform, these changes proved transitory. In addition, France did not fight a major land war between 1763 and 1789, meaning they were never put into practice.

Cavalry organization reflected the roots of the arm, both in resistance to change and the relative simplicity compared to the infantry. Cavalry regiments were usually smaller than infantry units and divided into squadrons, the cavalry equivalent of the battalion. Because the cavalry tended to be the province of the upper nobility and composed a relatively small portion of the army, less reform attention was directed towards it during the eighteenth century. It did not develop the same subdivisions as the infantry, meaning its internal organization was less complex but also more resistant to centralized control.

Because of the nature of the light forces, few were standardized in any way during the period. They remained largely the province of their commanders, both in their organization and their practice, even after the issuing of documents like the 1769 *Instructions for Light Troops*. The exception to this is the creation of the chasseur company within infantry battalions in the 1770s, which signaled the blurring of the lines between line and light forces that would continue throughout the Revolutionary and Napoleonic Wars and the ultimate disappearance of light forces as a discrete arm within the French army.

Like the cavalry, the artillery generally resisted centralized control. Because it was the most technical of the services, most commanders and even War Department bureaucrats did not have much knowledge of its workings. As a result, they left it largely to itself when compared to the infantry. The artillery technically comprised a "corps," meaning it was a single unit, or it was combined with the *génie*. The exception to this was the presence of small guns, usually 3- or 6-pound cannon, that were attached to battalions and regiments sporadically throughout the century; contemporaries bemoaned both their weight and lack of effective firepower. Eighteenth-century theorists, when they addressed artillery at all, generally referred to batteries as analogs for companies and squadrons, which loosely conformed with field artillery practice from the middle of the century onwards. However, the true integration of field artillery with the combat arms would not occur during the Old Regime.

Above the level of the regiment, organization became significantly less prescribed, largely because the regiment was the largest permanent organization in the French army prior to 1787. This was long tradition, as placing an echelon above the regiment would necessarily infringe on the rights of the regimental proprietors to dispose of their units as they saw fit. During peacetime, most regiments only encountered other regiments in the training camps that were held sporadically throughout the kingdom, particularly on its frontiers. The senior commander would divide the forces as he saw fit to achieve the purpose of the camp, which was usually to test a new theory or innovation in tactics.

A further complication was the presence of the foreign regiments, free companies, and the *Maison du roi* (king's household). Over the centuries, the French army had accumulated several regiments of foreign extraction, most notably from Switzerland and Flanders. These units originated as mercenary companies manned from their place of origin, but they gradually evolved into French army units that still drew on non-French manpower. Around twenty percent of the French army's line units were foreign regiments, mostly infantry, but also cavalry. Free companies were similar units, ad hoc formations that were usually smaller than regiments and that were drawn into French service over the decades. Many of them were light formations, but some were line or cavalry units. Finally, the *Maison du roi* consisted of the elite units that ostensibly guarded the king and carried his honor onto the battlefield. Because of the prestige attached to these units, they were a favorite target of wealthy *anoblis* and robe nobles who purchased commissions in them in order to ensure their sons' nobility.

The presence of the foreign regiments, free companies, and the *Maison du roi* further complicated army organization. They resisted efforts to standardize the army and adopt doctrine, as they relied on their traditions as the foundation of their identity. In battle, the foreign regiments were generally reliable and even elite, but the free companies and the units of the *Maison du roi* were of questionable quality. By mid-century, commanders and theorists alike recognized that the *Maison du roi* served a largely ceremonial role and could not be relied on in a fight. However, they were still included in the order of battle, as leaving them behind would insult the king's majesty. Commanders thus had to balance the needs of the campaign with political and social mores in constructing and deploying their armies.

During war, regiments combined to form a field army under the command of a senior general and his subordinate general officers. There were no formal echelons above the regiment, but commanders had been in the habit of forming ad hoc brigades since at least the mid-seventeenth century. These formations were more akin to a task force than to a brigade, in modern parlance; the *Encyclopedia* article "Brigadier" notes that such an officer "has only a commission and not a charge, nor properly a grade in the army." Brigades, and brigadiers, were generally used to dispatch a group of regiments from the main army rather than within the army itself, although they could be used for that purpose as well. Officers also sought the title of "brigadier" as a method of promotion, particularly in peacetime. On the march, officers generally commanded a portion of the march order, from their individual companies all the way up to a full march column. In battle, commanders usually assigned a wing of the army to a subordinate, especially if the army exceeded 40,000, as they often did.

The beginnings of operational-level warfare appeared during the Seven Years War in the French army. In 1759, Victor-François, duc de Broglie, divided his army into divisions containing two or more arms, the first formal use of the term and concept in French history. However, the usage did not last beyond the war, and echelons above the regiment would have to wait for the Revolutionary Wars. As a result, French armies of the eighteenth century can be characterized as collections of regiments.

Command and Control

French armies were led by officers of varying educational levels, skills, and competencies. The lower ranks tended to be populated by long-service professionals, men who knew their craft and were seasoned by combat. The upper levels of command varied greatly depending on the skill and ability of the men who were available and held purchase at court. It was controlled by the War Department with the assistance of other parts of the royal government, and it answered to the king and his court, although individual officers could hold sway far above their rank if they maintained powerful patrons and/or clients at court. The result was a hybrid organization of dizzying complexity that defied easy understanding, even by contemporaries. Despite this, the rank structure and hierarchy, particularly at the regimental level and below, will be familiar to the modern reader, as several Western militaries base their rank structure on the French example.

Infantry

The junior officers and non-commissioned officers (*sous-* or *bas-officiers* and subalterns) were the men of captain rank and below. With the exception of the period before the War of the Polish Succession when France had not fought a major war for almost two decades, almost all junior and non-commissioned officers were experienced veterans. As with organization, their ranks were in constant flux throughout the century, but some generalities may be sketched. The lowest level of non-commissioned officer was the corporal, who oversaw a group of five to fifteen soldiers, often referred to as a squad. Each company had around ten corporals, with grenadier companies usually having more to provide a higher ratio of non-commissioned officers to soldiers. Above the corporal was the sergeant, with a typical company having half the number of sergeants as corporals. Each company also had one sergeant-major who was almost always the senior sergeant. Above the sergeants were the lieutenants. Like their counterparts in modern armies, the corporals and sergeants oversaw the daily affairs of the army, whether in camp, in garrison, or on the march.

Almost every eighteenth-century company had at least one lieutenant, and they often had several, whether supernumerary, junior (*sous-lieutenant*), or simply multiple. The lieutenants were often placed in command of subdivisions of the company and may be said to be the lowest-level tactical commanders of discrete units in this role. Commanding them was the company's captain, the senior officer in the unit. He was the chief executive of the company, responsible for its training and functioning, particularly when it was encamped or in a depot, as well as disbursing its funds, distributing its equipment, and, for most of the century, its manning.

The battalion level marked the transition from junior officers to field officers (*officiers-majeurs*). Each battalion maintained an officer responsible for ensuring the uniform training of the companies; he usually held the rank of major or battalion chief (*chef de bataillon*). For much of the period, this position was not a formal rank, nor was it standardized across the army, and it was often conferred on the senior captain, who continued to command his company along with his added responsibilities. Every regiment had a colonel who owned the regiment and was responsible for its maintenance, readiness, and direction. Many regiments maintained officers between the colonel and the major/battalion chief. Foremost among these was the position of lieutenant-colonel. A lieutenant-colonelcy was usually not a formal rank, and it was often granted as an honorific to a long-serving captain. This created situations where an officer could be a captain, major/battalion chief, and lieutenant-colonel at the same time. In addition, many colonels were not competent or experienced enough to lead their regiments into battle, so they employed experienced officers to do so for them. These could hold the position of lieutenant-colonel, colonel-in-second, or colonel-commandant, among others. Finally, there would be specialty officers and men within the regiment and in lower echelons, including aides, drummers, flag-bearers, surgeons, financial officials, and cadets, who were usually the young sons of the nobility.

Cavalry, Light Forces, Artillery, and the Génie

As with the infantry, only generalities may be sketched of the other arms and branches. Non-infantry units generally had officers who performed roles specific to the arm or branch like the cavalry *mestre-de-camp* or the technicians of the artillery and *génie*. Command and control varied by practice. Cavalry units closely resembled infantry units, with the important note that cavalry units carried fewer officers, as they were usually much smaller than infantry units. Artillery and engineering units engaged in far less linear drill than their counterparts in the infantry and cavalry, as it was not incumbent in the operation of their branch. Instead, they practiced the skills and techniques relevant to their purpose, particularly in siege warfare. Light forces were often under less strict control than the other arms and branches, as they often dispersed across the battlefield or theater, and thus trained according to the standards their commander desired.

Operational and Strategic Command and Control

As with organization, command and control above the regimental level largely ceased to be standardized, especially in peacetime. Generals assigned to command a field army were almost always granted the marshal's baton. While the position of marshal is often imagined to be a formal military rank, it was not; instead, it was a court honor that enabled the marshal to hold command over other generals. A general did not have to be a marshal, but if he were not, he would endure ceaseless complaints from his subordinate generals, who would take affront to being commanded by someone they viewed as a peer or even as an inferior, to the point of outright refusing orders from him.

Commanding generals were selected by the court, usually in consultation with the War Department, but not always. Often, especially during the reign of Jeanne-Antoinette Poisson, marquise de Pompadour, armies went to court favorites rather than the skilled or experienced candidate. Princes of the Blood expected to be assigned command of an army, even if such an assignment were only pro forma, and the king might even decide to command an army himself, as Louis XV did after 1744 in the Low Countries. These men rarely exerted control over the army, preferring to leave that to the accompanying marshal or general and commanding only in title. Court intrigues could also occasion the recall of a general, although very rarely formally, as such an action would offend the nobility of the commander. Much more common was the resignation of a command, whether desired or not, at the end of a campaign season, usually under pressure from the crown and/or court.

A commanding general received virtual carte blanche to conduct affairs within his army as he saw fit. He was dispatched with a strategic plan and knowledge of the other armies that might be operating in the same region, and he was expected to communicate regularly with the Secretary of State for War, the king and court, and his fellow army commanders. He expected to have supplies and reinforcements dispatched from his rear, which connected him and his army to the vast web of the French bureaucracy, military and civilian. Almost every other detail was left up to the general.

Assisting the general was an array of subordinates, officials, and bureaucrats. The senior officers of regiments and armies were referred to as the *état-major*, which is often translated as "staff." While the translation is accurate for the modern French army, the analogy is not exact in the eighteenth century. In modern English, "staff" connotes a formal organization with officers performing set duties in assigned roles. In contrast, the eighteenth-century *état-major* was simply the senior officers, many of whom had formal duties other than staff work. The regimental *état-major* included men who might be company commanders, while the *état-major de l'armée* included all men of rank.

The *état-major* consisted of many officers of varying rank and experience. Senior among them were the men who held the rank of lieutenant-general, the highest permanent rank. Collectively, they were known as the general officers (*officiers-généraux*). There were normally two lieutenants-general with the army, and they rotated command (technically, command of the watch) every day. Directly beneath them were the men named *maréchal-de-camp* whose job it was to translate the generals' orders into action, both by interpreting them and delivering them to subordinates. As their name indicates, the *maréchaux-de-camp* usually concerned themselves with details of march, subsistence, and encampment. If any brigadiers were present, they ranked below the *maréchaux-de-camp*. Officers could be formally commissioned brigadier, but they could also be breveted so; any field officer could be breveted brigadier, including the odd captain on rare occasion. In addition, generals often appointed a major-general to oversee the army's infantry, a practice sometimes expanded to include one each for the cavalry, dragoons, and the *état-major* during the mid-century wars. Each army also had a *maréchal-général des logis*, an officer tasked with ensuring the army's logistics throughout the campaign. Each of these officers had numerous aides; the *maréchaux* had *aides-maréchaux*, the general officers had their own aides, and the infantry regiments generally maintained at least one *aide-major*. Aides were aspiring officers, men of skill or experience, or the children of officers engaging in their military apprenticeship.

The *état-major* of the army may be generally divided into three categories: operational command, sustainment, and bureaucracy. The general officers, *maréchaux-de-camp*, and brigadiers comprised the first category. The second and third were collectively known as the *service*. The *maréchal-général des logis* supervised the second, but not solely on his own authority. The third was headed by a military intendant, a royal official appointed by the king to oversee the army's bureaucracy. Intendants headed the civilian portion of the army's bureaucracy and worked alongside the *maréchal-général des logis* to ensure supply and other sustainment needs, particularly via purchase forward of the army's advance. Assisting them were the army's *commissaires de guerre*, bureaucrats charged with overseeing the details of the army, from food and supply to discipline and punishment. Both men also maintained contacts with various *munitionnaires*, private men who ran supply companies and could always be found around armies in the field or at court. These positions were not regularized across time or armies, so officers could simultaneously belong to two or even all three categories at the same time, and contemporary commanders enjoyed complaining that the logisticians dictated strategy rather than vice-versa.

In addition to the *état-major*, the field army possessed numerous supernumerary officers at every level. These ranged from cadets up to lieutenants-general. These positions existed for two main reasons. First, they provided a rank that idle nobles and *anoblis* could purchase to burnish their social standing. Second, they constituted a pool of officers who could be tasked with duties like running messages, staff planning, commanding a detachment, or even assuming command of echelons within the army itself.

The commander's headquarters was thus a warren of officers and bureaucrats who worked to ensure the army's success, albeit not always in concert. As might be imagined, the civilian and military officials did not always agree, although far less friction existed between them than might be imagined. The more contentious relationships tended to be between the various lieutenants-general, as they often believed themselves to have the superior title and thus the right of command, even over an appointed marshal. A Prince of the Blood might also supersede his generals, as frequently occurred in the later wars of Louis XIV, as Guibert notes. Thus, the commander's task was to mediate between various individuals and factions, to ensure the functioning of his army, and to liaise with both the court and his fellow army commanders, if a friendly army was within range. The baggage trains added further to the confusion. Every officer maintained his lifestyle as much as possible in the field, necessitating a massive amount of baggage to keep him in relative luxury. Eighteenth-century French armies were axiomatically heavy, slow-moving, and ponderous as a result.

While the commander was physically separated from the War Department and the court, he was expected to maintain communication with both. Mail moved relatively quickly across the distance via highway and the trans-state postal system, but a delay of up to a week was still normal. Most importantly, supplies and reinforcements flowed from France to the front, requiring a great deal of coordination between the field army/armies and the government, hence the preponderance of logistics officers and men in the *état-major de l'armée*.

The Department of War was one of the most important departments in the French government. It was headed by a Secretary of State for War, one of the five to ten most-important non-royal men in the government. His chief role was to coordinate all of the available resources for the war effort, dispatching them to the field armies. To support him in this, he had an array of bureaus that worked within the War Ministry as well as various private individuals who either acted as *munitionnaires* or liaised with *munitionnaire* companies. The Secretary of State for War was also responsible for strategic planning, although no general staff structure existed to perform this duty. Instead, as with supply, he was expected to draw on his client network, official and unofficial, to see to the success of the armies.

The War Ministry answered to the king and the court. The three kings of the eighteenth century had different approaches to the task. Louis XIV preferred a small cabinet and direct intervention in affairs, even of detail, although his energy waned during the War of the Spanish Succession. Louis XV was more distant, ruling through ministers, particularly his First Minister but also including a wide array of men and women who competed with each other for his attention and favor. Louis XVI tended to rely most on his ministers, largely opting not to directly interfere in military affairs. Each had his favorites, and almost everyone at court competed to be counted in that number. Thus, command and control at the highest level could be a varying process subject to the court and its cabals. A skilled Secretary of State for War was required to navigate these various elements to ensure the success of the armies while maintaining both his grace and his position; the high rate of turnover during wartime indicates how difficult a position in which he often found himself.

Manning

Soldiers

Throughout the Old Regime, every French soldier had ostensibly volunteered for duty. In reality, manning took a variety of forms, many with elements of coercion. Wartime especially strained conventional methods of recruitment. Desertion also presented a significant barrier to maintaining manpower, necessitating frequent recourses to more forceful means.

For the first half of the eighteenth century, recruiting was the duty of company commanders. Captains would receive their company's pay and funds from the colonel and then deputize their subordinates to recruit from the populace. The stereotypical recruiting drive involved a sergeant spending lavishly on food and especially drinks for the young men in a public house, then signing them up for service as they grew both more grateful and more impaired. The new recruit found himself with both an enlistment bounty and a lengthy contract. If the recruiters' numbers were not met, they were not above clearing out the local prisons, enlisting deserters from other units, inventing paper soldiers, or even outright kidnapping men to fill the ranks. Recruiting was not "national;" soldiers were gladly accepted from any country as long as they could communicate with their officers in some common language, whether in a French unit or a foreign regiment, although non-French soldiers were normally taken in by a corresponding foreign regiment.

Wartime occasioned a variety of other manning methods. The most obvious and accessible was the *milice*, the royal militia. All military-age males were liable for militia service, at least in theory, by drawing of lots. Like most contemporary militias, the *milice* was territorial and designed to defend the kingdom in case of invasion. It was forbidden from operating outside the kingdom's borders or being used in regular army service. However, it frequently became a ready reserve for the army, despite the edicts forbidding such usage. In addition, the kingdom had recourse to the medieval *arrière-ban*, which was used infrequently throughout the seventeenth and eighteenth centuries to call men to the army, usually ineffectually. Numerous companies were also scattered throughout the kingdom to garrison its many fortresses; while these were usually manned by *invalides,* disabled men, they were scoured for manpower if necessary. The French Navy maintained significant manpower, including men trained in land combat; these occasionally appeared in the army, particularly to guard rear areas and man garrisons when those forces were sent to the front. Finally, the free companies could be amalgamated into the army's regular units if necessary, either wholly or by dispersing their manpower across existing companies.

Despite these measures, the French army was chronically short of manpower, as was the case with most contemporary armies. Desertion could consume up to twenty percent of manpower on campaign, but a portion of deserters returned to service, albeit perhaps not with the original company. Combat and disease casualties also took their toll, and although the French army had an excellent medical service by comparison to its contemporaries, medical and surgical knowledge was still rudimentary.

Officers

The major source of the manpower for the officer corps was the nobility. The French state and society had been constructed in part on the military relationship between the king and his nobility: the crown granted use of its land in exchange for military service. As a result, the nobles considered it a duty to send their sons to the military, especially the army. While exact numbers are difficult to determine, the French nobility comprised around one-and-a-half percent of the French population of around twenty million, providing a large manpower pool from which to draw officers. In addition, tens of thousands of people regularly entered the nobility via purchase of noble patents, including army commissions.

This provided a virtually inexhaustible supply of manpower to the officer corps, but not all officers were suited to command. Traditionalists held that the skill of command was in the blood, but even the most stringent recidivists acknowledged that nobles needed some form of education and training. Most nobles were sent to a school for basic education or received private tutoring; a large number also attended the *collèges* that were administered by the Church. After 1750, many were sent to the various incarnations of the *Ecole royale militaire*, a school designed to educate male, teenage members of the poor nobility in the art and science of warfare. If they were not a student in at the *Ecole royale militaire*, noble sons were expected to undergo a military apprenticeship by purchasing a commission in a company or regiment at the age of majority, around thirteen, and serving throughout the remainder of their able life. By this combination of basic education and experiential training and genetics, a noble became an officer suited to command. The exception to this was the highest nobility, particularly the Princes of the Blood, who may have had only an ineffectual private education at best.

The officer corps was almost exclusively noble. Around ninety to ninety-five percent of officers held a noble patent. The few common officers, known as *roturiers*, tended to rise no further than the rank of captain, and even then, only after many years' service. The nobility jealously guarded its position in the army, both out of class solidarity and because its members genuinely believed that noble status conferred some degree of military competence. However, there were divisions between the various noble classes, especially the poor provincial nobility and the rich robe nobles and *anoblis*. Nobles of older extraction resented the parvenus of the *anoblis* and railed against their perceived lack of education and experience, while the *anoblis* lobbied for a more open system and society, reflecting one of the fundamental disputes in French society during the period.

In addition, foreign officers frequently appeared in the French army, and the profession of officer may be said to have been a truly international one in the eighteenth century. As with the recruitment of soldiers, ideas of "nation" or even patriotism rarely prevented an immigrant from serving in France's military. Irish, Scottish, Swiss, and Flemish officers abounded, honoring the long tradition of service that each of their countries and societies had to the French crown. Geography also played a role in officer immigration: many Germans and Italians were found in the French officer corps, although Spanish officers tended to be less so.

By the eighteenth century, this timeworn system was increasingly under assault from a variety of sources and developments in French society. A major source of criticism came from Enlightenment *philosophes*, who called for technical education and training for all officers, especially as armies grew larger and war became more technical and complicated. Another was the increasing intrusion of the *anoblis* and *noblesse de la robe* into the officer corps. Their members frequently purchased commissions for their sons, especially in the *Maison du roi*. Most of these were supernumerary positions, but many were also in positions of authority. As officers were required to spend only the campaign season with their units in wartime and only a few months in peacetime, they increasingly knew little about the units they commanded, the responsibilities they held, or military affairs in general. Both traditionalists and progressives pushed to require education for all officers and that they spend more time with their units. However, none of these proposals permanently cohered both in regulation and practice during the Old Regime and would have to wait for the Revolution.

The French officer corps was thus a semi-professional caste with a porous floor and borders. French officers served in non-French armies, and non-French officers served in the French army. Officers may have had some experience, training, and education, but none was required. Every year, thousands of young men entered the officer corps, prepared or not. Supernumerary officers abounded, leading to rancorous arguments over the propriety of officer commissions, the proper nature of an officer, and the direction of the future officer corps.

Services

The various services that supported the French army relied on the same convoluted bureaucracy that produced its command and control. Supply systems, equipment, and medical services occupied much of the time and energy of the Department of War and the functionaries of the army *état-major*. They also cost a great deal, which proved increasingly onerous throughout the century as the financial crisis loomed.

Supply systems relied almost entirely on private companies, both in France and abroad. While armies usually had *commissaires* overseeing munitions in the army *état-major*, supply was not provided directly by the government. Instead, the Department of War contracted with *munitionnaires*, individuals who could provide supply, transport, and storage to the army. The War Department also purchased food, fodder, and warehousing in advance of the army, which were almost always available no matter how hostile the population might be in the invaded area. This was largely systematized through court figures who built client networks of *munitionnaires* and could efficiently direct supply to the armies. The most famous example of this was the Pâris brothers, all four of whom were deeply entrenched in the government of the early half of the century and oversaw supply and finance for the wars of the period.

Equipment relied on a vast web of manufactories and distributors, both within France and in other countries. Certain resources, like saltpeter, could be found domestically, but others, like iron, had to be found elsewhere. Most equipment was manufactured in France in a variety of government-supported workshops, particularly in the more industrialized region in the north and east. It would be stored in garrisons or warehouses in anticipation of war, then dispatched to the armies by the War Department.

Supply and equipment reached the soldier through a variety of means. Soldiers' equipment needs were usually met on campaign via the *état-major*, with the exception of shoes and weatherproof clothes, on occasion. Official sources usually provided a minimum of sustenance, although frequently not of high quality. While the vast clouds of camp followers of the previous century had largely evaporated, many survived, including the *cantinières* and *vivandières* that seem to be ubiquitous in military history. Soldiers supplemented their supply with items bought or taken from locals. Pillage was not as common during the eighteenth century as the prior, largely due to changing social mores, but it certainly occurred, especially of food and clothes.

Regimental Manpower per Choiseul Reforms of the 1760s

Etat-major	Fusilier company	Grenadier company	Battalion strength	
At the discretion of the Colonel; approximately 10 officers	1 Captain	1 Captain	8 Fusilier Companies	528
	1 Lieutenant	1 Lieutenant	1 Grenadier Company	63
	1 *Sous-Lieutenant*	1 *Sous-Lieutenant*	Total:	591
	1 Supply Officer	1 Supply Officer		
	4 Sergeants	2 Sergeants		
	8 Corporals	8 Corporals		
	8 *Appointés* (trainee officers)	8 *Appointés* (trainee officers)		
	2 Drummers	1 Drummer		
	40 Fusiliers (peacetime strength; raised as necessary during war)	40 Grenadiers (peacetime strength; raised as necessary during war)	**Regimental Strength**	
			2 Battalions	1182
			Etat-major	10
Total:	66	63	Total:	1192

Regimental Manpower per 1776 Ordinance

Regiments of 2 Battalions; Battalions of 4 Fusilier Companies, 1 Chasseur Company, 1 Grenadier Company, 1 Depot Company

Etat-major	Fusilier/Chasseur company	Grenadier company	Battalion strength	
1 Colonel	1 Captain	1 Captain	4 Fusilier Companies	684
1 Colonel-in-Second	1 Captain-in-Second	1 Captain-in-Second	1 Chasseur Company	171
1 Lieutenant-Colonel	1 Lieutenant	1 1st Lieutenant	1 Grenadier Company	108
1 Major	1 Lieutenant-in-Second	1 2nd Lieutenant	Depot Company	171
1 Quartermaster-Treasurer	2 *Sous-Lieutenants*	2 *Sous-Lieutenants*	Total:	1134
2 Flagbearers	1 Sergeant-Major	1 Sergeant-Major		
1 Adjutant	1 Supply-Writer	1 Supply-Writer		
1 Surgeon-Major	5 Sergeants	4 Sergeants		
1 Almoner	10 Corporals	8 Corporals		
1 Drum-Major	1 *Cadet-gentilhomme*	1 *Cadet-gentilhomme*		
1 Armorer	1 Barber	1 Barber	**Regimental Strength**	
	144 Fusiliers/Chasseurs	84 Grenadiers	2 Battalions	2268
	2 Drummers	2 Drummers	*Etat-major*	12
Total:	171	108	Total:	2280

ADAPTED FROM BACQUET, *L'INFANTERIE AU XVIIIE SIÈCLE*

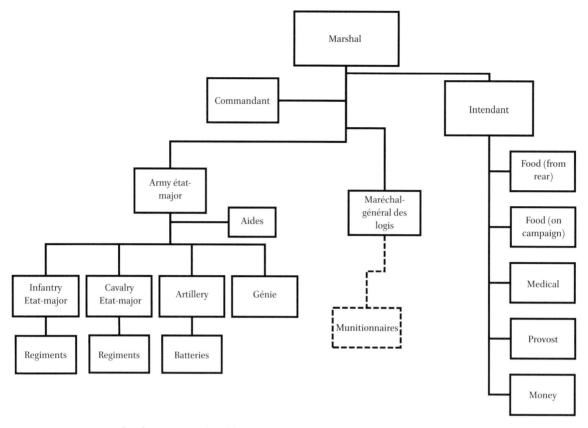

FIGURE 10   Prototypical Midcentury French Field Army Organization
ADAPTED FROM KENNETT, *THE FRENCH ARMY IN THE SEVEN YEARS WAR*.

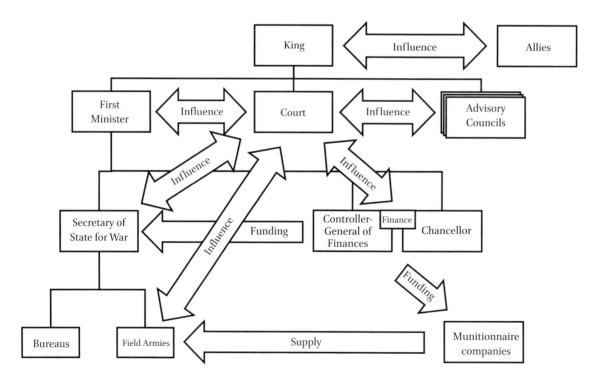

FIGURE 11   Generalized Diagram of French Strategic Command and Control
ADAPTED FROM KENNETT, *THE FRENCH ARMY IN THE SEVEN YEARS WAR*.

Appendix C: Glossary of Terms

ANOBLIS   A person who has a noble patent but is not fully accepted as noble; the classes of such people who formed the liminal space between the upper classes of commoners and the nobility.

ARME BLANCHE   Generic term for melee combat; originates from the cavalry, which was the exclusive province of the nobility in the medieval period, and white was the color of nobility, signifying pure blood.

AVANT-PROPOS   A form of introduction often used in French academic writing that outlines the work's purpose and approach and situates it within its larger field.

BANDIÈRE   Unit flag, ensign, pennant, or other symbol

BREAK   To separate the constituent parts of a unit, usually from closed order for deployment. Usually synonymous with "shake" and "tear."

CARABINIER   Literally, a soldier who carries a carbine, but not all carried actual carbines during the period; instead, often a general term for light troops and/or skirmishers, as distinguished from fusiliers/*fantassins*

CHANGE, GIVE OR MAKE   To induce an opponent to change his formation or position, preferably to his disadvantage.

CLOSED ORDER   A formation in which no interval is left between the constituent units. Closed order only became possible after the adoption of the cadenced step, as it required precision in march and maneuver to avoid units' becoming entangled.

COMBINE/COMBINATION   In eighteenth-century military theory, "combine" and "combination" denoted how a commander arranged his forces in formations and for action; for example, a general may combine his forces on a place to receive an oncoming army.

COMMISSAIRE   Officer within the army charged with ensuring the troops' discipline, pay, and provision. Guibert usually use the term to refer to a munitions officer, but not always. The term should not be confused with the later commissar/*komissar*/*commissaire de guerre*, which usually denotes a political officer separate from the military hierarchy.

CONSTITUTION   While the modern term generally denotes a written plan of government, the eighteenth-century definition of the word is more general, meaning a systematic concept or fundamental ideas and mores. Montesquieu's *Spirit of the Laws* would have been considered a political constitution by contemporaries, for example. Guibert most often uses the term to refer to what would now be called doctrine in military institutions, but he also uses it in the political sense, especially in the last chapter of the book.

COUP D'ŒIL   The ability of a commander to envision when and where enemy and friendly forces will be positioned before and during a battle. The French, especially in the eighteenth century, usually use the term to refer specifically to the commander's ability to judge the terrain and how forces may be placed on it; the English use of the term is more broad, largely reflecting the expansion of the term by Clausewitz to include ephemeral factors like morale and enemy psychology.

DEPLOY   See Ploy and Deploy.

ETAT-MAJOR   The senior officers of a unit, usually battalion-sized or larger, some of whom were expected to perform staff functions. While the term is commonly translated as "staff," it does not align directly with the modern definition of staff, which is a much more rigid system with staff officers in assigned roles under the direction of the unit commander and chief of staff.

EN BASTION   "As a bastion;" a formation that resembles a bastion.

EN BATAILLE   Sometimes translated as "in battle order," particularly when paired with "in march order;" also as "in line" or "in battle line." John Lynn, *The Bayonets of the Republic*, provides a persuasive case for leaving the term in French, as it can have multiple meanings that do not always translate.

EN BATTERIE   "In battery." As with *en bataille*, this term refers to preparing artillery for battle but does not have a direct translation that would make sense to a modern Anglophone.

EN ÉCHIQUIER   "In a quincunx or checkerboard formation."

EN MURAILLE   "In a wall;" to stand shoulder-to-shoulder without intervals. The term recalls siegecraft.

EN PLAINE   In a plain, exposed to enemy fire.

EN ROUAGE   In a position to fire on the enemy, particularly enemy artillery and using enfilading fire. Usually used in reference to artillery.

EVOLUTION   Essentially, a tactical maneuver. "Evolutions" generally refers to the suite of maneuvers available to a commander to prepare for and engage in battle, particularly at the battalion level.

FACILE   While the modern English definition of the word connotes a negative simplicity or lack of sophistication, Guibert uses it to mean "simple" or "easy," with a positive rather than a negative connotation.

FANTASSIN   Line infantryman who is not a member of a light or elite company; eighteenth-century equivalent of "general infantry." See fusilier.

FILE   The men in a line in front of and behind a soldier in formation; a line perpendicular to the unit's front.

FLANK MARCH   A march to the right or left, along a line perpendicular to the center of the unit and projected forwards and backwards.

FLOATING   The drifting apart of men or sub-units within a formation that required redressing it; usually paired with "disorder."

FRONT DE BANDIÈRE   A line of *bandières* planted in front of the line of troops in a maneuver camp.

FRONT MARCH   A march forward or backwards, along a line parallel to the center of the unit and projected forwards and backwards.

FUSIL   The technical term for a period weapon, even though they are popularly referred to as "muskets." A fusil was a smoothbore flintlock musket around four-and-a-half feet long, which would reach six feet with socket bayonet attached. Its effective range was around two-hundred yards, or thirty-five *toises*.

FUSILIER   A soldier who uses a fusil; can sometimes be used to distinguish from a *carabinier* or other specialized unit; also a generic term for infantry, interchangeable with *fantassin*.

GRANDS   Grandees; originally, lords who controlled a large demesne; by Guibert's time, simply people who held power, especially at court.

HEIGHT   A geometrical term referring to the placement of a unit in formation, usually the unit of alignment. The height of a formation would be the position of its front rank. Subsequent units could deploy to the same height, meaning by aligning their front ranks on a line drawn through the first rank of the original unit and extending to its right and left, which would usually be perpendicular to its files.

HUGUENOT   a French Protestant.

INTERVAL   The distance between divisions of men within a unit or between units. When marching or deploying, "full interval" would be an interval equal to the units' frontage, and "half interval" would be a lesser interval, although likely not exactly half.

INVERSION   Changing the prescribed method of deployment, especially via maneuvers that did not end with the most prestigious unit deployed on the formation's right.

MARINE   The Ministry of the Marine, which encompassed both the French Navy and the administration of all French colonies. Military writers generally use the term as shorthand for the Navy, but not always.

MILITAIRE   A person engaged in military activities, usually as a serious hobby or profession. While the term is occasionally translated as "military man," it is clunky to translate into de-gendered English, which is why it remains in the French.

MUNITIONNAIRE   A businessman who contracts with the army to provide provisions on campaign.

NOBLESSE DE L'ÉPEE   "Sword nobles," nobles of old extraction, particularly those who could trace their lineage back to the traditional feudal exchange of fealty and military service for protection and a fief.

NOBLESSE DE LA ROBE   "Robe nobles," nobles of recent extraction who had purchased ennobling offices, especially within the judicial and financial administrations. Many members of the *noblesse de la robe* were considered to be *anoblis*.

NOBLESSE DU SANG   "Nobles of the Blood," members of the royal family, which had several cadet branches and thus comprised several hundred members at any given time.

OFFICIER-MAJOR   The officer responsible for a battalion's discipline and order; often shortened to simply "major."

OPEN ORDER   A formation in which an interval is left between the constituent units. Open order, especially in column, was easier to maneuver in, as it left a margin for error, but it required several more steps to deploy into line, as the intervals would first have to be closed.

PARLEMENT   A regional law court located in a major province; traditionally, France had thirteen, but the number was never fixed. Its members were almost exclusively jurists from wealthy families, both common and *anoblis*. During the eighteenth century, the parlementaires were one of the major groups of rising bourgeoisie, and many of them wished to make the parlements, or the Parlement of Paris, into a quasi-legislative body or bodies. Despite the similar name and frequent equation, a parlement is not a parliament, nor is it at all akin to the English Parliament, even though they are sometimes equated or confused.

PATRIE   Generally translated as "fatherland;" the French is usually retained in order to draw a distinction from other cultures that use a similar term, particularly Germany during the Nazi period.

PHILOSOPHE   Literally "philosopher" but denotes a supporter of the Enlightenment and its thought patterns during the period. While the terms "Enlightenment" and "enlightened" were used, most contemporaries referred to them simply as "philosophy" and their practitioners as "philosophers," hence the retention of the French term for the specific period.

PIVOT   Point on which a unit turns. A fixed pivot requires all units in a formation to turn on the same point, while a moving pivot assigns a separate point to each man, subdivision, or unit at the discretion of the officers.

PLACE (OF WAR)/POINT   A defensive and/or fortified position, ranging from a small and temporary battlefield emplacement to entire fortified cities and fortress complexes.

PLOY AND DEPLOY   Drill-specific verbs that refer to the movements from column to line (deploy) and line to column (ploy). "Ploy" has fallen out of common usage, even among militaries, and "deploy" has become a more generalized term analogous to preparation. The technical meanings are intended throughout Guibert's book.

POINT-BLANK (BUT EN BLANC)   Like ploy and deploy, point-blank is a general term with a more technical meaning in military ballistics. Its common modern definition is simply "very close," but in ballistics, it refers to the distance over which a projectile will travel and still hit the target without needing to compensate for gravity. In most cases, Guibert intends the technical meaning of the term.

RANK   The men in a line to the right and left of a soldier in formation; a line parallel to the unit's front.

SHAKE   see break.

SERRE-FILE   The last man in a file.

SYSTEM   Guibert usually uses "system" to refer to prescriptive doctrines, especially those crafted in imitation of the ideas of Jean-Charles, Chevalier Folard. He condemns them as "makers of systems" and rejects their rigid nature. However, the word does not always mean this in Guibert's writing; the difference should be apparent in context.

TEAR   see break.

TIRAILLERIE   "Skirmishings;" to deploy in skirmish order or for skirmishing.

TOISE   a measurement of land distance, akin to a nautical fathom, equaling around two modern meters.

Bibliography

Archival

Service Historique – Armée de Terre, Vincennes, France.

Primary

Abel, Jonathan. *Guibert's General Essay on Tactics*. Leiden: Brill, 2022.

ADP 6–0 *Mission Command*. 2019.

Analyse de la philosophie du chancelier François Bacon. 2 Volumes. Leiden: Libraires Associés, 1756.

Arcq, Philippe-Auguste de Sainte-Foy, chevalier d'. *La noblesse militaire ou le patriote français*. Paris, 1756.

Aulnay, Louis Dupré de. *Traité des subsistences militaires*. Paris: Prault, 1744.

Bayle, Pierre. *Dictionnaire historique et critique*. 4 Volumes. Basle: Brandmuller, 1738.

Bernis, François-Joachim de Pierre, Cardinal. *Memoirs and Letters*. 2 Volumes. Translated by Katharine Wormeley. Boston: Hardy, Pratt, & Co.

Besenval, Pierre-Victor, baron. *Mémoires*. Paris: 1821.

Bossuet, Jacques-Bénigne. *An Universal History from the Beginning of the World to the Empire of Charlemagne*. Translated by James Elphinston. Dublin: Marchbank, 1785.

Bourcet, Pierre-Joseph. *Mémoires historiques sur la guerre que les français ont soutenue en Allemagne depuis 1757 jusqu'en 1762*. Paris: Maradan, 1792.

Bourcet, Pierre-Joseph. *Mémoires militaires sur les frontières de la France, du Piémont, et la Savoie, depuis l'embouchure du Var jusqu'au Lac de Genève*. Paris: Chez Levrault, 1802.

Bourcet, Pierre-Joseph. *Principes de la guerre de montagne*. Paris: Imprimerie Nationale, 1888.

Brézé, Argentero. *Observations historiques et critiques sur les commentaires de Folard et sur la cavalerie*. 2 Volumes. Torino: Revcend, 1772.

Broglie, Victor-François, duc de. *Campagnes du maréchal duc de Broglie en Allemagne 1759–1761*. Frankfurt et Leipzig, 1761.

Broglie, Victor-François, duc de. *Correspondance inédite de Victor-François de Broglie avec le prince Xavier de Saxe, comte de Lusace, pour servir à l'histoire de la guerre de sept ans*. 4 Volumes. Paris: Albin Michel, 1905.

Caesar, Gaius Julius. *Civil Wars*. Perseus Digital Library. http://www.perseus.tufts.edu/hopper/text?doc=Perseus:text:1999.02.0076

Caesar, Gaius Julius. *Gallic Wars*. Perseus Digital Library. http://www.perseus.tufts.edu/hopper/text?doc=Perseus:text:1999.02.0001

Caesar, Gaius Julius. *On the African War*. LacusCurtius. https://penelope.uchicago.edu/Thayer/E/Roman/Texts/Caesar/African_War/home.html

Chastellux, François-Jean de Beauvoir, marquis de. *Travels in North America in the Years 1780, 1781, and 1782*. London: Robinson, 1787.

Chevert, François de. *Journal en vers de ce qui s'est passé au camp de Richemont, commandé par Chevert*. Paris Lambert, 1755.

Choiseul, Etienne-François, duc de. *Mémoires*. Paris: Mercure de France, 1982.

Cicero, Marcus Tullius. *De oratore*. 3 Volumes. Cambridge: Harvard University Press, 1979.

Clausewitz, Carl von. *On War*. Edited and Translated by Michael Howard and Peter Paret. Princeton: Princeton University Press, 1989.

Correspondance littéraire, philosophique, et critique. Edited by Denis Diderot and Friedrich Melchoir, baron Grimm.

Coudray, Philippe-Charles-Jean-Baptiste Tronson du. *L'ordre profonde et l'ordre mince considérés par rapport aux effets de l'artillerie: réponse de l'auteur de l'Artillerie nouvelle à Mesnil-Durand et Maïzeroy*. Paris: Rualt et Esprit, 1776.

Coyer, Gabriel-François. *La noblesse commerçante*. Paris: Duchesne, 1756.

Crissé, Lancelot Turpin, comte de Sanzay et. *Commentaire sur les institutions de Végèce*, 3 Volumes. Montargis: 1779.

Crissé, Lancelot Turpin, comte de Sanzay et. *Commentaires de César*. 3 Volumes. Montargis, 1785.

Crissé, Lancelot Turpin, comte de Sanzay et. *Commentaires sur les Mémoires de Montecuccoli*. 3 Volumes. Paris: 1769.

Crissé, Lancelot Turpin, comte de Sanzay et. *Essai sur l'art de la guerre*. 2 Volumes. Paris: 1754.

Dryden, John. *Alexander's Feast, or The Power of Musique*. London: Tonson, 1697.

Dumas, Alexandre. *The Three Musketeers*. New York: Oxford University Press, 2009.

Dumas, Alexandre. *Twenty Years After*. New York: Oxford University Press, 2009.

Dumas, Alexandre. *The Vicomte de Bragelonne*. New York: Oxford University Press, 2009.

Dumouriez, Charles-François du Périer. *Life*. 3 Volumes. London: Johnson, 1796.

Encyclopédie ou dictionnaire raisonné des sciences, des arts, et des métiers. Paris: 1751–1772.

Feuquières, Antoine de Pas, marquis de. *Mémoires contenants ses maximes sur la guerre et l'application des exemples aux maximes*. 4 Volumes. London: Dunoyer, 1736.

Feuquières, Antoine de Pas, marquis de. *Memoirs Historical and Military, Containing a Distinct View of all the Considerable States of Europe*. 2 Volumes. London: Woodward, 1736.

Flavii Vegetii Renati uiri illustris de re militari. Sexti Iuln Frontini uiri consularis de strategematis. Æliani de instuedis aciebus modesti de uocabulis rei militaris, præclara opera nunc demu ad multoru uetustissimoru codicu fide recognita & castigate. Index capiti præfixus est. 1524.

FM 6-0: *Commander and Staff Organization and Operations*. Washington, DC: US Army Publishing Directorate, 2014.

Folard, Jean Charles, chevalier. *Histoire de Polybe*. 7 Volumes. Various, 1753.

Folard, Jean Charles, chevalier. *Nouvelles découvertes sur la guerre, dans une dissertation sur Polybe, où l'on donne une idée plus étendue du commentaire entrepris sur cet auteur, et deux dissertations importantes détaches du corps de l'ouvrage*. Paris: Josse and Labottiere, 1724.

Folard, Jean Charles, chevalier. *Traité de la colonne, la manière de la former et de combattre dans cet ordre*. Amsterdam, 1774.

Friedrich II. *Recueil de lettres de S.M. le Roi de Prusse pour servir à l'histoire de la guerre dernière*. Leipzig, 1772.

FT-05: *The Tactical Commander's Guide to Command and Control in Operations*. Vincennes: Armée de Terre Centre de Doctrine et d'Enseignement du Commandement, 2011.

Guibert, Jacques-Antoine-Hippolyte, comte de. *A General Essay on Tactics*. 2 Volumes. London, 1780.

Guibert, Jacques-Antoine-Hippolyte, comte de. *Considérations militaires et patriotiques*. Avignon.

Guibert, Jacques-Antoine-Hippolyte, comte de. *De la force publique, considérée dans tous ses rapports*. Paris, 1790.

Guibert, Jacques-Antoine-Hippolyte, comte de. *Eloge de Maréchal de Catinat*. Edinburgh, 1775.

Guibert, Jacques-Antoine-Hippolyte, comte de. *Eloge du roi de Prusse*. London, 1787.

Guibert, Jacques-Antoine-Hippolyte, comte de. *Eloge historique de Michel de l'Hôpital, Chancelier de France*. 1777.

Guibert, Jacques-Antoine-Hippolyte, comte de. *Essai général de tactique*. 2 Volumes. Liège: Plomteaux, 1773.

Guibert, Jacques-Antoine-Hippolyte, comte de. *Essai général de tactique*. 2 Volumes. London: Librairies Associés, 1772.

Guibert, Jacques-Antoine-Hippolyte, comte de. *Journal d'un voyage en Allemagne*. 2 Volumes. Paris: Treuttel et Würtz, 1803.

Guibert, Jacques-Antoine-Hippolyte, comte de. *Lettre à M. le comte de Guibert sur les précis de ce qui est arrivé à son égard à l'assemblée du Berry*. 1789.

Guibert, Jacques-Antoine-Hippolyte, comte de. *Œuvres dramatiques*. Paris: Persan, 1822.

Guibert, Jacques-Antoine-Hippolyte, comte de. *Œuvres militaires*. Paris: Magimel, 1803.

Guibert, Jacques-Antoine-Hippolyte, comte de. *Projet de lettre à un citoyen sur son discours projeté aux trois ordres de l'Assemblée de Berry*. 1789.

Guibert, Jacques-Antoine-Hippolyte, comte de. *Voyages de Guibert, dans diverses parties de la France et en Suisse faits en 1775, 1778, 1784, et 1785*. Paris: D'Hautel, 1806.

Guichard, Karl Gottleib. *Mémoires militaires sur les Grecs et les Romains*. 2 Volumes. Den Haag: Hondt, 1758.

Herodotus. *The Histories*. Perseus Digital Library. http://www.perseus.tufts.edu/hopper/text?doc=Perseus:text:1999.01.0126.

Homer, *L'iliade*. Translated by Anne Dacier. Paris: 1699.

Homer. *The Odyssey*. Perseus Digital Library. https://www.perseus.tufts.edu/hopper/text?doc=Perseus:text:1999.01.0136.

Houssaye, Abraham-Nicolas Amelot de la. *Histoire du gouvernement de Venise*. Paris: Léonard, 1676.

Houssaye, Abraham-Nicolas Amelot de la. *Mémoires historiques, politiques, critiques, et littéraires*. 2 Volumes. Amsterdam: Charles le Cene, 1722.

Houssaye, Abraham-Nicolas Amelot de la. *Le prince de Nicolas Machiavel, citoyen de Florence*. Amsterdam: Wetstein, 1684.

Jomini, Antoine-Henri, baron. *The Art of War*. Translated by G.H. Mendell. Boston: Lippincott, 1962.

La Fontaine. *La doctrine militaire ou le parfait général d'armée*. Paris: Loyson, 1671.

The Landmark Herodotus. Edited by Robert Strassler. Translated by Andrea Purvis. New York: Vintage Books, 2007.

The Landmark Thucydides: A Comprehensive Guide to the Peloponnesian War. Edited by Robert Strassler. New York: Free Press, 1996.

Lespinasse, Julie de. *The Love Letters of Mlle. de Lespinasse to and from the Comte de Guibert*. Edited by Armand Villeneuve-Guibert. Translated by E.H.F. Mills. London: Routledge, 1929.

Le Blond, Guillaume. *L'artillerie raisonnée*. Paris: Jombert, 1761.

Le Blond, Guillaume. *The Elements of Fortification*. Philadelphia: Wayne, 1801.

Le Blond, Guillaume. *A Treatise of the Attack of Fortified Places*. London: Cave, 1748.

"Lettre d'un officier-général d'artillerie aux auteurs de ce journal au sujet d'un livre nouveau en deux volumes qui à pour titre *Défense du système de la guerre moderne ou réfutation complette du système de Mesnil-Durand* par l'auteur de l'*Essai général de tactique*." *Journal encyclopédique ou universel* 4 (1779): 300–306.

Livius, Titus. *The History of Rome*. Perseus Digital Library. http://www.perseus.tufts.edu/hopper/text?doc=Perseus:text:1999.02.0145.

Lloyd, Henry. *The History of the Late War in Germany between the King of Prussia and the Empress of Germany and her Allies*. London, 1766.

Lloyd, Henry. *War, Society, and Enlightenment: The Works of General Lloyd*. Patrick Speelman, editor. Leiden: Brill, 2005.

Louis XVI and the comte de Vergennes: Correspondence, 1774–1787. Edited by John Hardman and Munro Price. Liverpool: Liverpool University Press, 1998.

Machiavelli, Niccolò. *Œuvres de Machiavel*. 8 Volumes. Paris: Volland, 1793.

Maïzeroy, Paul-Gédéon Joly de. *Cours de tactique théorique, pratique, et historique*. 2 Volumes. Paris, 1766.

Maïzeroy, Paul-Gédéon Joly de. *Institutions militaires de l'empereur Léon le Philosophe*. 2 Volumes. Paris: Jombert, 1771.

Maïzeroy, Paul-Gédéon Joly de. *Mémoire sur les opinions qui partagent les militaires*. Paris: Jombert, 1773.

Maro, Publius Vergilius. *The Aeneid*. New York: Oxford University Press, 2015.

Melfort, Louis Drummond, comte de. *Traité sur la cavalerie*. Paris: Desprez, 1776.

Mesnil-Durand, François-Jean de Graindorge d'Orgeville, baron de. *Collection de diverses pièces et mémoires*. 2 Volumes. Amsterdam, 1780.

Mesnil-Durand, François-Jean de Graindorge d'Orgeville, baron de. *Fragments de tactique* [mémoires 7–9]. Paris: Jombert, 1776.

Mesnil-Durand, François-Jean de Graindorge d'Orgeville, baron de. *Fragments de tactique: ou six mémoires*. Paris: Jombert, 1774.

Mesnil-Durand, François-Jean de Graindorge d'Orgeville, baron de. *Observations sur le canon par rapport à l'infanterie en général et à la colonne en particulier, suives de quelques extraits de l'essai sur l'usage de l'artillerie*. Paris: Jombert, 1772.

Mesnil-Durand, François Jean de Graindorge d'Orgeville, baron de. *Projet d'un ordre français en tactique, ou la phalange coupée et doublée soutenue par le mélange des armes*. Paris: Boudet, 1755.

Mesnil-Durand, François-Jean de Graindorge d'Orgeville, baron de. *Réflexions sur l'ordre et les manœuvres de l'infanterie: extraites d'un mémoire écrit en 1776*. Paris: Nicolle, 1778.

Mesnil-Durand, François-Jean de Graindorge d'Orgeville, baron de. *Suite du projet d'un ordre français n tactique pour servir de supplément à cet ouvrage et preparer à en faire usage pour le service du roi*. Paris: Jombert, 1758.

Moheau, Jean-Baptiste. *Recherches et considerations sur la population de la France*. Paris: Moutard, 1778.

Montecuccoli, Raimundo. *Mémoires*. Edited by Lancelot Turpin de Crissé. Amsterdam/Leipzig: Artkée & Merkus, 1770.

Montesquieu, Charles-Louis Secondat, baron de la Brède et de. *De l'esprit des lois*. Paris: Gallimard, 1995.

Montesquieu, Charles-Louis Secondat, baron de la Brède et de. *Lettres persanes*. Paris: Garnier, 1960.

Montesquieu, Charles-Louis Secondat, baron de la Brède et de. *The Spirit of the Laws*. New York: Cambridge University Press, 1989.

Morogues, Sébastien-François bigot, vicomte de. *Tactique navale, ou traité des évolutions et des signaux*. Paris: Guerin & Delatour, 1763.

Morris, Gouverneur. *Diary and Letters*. 2 Volumes. New York: C. Scribner's Sons, 1888.

Naso, Publius Ovidius. *Metamorphosis*. 2 Volumes. New York: Harper & Brothers, 1872.

Ordonnance du roi pour régler l'exercice de ses troupes d'infanterie du 1er juin 1776. 1776.

Orval, Edmé-Jean-Antoine du Puget d'. *Essai sur l'usage de l'artillerie dans la guerre de campagne et dans celle des sieges*. Amsterdam: Arckstée et Merkus, 1771.

Pictet, Gabriel. *Essai sur la tactique de l'infanterie: ouvrage méthodique où l'on trouve en detail et par ordre*. 2 Volumes. Amsterdam/Geneva, 1761.

Pollio, Marcus Vitruvius. *Ten Books of Architecture*. Perseus Digital Library. http://www.perseus.tufts.edu/hopper/text?doc=Perseus:text:1999.02.0073

Polybius. *Histories*. Perseus Digital Library. http://www.perseus.tufts.edu/hopper/text?doc=Perseus:text:1999.01.0234

Puységur, Jacques-François de Chastenet, marquis de. *Art de la guerre par principes et par règles*. 2 Volumes. Paris, 1749.

Puységur, Louis-Pierre de Chastenet, comte de. *Etat actuel de l'art et de la science militaire à la Chine*. Paris: Didot, 1773.

Raynal, Guillaume-Thomas-François. *A Philosophical and Political History of the Settlements and Trade of the Europeans in the East and West Indies*. 10 Volumes. London Strahan and Cadell, 1783.

Recueil des nouvelles ordonnances du roi relatives à la constitution actuelle de l'état militaire. 5 Volumes. Collignon: Metz, 1776–1777.

Regnard, Jean-François. *Œuvres complètes*. 6 Volumes. Paris: Brière, 1832.

Richelieu, Armand Cardinal Jean du Plessis, duc de Fronsac et de. *The Political Testament of Cardinal Richelieu*. Translated by Henry Hill. Madison: University of Wisconsin Press, 1961.

Rochambeau, Jean-Baptiste-Donatien de Vimeur, comte de. *Mémoires militaires, historiques, et politiques*. 2 Volumes. Paris: Fain, 1809.

Roguet, François, comte. "Etude sur l'ordre perpendiculaire." *Le spectateur militiaire* 18 (1934): 484–527.

Rohan, Henri, duc de. *Le parfait capitaine*. Paris: 1639.

Rules and Regulations for the Field Exercise and Maneuvers of the French Infantry issued August 1, 1791, and the Maneuvers Added which has been since Adopted by the Emperor Napoleon; also, the Maneuvers of the Field Artillery with the Infantry. Edited and Translated by Irenée Amelot de Lacroix, Irenée Amelot. Boston: T.B. Wait, 1810.

Saint-Germain, Claude-Louis, comte de. *Mémoires et commentaires*. London, 1781.

Saint-Pierre, Charles-Irénée Castel de. *Projet pour render la paix perpétuelle en Europe*. 3 Volumes. Utrecht: Schouten, 1713–1717.

Saint-Remy, Pierre Surirey de. *Mémoires d'artillerie*. 6 Volumes. Paris: Rollin, 1745.

Santa Cruz de Marcenado, Alvaro de Navia-Orosio y Virgil de la Rúa, vizconde del Puerto, marqués de. *Réflexions militaires et politiques*. 12 Volumes. Various, 1724–1730.

Saxe, Maurice de. *Mes rêveries*. Amsterdam: Arkstée et Merkus, 1751.

Siculus, Diodorus. *Library of History*. LacusCurtius. http://penelope.uchicago.edu/Thayer/E/Roman/Texts/Diodorus_Siculus/23*.html

Staël-Holstein, Anna-Louise-Germaine. *Mémoires*. Paris: Charpentier, 1843.

Tacticus, Æneas. *On the Defense of Fortified Positions*. London: Loeb, 1928.

Toulongeon, François-Emmanuel. "Notice historique de Jacques-Antoine-Hippolyte Guibert, écrit en 1790." *Journal d'un voyage en Allemagne*. Paris: Treuttel et Würtz, 1803. 1–85.

Tranquillus, Gaius Suetonius, *Lives of the Caesars*. Perseus Digital Library. http://www.perseus.tufts.edu/hopper/text?doc=Perseus:text:1999.02.0132

Vauban, Sébastien le Prestre, siegneur de. *The New Method of Fortification*. Abel Swall, translator. London, 1691.

Vegetius, Flavius Renatus. *Epitome of Military Science*. Translated by N.P. Milner. Liverpool: Liverpool University Press, 2001.

Vernon, Simon François Gay de. *Traité élémentaire d'art militaire et de fortification, à l'usage des élèves de l'Ecole Polytechnique et des élèves des écoles militaires*. 2 Volumes. Paris: Allais, 1805.

Voltaire. *History of Charles XII, King of Sweden*. Edinburg: Black, 1887.

Voltaire. *Letters Concerning the English Nation*. New York: Oxford University Press, 2009.

Voltaire. *Oeuvres completes*. Volume 1. Paris, 1830.

Secondary

A Cultural History of Peace in the Age of Enlightenment. Edited by David Armitage and Stella Ghervas. New York: Bloomsbury, 2023.

Abel, Jonathan. "An Aspect of the Military Experience in the Age of Reason: The Evolution of the Combined-Arms Division in Old-Regime France." In *The Changing Face of Old Regime Warfare: Essays in Honor of Chirstopher Duffy*, 140–160. Warwick: Helion, 2022.

Abel, Jonathan. "Jacques Antoine Hippolyte, comte de Guibert." *Oxford Bibliographies Online*, 2014. http://www.oxfordbibliographies.com/view/document/obo-9780199791279/obo-9780199791279-0037.xml

Abel, Jonathan. *Guibert: Father of Napoleon's Grande Armée*. Norman: University of Oklahoma Press, 2016.

Adamson, Peter. *Medieval Philosophy*. New York: Oxford University Press, 2019.

Aksan, Virginia. *Ottoman Wars 1700–1870: An Empire Besieged*. New York: Pearson, 2007.

Allmand, Christopher. *The De re militari of Vegetius: The Reception, Transmission, and Legacy of a Roman Text in the Middle Ages*. Cambridge, UK: Cambridge University Press, 2011.

Anderson, M.S. *War and Society in Europe of the Old Regime, 1617–1789*. New York: St. Martin's Press, 1988.

Anderson, M.S. *The War of the Austrian Succession, 1740–1748*. New York: Longman, 1995.

Antoine, Michel. *Louis XV*. Paris: Fayard, 1989.

Aragon, Marie-Christine d'. *Julie de Lespinasse*. Paris: Ramsay, 1980.

Asprey, Robert. *Frederick the Great: The Magnificent Enigma*. New York: Ticknor & Fields, 1986.

Baer, Friederike. *Hessians: German Soldiers in the American Revolutionary War*. New York: Oxford University Press, 2022.

Bainville, Jacques. *Napoléon*. Digicat, 2022.

Barbiche, Bernard. *Les institutions de la monarchie française à l'époque moderne*. Paris: Presses Universitaires de France, 1999.

Bardin, Etienne-Alexandre, baron. *Dictionnaire de l'armée de terre ou recherches historiques sur l'art et les usages militaires des anciens et modernes*. 17 Volumes. Paris: Corréard, 1841–1851.

Bardin, Etienne-Alexandre, baron. *Notice historique sur Guibert*. Paris: Corréard jeune, 1836.

Barker, Juliet. *Conquest: The English Kingdom of France, 1417–1450*. Cambridge: Harvard University Press, 2013.

Baugh, Daniel. *The Global Seven Years War 1754–1763: Britain and France in a Great Power Contest*. New York: Routledge, 2011.

Beasley, Faith. *Salons, History, and the Creation of Seventeenth-Century France: Mastering Memory*. Burlington, VT: Ashgate, 2006.

Bégin, Emile-August. *Biographie de la Moselle*. 4 Volumes. Metz, 1832.

Beik, William. *Urban Protest in Seventeenth-Century France: The Culture of Retribution*. New York: Cambridge University Press, 1997.

Berkovich, Ilya. *Motivation in War: The Experience of Common Soldiers in Old-Regime Europe*. New York: Cambridge University Press, 2017.

Best, Geoffrey. *War and Society in Revolutionary Europe, 1770–1870*. New York: St. Martin's Press, 1982.

Bien, David, et al. *Caste, Class, and Profession in Old Regime France: The French Army and the Ségur Reform of 1781*. St. Andrews: Centre for French History and Culture, 2010.

Bien, David. "Military Education in 18th Century France: Technical and Non-Technical Determinants." *Science, Technology,* and Warfare: Proceedings of the Third Military History Symposium, U.S. Air Force Academy, 8–9 May 1969.* Edited by Monte D. Wright and Lawrence J. Paszek. (1971): 51–59.

Bien, David. "The Army in the French Enlightenment: Reform, Reaction, and Revolution." *Past & Present* 85 (1979): 68–98.

Bien, David, and Godneff, Nina. "Les offices, les corps et le crédit d'état: l'utilisation des privilèges sous l'Ancien Régime." *Annales. Histoire, Sciences Sociales* 43e Année. (1988): 397–404.

Bien, David, and Rovet, J. "La réaction aristocratique avant 1789: L'exemple de l'armée." *Annales. Histoire, Sciences Sociales* 29ᵉ Année no. 3 (1974): 505–534.

Bien, David. and Rovet, J. "La réaction aristocratique avant 1798: L'exemple de l'armée." *Annales. Histoire, Sciences Sociales* 29ᵉ Année no. 2 (1974): 23–48.

Billows, Richard. *Julius Caesar: The Colossus of Rome.* London: Routledge, 2009.

Biographie universelle ancienne et moderne. Edited by Louis-Gabriel Michaud. 45 Volumes. Paris: Desplaces, 1842–1865.

Black, Jeremy. *European Warfare, 1660–1815.* New Haven, CT: Yale University Press, 1994.

Black, Jeremy. *Warfare in the Eighteenth Century.* London: Cassell, 1999.

Blanchard, Joël. "Louis XI, King of France." *Oxford Bibliographies Online,* 2022. https://www.oxfordbibliographies.com/display/document/obo-9780195399301/obo-9780195399301-0491.xml.

Blanning, T.C.W. *The Culture of Power and the Power of Culture: Old Regime Europe 1660–1789.* New York: Oxford University Press, 2006.

Blaufarb, Rafe. "Noble Privilege and Absolutist State Building: French Military Administration after the Seven Years War." *French Historical Studies* 24 (2001): 223–246.

Blaufarb, Rafe. *The French Army, 1750–1820: Careers, talent, merit.* New York: Manchester University Press, 2002.

Bond, Brian. *War and Society in Europe, 1870–1970.* Montreal: McGill-Queen's University Press, 1998.

Bouissounouse, Janine. *Julie: The Life of Mademoiselle de Lespinasse: her Salon, her Friends, her Loves.* Translated by Pierre de Fontnouvelle. New York: Appleton-Century-Crofts, 1962.

Brewer, John. *The Sinews of Power: War, Money, and the English State.* Cambridge: Harvard University Press, 1990.

Brialmont, Alexis. *Précis d'art militaire.* Brussels, 1850.

Broglie, Albert. *Le secret du roi.* New York: Cassel, 1879.

Brown, Howard. *War, Revolution, and the Bureaucratic State: Politics and Army Administration in France 1791–1799.* New York: Oxford University Press, 2004.

Browning, Reed. *The War of the Austrian Succession.* New York: St. Martin's Griffin, 1995.

Buffington, Arthur H. *The Second Hundred Years War, 1689–1815.* New York: Holt and Co., 1929.

Buisseret, David. *Henry IV.* London: Allen & Unwin, 1984.

The Cambridge New Medieval History. 7 Volumes. New York: Cambridge University Press, 2008.

Cameron, Iain. "The Police of Eighteenth-Century France." *European Studies Review* 7 (1977): 47–75.

Camon, Hubert. *Quand et comment Napoléon a conçu son système de bataille.* Paris, 1935.

Camon, Hubert. *Quand et comment Napoléon a conçu son système de manœuvre.* Paris: 1931.

Carlyle, Thomas. *History of Friedrich the Second, Called Frederick the Great.* 8 Volumes. New York: John B. Alden, 1885.

Cartledge, Paul. *Thermopylae: The Battle that Changed the World.* Woodstock, NY: Overlook, 2006.

Cassirer, Ernst. *The Philosophy of the Enlightenment.* Boston: Beacon Press, 1955.

Censer, Jack. *The French Press in the Age of Enlightenment.* New York: Routledge, 1994.

Chagniot, Jean. *Le chevalier de Folard: la stratégie de l'incertitude.* Paris: Editions du Rocher, 1997.

Chartier, Roger. *The Cultural Origins of the French Revolution.* Translated by Lydia Cochrane. Durham, NC: Duke University Press, 1991.

Chet, Guy. *Conquering the American Wilderness: The Triumph of European Warfare in the Colonial Northeast.* Amherst: University of Massachusetts Press, 2003.

Childs, John. *Armies and Warfare in Europe, 1648–1789.* Manchester: Manchester University Press, 1982.

Childs, John. *Warfare in the Seventeenth Century.* Washington, DC: Smithsonian Books, 2006.

Citino, Robert. *The German Way of War: From the Thirty Years War to the Third Reich.* Lawrence: University Press of Kansas, 2012.

Clark, Christopher. *Iron Kingdom: The Rise and Downfall of Prussia, 1600–1947.* Cambridge: Belknap, 2006.

Clausewitz, Carl von. *On War.* Edited by Michael Howard and Peter Paret. Princeton: Princeton University Press, 1984.

Cole, Charles. *Colbert and a Century of French Mercantilism.* 2 Volumes. New York: Columbia University Press, 1939.

Colin, Jean. *L'éducation militaire de Napoléon.* Paris: R. Chapelot, 1901.

Colin, Jean. *L'infanterie au XVIIIᵉ siècle. La tactique.* Paris: Berger-Levrault, 1907.

Collins, James. *The Fiscal Limits of Absolutism: Direct Taxation in Early Modern France.* Berkeley: University of California Press, 1988.

Collins, James. *The State in Early Modern France.* New York: Cambridge University Press, 2009.

Corvisier, André. *Armies and Societies in Europe, 1494–1789.* Translated by Abigail T. Siddall. Bloomington: Indiana University Press, 1979.

Corvisier, André. *Les contrôles des troupes de l'ancien régime.* 2 Volumes. Paris, 1970.

Craveri, Benedetta. *Madame du Deffand and Her World.* Translated by Teresa Waugh. Boston: David R. Godine, 1994.

The Crisis of the Absolute Monarchy. Edited by Julian Swann and Joël Félix. New York: Oxford University Press, 2013.

Cultures of Power in Europe during the Long Eighteenth Century. Edited by Hamish Scott and Brendan Simms. New York: Cambridge University Press, 2007.

The Culture of Print: Power and the Uses of Print in Early Modern Europe. Edited by Roger Chartier. Translated by Lydia Cochrane. Princeton: Princeton University Press, 1987.

D'Auria, Matthew. *The Shaping of French National Identity: Narrating the Nation's Past, 1715–1830.* New York: Cambridge University Press, 2020.

Daly, Kevin. "Ancient Thebes." *Oxford Bibliographies Online*, 2021. https://www.oxfordbibliographies.com/display/document/obo-9780195389661/obo-9780195389661-0362.xml.

The Darnton Debate: Books and Revolution in the Eighteenth Century. Edited by Haydn Mason. Oxford: Voltaire Foundation, 1998.

Darnton, Robert. *The Business of the Enlightenment: A Publishing History of the "Encyclopédie."* Cambridge, MA: Harvard University Press, 1979.

Darnton, Robert. *The Corpus of Clandestine Literature in France, 1769–1789.* New York: W.W. Norton & Co., 1995.

Darnton, Robert. *The Forbidden Bestsellers of Pre-Revolutionary France.* New York: W.W. Norton & Co., 1995.

Darnton, Robert. *The Literary Underground of the Old Regime.* Cambridge: Harvard University Press, 1982.

David, Alexandre. *Joly de Maïzeroy: l'inventeur de la stratégie.* Paris: Ecole de Guerre, 2018.

Davies, Brian. *Warfare, State, and Society on the Black Sea Steppe, 1500–1700.* New York: Routledge, 2007.

Davies, Norman. *God's Playground: A History of Poland.* Volume 1: *Origins to 1795.* New York: Oxford University Press, 2005.

DeJean, Joan. *Ancients Against Moderns: Culture Wars and the Making of a Fin de Siècle.* Chicago: University of Chicago Press, 1997.

Delbrück, Hans. *History of the Art of War.* Lincoln: University of Nebraska Press, 1990.

Devos, Jean-Claude, et al. *Inventaire des archives de la guerre: sous-série Y^a.* Vincennes, 2003.

DeVries, Kelly. "Catapults are not Atomic Bombs: Towards a Redefinition of 'Effectiveness' in Premodern Military Technology." *War in History* 4, no. 4 (1997): 454–470.

DeVries, Kelly. *Guns and Men in Medieval Europe, 1200–1500: Studies in Military History and Technology.* Burlington, VT: Ashgate, 2002.

DeVries, Kelly. *Infantry Warfare in the Early Fourteenth Century: Discipline, Tactics, and Technology.* Woodbridge, UK: Boydell Press, 1996.

Dewald, Jonathan. *The French Nobility in the Eighteenth Century: Reassessments and New Approaches.* University Park, PA: Pennsylvania State University Press, 2006.

Dictionnaire de l'Académie française. First through Ninth Editions. Paris: Académie française, 1694–2020.

Dictionnaire militaire portatif contenant tous les termes propres à la guerre. 3 Volumes. Paris: Duchesne, 1758.

Doniol, Henri. *Histoire de la participation de la France à l'établissement des Etats-Unis d'Amérique.* 6 Volumes. Paris: Imprimerie nationale, 1886–1892.

Doyle, William. *Jansenism: Catholic Resistance to Authority from the Reformation to the French Revolution.* New York: St. Martin's, 2000.

Doyle, William. *The Origins of the French Revolution.* New York: Oxford University Press, 1980.

Doyle, William. *The Oxford History of the French Revolution.* New York: Oxford University Press, 2018.

Doyle, William. *Venality: The Sale of Offices in Eighteenth-Century France.* Oxford: Oxford University Press, 1966.

Duby, Georges. *The Legend of Bouvines: War, Religion, and Culture in the Middle Ages.* Translated by Catherine Tihanyi. Berkeley: University of California Pres, 1990.

Duffy, Christopher. *Fire & Stone: The Science of Fortress Warfare 1660–1860.* Edison, NJ: Castle Books, 2006.

Duffy, Christopher. *Russia's Military Way to the West: Origins and Nature of Russian Military Power, 1700–1800.* New York: Routledge, 1985.

Duffy, Christopher. *The Army of Frederick the Great.* Warwick: Helion, 2018.

Duffy, Christopher. *The Army of Maria Theresa: The Armed Forces of Imperial Austria, 1740–1780.* New York: Hippocrene, 1977.

Duffy, Christopher. *The Austrian Army in the Seven Years War.* 2 Volumes. Chicago: Emperor's Press, 2000–2008.

Duffy, Christopher. *The Military Experience in the Age of Reason.* New York: Atheneum, 1988.

Duffy, Christopher. *The Military Life of Frederick the Great.* New York: Atheneum, 1986.

Duffy, Christopher. *Prussia's Glory: Rossbach and Leuthen 1757.* Rosemont, IL: Emperor's Press, 2004.

Dull, Jonathan. *A Diplomatic History of the American Revolution.* New Haven: Yale University Press, 1985.

Dull, Jonathan. *The French Navy and American Independence: A Study of Arms and Diplomacy.* Princeton: Princeton University Press, 1975.

Easum, Chester Verne. *Prince Henry of Prussia, Brother of Frederick the Great.* Madison: WI: University of Wisconsin Press, 1942.

Eckberg, Carl. *The Failure of Louis XIV's Dutch War.* Chapel Hill: University of North Carolina Press, 1979.

Egret, Jean. *The French Pre-Revolution 1787–1789.* Translated by Wesley Camp. Chicago: University of Chicago Press, 1994.

Elliot, John. *Imperial Spain, 1469–1716*. New York: St. Martin's, 1964.

Elting, John. *Swords Around a Throne: Napoleon's Grande Armée*. New York: Free Press, 1988.

Ermus, Cindy. *THe Great Plague Scare of 1720: Disaster and Diplomacy in the Eighteenth-Century Atlantic World*. New York: Cambridge University Press, 2023.

The European Fiscal-Military System 1530–1870. https://fiscalmilitary.history.ox.ac.uk/.

The Evolution of Operational Art: From Napoleon to the Present. Edited by John Andreas Olsen and Martin van Creveld. New York: Oxford University Press, 2011.

Farge, Arlette. *Subversive Words: Public Opinion in Eighteenth-Century France*. Translated by Rosemary Morris. University Park, PA: Penn State University Press, 1995.

Ferling, John. *Almost a Miracle: The American Victory in the War of Independence*. New York: Oxford University Press, 2007.

Finkel, Caroline. *Osman's Dream: The Story of the Ottoman Empire, 1300–1923*. New York: Basic Books, 2003.

Foucault, Michel. *Discipline and Punish: The Birth of the Prison*. Translated by Alan Sheridan. New York: Vintage Books, 1995.

Forestié, Emerand. *Biographie du Cte. de Guibert*. Montauban, 1855.

France, John. *Western Warfare in the Age of the Crusades, 1000–1300*. Ithaca: Cornell University Press, 1999.

Francis, Alan. *The First Peninsular War 1702–1713*. London: Benn, 1975.

French Women and the Age of Enlightenment. Edited by Samia I. Spencer. Bloomington, IN: Indiana University Press, 1984.

Frost, Robert. *The Northern Wars: War, State, and Society in Northeastern Europe, 1558–1721*. New York: Longman, 2000.

Furet, François. *Interpreting the French Revolution*. New York: Cambridge University Press, 1981.

Gambier-Parry, Mark. *Madame Necker: Her Family and her Friends*. London: W. Blackwood and Sons, 1913.

Garros, Louis. *Napoléon, cet inconnu*. Paris: Beaudart, 1950.

Gat, Azar. *A History of Military Thought from the Enlightenment to the Cold War*. New York: Oxford University Press, 2001.

Gay, Peter. *The Age of Enlightenment*. New York: Time, 1996.

Gay, Peter. *The Enlightenment: A Comprehensive Anthology*. New York: Simon and Schuster, 1973.

Gay, Peter. *The Enlightenment: An Interpretation: The Rise of Modern Paganism*. New York: Knopf, 1969.

Geary, Patrick. *Before France and Germany: The Creation and Transformation of the Merovingian World*. New York: Oxford University Press, 1988.

Gebelin, Jacques. *Histoire des milices provinciales (1688–1791): le tirage au sort sous l'ancien régime*. Paris: Hachette, 1882.

Ghervas, Stella. *Conquering Peace from the Enlightenment to the European Union*. Cambridge: Harvard University Press, 2021.

Gibbon, Edward. *The History of the Decline and Fall of the Roman Empire*. 3 Volumes. New York: Penguin, 2005.

Goldsworthy, Adrian. *Caesar: Life of a Colossus*. New Haven: Yale University Pres, 2006.

Goldsworthy, Adrian. *The Punic Wars*. London: Cassel, 2000.

Goldsworthy, Adrian. *The Roman Army at War, 100 BC-AD 200*. New York: Oxford University Press, 1996.

Gooch, G.P. *Louis XV: The Monarchy in Decline*. New York: Longmans, 1956.

Goodman, Dena. *The Republic of Letters: A Cultural History of the French Enlightenment*. Ithaca, NY: Cornell University Press, 1994.

Granier, Raymond. "Ou est né le Maréchal Guibert?" *Actes du congrès des sociétés savantes. Section d'histoire moderne et contemporaine* 77 (1952): 29–33.

Green, Peter. *Alexander of Macedon, 356–323 BC: A Historical Biography*. Berkeley: University of California Press, 1991.

Green, Peter. *The Greco-Persian Wars*. Berkeley: University of California Press, 2008.

Grenier, John. *The First Way of War: American War Making on the Frontier, 1607–1814*. New York: Cambridge University Press, 2005.

Griffith, Paddy. *The Art of War of Revolutionary France 1789–1802*. Mechanicsburg, PA: Stackpole Books, 1998.

Groffier, Ethel. *Le stratège des lumières: le comte de Guibert (1743–1790)*. Paris: Editions Champion, 2005.

Guibert ou le soldat philosophe. Edited by Jean-Paul Charnay. Paris: Chateau de Vincennes, 1981.

Guízar, Haroldo, *The Ecole Royale Militaire: Noble Education, Institutional Innovation, and Royal Charity, 1750–1788*. New York: Palgrave Macmillan, 2020.

Guyot-Desfontaines, Pierre. *Histoire des ducs de Bretagne et des différentes revolutions arrives dans cette province*. 6 Volumes. Paris: Clousier, 1739.

Habermas, Jürgen. *The Structural Transformation of the Public Sphere: An Inquiry into a Category of Bourgeois Society*. Translated by Thomas Burger. Cambridge: MIT Press, 1989.

Haldon, John. *Warfare, State, and Society in the Byzantine World 565–1204*. New York: Routledge, 1999.

Hall, Thadd. *France and the Eighteenth-Century Corsican Question*. New York: New York University Press, 1971.

Hardman, John. *French Politics 1774–1789: From the Accession of Louis XIV to the Fall of the Bastille*. New York: Longman, 1995.

Hardman, John. *Louis XVI*. New York: Cambridge University Press, 1993.

Hardman, John. *Overture to Revolution: The 1787 Assembly of Notables and the Crisis of France's Old Regime*. New York: Oxford University Press, 2010.

Hayter, Tony. *The Army and the Crowd in Mid-Georgian England*. Totowa, NJ: Rowman and Littlefield, 1978.

Heath, Thomas. *Aristarchus of Samos: A History of Greek Astronomy to Aristarchus*. New York: Cambridge University Press, 2013.

Heuser, Beatrice. *The Evolution of Strategy: Thinking War from Antiquity to the Present*. New York: Cambridge University Press, 2010.

Heuser, Beatrice. "Guibert: Prophet of Total War?" *War in an Age of Revolution, 1775–1815*. Edited by Roger Chickering and Stig Förster, 49–67. New York: Cambridge University Press, 2010.

Heuser, Beatrice. *The Strategy Makers: Thoughts on War and Society from Machiavelli to Clausewitz*. Santa Barbara, CA: Praeger, 2010.

Hickson, Michael. "Pierre Bayle." *Oxford Bibliographies Online*, 2022. https://www.oxfordbibliographies.com/display/document/obo-9780195399301/obo-9780195399301-0482.xml.

Higgonet, Patrice. "The Origins of the Seven Years War." *Journal of Modern History* 40, number 1. (1968): 57–90.

Histoire du 1er régiment de cuirassiers. Angers: Lachèse & Dolbeau, 1889.

Holt, Mack. *The French Wars of Religion, 1562–1629*. New York: Cambridge University Press, 2005.

Hoock, Holger. "Mangled Bodies: Atrocity in the American Revolutionary War." *Past & Present* 230 (2016): 123–159.

Hornung, Eric. *History of Ancient Egypt*. Edinburgh: Edinburgh University Press, 1999.

Hughes, Lindsey. *Russia in the Age of Peter the Great*. New Haven: Yale University Press, 2000.

Hume, David. *Histoire d'angleterre depuis l'invasion de Jules César jusqu'à l'avenement de Henri VII*. 6 Volumes. Amsterdam, 1765.

Hume, David. *The History of England from the Invasion of Julius Caesar to the Abdication of James II, 1688*. 8 Volumes. London: Cadell, 1770.

Huntington, Samuel P. *The Soldier and the State: The Theory of Politics and Civil-Military Relations*. Cambridge: Harvard University Press, 1957.

Imber, Colin. *The Ottoman Empire: 1300–1650: The Structures of Power*. New York: Palgrave, 2009.

Impey, Oliver. *Chinoiserie: The Impact of Oriental Styles on Western Art and Decoration*. New York: Oxford University Press, 1977.

"L'influence de la pensée militaire antique dans la réforme oranienne: entre appel au passé et recherche de solutions nouvelles," *La revue d'histoire militaire*, 2022. https://larevuedhistoiremilitaire.fr/2022/05/25/linfluence-de-la-pensee-militaire-antique-dans-la-reforme-oranienne-entre-appel-au-passe-et-recherche-de-solutions-nouvelles/.

Israel, Jonathan. *The Dutch Republic: Its Rise, Its Greatness, and Fall, 1477–1806*. New York: Oxford University Press, 1995.

Jacobs, Paul, and Conlin, Diane Atnally. *Campus Martius: The Field of Mars in the Life of Ancient Rome*. New York: Cambridge University Press, 2015.

James, Edward. *The Franks*. New York: Blackwell, 1988.

Janin, Hunt. *Medieval Justice: Cases and Law in France, England, and Germany, 500–1500*. Jefferson, NC: McFarland, 2009.

Jaurgain, Jean de. *Notice sur les familles Vallet et Villeneuve-Guibert*. Paris: Imprimerie de la Cour d'Appel, 1893.

Jebb, Camilla. *The Star of the Salons: Julie de Lespinasse*. New York: G.P. Putnam's Sons, 1908.

Jombert, Charles-Antoine. *Dictionnaire portatif de l'ingénieur et de l'artilleur*. Paris: Jombert, 1768.

Jomini, Antoine Henri, baron de. *Précis sur l'art de guerre*. Paris, 1836.

Kale, Steven. *French Salons: High Society and Political Sociability from the Old Regime to the Revolution of 1848*. Baltimore: Johns Hopkins University Press, 2004.

Kaplan, Herbert. *The First Partition of Poland*. New York: Columbia University Press, 1962.

Karges, Caleb. "Eugene of Savoy," *Oxford Bibliographies Online*, 2023. https://www.oxfordbibliographies.com/display/document/obo-9780199791279/obo-9780199791279-0238.xml.

Kennett, Lee. *The French Armies in the Seven Years War: A Study in Military Organization and Administration*. Durham: Duke University Press, 1967.

Kettering, Sharon. *French Society, 1589–1715*. London: Routledge, 2017.

Kiley, Kevin. *Artillery of the Napoleonic Wars 1792–1815*. Mechanicsburg, PA: Stackpole Books, 2004.

Knox, MacGregor and Murray, Williamson. *The Dynamics of Military Revolution, 1300–2050*. New York: Cambridge University Press, 2001.

Komlos, John; Hau, Michael; and Bourguinat, Nicolas. "An Anthropometric History of Early-Modern France." *European Review of Economic History* 7, no. 2 (2003): 159–189.

Kwass, Michael. *Privilege and the Politics of Taxation in Eighteenth-Century France*. New York: Cambridge University Press, 2000.

Lacour-Gayet, Georges. *La marine militaire de la France sous le règne de Louis XIV*. Paris: Champion, 1905.

Latreille, Albert. *L'œuvre militaire de la révolution: l'armée et la nation à la fin de l'ancien régime; les derniers ministres de la guerre de la monarchie*. Paris: Chapelot, 1914.

Lauerma, Matti. *Jacques-Antoine-Hippolyte de Guibert (1743–1790)*. Helsinki: Suomalainen Tiedeakatemia, 1989.

Le Beau, Charles. *Histoire du Bas-Empire en commençant à Constantin le Grand*. 27 Volumes. 1757–1811.

Le Roux, Nicholas. *Les guerres de religion (1559–1629)*. Paris: Bellin, 2009.

Le Roy Ladurie, Emmanuel. *The Ancien Régime: A History of France, 1610–1774*. Translated by Mark Greenglass. New York: Wiley-Blackwell, 1998.

Le Roy Ladurie, Emmanuel. *The Royal French State, 1460–1610*. Translated by Juliet Vale. Oxford: Blackwell, 1987.

Lendon, J. E. *Soldiers and Ghosts: A History of Battle in Classical Antiquity*. New Haven: Yale University Press, 2005.

Les ministres de la guerre 1570–1792. Edited by Thierry Sarmant. Paris: Bellin, 2007.

Liddel-Hart, Basil. *Strategy*. New York: Praeger, 1967.

Lintott, Andrew. *The Constitution of the Roman Republic*. New York: Oxford University Press, 2009.

Lomas, Kathryn. *The Rise of Rome from the Iron Age to the Punic Wars*. Cambridge: Harvard University Press, 2018.

Luvaas, Jay. *Napoleon on the Art of War*. New York: Simon & Schuster, 1999.

Lynn, John. "Recalculating French Army Growth during the Grand Siècle, 1610–1715." *French Historical Studies* 18 (1994): 881–906.

Lynn, John. "Toward an Army of Honor: The Moral Evolution of the French Army, 1789–1815." *French Historical Studies* 16 (1989): 152–173.

Lynn, John. *Giant of the Grand Siècle: The French Army, 1610–1715*. New York: Cambridge University Press, 2006.

Lynn, John. *The Bayonets of the Republic: Motivation and Tactics in the Army of Revolutionary France, 1791–94*. Urbana: University of Illinois Press, 1984.

Lynn, John. *The Wars of Louis XIV 1667–1714*. New York: Longman, 1999.

Mackesy, Piers. *The Coward of Minden: The Affair of Lord George Sackville*. London, 1979.

Mahan, Alfred. *The Influence of Sea Power upon History 1660–1783*. Boston: Little, Brown, and Co., 1898.

Makers of Modern Strategy: Military Thought from Machiavelli to the Nuclear Age. Edited by Peter Paret. Princeton: Princeton University Press, 1986.

Mallet, Michael, and Shaw, Christine. *The Italian Wars, 1494–1559: War, State, and Society in Early Modern Europe*. New York: Routledge, 2019.

March, Jennifer. *Dictionary of Classical Mythology*. Oxford: Oxbow Books, 2014.

Marcia Young. "The Enlightenment and the French Military Aristocracy." Doctoral dissertation, Harvard University, 1984.

Marvin, Nathan, and Smith, Blake. "France and its Empire in the Indian Ocean." *Oxford Bibliographies Online*, 2019. https://www.oxfordbibliographies.com/display/document/obo-9780199730414/obo-9780199730414-0318.xml.

Mas, Raymond. "L'éssai général de tactique (1770) de Guibert ou le rationalism des Lumières face à la guerre." *La Bataille, l'armée, la gloire, 1745–1871: actes du colloque international de Clermont-Ferrand*. Edited by Paul Viallaneix and Jean Ehrard (1985): I:119–134.

Massie, Robert. *Catherine the Great: Portrait of a Woman*. New York: Random House, 2011.

Massie, Robert. *Peter the Great: His Life and World*. New York: Random House, 1981.

Maude, Frederic Natusch. *The Leipzig Campaign, 1813*. New York: MacMillan, 1908.

Mayer, E. "Le général Jean Colin." *Revue de Paris* 4 (1918): 827–849.

McConachy, "The Roots of Artillery Doctrine: Napoleonic Artillery Tactics Reconsidered." *The Journal of Military History* 65, no. 3 (2001): 614–640.

McCullough, Roy. *Coercion, Conversion, and Counterinsurgency in Louis XIV's France*. Leiden: Brill, 2007.

McLaren, Moray. *Corsican Boswell: Paoli, Johnson, and Freedom*. London: Secker & Warburg, 1966.

Menard. "De la force publique ou le testament militaire du comte de Guibert." *Revue de défense nationale* (1969).

Miakinkov, Eugene. *War and Enlightenment in Russia: Military Culture in the Age of Catherine II*. Buffalo: University of Toronto Press, 2020.

Middleton, Robert Nelson. *French Policy and Prussia after the Peace of Aix-la-Chappelle, 1749–1753*. Doctoral dissertation, Columbia University, 1968.

Mikaberidze, Alexander. *Conflict and Conquest in the Islamic World: A Historical Encyclopedia*. Volume I. New York: ABC-CLIO, 2011.

Mikaberidze, Alexander. *The Napoleonic Wars: A Global History*. New York: Oxford University Press, 2020.

The Military Revolution Debate: Readings on the Military Transformation of Early Modern Europe. Clifford Rogers, editor. Boulder, CO: Westview Press, 1995.

Mitchell, Stephen. *A History of the Later Roman Empire, AD 284–641*. Malden, MA: Wiley Blackwell, 2015.

Mitchener, Margaret. *A Muse in Love: Julie de Lespinasse*. London: The Bodley Head, 1962.

Monahan, W. Gregory. *Let God Arise: The War and Rebellion of the Camisards*. New York: Oxford University Press, 2014.

Mousnier, Roland. *The Institutions of the Absolute Monarchy*. 2 Volumes. Translated by Arthur Goldhammer and Brian Pearce. Chicago: University of Chicago Press, 1979–1984.

Mukherjee, Mithi. "The Colonial and the Imperial: India and Britain in the Impeachment Trial of Warren Hastings." *India in the Shadows of Empire: A Legal and Political History (1774–1950)*. New York: Oxford University Press, 2012.

Murphey, Rhoads. *Ottoman Warfare, 1500–1700*. New Brunswick: Rutgers University Press, 1999.

Murphy, Orville. *Charles Gravier, comte de Vergennes: French Diplomacy in the Age of Revolution, 1719–1787*. New York: State University of New York Press, 1982.

Napoleon and the Operational Art of War: Essays in Honor of Donald D. Horward. Michael Leggiere, editor. Leiden: Brill, 2016.

Nayar, Pramod. "English Colonial Discourse and India." *Oxford Bibliographies Online*, 2021. https://www.oxfordbibliographies.com/display/document/obo-9780190221911/obo-9780190221911-0114.xml.

Nelson, Eric. "Henri IV, King of France." *Oxford Bibliographies Online*, 2021. https://www.oxfordbibliographies.com/display/document/obo-9780195399301/obo-9780195399301-0087.xml.

Nelson, Janet. "The Dark Ages." *History Workshop Journal* 63, no. 1 (2007): 191–201.

Nelson, Janet. *King and Emperor: A New Life of Charlemagne*. Berkeley: University of California Press, 2019.

Nosworthy, Brent. *The Anatomy of Victory: Battle Tactics 1689–1763*. New York: Hippocrene Books, 1990.

Nouveau dictionnaire pour servir de supplement aux dictionnaires des sciences, des arts, et des métiers. 4 Volumes. Various, 1776.

Oakeshott, Ewart. *The Archaeology of Weapons: Arms and Armour from Prehistory to the Age of Chivalry*. Mineola, NY: Dover, 2019.

Oakley, Stewart. *War and Peace in the Baltic, 1560–1790*. New York: Routledge, 1992.

Onofrei, Cosmin. "Thracians in Roman Dacia. Military and Civilian Elements." https://arheologie-istoriaartei-cluj.ro/Articole/eph-XVIII-05.pdf.

"L'origine des grandes manœuvres—les camps d'instruction aux XVIIe et XVIIIe siècles." *Revue militaire* and *Revue d'histoire* (1899–1900, 1901–1903).

Osman, Julia. "Ancient Warriors on Modern Soil: French Military Reform and American Military Images in 18th Century France." *French History* 22 (2008): 223–246.

Osman, Julia. "Guibert vs. Guibert: Competing Notions in the *Essai général de tactique* and the *Défense du système de guerre moderne*." *Journal of Military History* 83, no. 1 (2019): 43–66.

Osman, Julia. "Patriotism as Power: The Old Regime Foundation for Napoleon's Army. *International Congress of Military History Conference Proceedings* 2009 (2010).

Osman, Julia. *Citizen Soldiers and the Key to the Bastille: War, Culture, and Society, 1750–1850*. New York: Palgrave Macmillan, 2015.

Ostwald, Jamel. *Vauban under Siege: Engineering Efficiency and Martial Vigor in the War of Spanish Succession*. Boston: Brill, 2007.

Outram, Dorinda. *The Enlightenment*. New York: Cambridge University Press, 2019.

Ovalle, Alonso de. *An Historical Relation of the Kingdom of Chile*. London: Churchill, 1703.

The Oxford Handbook of Warfare in the Classical World. Edited by Brian Campbell and Lawrence Tritle. New York: Oxford University Press, 2013.

Pâris de Bollardière, Bernard. *Joseph Pâris Duverney et ses frères: financiers dauphinois à la cour de Louis XV*. Toulon: Presses du Midi, 2006.

Parker, Geoffrey. *The Army of Flanders and the Spanish Road, 1567–1659*. New York: Cambridge University Press, 2004.

Parker, Geoffrey. *The Military Revolution: Military Innovation and the Rise of the West, 1500–1800*. New York: Cambridge University Press, 2016.

Parker, Geoffrey. *The Thirty Years War*. New York: Barnes & Noble, 1987.

Parrott, David. *The Business of War: Military Enterprise and Military Revolution in Early Modern Europe*. New York: Cambridge University Press, 2012.

Parrott, David. *Richelieu's Army: War, Government, and Society in France, 1624–1642*. New York: Cambridge University Press, 2008.

Pattou, Etienne. "Maisons de Maingot de Surgères et Granges de Surgères," *Racines Histoire*, 2022. http://racineshistoire.free.fr/LGN/PDF/Maingot_de_Surgeres.pdf.

Pavlov, Andrei, and Perrie, Maureen. *Ivan the Terrible*. London: Routledge, 2003.

Pavlovitch, Théodore. *L'idéal démocratique et la discipline militaire*. Paris: Chapelot, 1911.

Perrault, Charles. *Les hommes illustres qui ont paru en France pendant ce siècle*. 2 Volumes. Paris: Dezallier, 1697.

Pichichero, Christy. *The Military Enlightenment: War and Culture in the French Empire from Louis XIV to Napoleon*. Ithaca: Cornell University Press, 2017.

Pitts, Vincent. *Henri IV of France: His Reign and Age*. Baltimore: Johns Hopkins University Press, 2012.

Poirier, Lucien. *Les voix de la stratégie*. Paris: Fayard, 1985.

Popkin, Jeremy. *A New World Begins: The History of the French Revolution*. New York: Basic Books, 2019.

Price, Roger. *A Concise History of France*. New York: Cambridge University Press, 2005.

Quimby, Robert. *The Background of Napoleonic Warfare: The Theory of Military Tactics in Eighteenth-Century France*. New York: Columbia University Press, 1957.

Ranum, Orest. *The Fronde: A French Revolution, 1648–1652*. New York: W.W. Norton, 1993.

Rapin, Ami-Jacques. "The Invention of Strategy at the Turn of the 18th to 19th Centuries." Unpublished, 2023.

Revue militaire rédigée à l'Etat-major de l'armée. 11 Volumes. Paris: Chapelot, 1899–1900.

Riley, James. *The Seven Years War and the Old Regime in France: The Economic and Financial Toll*. Princeton, NJ: Princeton University Press, 1986.

Roberts, Michael. *Gustavus Adolphus*. London: Routledge, 2016.

Roberts, Michael. "The Military Revolution, 1560–1660." Belfast, 1956.

Roberts, Michael. *Sweden as a Great Power: Government, Society, Foreign Policy*. New York: St. Martin's Press, 1968.

Roche, Daniel. *France in the Enlightenment*. Translated by Arthur Goldhammer. Cambridge: Harvard University Press, 1998.

Roczniak, Wladyslaw. "The Polish-Lithuanian Commonwealth." *Oxford Bibliographies Online*, 2019. https://www.oxfordbibliographies.com/display/document/obo-9780195399301/obo-9780195399301-0119.xml.

Roemer, J. *Dictionary of English and French Idioms Illustrating, by Phrases and Examples, the Peculiarities of Both Languages*. New York: Huntington and Mason Brothers, 1853.

Rogers, Cliff. "The Efficacy of the English Longbow: A Reply to Kelly DeVries." *War in History* 5, no. 2 (1998): 233–242.

Rogister, John. *Louis XV and the Parlement of Paris, 1737–1755*. New York: Cambridge University Press, 1995.

Rohan Chabot, Alix de. *Le maréchal de Belle-Isle ou la revanche de Foucquet*. Paris: Perrin, 2005.

Roper, L.H. "English Overseas Empire." *Oxford Bibliographies Online*. 2023. https://www.oxfordbibliographies.com/display/document/obo-9780195399301/obo-9780195399301-0468.xml.

Ross, Steven. "The Development of the Combat Division in Eighteenth-Century French Armies." *French Historical Studies* no. 1 (1965): 84–94.

Ross, Steven. *From Flintlock to Rifle: Infantry Tactics, 1740–1866*. London: Frank Cass, 1996.

Rothenberg, Gunther. *The Military Border in Croatia, 1740–1881: A Study of an Imperial Institution*. Chicago: University of Chicago Press, 1966.

Rowlands, Guy. *Dangerous and Dishonest Men: The International Bankers of Louis XIV's France*. London: Palgrave Macmillan, 2015.

Rowlands, Guy. *The Dynastic State and the Army under Louis XIV: Royal Service and Private Interest, 1661–1701*. New York: Cambridge University Press, 2010.

Rowlands, Guy. *The Financial Decline of a Great Power: War, Influence, and Money in Louis XIV's France*. New York: Oxford University Press, 2013.

Royde-Smith, Naomi Gwladys. *The Double Heart: A Study of Julie de Lespinasse*. New York: Harper, 1831.

Rufus, Quintus Curtius. *The History of Alexander*. 2 Volumes. Translated by John Rolfe. Cambridge: Harvard University Press, 1946.

Savkin, Vasilii Efimovich. *The Basic Principles of Operational Art and Tactics: A Soviet View*. Washington, DC: US Government, 1974.

Savory, Reginald Arthur. *His Britannic Majesty's Army in Germany during the Seven Years War*. Oxford: Clarendon Press, 1966.

Schieder, Theodor. *Frederick the Great*. Translated by Sabina Berkeley and H.M. Scott. New York: Longman, 2000.

Scott, H.M. *The Birth of a Great Power System, 1740–1815*. Harlow, UK: Pearson Longman, 2005.

Scott, Samuel. *From Yorktown to Valmy: The Transformation of the French Army in the Age of Revolution*. Boulder: University Press of Colorado, 1998.

Scott, Tom. *The Swiss and their Neighbours, 1460–1560: Between Accommodation and Aggression*. Oxford: Oxford University Press, 2019.

Scullard, H.H. *A History of the Roman World from 753 to 1446 BC*. London: Meuthen, 1961.

Scullard, H.H. *From the Gracchi to Nero: A History of Rome from 133 B.C. to A.D. 68*. London: Methuen, 1970.

Ségur, Philippe-Marie-Maurice Henri, marquis de. *Julie de Lespinusse*. New York: E.P. Dutton, 1927.

The Seven Years War: Global Views. Edited by Mark Danley and Patrick Speelman. Leiden: Brill, 2012.

Shrier, Patrick. "Frederick the Great." *Oxford Bibliographies Online*, 2013. https://www.oxfordbibliographies.com/display/document/obo-9780199791279/obo-9780199791279-0094.xml.

Showalter, Dennis. *Railroads and Rifles: Soldiers, Technology, and the Unification of Germany*. Warwick: Helion, 2013.

Showalter, Dennis. *The Wars of Frederick the Great*. New York: Longman, 1996.

Smith, Jay. *The Culture of Merit: Nobility, Royal Service, and the Making of Absolute Monarchy in France, 1600–1789*. Ann Arbor: University of Michigan Press, 1996.

Smith, Jay. *The French Nobility in the Eighteenth Century: Reassessments and New Approaches*. University Park: Pennsylvania State University Press, 2006.

Smith, William. *Historical Account of Bouquet's Expedition against the Ohio Indians in 1764*. Cincinnati: Clarke, 1868.

Southern, Patricia. *The Roman Army: A Social & Institutional History*. New York: Oxford University Press, 2006.

Southern, Patricia, and Dixon, Karen. *The Late Roman Army*. London: Routledge, 2014.

Southern, Patricia. *Ancient Rome: The Empire, 30 BC-AD 476*. Stroud, Gloucestershire: Amberley, 2011.

Southern, Patricia. *The Roman Army: A History 1753 BC – AD 476*. Stroud: Amberley, 2014.

Spalding, Oliver. "The Military Studies of George Washington." *The American Historical Review* 29, number 4 (1924): 675–680.

Speelman, Patrick. *Henry Lloyd and the Military Enlightenment of Eighteenth-Century Europe*. Westport, CT: Greenwood Press, 2002.

Starkey, Armstrong. *War in the Age of Enlightenment, 1700–1789*. Westport, CT: Praeger, 2003.

Starobinski, Jean. *The Invention of Liberty, 1700–1789*. New York: Rizzoli, 1987.

Stevens, Carol. *Russia's Wars of Emergence, 1460–1730*. New York: Pearson Longman, 2007.

Stinchcombe, William. *The American Revolution and the French Alliance*. Syracuse: Syracuse University Press, 1969.

Stone, Bailey. *The French Parlements and the Crisis of the Old Regime*. Chapel Hill, NC: University of North Carolina Press, 1986.

Stone, David. *A Military History of Russia from Ivan the Terrible to the War in Chechnya*. Westport, CT: Praeger, 2006.

Stone, Lawrence. *An Imperial State at War: Britain from 1689 to 1815*. New York: Routledge, 1994.

Storring, Adam. "'The Age of Louis XIV': Frederick the Great and French Ways of War." *German History* 38, no. 1 (2020): 24–46.

Sturgill, Claude. *Marshal Villars and the War of the Spanish Succession*. Lexington: University of Kentucky Press, 1965.

Sumption, Jonathan. *The Hundred Years War*. 5 Volumes. Philadelphia: University of Pennsylvania Press, 1990–2015.

Sutton, John L. *The King's Honor & the King's Cardinal: The War of the Polish Succession*. Lexington, KY: University Press of Kentucky, 1980.

Swann, Julian. *Politics and the Parlement of Paris under Louis XV, 1755–1774*. New York: Cambridge University Press, 1995.

Syrett, David. "The British Landing at Havana: An Example of an Eighteenth-Century Combined Operation." *Mariner's Mirror* 55, no. 3 (1969): 325–331.

Szabo, Franz. *The Seven Years War in Europe, 1756–1763*. New York: Routledge, 2013.

Tapie, Victor-Lucien. *France in the Age of Louis XIII and Richelieu*. Translated by D. McN Lockie. New York: Cambridge University Press, 1995.

Telp, Claus. *The Evolution of Operational Art, 1740–1813: From Frederick the Great to Napoleon*. New York: Frank Cass, 2005.

Thompson, I.A.A. *War and Government in Habsburg Spain 1560–1620*. London: University of London Press, 1976.

Thrasher, Peter Adam. *Pasquale Paoli, an Enlightened Hero, 1725–1807*. Hamden, CT: Archon, 1970.

Valois, Marguerite de. *Memoirs*. Translated by Violet Fane. New York: Scribner's, 1842.

Van Creveld, Martin. *Supplying War: Logistics from Wallenstein to Patton*. New York: Cambridge University Press, 2004.

Van Creveld, Martin. *The Transformation of War*. New York: Free Press, 1991.

Van Wees, Hans. *Greek Warfare: Myths and Realities*. London: Bloomsbury, 2016.

Vivent, Jacques. "Un précurseur de la tactique moderne: le comte de Guibert." *Revue historique de l'armée; revue trimestrielle de l'état-major de l'armée, service historique*.

Volpilhac-Auger, Catherine. "Montesquieu." *Oxford Bibliographies Online*, 2020. https://www.oxfordbibliographies.com/display/document/obo-9780195396577/obo-9780195396577-0275.xml.

Vries, Kelly de. *Medieval Warfare 1300–1450*. Aldershot: Ashgate, 2008.

Waddington, Richard. *La guerre de sept ans: historique politique et militaire*. 5 Volumes. Paris: Firmin-Didot, 1899–1914.

Wasson, James N. *Innovator or Imitator: Napoleon's Operational Concepts and the Legacies of Bourcet and Guibert*. Fort Leavenworth, KS: US Army Command and General Staff College, 1998.

War and Competition between States. Edited by Philippe Contamine. New York: Oxford University Press, 2000.

Waterfield, Robin. *Dividing the Spoils: The War for Alexander the Great's Empire*. New York: Oxford University Press, 2011.

Waters, Matthew. *A Concise History of the Achaemenid Empire, 550–330 BCE*. New York: Cambridge University Press, 2016.

Wawro, Geoffrey. *The Franco-Prussian War: The German Conquest of France in 1870–1871*. New York: Cambridge University Press, 2003.

Weigley, Russell. *The Age of Battles: The Quest for Decisive Warfare from Breitenfeld to Waterloo*. Bloomington: Indiana University Press, 1991.

White, John. *Marshal of France: The Life and Times of Maurice, comte de Saxe, 1696–1750*. London: Hamilton, 1960.

Wilkinson, Spenser. *The Defense of Piedmont, 1742–1748: A Prelude to the Study of Napoleon*. Oxford: Clarendon Press, 1927.

Wilkinson, Spenser. *The French Army before Napoleon: Lectures Delivered before the University of Oxford in Michaelmas Term, 1914*. Oxford: Clarendon Press, 1915.

Wilson, Peter. *The Thirty Years War: Europe's Tragedy*. Cambridge: Harvard University Press, 2011.

Winkler, Albert. "The Battle of Murten: The Invasion of Charles the Bold and the Survival of the Swiss States." *Swiss American Historical Society Review* 46, no. 1 (2010): 8–34.

Wolf, John. *Louis XIV: A Profile*. New York: Palgrave Macmillan, 2014.

Worthington, Ian. *By the Spear: Philip II, Alexander the Great, and the Rise and Fall of the Macedonian Empire*. New York: Oxford University Press, 2016.

Wright, John. "Skepticism and Incomprehensibility in Bayle and Hume." https://philarchive.org/archive/WRISAI-2.

Index

Ajax   11
Alexander III, King of Macedon   24n33, 77–78, 117
Ancre, marquis d'   159
Aphrodite   11
Archimedes   171–172
Athens/Athenians   77, 116
Atilla   124
Austria/Austrians   XVI, XIX, 23, 61–62, 76–80, 85, 109, 129, 135–136, 143–144, 160, 166–168, 170

Bacon, Francis   176
Barca, Hannibal   67, 76–77, 116–117, 153, 173
Battle of Agnadello   124–125, 169n50.
Battle of Azincourt   62, 118
Battle of Bergen   57, 62n9, 75, 84–85, 102, 150
Battle of Blenheim   20n15, 62–63, 129, 149, 161
Battle of Breitenfeld   12
Battle of Cannae   67, 125, 173
Battle of Crécy   62, 169n49
Battle of Freiburg   78, 105
Battle of Grünberg   79
Battle of Hochkirch   135
Battle of Khotyn   63
Battle of Kolin   78–79, 135
Battle of Krefeld   23–24, 129
Battle of Kunersdorf   78–79, 135n46
Battle of Lauffeld   61–62, 128–129
Battle of Leuctra   77n5, 172
Battle of Leuthen   23–24, 62n4, 78n10, 109, 129, 143–144
Battle of Lützen   12
Battle of Mantinea   77, 172
Battle of Marignano   124–125, 169
Battle of Maxen   135
Battle of Minden   XVII, 62
Battle of Narva   63
Battle of Pavia   124–125
Battle of Pharsalus   23–24, 77, 83
Battle of Poitiers   62, 169n49
Battle of Poltava   63
Battle of Rossbach   XV, XVII, 3n13, 21n20, 23n32, 62n4, 78
Battle of Steenkerque   63
Battle of Sandershausen   57, 85
Battle of the Ticinus   67
Battle of the Trebbia   67
Battle of Tucapel   20–21
Battles of Saratoga   161
Bayezid I, Ottoman Sultan   63
Bélidor, Bernard de   171–172
Belle-Isle, duc de   XVI, 28
Berwick, duc de   107–108, 174
Bessi   171
Broglie, duc de   XV, XX, 1–3, 15, 27–29, 31, 33–34, 51, 57–58, 62n9, 75, 79n14, 84–85, 99, 101–103, 105, 112, 117, 150, 181
Brunswick, Hereditary Prince of   79
Brunswick, Prince Ferdinand of   XVII, 23–24, 57n32, 62n9, 102, 112, 126, 129
Burgoyne, John   161

Caesar, Gaius Julius   23, 28, 77, 83, 116–117

Calmet, Antoine   10
Camillus, Marcus Furius   173
Carthage/Carthaginians   67, 77, 173. *See also* Barca, Hannibal
Catinat, Nicholas   107–108, 174
Charlemagne, Holy Roman Emperor   125
Charles, duc de Bourbon   168–169
Chastellux, marquis de   2–3, 111–112
Chile   20–21, 45, 101
Choiseul, duc de   XVIII–XX, 1–3
Clermont, comte de   23–24
Clovis I, King of the Franks   124
Condé, Louis de Bourbon, prince de   105, 107, 117, 139
Contades, marquis de   57n32, 62n9
Créqui, François de   105–109, 174

Dacians   171
David, King of Israel   21
Douai   13–14, 87n5

Epaminondas   77, 172
Eugene, Prince of Savoy   14

Feuquières, marquis de   9–10, 72, 79, 103–104
Finck, Friedrich von   135
François I, King of France   124–125, 169n50
Friedrich II, King of Prussia   XVI–XVII, 1, 13, 21, 23–24, 27–28, 50–51, 71, 74, 78–80, 85, 86, 98, 107–109, 112, 116, 122, 126, 130, 135–136, 143–144, 156, 158, 162–163, 165–168, 175

Galen, Bishop of Münster   169
Gates, Horatio   161
Gideon   122
Greece/Greeks   9–10, 17–18, 66–67, 76–78, 171–173
Guesclin, Bertrand du   168–169
Guichard, Karl-Gottleib   10
Gustav II Adolph, King of Sweden   12, 81, 105, 169n51, 173–174

Hamelin   102
Henri III, King of France   81n18, 159
Henri IV, King of France   81, 159
Horatii

Invasion of Menorca   61–62

Jansenism   9

La Chappelle, comte de   2
"La Fontaine"   2
La Motte Fouqué, Freiherr de   116
Le Beau, Charles   121
Loudon, Freiherr von   78–79
Louis IX, King of France   156
Louis XI, King of France   159
Louis XIII, King of France   107n2, 159n19
Louis XIV, King of France   XV, 2n8, 14n30, 20n15, 27n2, 79, 81n18, 105n7, 107–108, 159, 161–162, 169n53, 172n65, 174
Louis XV, King of France   2–3, 172n65, 175n80
Louis XVI, King of France   XX
Lusace, comte de   112

INDEX

Maccabees   121–122
Martel, Charles, King of the Franks   124
Mercy, Freiherr von   105
Metz   2–3, 28, 30–60, 86, 105n9
Montauban   XV
Montecuccoli, Raimondo   79, 81, 105, 108–109, 116
Muy, comte de   2–3, 112

Narses   121–122
Nero, Emperor of Rome   159–161
Numidia/Numidians   77

Odysseus   11

Parma, duca di   81, 173
Pompey (Sextus Pompeius)   23, 77
Puységur, marquis de   27

Raynal, Guillaume   157–158
Regulus, Marcus Atilius   77
Richelieu, cardinal   159
Richelieu, duc de   61
Robbins, Benjamin   171–172
Rochambeau, comte de   XX, 57–58, 115–117
Rome/Romans   XVIII, 9–12, 20–25, 45, 66–67, 76–80, 101, 105, 117, 124–125, 157, 161–167, 171–175
Rugy, Goullet de   171–172
Russia/Russians   63, 80–81, 156, 158, 160n24, 165, 167

Saint Bartholomew's Day Massacre   159
Saschen-Weimar, Bernhard von   169
Savornin, Johannes van   13
Saxe, comte de   XVIII, 14–15, 61–62, 78n12, 107, 117, 129, 141n52
Scipio Africanus, Publius Cornelius   117
Seizure of Bender   61–63

Seven Years War   XVII-XXI, 27, 79, 99, 119, 125, 134–135, 170–171
Seydlitz, Freiherr von   21n20, 78
Siege of Bergen-op-Zoom   61–62, 171n60
Siege of Havana   61
Siege of Magdeburg   171
Siege of Ochakov   61–62
Siege of Schweidnitz   61–62
Siege of Torino   62–63
Soubise, prince de   57n32
Spain/Spanish   20–21, 62, 77, 79n16, 81n18, 105n7, 173–174
Sparta/Spartans   63, 77
Suleiman I, Ottoman Sultan   63

Tallard, duc de   20, 61, 129
Thessaly/Thessalians   76–77
Thucydides   63
Thuillier, Vincent   10

Valdivia, Pedro Gutiérrez de   20–21
Vauban, seigneur de   171–172, 179–180
Vegetius, Flavius Renatus   21n24, 24–25, 77, 118–124, 155–162
Vendôme, duc de   107
Villars, duc de   14, 107, 162

War of Austrian Succession   XVI, 1, 14–15, 27, 61–62, 99, 129, 141
War of Bavarian Succession   1n4, 76n3, 109n7, 135, 156, 162n29, 170n55
War of Polish Succession   14, 27, 107–108
War of Spanish Succession   XV, XVII, 9n3, 14, 20n15, 27, 62n7, 107–109, 149n59, 174, 184
Washington, George   161

Xanthippus   77, 173

Zeno of Elea   73